WORK & FAMILY: A CHANGING DYNAMIC

A BNA SPECIAL REPORT

Extra copies of this report (Product Code 45 LDSR-37) are $40.00 each, and may be obtained from BNA's Response Center, toll-free (800) 372-1033; Maryland, (800) 352-1400; Washington, D.C., area, 258-9401; or by mail from BNA's Customer Service Center, 9435 Key West Ave., Rockville, Md. 20850, with the following quantity discounts available: 6-10 copies, 10%; 11-25 copies, 15%; 26-50 copies, 20%; 51-500 copies, 25%; 501-1,000 copies, 30%; and more than 1,000 copies, 35%.

TABLE OF CONTENTS

PREFACE

This special report, *Work & Family: A Changing Dynamic*, is published under a cooperative agreement with the Bureau of Labor-Management Relations and Cooperative Programs of the U.S. Department of Labor. The Department's project officer was Richard P. Shore.

This report was released in conjunction with a national conference on *Work and Family: Seeking a New Balance*, co-sponsored by The Bureau of National Affairs, Inc., and the U.S. Department of Labor, and held in Washington, D.C., April 14-15, 1986. The conference was presented in cooperation with The American Federation of Labor-Congress of Industrial Organizations and the National Association of Manufacturers.

Editorial contributors to the report include the following individuals: Michelle Amber, Tim Bevins, Karen Breslin, Raymond Ertel, A. Kelley Fead, James Fitzpatrick, Neil Gilbride, Elaine Kessler, Martha Kessler, Karen Kurt, Jean Linehan, David McShea, Craig Mellow, Marilyn Modlin, Ross Ramsey, Bebe Raupe, Nancy Sainburg, Susan Sala, Stephen Siciliano, Gerald Silverman, Glenn Totten, Janice Valverde, Julia Whitmore, and Paula Zimlicki.

Jean Shapiro was the principal photographer for the report.

Michael Levin-Epstein served as project coordinator, Fitzpatrick served as principal researcher and editorial coordinator, and Bevins edited and coordinated production of the report.

Economic, social, and demographic changes in recent decades have upset the once-established dynamic of work and family life. In the past, fathers worked and mothers stayed home. Now, it is more and more likely that the mother also works.

The influx of women into the work force is the most significant of a number of changes. However, the care of the children of working parents and the ways in which employers, unions, and government support working parents are not just women's issues. How these issues will be addressed has far-reaching implications for employers, unions, and public policymakers, who already have begun to rethink traditional approaches to child and dependent care assistance. Policies on pregnancy leave, parental leave, work schedules, and fringe benefit packages also are being reexamined.

This report explores the broad range of responses that are being adopted, and advocated, to meet the reality of the new American workplace. The report's major highlights are summarized in Chapter II. Chapter III discusses the character and composition of the new family and the new workplace, as well as the question of who is responsible for accommodating the specific needs of working parents.

Chapter IV presents background information and more than 30 case studies illustrating specific responses by private and public sector employers and unions in the following areas:

- Child and Dependent Care;
- Alternative Work Schedules;
- Employee Assistance Programs;
- Parental Leave; and
- Relocation Assistance Programs.

Trends and developments in the family-and-work area are examined in Chapter V. One section of this chapter is devoted to a discussion of major federal legislative proposals on parental leave and child care. Another section presents a listing of legislative and executive actions on family and work and related issues by some 15 states. Chapter V also includes a discussion of trends and developments in flexible benefits. Some observers maintain that "cafeteria-style" benefits are an inexpensive way for employers to tailor benefits more appropriately to the diverse needs of women, single parents, and two-earner couples. A look at international trends and developments on family and work and leave policies is also found in Chapter V, including a look at work and family policies in Sweden — considered by many to be the trendsetter in this area. The last two sections of the chapter present a survey of parental leave in Western Europe, and a global survey of maternity benefits.

Labor-management approaches to work-and-family issues, including cooperative efforts, are discussed in Chapter VI.

For this report, a number of experts on work and family were asked to state what the specific responsibilities and responses of business, labor, and government should be toward family concerns of workers. Their responses can be found in Chapter VII. A variety of individuals responded, including representatives of the U.S. Chamber of Commerce, labor unions, academia, the federal government, and private organizations. The experts' views ranged from that expressed by Chamber representatives, who said new benefits should not be legislatively mandated, to an endorsement by a labor union official of federal legislation that would require employers to grant parental leave.

A listing of more than 60 resource organizations is found in Chapter VIII.

Chapter IX, the Appendix, contains text of a number of documents, including proposed federal legislation on parental leave and AFL-CIO-endorsed resolutions on family and work. The Appendix also carries an interview with noted pediatrician, Dr. T. Berry Brazelton, as well as a detailed explanation of the tax aspects of dependent care assistance plans. Corporate policy statements on work-and-family issues, and examples of collectively bargained contract clauses also are included in the Appendix.

A comprehensive bibliography is set out in Chapter X. Chapter XI contains an Index.

The dynamics of the American family and the American workplace are undergoing major adjustments. Both the family and workplace have changed dramatically in the last three decades. (See "A Look at the Numbers" at the end of this chapter.) Fewer than 10 percent of the population now live in the "classic" 1950s-style family — the household headed by a male as the sole breadwinner. In the fourth quarter of 1985, nearly 60 percent of the mothers of children under age 18 were in the work force. By 1995, more than 80 percent of women between the ages of 25 and 44 are expected to be working, according to Labor Department statistics.

This BNA special report examines the ways in which employers, unions, and governments are dealing with the special concerns of working parents. Following are the general conclusions of the report:

1. Economic, social, and demographic changes in the last 30 years have resulted in a massive restructuring of the American work force. Within the last decade, for example, the labor participation rate for married women with children under one year of age increased 70 percent.

2. More employees can be expected to experience difficulties balancing family-and-work concerns. According to one survey, almost one-half of all employees who separated from their spouses said they had some difficulty in dealing with the responsibilities of family and work.

3. There is no consensus in the United States on the responsibility for helping employees balance work and family. Corporations, unions, governments, schools, and community organizations are being called upon to come up with programs to help individuals deal with real-life problems resulting from the changing dynamic of work and family.

4. Several states have created task forces specifically to address family-and-work problems. In Massachusetts, for example, a task force report led to the establishment of five child care resource and referral agencies serving parents, providers, and potential providers in the public and private sector, and establishment of at least 12 new child care facilities.

5. Parental leave has become a national issue. Congress is considering legislation that would mandate up to 18 weeks of unpaid leave to employees who choose to stay home to care for a newborn, newly adopted, or seriously ill child.

6. Although there are studies showing that certain family-oriented programs, such as flextime or employee assistance plans, can increase productivity and enhance the corporate bottom line, some corporate officials remain skeptical about whether the potential benefits are worth the actual costs of such programs. Corporate decisionmakers point out that there is a fine line that a company must walk in response to work/family problems — the line between interfering with employees' personal lives and being responsive to their needs.

7. In general, corporate America has not kept pace with the changing dynamic of work and family. For example, only 2,500 companies offer *any* kind of child care assistance to employees.

8. In the last few years, however, many corporations have become aware of, and have responded to, the increasing interrelationship between work and family. As the case studies in this report illustrate, some employers have initiated innovative and successful programs in the areas of child care, alternative work schedules, employee assistance plans, parental leave, and relocation assistance.

9. Unions are expected to demand that employers strengthen their family-oriented programs. The AFL-CIO has urged affiliates to press for programs such as joint employer-union sponsored day care centers and establishment of flexible working hours to accommodate employees' need to care for children and other dependents.

10. Occasionally, as the result of joint labor-management committees or collective bargaining, labor and management have cooperated to implement creative workplace policies that enable employees to handle job and family responsibilities in mutually beneficial ways. Secretary of Labor William Brock, however, remarked in 1985: "We still act as though workers have no families . . . Labor and management haven't faced that adequately, or at all. They don't understand it, and I think that's dumb."

Following are summaries of the case studies used to illustrate how employers, unions, and governments are addressing work-and-family concerns.

CHILD AND DEPENDENT CARE

The pressure on employers, unions, and government to help provide child and dependent care will continue to grow as long as the number of couples and single parents in the work force continues to rise. Although the number of employers providing child care assistance to employees increased fourfold from 1982 to 1985, the total number of employers taking such action is still quite small. Working parents still face the unresolved problems of care for children who are sick, infant care, and after-school and summer care for school-age children. A number of studies have found a relationship between child care resources, company policy, and the level of absenteeism, productivity, and morale among employees.

Employers, unions, and government have begun to fashion responses to the child care needs of working parents. Child care information and referral services, on-site parenting seminars, employer financial contributions for child care, flexible benefits plans, and other means of helping families appear to be yielding benefits for some firms. Following are highlights of case studies documenting some of these actions:

• *On-site day care* for employees was negotiated in the 1982 contract between Boston City Hospital and Local 285 of the Service Employees International Union. Demand for the service has grown so that the union is now negotiating to expand the number of slots for infants and toddlers.

• *Summer camp* for employees' children age seven through 15 has been provided since 1970 by Fel-Pro, Inc., an automotive supplier. Fel-Pro also opened its own on-site day care center in 1983.

• *Near-site day care* is provided by the Boston advertising firm of Hill Holliday Connors Cosmopulos, Inc. The care is largely subsidized by the firm; individual fees are determined by a sliding scale based on salary and age of the child.

• *The California Child Care Initiative*, a public/private consortium headed by BankAmerica Foundation in San Francisco, raised $700,000 to bankroll six pilot projects aimed at increasing the availability and quality of child care statewide.

• A *voucher system* for day care was begun by Polaroid Corp. in 1970. Polaroid pays a direct subsidy to cover a percentage of an employee's day care bill. The percentage varies according to a sliding scale based on income.

• *A day care subsidy* was provided by Procter & Gamble to help establish two day care centers and a community child care referral service in Cincinnati, where the firm is headquartered.

• *An information and referral service* to help parents find out about child care services is being provided by Metropolitan Washington Child Care Network, which is funded by corporate and other contributions.

• *Parenting seminars* conducted by an outside consultant have allowed some 400 employees of PSFS Bank in Philadelphia to express their feelings about problems such as child care, and then to discuss solutions.

• *Sick child care* is being provided by several organizations. One such operation is Chicken Soup in Minneapolis, Minn. Another is Sniffles 'n' Sneezes, run by the Southeastern Medical Center in Miami, Fla. The 3M Corp., also located in Minneapolis, has set up a program to help employees pay for care for sick children.

• *A labor-management child care program* is found in the contract between Kaiser Permanente Medical Group in Los Angeles and Local 399 of the Service Employees International Union. The program is primarily a resource and referral service. Management estimates that 5 percent of its 4,600 employees make use of the service.

• *After-school programs for children* are being funded by the Houston Committee for Private Sector Initiatives, which has awarded start-up grants and conducted training for program coordinators.

• *A child care ordinance* in San Francisco requires new office developers either to provide space for an on-site child care facility or to contribute to city's Affordable Child Care Fund.

• *Elderly dependent care* is a major responsibility for many employees at The Travelers Corp., which is studying several options to help workers better deal with these responsibilities.

ALTERNATIVE WORK SCHEDULES

More and more workers have child care responsibilities. And more and more workers are commuting longer distances. Time off from work is increasingly being requested by workers who want to reconcile their simultaneous and often conflicting roles as workers and parents.

One type of alternative scheduling option — flextime — is improving productivity and employee morale, according to the American Management Association. To help employees, and to help the corporate bottom line, employers are considering other work scheduling options, including:

• compressed workweeks;
• job-sharing;
• permanent and temporary part-time employment;
• voluntary reduced work-time programs (V-time);
• telecommuting; and
• flexible use of vacation time and personal days.

Some employers, however, remain skeptical about the potential benefits versus the actual costs of such programs. Unions, too, have some reservations about alternative work schedules. Nevertheless, a number of programs have worked, and are working, successfully:

• *Flextime*, initiated by the federal government on an experimental basis in 1979, was made a permanent feature of employment for federal government employees in 1985. It is estimated that flexible work schedules and compressed work schedule programs are being used by up to 500,000 federal employees, and that more than 10 million private sector workers enjoy such programs.

• *A flextime program*, instituted on a pilot project basis at Transamerica Occidental Life Insurance Co. in 1972, was so well received that 90 percent of the company's 3,800 Los Angeles-area workers now participate.

• *Flexible work scheduling* has been offered for more than a decade to most employees of SmithKline Beckman Corp., which reports that the program has eased employees' child care burdens, reduced absenteeism, and improved productivity.

• *A job-sharing "team program"* was instituted for factory and some clerical workers in 1975 by Rolscreen Co. Employees are expected to work at least 1,000 hours per year, but the Pella, Iowa, manufacturer allows members of the job-sharing team to decide how those hours will be divided up.

• *A part-time employment strategy* called Peak-Time was pioneered by Provident Bank of Cincinnati in 1983. By paying part-time employees who work during the busiest period of the day at a higher hourly rate than those who work during the remaining bank hours, the bank has attracted many early retirees as well as mothers looking to re-enter the labor force.

• *Voluntary reduced work time (V-time)* is offered by Shaklee Corp. The typical V-time agreement at the San Francisco health products company calls for three- or four-day workweeks.

• *A telecommuting program* was instituted by Pacific Bell in 1985 for about 80 managerial employees, most of whom wanted to work at home or at remote work sites for family-related reasons.

• *A flexible leave policy* that does away with the distinction between vacation leave and sick leave has been adopted by Hewlett-Packard Co. Personal leave time, which is accrued on the basis of length of service, can be taken for any purpose, including childbirth, adoption, or care for sick relatives.

EMPLOYEE ASSISTANCE PROGRAMS

Employers are becoming more aware that employees' personal problems can have an adverse effect on their work performance. Some employers are turning to employee assistance programs (EAPs) to help employees deal with personal problems, including the stress resulting from conflicting work and homelife demands:

• *New York State's employee assistance program* is part of overall effort by the State and unions representing state workers to help employees deal with a wide variety of personal problems, including family difficulties and alcohol and substance abuse. Of the 20,958 referrals made from September 1984 to September 1985, 3,025 were for family counseling services.

• *Family counseling* has been part of the International Longshoremen's Association's alcoholism treatment program in New York City since its inception in 1974. Members of a recovering alcoholic's family are strongly encouraged to participate in the treatment program and to attend the local branch of Al Anon for family members of alcoholics.

• *Contract EAP services* are being provided to more than 55 client organizations in 40 states by the EAP division of Parkside Medical Services Corp. in Park Ridge, Ill. The firm believes that helping employees deal with problems that affect their performance boosts morale and pays off on the bottom line.

• *A counseling and assistance program* has been helping employees at Ameri-Trust Bank to balance family and work responsibilities for more than 10 years. The Cleveland, Ohio, bank also offers parenting and childbirth preparation classes to provide peer support as well as counseling for workers.

PARENTAL LEAVE

There are more parents in the work force than ever before. Whether out of concern or necessity, employers now are taking a closer look at policies on maternity, parental leave, and adoption. And, according to a 1985 Congressional Research Service report, "[U]nions may press with added vigor for maternity leaves." A growing number of companies also are beginning to offer unpaid leaves with job guarantees to fathers and adoptive parents, a Catalyst report concludes, but the report also notes that few men are taking such leave.

According to the special report, parental leave has become a national issue:

• A parental leave bill, proposed in 1985 (HR 2020), and again in 1986 (HR 4300), would require employers to provide 18 weeks of leave to employees who choose to stay home to care for a newborn, newly adopted, or seriously ill child.

• Infant care leave should be available for at least six months, with about 75 percent of salary paid for three months, according to recommendations made in 1985 by the Advisory Committee on Infant Care Leave at the Yale-Bush Center in Child Development and Social Policy. The committee suggested that such leave could be financed through employer and employee contributions to an insurance fund.

• Federal legislation requiring public and private employers to provide temporary disability insurance to all employees should be enacted, the Family Policy Panel of the Economic Policy Council of UNA-USA recommended in a 1986 report. The panel also recommended that jobs of employees on disability should be fully protected, and that employers should consider providing unpaid parenting leave and should guarantee employees their former job or a comparable job if they return from parenting leave within six months after the child is born.

• In early 1986, the Supreme Court agreed to decide whether states are free to grant pregnant women special employment protections beyond those afforded by federal law.

This section includes the following case studies:

• *Paid maternity leave* of at least eight weeks is provided by Foley, Hoag & Eliot to any of its attorneys who is unable to work because of pregnancy, childbirth, or other conditions related to pregnancy. The Boston law firm also allows a part-time work schedule to facilitate a parent's return to work after leave, and unpaid parenting leave to male as well as female attorneys.

• *Paid parental leave* of up to three months is provided by Bank Street College of Education to workers who are the primary caregivers for their biological or adopted children. Additional unpaid leave of up to a year also is available.

• *Parenting and "bonding" leave* of up to four weeks is provided by Lotus Development Corp. to employees who are biological or adoptive parents. The Cambridge, Mass., computer software company requires employees to negotiate with department managers on whether leave is possible, and on the length of leave.

• *Adoption assistance* has been provided to some 40 Bank of America employees since 1983 when the San Francisco financial institution began providing reimbursement for adoption expenses of more than $250 and up to $2,000 to employees adopting foster children or step-children and children from overseas.

RELOCATION ASSISTANCE PROGRAMS

Employee relocation inevitably causes pressure and anxiety for transferred employees, especially those with working spouses, children and other dependents. In the 1990s, companies will be forced to adapt to employees' growing resistance to relocation, several experts maintain in this report. The resistance is due to working-spouse considerations, potential family disruptions, and the desire to be close to parents or other extended family members.

Spousal job assistance is being requested more and more, even in the recruitment setting. Some industry observers recommend that corporations offer a flexible relocation package, which includes an option for quality job search assistance for spouses.

Employer assistance is taking several forms:

• *A community support network* is being provided by the United Auto Workers and General Motors to orient workers who are relocating from cities in Missouri and Wisconsin to Fort Wayne, Ind., the site of a new truck manufacturing plant. The support network provides newcomers with counseling and information on the community.

• *A mortgage assistance program* at Diamond Shamrock Corp. has helped some 300 employees annually since 1975. By serving in several capacities from real estate broker to home seller, the company tries to bring the employees' cost of moving as close to zero as possible.

• *Spousal relocation assistance* — including resettlement and career continuance help for up to 12 months — is offered by The Standard Oil Company to spouses of recruited employees. Recruiters act as career counselors assisting with resumé preparation, interview coaching, and feedback on job search experiences.

WORK & FAMILY: A LOOK AT THE NUMBERS

The statistics below reflect the extent of transformations of the work force and the family, and the impact of these changes on the workplace.

FAMILIES AND THE WORKPLACE

Nearly 60 percent of the mothers of children under age 18 were employed in the fourth quarter of 1985.

The Bureau of Labor Statistics

Within the last decade, the labor force participation rate for married women with children under one year of age increased 70 percent.

Professors Sheila Kamerman and Alfred Kahn, Columbia University

By 1995, more than 80 percent of women between the ages of 25 and 44 are expected to be working.

U.S. Department of Labor

Fifty-two percent of women over age 30 in June 1984 who reported to a Census Bureau survey that they had given birth during the previous 12 months were in the labor force as of the survey date.

Census Bureau

Fewer than 10 percent of our population lives in the "classic" family headed by a single male breadwinner.

Jerome M. Rosow, Work in America Institute

More than half of the children 13 years old and under live in a family with both parents or the only parent present in the work force.

House Select Committee on Children, Youth, and Families

In 1984, 60 percent of all working women had no paid maternity leave. Yet, 80 percent of women currently in the work force are of child-bearing age and an estimated 93 percent of them will become pregnant during their careers.

Jack Golodner, Department for Professional Employees, AFL-CIO

More than 100 countries, including almost every industrial nation, have laws that protect pregnant workers and allow new mothers a job-protected leave at the time of childbirth with full or partial wage replacements, but the United States does not.

Family Policy Panel of the Economic Policy Council of the UNA-USA

CORPORATE POLICIES

A 1985 survey of medium-sized and large companies showed that less than 20 percent offered flexible benefits plans, but that 46 percent of the management personnel expected their companies to introduce flexible benefits plans in the next two years.

Louis Harris & Associates, Inc

More than half of the 400 companies responding to a survey had changed their policies on maternity, paternity, infant care, and adoption leave in the past five years.

Catalyst

Relocation services estimate that 30 to 40 percent of employee relocations involve two-earner couples. And, in 1983 the executive transfer refusal rate was 24 percent.

Catalyst

As of October 1985, some 2,500 companies were providing some form of child care assistance. This is a fourfold increase over the 600 in 1982.

The Conference Board

In a survey of more than 1,400 employees aged 30 or older, 20 percent were providing some form of care for elderly relatives or friends.

The Travelers Corp

WORK-AND-FAMILY PROBLEMS

More than one-third of a survey of 651 employees reported significant difficulties with managing family responsibilities.

Boston University School of Social Work

Family/marital problems, which include those associated with the conflicts between home and job responsibilities, are in the range of 30 to 35 percent of the caseload of employee assistance programs.

Don Phillips, president of COPE, Inc., Washington, D.C.

Eighteen percent of the 651 employees responding to a 1985 survey cited responsibility for an aging parent as a very serious problem.

Boston University School of Social Work

Forty-six percent of women with children under age two, and 23 percent of the male counterparts, said child care concerns would influence their decision on whether to accept a promotion.

John Fernandez, author of Child Care and Corporate Productivity

Child care problems force working parents to be off the job a total of about eight days a year.

1985 study by Child Care Systems, Inc., Lansdale, Pa.

Women are six times more likely to stay home with a sick child than are men.

Boston University School of Social Work

Sixty-five percent of 5,000 employees surveyed believe that child care problems are costing their corporations a great deal in lost productivity.

John Fernandez

III. BACKGROUND

The family and the workplace — sweeping change has transformed both in recent years. This chapter examines the extent of the transformations, and discusses the question of who is responsible for accommodating the specific needs of working parents.

A. CHANGES IN THE LABOR FORCE

For many years, the "typical" American family was depicted as a father at work and a mother at home with the children. That description no longer accurately fits a large portion of American families. The number of American families in which the father works and the mother stays home with the children is now a small minority of the total, the Bank Street College of Education noted in its Fall 1985 *Alumni News*.

Major Demographic Changes

Economic, social, and demographic changes in the last several decades have resulted in dramatic changes in the American work force and, in the process, the American family. A surge in the number of working women is just one of these changes. Another is that more women are returning to the work force after giving birth.

The number of women in the work force has increased 173 percent from 1947 to 1980, according to data compiled by the Congressional Caucus for Women's Issues. Women, who accounted for less than a third of all workers 30 years ago, now account for considerably more than two-fifths of all workers, the Conference Board noted in a 1985 research report, "Corporations and Families: Changing Practices and Perspectives."

Women will account for the majority of labor-force growth from 1984 to 1995, the Labor Department projects. In 1970, only half the women between the ages of 25 and 44 were in the work force. By 1995, more than 80 percent of women in that age range are expected to be working. This growth is reflected in the following Department of Labor graphs.

Labor force participation rates of
men and women age 16 and over, 1975–95

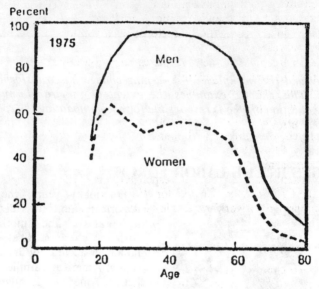

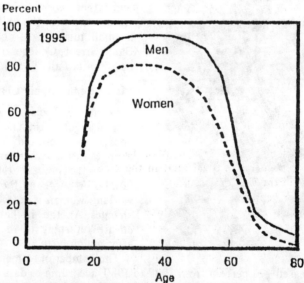

Source: *Monthly Labor Review* (November 1985).

The 1990s will be the first decade in which, at the start, a majority (55 percent) of mothers of children under age six, in families where the husband is present, will be in the labor force, according to the House Select Committee on Children, Youth, and Families. In 1970, fewer than one-third of all married mothers of children under age six worked, the Committee reported in a fact sheet it prepared on the Child Care Opportunities for Families Act of 1985. (See Chapter VI for a discussion of this bill.)

"The influx of mothers into the labor force has been one of the most dramatic and far-reaching social changes in recent times," says The Union Work and Family Life Study, a joint project of Bank Street College of Education in New York City and Oil, Chemical and Atomic Workers Local 8-149. The study notes the "astounding" increases in the labor force participation rate of mothers with children under 18 years of age:

- in 1940, 8.6 percent of mothers in this category were part of the work force;
- in 1950, the rate was 21.6 percent;
- in 1970, it was 42.9 percent; and
- in 1977, it was 50 percent.

By the fourth quarter of 1985, nearly 60 percent of mothers with children under 18 were employed, the Bureau of Labor Statistics of the Department of Labor reported in early 1986. (See Appendix J for selected data from BLS on family employment and earnings.)

Working women increasingly are responsible for providing family income, according to the Congressional Caucus for Women's Issues. More than six million families are supported by working female heads-of-households, the Caucus reported in 1985.

Mothers of Infants Working in Record Numbers

The most rapid change in labor force participation has been among mothers of infants and toddlers, Bank Street College noted in its study. In 1976, 35 percent of these women were in the labor force; in 1984, that proportion had risen to 48 percent, the College said.

"Mothers of infants and toddlers make up the fastest-growing segment in the labor force."

"More than half of the mothers of children under six are employed outside the home," the College pointed out, adding, "Mothers of infants and toddlers make up the fastest-growing segment in the labor force." These trends in labor force participation by women are illustrated in the chart on the following page. The chart appeared in the Conference Board's "Corporations and Families: Changing Practices and Perspectives."

"Within the last decade, the labor force participation rate for married women with children under one year of age has increased by an astonishing 70 percent," Columbia University School of Social Work Professors Sheila B. Kamerman and Alfred J. Kahn told a 1985 Congressional hearing on a bill that would provide a national parenting and temporary disability leave policy.

Eighty percent of working women are likely to become pregnant during their working lives, according to the Congressional Caucus for Women's Issues. Over half of those women will return to work within a year of childbirth, the Caucus noted. Bank Street College reports that, on average, a working mother takes about six weeks off her job to have her baby.

The notion that most mothers stay at home until their children begin school is no longer valid. Half the mothers of pre-school children were working in 1982, the Congressional Caucus said. Fifty-two percent of women over age 30 in June 1984 who reported to a Census Bureau survey that they had given birth during the previous 12 months were in the labor force as of the survey date. The corresponding figure in 1976 was only 28 percent, Census reported in "Fertility of American Women: June 1984."

"The working mother is now the rule rather than the exception," the Women's Bureau of the Department of Labor declared in a pamphlet describing its efforts to promote employer-sponsored child care systems.

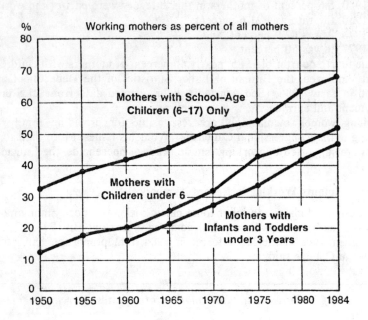

[Reprinted with permission of the Conference Board.]

*   *   *

B. CHANGES IN THE FAMILY

The structure and character of the American family have undergone dramatic changes in the last few decades. These changes have far-reaching implications for the workplace.

"American families today are living under circumstances much different than even a few years ago. Every income group and geographic region is affected," according to Rep. George Miller (D-Calif), chairman of the House Select Committee on Children, Youth, and Families. Data compiled by the Committee, Miller noted, show that more than half of children 13 years old and under live in a family in which either both parents or the only parent present are members of the work force.

Demand for Child Care Particularly Acute

At oversight hearings on job training late in 1985, Sen. Paula Hawkins (R-Fla) remarked, "Since the 1950s our country has gone through many changes that have strongly influenced the family structure and increased the need for quality child care." For instance, she said, families have become increasingly mobile. Many of us live far from where we grew up and far from the support of our families. This means that often we cannot rely on grandparents and aunts and uncles to care for our children in time of need, said Hawkins, who chairs the Subcommittee on Children, Family, Drugs and Alcoholism.

The structure of the family has been changed. No matter what our philosophical views are, this is a fact, Hawkins said. "By 1990 . . . it is expected that fully one-fourth of our children will be living in families where the sole support and sole nurturer is a single parent. Even in the traditional family, it is often necessary for both parents to be employed."

Rise in Number of Single-Parent Households

Increases in the rates of separation and divorce, among other things, have led to an increase in the number of single-parent households in the United States.

From 1870 to 1970, single-parent households represented about 10 percent of U.S. households with children under age 18, the *Journal of Home Economics* noted in its Spring 1985 issue. By 1980, single-parent households exceeded 20 percent of all such households, the *Journal* said, noting that, in 1984, nearly 10.9 million children were in such families.

The number of households headed by working mothers in 1970 was almost two million, according to Helen Axel, director of the Work and Family Information Center at the Conference Board. In 1985, the number was more than five million, she said.

"This is a huge change in our social structure," Sen. Daniel Patrick Moynihan (D-NY) said in a speech in Washington, D.C., in early 1986. Moynihan noted forecasts that 67 percent of children born in 1984 can expect to live in a one-parent household for some portion of their lives.

In his book, *Family and Nation*, published in 1986, Moynihan says, "In the final two decades of the century, we project the number of families will increase from 59.5 million to 72.5 million." Of these families, only 5.9 million are expected to be "traditional" husband-wife families.

The number of children living with a divorced mother more than doubled between 1970 and 1982, and the number of children living with a never-married mother increased more than fourfold, the Department of Labor has reported.

A November 1985 study by the Joint Economic Committee of the Congress noted that of the 7.1 million female family heads in 1984, 22.1 percent had never been married, 64.3 percent were divorced or separated, and 11.3 percent were widows. "Thus, the vast majority of children currently living in families headed by their mothers previously lived in two-parent families which had, on average, much higher average incomes." The report — "How Have Families with Children Been Faring?" — stated that average real income for families declined between 1973 and 1984, and noted the importance of women's earnings to the family. "The disappointing experiences of families over the recent past would have been even worse had it not been for the increased earnings of wives and of women heading households."

Redefinition of Fatherhood

Another dramatic change in the character of the American family is the "redefinition of fatherhood" that has been going on for well over 10 years, according to James A. Levine, director of The Fatherhood Project at the Bank Street College of Education in New York City. "Men *are* becoming more involved with the child-rearing, albeit slowly," says Levine. In the March 1986 issue of *Across the Board*, Levine states: "There is no revolution under way, but there is a significant evolution. By 1995, when . . . over 85 percent of women under 45 will be in the labor force, the issue of who is caring for the children and how the work force is supporting the family will not be just for 'working mothers.' "

Levine told BNA that research done by The Fatherhood Project, which, among its other activities, serves as an information clearinghouse, shows that the changes in the definition of fatherhood have been gradual and subtle. For instance, he said, baby products and other household goods advertisers often include fathers in the "pitch." Men also are attending workplace parenting seminars in greater numbers and talking about concerns that would have been "underground issues" a decade ago, Levine said. Women, Levine added, also are becoming more aware of the father's role and are more willing to admit openly that they unconsciously might have been "holding onto everything — not wanting to be supermom, but acting that way."

Another indicator of the changing role of fathers is the amount of housework done by men, Levine said. Although the data show that women are still doing the lion's share of household chores, "we are seeing men do more."

Levine said that the percentage of households headed by the male parent has held fairly constant at about 10 percent. The number, however, has increased and single-parent fathers have become more vocal about their concerns in balancing work-and-family responsibilities.

Response to Change Is Slow

"The family has changed, yet the institutions affecting the family . . .have been slow in responding," according to Bank Street College's Union Work and Family Life Study. "Workplaces require last-minute overtime, thus causing a dilemma for employed parents who must pick up their children promptly at day care centers. Schools schedule teacher conferences and school performances during the day, making it virtually impossible for employed parents to attend. Television shows and newspaper and magazine articles report on superfamilies — parents and children who are able to have it all and do it all — while the realities in most families' lives are very different," according to the study.

Throughout the developed world, changes in work force and family patterns, similar to those in the United States, have been occurring, noted the Economic Policy Council of the United Nations Association of the United States of America. In a report released early in 1986, the Association's Family Policy Panel stressed that many countries have responded to the change by implementing a coordinated set of public and private "family" policies. "Among industrialized countries, the United States is conspicuous for its slow response in policy and program to the impact that recent structural changes have had on the family, the workplace, and the schools."

The EPC panel's recommendations on national family policy options, as well as the recommendations of other organizations, are discussed throughout this report.

*   *   *

C. WORK AND FAMILY: SHARED RESPONSIBILITY

Balancing work and family responsibilities is difficult because everyone thinks it's someone else's problem, Sarah Lawrence College President Alice S. Ilchman told a Washington, D.C., audience in 1986. Management thinks it's a workers' problem, men think it's women's, and older parents think it's the problem of younger parents, she said.

"Who has responsibility in so personal and intimate a setting?" Ilchman asked in remarks on the release of the Family Policy Panel's report. Ilchman and Service Employees International Union President John J. Sweeney co-chaired the panel.

All sectors of U.S. society — government, schools, employers, unions, and community groups — must take an active role in setting family policy, the EPC panel of business, labor, and academic leaders concluded. Government should set standards, guarantee and enforce minimum statutory rights and benefits, and create "incentives for the private sector to address these issues in a serious, pragmatic manner," the EPC panel said.

"Employers and unions can implement creative workplace policies that will help their employees (or members) handle job and family responsibilities in mutually beneficial ways," the panel commented.

"Changes in family structure have affected the majority of children and adults, yet with very few exceptions, the schools, the workplace, the relevant government agencies and legislation, and our attitudes as a nation have not fully recognized or addressed the widespread social and economic implications of these changes," the Family Policy Panel concluded. Traditional attitudes and policies in the workplace "often militate against long-run economic efficiency, while failing to respond to the present social reality and the concerns of today's workers." The EPC panel called for the reorientation of training programs, benefit systems, and work rules and attitudes "to respond to what is soon to be the typical American worker: the working parent."

Labor Secretary on Problems of Working Parents

"We still act as though workers have no families .... Labor and management haven't faced that adequately, or at all. They don't understand it, and I think that's dumb," said Secretary of Labor William Brock in a 1985 address at ceremonies marking the 65th anniversary of DOL's Women's Bureau. Although women have made great strides in the labor market, American managers and labor organizations are paying too little attention to the problems of working parents, Brock said. Although he did not offer any specific proposals for dealing with problems of working parents, Brock did observe, "Secure parents who aren't worried about their kids are better workers."

"We still act as though workers have no families .... Labor and management haven't faced that adequately, or at all."

"Corporate policy is severely behind the times," according to Anne Ladkey, director of the Women Employed Institute in Chicago. Women are in jobs in greater numbers than ever and in jobs that they never had, she noted. "They are not replaceable now and yet companies still haven't moved along on this." There is a societal responsibility, Ladkey said, for a company to provide humane policies

that support families of all kinds, whether it's a worker
responsibility for an elderly parent, or a child. "It's not
pollution. They have a duty to respond," she maintained.

Men are going to play a role in changing corporate polic
but the front lines will be staffed by women. Women, not men, a๛
concerned with family issues, she said. Although there are now more wo๛๛
women and two-career couples than ever, Ladkey said, when women break the
barrier to top management, they will be in a stronger position to be influential on
the family concerns of workers.

Most corporations are still run by men with stay-at-home wives, Ladkey said,
and many of these executives have not grasped the problem of balancing work and
family.

Working women's problems are too often "painted as male-vs.-female issues, but
they are not," Rep. Patricia Schroeder (D-Colo) told a November 1985 conference
at Northeastern University. They are family issues, human issues, quality-of-life
issues, everybody's issues, said Schroeder, who urged employers to develop policies
that accommodate the families and lifestyles of today.

(Legislation providing for parental and disability leave, introduced as HR 2020
in 1985 and reintroduced by Schroeder as HR 4300 in March 1986, is discussed in
Chapters IV and V. Full text of HR 2020 can be found in the Appendix.)

Employers Need to Catch Up

Sensitivity to family concerns by employers has lagged behind the emergence of
family concerns as an issue for employees, according to John Fernandez, author of
Child Care and Corporate Productivity. "The higher you go in the corporate
structure, the less likely are the department heads to want to provide some type of
child care," said Fernandez. Of those managers and officers well up on the
corporate ladder, "a much higher percentage have wives who do not work, or if
they do work, it's only part time," he told BNA. If they have child care needs,
they have an ample income to meet that need, even to the extent of having a live-in
housekeeper, Fernandez maintained.

"In addition," according to Fernandez, "there's the attitude, 'I didn't have any
problems with child care, my wife stayed home. Why can't other people solve their
child care problems?' " He remarked, "I'd say that's the dominant opinion up
there."

"At this point the family needs to have an impact on the workplace . . . to keep . . . from going under."

Fernandez suggested that a small but growing number of employers have begun
to recognize that, to be efficient and effective, they will have to begin assisting employees with child care.

A lot of chief executive officers in their 40s and 50s weren't sensitized to
work/family concerns when they were growing up because the workplace was
different when they were moving up the corporate ladder, said Irma Finn
Brosseau, executive director of BPW/USA, an advocacy branch of The National
Federation of Business and Professional Women. Many corporate officers are just
not aware of the changes that have taken place in the workplace, she said. The
workplace has an enormous impact on the family, Brosseau observed. "At this

ne family needs to have an impact on the workplace . . . to keep . . . from
under."

art of BPW/USA's role in encouraging accommodation of the family in
orporate policy, Brosseau said, will be to show that it's economically feasible. "I
believe that companies have a natural motivation to see the workplace more
productive."

If there is to be a new understanding of the shared responsibility for child and
elderly dependent care, the issue must be made relevant to men in decisionmaking
positions, Dana Friedman of the Conference Board maintains. At the least,
include them in the debate and acknowledge that there is a potential role for them,
she said.

The only way to spark a corporate response on work-and-family issues, Friedman told BNA, is to present those issues in terms of self-interest. Some companies
have a "gut" feeling that it is an appropriate thing to do because it will make them
more productive. "For those who don't believe it or don't want to see it, it's a very
hard thing to prove. There has to be some leap of faith because the data are so
lacking," Friedman said.

Walking a Fine Line on Work/Family Problems

As part of its study of work and family life, Bank Street College of Education in
New York City surveyed corporate decisionmakers in 1984, asking the following
question: How do you view the influx of women into the labor market and the role
of the corporation in making changes on behalf of these families?

---

*"Most managers think there is a fine line that a company must walk in
response to work/family problems — the line between being paternalistic or
interfering, and being responsive. That line has changed in the past few years as a
result of companies' greater involvement in developing work/family innovations."*

Ellen Galinsky, principal investigator, reported the initial findings of the study
in 1984. "Most managers think there is a fine line that a company must walk in
response to work/family problems — the line between being paternalistic or
interfering, and being responsive. That line has changed in the past few years as a
result of companies' greater involvement in developing work/family innovations. It
was agreed that whenever an employee's productivity or performance was affected
by personal problems, the company should step in," Galinsky said.

In a report released in 1985, the National Commission on Working Women
concluded: "The message to business, labor and government is clear: They must
break into the circle and assume more responsibility for child care . . . Employers
and policymakers must offer their own leadership and creativity in order for
affordable solutions to be found."

In addition to the expansion of direct child care assistance, a number of
companies are changing work-time arrangements to allow greater flexibility for
family responsibilities, the Commission noted.

Piecemeal Approach to Policymaking Scored

While the response of most employers to the child care needs of their employees
is disappointing to many employees and unions, the Commission said, advocates of
change are maintaining the drive to solicit employer support.

"Working parents feel a strong need for societal supports, a need which thus far has not been met," said Catalyst in its "Report on a National Study of Parental Leaves." The need has not been met, in part, because of a piecemeal approach to policymaking, according to the New York-based organization, which examines work and family issues. "Companies have tried to address one or two problems, but have failed to evolve a comprehensive plan that would meet the needs of this new, and by no means insignificant, segment of the work force."

In considering policy changes, Catalyst said, companies are torn between two opposing forces. One is the changing nature of the work force and the demand for policies designed to accommodate employees' needs. The other is management's concern about the rise in costs and the loss in short-term productivity that can result from increased leave-taking.

Catalyst concluded:

"In recent years, working parents have changed in their perceptions of themselves and their ability to manage work and family. The time when they felt obliged to shoulder their responsibilities with a minimum of outside help has passed. Working parents now realize that fulfilling their responsibilities as workers or as parents is unlikely without some type of societal supports. Because perceived needs have changed, working parents — particularly women — are now more likely to assess employer attitudes and to scrutinize benefits packages.

"Meanwhile, companies are discovering that meeting the needs of today's working parents can conflict with such corporate concerns as maintaining short-term productivity and containing costs. Future policy changes will depend on the outcome of this tug-of-war between two divergent constituencies."

IV. CASE STUDIES

The number of working mothers in the United States has risen dramatically since 1970. Coinciding with that increase is an increased demand by employees for child care assistance. Some employers have fashioned their own responses to help employees meet responsibilities for their children, other dependents, and spouses. Other firms are supporting existing community-based resources, or helping to fund new ones, to ensure that adequate, affordable options will be available to employees.

Employers, labor unions, and public policymakers all have begun to focus attention on the unmet needs of an increasingly diverse American work force. This chapter examines some of the options adopted by employers that are trying to fashion ways of accommodating workers' family obligations. The case studies that follow reflect the trends in employer responses in five areas: child and dependent care programs, alternative work schedules, employee assistance programs, parental leave, and relocation assistance programs.

A. CHILD AND DEPENDENT CARE PROGRAMS

As long as the number of couples and single parents in the work force continues to climb, the pressure on employers, unions, and government to provide for adequate, affordable child and dependent care will continue to mount. Since 1980, there has been dramatic growth in the proportion of the U.S. labor force that must rely on child care services in order to work, Dana Friedman, senior research associate with the Work and Family Information Center at the Conference Board, told BNA. Furthermore, a 1985 Conference Board study shows that child care expenses are the fourth-largest budget item for most American households, behind food, housing, and taxes. Away-from-home care for one child can range from $1,500 to $10,000 a year, with most parents paying an average $3,000, the board said.

Trend Is toward Assistance, but Real Numbers Small

Although the employer response to the mounting pressure for child care assistance has grown dramatically in recent years, the number of employers providing such assistance is still quite small. As of October 1985, the Conference Board reported, some 2,500 companies were providing some form of child care assistance. This is a fourfold increase over the 600 in 1982, said Friedman, of the New York-based research organization. The increase in the number of companies adopting such options has not leveled off, Friedman said, and is not likely to do so.

The breakdown of the options these companies are using, according to the Conference Board, is as follows:
- flexible spending accounts, salary reduction — 800;
- information and referral — 500;
- on- or near-site day care centers
  — hospitals - 400
  — corporations - 150
  — public agencies - 30;
- discounts (50% with corporate contributions) — 300;
- comprehensive cafeteria benefit plans — 150;
- after-school child care — 75;
- family day care support — 50;
- sick child care initiatives — 20;
- financial assistance vouchers — 25.

The Conference Board also says that as many as 1,000 employers provide corporate contributions to local child care programs and another 1,000 offer parent education seminars at the workplace.

Child Care: The Critical Factor in Returning to Work

The critical factor in being able to return to work after childbirth and to stay on the job is adequate child care. That's what working women told Catalyst, a non-profit career and family resource center. "A management consultant who had an excellent child care arrangement that fell through said, 'The hardest thing is to go to work with doubts about what's happening at home. If your child care is good,

---

" 'The hardest thing is to go to work with doubts about what's happening at home. If your child care is good, you can be yourself. If it isn't, you can't function.' "

---

you can be yourself. If it isn't, you can't function.' Many women reported having difficulty locating and maintaining satisfactory child care. They also complained about the lack of support systems when an arrangement collapsed or a child became ill. These factors combined to make many employees continuously apprehensive about their return to work," Catalyst stated in its 1986 "Report on a National Study of Parental Leaves."

In its 1985 profile of child care workers, *Who Cares For Kids?*, the National Commission on Working Women concluded that the supply of child care centers has not kept up with the demand created by "the explosion of mothers into the labor force in the last decade." The shortage of child care slots is particularly acute for infant care, the Commission noted.

"It appears that employers have a major challenge in responding to the child care issue," Catalyst observed. Noting that working parents are expected to make up more than 66 percent of the U.S. work force by 1990, Catalyst said that, if its findings "are any indication, the child care issue is not going to disappear for employers, but rather can only grow in scope and impact."

The Dependent Care Woes of Working Parents

More than one-third of 651 employees responding to a 1985 Boston University study reported they had significant difficulties in managing family responsibilities. According to the study, conducted by the university's School of Social Work and C.O.P.E., a Boston-based licensed family counseling center, the problems that parents found most difficult were:
- not being able to be home when children return from school;
- staying home with a sick child;
- going to school events for children;
- taking children to health care appointments; and
- getting children to and from child care.

In addition, 18 percent of employees cited responsibility for an aging parent as a very serious problem. One-third said they provided financial assistance to their parents and spent considerable time making arrangements for their care.

Results of a 1985 study of 8,083 employees in the greater Kansas City, Mo., area support the Boston University findings on the difficulty of combining work and family responsibilities. According to preliminary findings, 37 percent of women employees with children, and 45 percent of the employees who were

---

"Affordable child care of satisfactory quality is difficult to find . . . "

---

separated from their spouses said they had some difficulty in combining work and family responsibilities, according to a report by the Metropolitan Child Care Project (MCCP), which conducted the study.

"Parents responding to the survey seem to experience the most difficulty in finding child care," the MCCP report said. Overall, 56 percent of the women employees and 41 percent of the men employees said they had difficulty finding child care. Care for children who are sick, infant care, and summer care for school age children were the types of child care that appeared to be most in demand, the report stated. "Affordable child care of satisfactory quality is difficult to find," the MCCP report concluded.

The Problem of Caring for Sick Children

A particularly difficult part of the overall child care problem for parents is the matter of care for sick children. Parents have no alternatives to staying home from work when their children are sick.

According to a 1985 study by Karen Skold, a researcher at Stanford University's Center for Research on Women, the problem has not been solved in the last 15 years. In 1970, Skold said, a survey sponsored by the City of Berkeley, Calif., revealed that 63 percent of the responding parents stayed home with a sick child. Fifteen years later, a survey of its members in San Jose, Calif., by Local 715 of the Service Employees International Union showed that 60 percent of its members stayed home when a child was sick, reported Skold. The rest said their spouse stayed home, another relative took care of the child, or they relied on a child care provider. "Again, only a minority had a satisfactory alternative to missing work," Skold pointed out.

Most employers do not know whether child illness is a significant cause of employee absence, since workers typically report such absences as due to their own illness, Skold wrote. There is evidence, however, that sick children may be an important hidden cause of absence, she added.

A certain amount of mild illness is a normal part of childhood. Medical studies have shown that young children typically get eight to 10 viral infections a year, according to the study by the Stanford scholar.

"In the absence of any satisfactory alternatives for care of a sick child, working parents find that the inevitable bouts of flu and colds cause family crises," the Stanford researcher said. "Torn between job and child, parents feel they cannot do the right thing no matter what they do."

The Boston University study reached the same conclusion: No formal child care arrangements exist when children are sick. Moreover, women are six times more likely to have to stay home with a sick child than are men, according to its findings.

Although a parent staying home from work may be the best alternative for meeting the needs of a sick child, in cases of excessive absence, there are negative consequences both to the parent and the employer.

Further evidence of how parents deal with the problem of sick children is presented in the MCCP report. When their children were sick, 66 percent of the men in the Metropolitan Child Care Project reported that their spouse or an older child stayed home with the sick child. Women said that they took their children to the regular child care arrangement (24 percent) or that their spouse or an older child stayed home with the sick child (24 percent). Half of the employees who stayed home with their sick child reported that they used vacation or personal leave. Only 16 percent stated that they use sick leave.

Although staying home from work may be the best way for a parent to meet the needs of a sick child, excessive absence can bring negative consequences both to the parent and the employer, said the Stanford University report. In the worst cases, parents lose their jobs. "Particularly vulnerable are those in entry-level positions, in probationary periods, and in jobs where work cannot be taken home or made up at a different time."

Excessive absence also causes problems for employers, the Stanford study pointed out. Although most workplaces can adjust to an occasional unplanned absence, frequent absences disrupt work. Co-workers may feel frustrated and the employer incurs productivity losses, the report said. "Small organizations, where each employee plays a key role, are especially vulnerable to frequent, unplanned absences."

One of the approaches the Stanford report advocated for responding to the problem of sick child care is to involve employers in the effort to create more options. Employers, the study said, can respond by:

• adopting flexible, occasional absence policies which recognize that sometimes employees must take care of a sick family member;

• working with other community groups to stimulate the development of new sick child care services so that their employees have an alternative to staying home; and

• sharing the cost of using such a service with their employees, so that the option of coming to work is financially feasible.

Child Care Concerns: More Prominent Among Women

For most women, child care concerns figure prominently in career decisions, according to John Fernandez, author of *Child Care and Corporate Productivity*, a report on a survey of 5,000 management and non-management employees. Among the women respondents with children under the age of two, 46 percent said that "at least to some extent" child care concerns would influence their decision on whether to accept a promotion; only 23 percent of the male respondents with children in the same age group said child care concerns would have any effect on such a decision. Of the women respondents with children age two to five, 51 percent said they considered child care concerns a factor in making promotion decisions, while only 20 percent of the men considered such concerns a factor. "When you look at what it costs to train highly competent people — $25,000 for an average employee and $50,000 for a competent employee — to lose someone because of child care needs is just wasting the corporation's resources," Fernandez said.

Eight Work Days a Year

In addition to problems of caring for sick children, working parents also face problems ranging from the illness of a care provider to problems with transportation and school holidays. Such child care problems force working parents to be off the job a total of about about eight work days a year, according to a 1985 study by Child Care Systems, Inc., a corporate child care consultant based in Lansdale, Pa. CCS serves 65 employers and 135,000 families in eight states.

Among the 1,888 working parents who participated in the study, 33 percent said they took vacation leave to cope with child care problems, 31 percent took sick leave, and 24 percent took personal days off. The respondents also reported losing an average of just over eight hours a year due to leaving work early or arriving late because of child care problems. Forty percent said they have considered quitting their jobs because of child care issues.

CCS also concluded that workers needed an average of nine hours to locate care, lost a day a year in tardiness and phone calls, and were absent five days because of child care problems.

Women: More Stress, More Absenteeism

The Metropolitan Child Care Project in Kansas City concluded that women with children were found to have the highest incidence of absenteeism of all employees. The project's report noted a relationship between child care resources and company policy and the number of work days missed, late arrivals, early departures, and interruptions while at work.

Women with children in the Kansas City study also reported experiencing more overall stress in life than men with children. When asked whether or not child care and five other areas of life had created stress during the previous four weeks, 40 percent of women with children and 24 percent of men with children reported stress related to child care. Job stress and family finances were identified as the greatest sources of pressure.

Professors Arthur Emlen and Paul Koren of the Regional Research Institute for Human Services at Portland State University in Oregon surveyed employees in 33 companies and agencies in the Portland area in 1984-85 to determine the impact of child care concerns on the workplace.

The professors found that women assumed most of the responsibility for child care arrangements. "Absenteeism for men was low because women's was high," Emlen and Koren wrote in *Hard to Find and Difficult to Manage: The Effects of Child Care on the Workplace.* Furthermore, they said, "[I]n families where both spouses earned incomes, women still appeared to carry a disproportional share of the child care responsibilities."

"[I]n families where both spouses earned incomes, women still appeared to carry a disproportional share of the child care responsibilities."

When latchkey children — children who come home to an empty house after school — telephone a parent at work, it's usually the mother who receives the call, agreed researcher Thomas Long. The Koren/Emlen survey revealed that women with children under 18 were interrupted at work two times as often as men. "We still look toward women as the main child care giver in the family," Long explained. For this reason, mothers tend to work closer to home than do fathers, Long maintained.

Emlen said he doubts that productivity is severely diminished during the day because of telephone interruptions from latchkey children. "They certainly do get interruptions, but people compensate."

Emlen's advice is for companies to "roll with it." With regard to corporate policy, "it's better to try to remove the barrier to accommodate the needs of kids calling the workplace, or to find an alternative to their being alone at all," he said. There are companies that are very severe in their policy against taking calls at work, and "they pay the price," Emlen said. Employee dissatisfaction is the result of inflexible corporate policies that ignore an employee's family responsibilities, Emlen told BNA.

Children Alone: The Effects

The welfare of children at home alone after school is becoming a national social issue. Despite the growing number of after-school programs serving an estimated five to 10 million of these so-called latchkey children, the need for after-school care isn't being met for all such children.

The long-term effects that caring for themselves may have on elementary school-age children is the subject of study by Thomas and Lynette Long, co-directors of the non-profit National Institute for Latchkey Children and Youth. For certain children, the after-school hours are suffused with loneliness, fear, and boredom, according to the Longs. Thomas Long said he believes that "kids need continuous loving, adult supervision, especially elementary school-age children," and said he supports extended day care programs offered in certain communities by schools, by YMCAs and YWCAs, and by churches and other organizations. While such programs are becoming more common, a number of barriers — among them, lack of transportation and insufficient funds — still prevent the inclusion of all latchkey children.

Employers, and employees, are just now beginning to recognize the costs associated with child care concerns. Productivity declines can be documented by examining absenteeism rates and incidents of tardiness and "leaving early," John Fernandez maintains, but he told of another cost — the decline in job performance among parents who are under stress because of concerns about children. "We have data which clearly show that people who are having trouble finding child care, or who have latchkey children, are having a difficult time balancing family and work," Fernandez said. "They have an extreme amount of stress on the job, and also at home." He advised:

"[I]f you're a corporation, and you want to make certain you have the most productive, efficient organization, especially in a new competitive arena, you want to make sure people are working at their highest capacity. Then you have to look at child care not as a way to help women work, but as a concrete decision to allow your corporation and your employees to be more competitive."

Sixty-five percent of all respondents in his survey said "[they] believe that child care problems are costing their corporations a great deal in lost productivity," Fernandez told BNA. "If [corporations] wanted to look, they could find the dollar value," he said.

Child Care: Benefits for Employers and Employees

Companies that invest in child care programs for their employees who are parents reap a number of benefits, according to Catalyst. "When the adequate care of children is not a parental concern, companies can expect improved concentration and performance. In addition to boosting workplace morale and productivity, employers providing child care assistance have the recruitment edge with a gradually shrinking labor pool," Catalyst maintained. Steve Marcus, manager of IBM's employee assistance programs, told BNA that the computer firm in April 1985 directed its recruiters to cite the firm's nationwide child care referral service as a company benefit when luring new talent to IBM.

The assurance of adequate child care enhances employment opportunities for individuals not now in the work force, according to the House Select Committee on Children, Youth, and Families. A committee fact sheet reported that a June 1982 survey conducted by the Census Bureau showed that 45 percent of single mothers with children under five and 36 percent of mothers in families with incomes less than $15,000, who were not working, said they would work if affordable child care were available. The same survey showed that 26 percent of unemployed mothers with children under age five said they would seek employment if affordable child care were available.

CHILD CARE OPTIONS

Dana Friedman of the Conference Board said that, with increasing pressure on companies to deal with the child care needs of parents, many companies are finding it easier to respond with contributions to existing child care systems than to make a change in internal policy. Friedman predicted three options would grow in popularity: information and referral services, employer financial contributions, and flexible benefits plans. Employers want to help employees "buy into" the existing systems, she said. This procedure leaves the burden for selecting up to the parents and avoids some of the liability issues, Friedman explained, noting that it also allows a greater number of employees to be served.

The percentage of employees that use employer-provided child care benefits is low, Friedman said. The rate of use is under 5 percent in the case of dependent care assistance plans, she said.

Among the options for dealing with child care needs, information services and financial support for community-based child care are considerably more popular among employers than subsidies for employees' child care and on- or near-site child care, according to Catalyst's 1986 final "Report on a National Study of Parental Leaves." Catalyst stated that "[c]oncern over equity may explain these preferences . . . . Direct subsidies for child care and on- or near-site day care could be considered special benefits, since non-parents are obviously excluded. Moreover, on- or near-site day care entails a substantial start-up cost and company involvement."

A 1985 survey by New York City's Human Resources Administration found employers there prefer not to give cash assistance to workers, but to provide information on child care facilities by means of seminars or workshops and to participate in a referral and placement system.

Of 156 northeastern Ohio companies responding to a 1983 phone survey by RESOURCE: Careers, 32.9 percent said they had an information and referral service, 12.8 provided financial support to community-based child care facilities, and 0.6 percent provided subsidies for child care.

Trends

The two most popular forms of child care assistance provided by employers appear to be flexible benefits plans and information and referral services, said Tom Copeland, director of employer services for Resources for Child Caring in St. Paul, Minn. More and more companies are taking some responsibility for collecting and passing on the information to employees, he said.

The Metropolitan Child Care Project survey in Kansas City revealed that parents' greatest need was better information and referral services, Shirley Stubbs, manager of child care services for Family and Children Services of Kansas City, Inc., and a staffer on the project, told BNA.

One reason for the growth in popularity of child care information and referral is that employers aren't ready to choose the more expensive options because they fear the issue of equity will be raised.

"It is confusing out there," said Connie Bell, director of the Greater Minneapolis Day Care Association. "We have 2,000 child care providers in Hennepin County." One reason for the growth in popularity of child care information and referral, according to Bell, is that employers aren't ready to choose the more expensive options because they fear the issue of equity will be raised.

Information and Referral: Some Drawbacks

Although she said information and referral services are one of the child care "growth industries," Bell remarked that these systems don't solve all parents' problems. "The only drawback is that there also needs to be a recruitment component. You can't solve the problem if you can't make the referral," Bell said, pointing out that there is a continuing need for more child care providers. More companies need to contribute funding to help add additional providers, she said, adding that the need is particularly acute for infant and sick child care.

IBM's national information and referral project is one that is helping increase the supply of care providers, maintained Steve Marcus, manager of the firm's employee assistance programs. Marcus said that agencies with which IBM has contracts are supporting the efforts to open 300 new centers, and have recruited and trained about 240 people to provide care in the home of the child. Employers

---

Employers who provide child care information and services have a moral obligation to create new resources, and shouldn't simply overload existing ones.

---

who provide child care information and services, Marcus said, have a moral obligation to create new resources, and shouldn't simply overload existing ones.

Work-Family Seminars

A growing number of employers are offering seminars or employee education programs to help employees better integrate their work and family lives, and more efficiently deal with the conflicts that arise.

Seminars on work-and-family issues often are conducted at the workplace by a professional facilitator or consultant, who educates and trains employees how to combine work and family responsibilities, Catalyst reported in a paper on the subject. At the seminars, employees discuss how family life affects work and how work-and-family conflicts can be handled, said Catalyst.

Bell said the Greater Minneapolis Day Care Association has had "good luck" with parenting seminars and materials for on-site parenting information centers. Nevertheless, Bell said, seminars — like information and referral services — are short-term solutions to the bigger problems of availability and affordability.

One way employers can be more responsive to the needs of working parents at minimal costs is to set up working-family information centers at worksites, according to Dorothy Rich, who formed Dorothy Rich Associates, Inc., a firm that helps parents manage the demands of family and work. These can be as simple as providing child care magazines and pamphlets or as complex as offering parent training on topics such as effective discipline, said Rich. "Concern about children and lack of time to be with them are sources of anxiety and tension for working parents. These, of course, can lead to job-performance problems. Parents need the tools that can help them manage the demands of their work and home lives," according to Rich.

A survey of more than 400 Minnesota businesses revealed that many are interested in offering seminars to address work-family issues. The 1982 survey, conducted by the Vocational Education Work & Family Institute, which helps businesses obtain education services on work-and-family issues, showed that 62 percent of the respondents said they would consider offering such seminars. The respondents who said they were likely to offer seminars indicated that they had two primary reasons for doing so: one, to demonstrate that they were concerned about their employees, and two, to help improve productivity.

The most popular seminars among employers, according to the Minnesota survey, were:

- managing financial resources;
- assessing family goals and values;
- identifying the concerns of dual-earner families; and

● enhancing personal relationships.

If seminars were offered, the survey report concluded, "it is clear that the company may be willing to support them financially at least in part. Only five percent of respondents said they would expect employees to financially support them alone."

Child Care Centers: Pluses and Minuses

The provision of a quality child care facility can provide significant benefits to companies, although there are also disadvantages.

Child care is attractive to many prospective employees, and can help recruitment, noted Catalyst, which also contended that enhanced productivity, reduced absenteeism, and high employee morale are other benefits yielded by on-site day care. "[E]mployees with satisfactory child care are often unwilling to give it up, and are therefore less likely to seek new employment," added Catalyst. Firms also can generate positive publicity and enhance their public profile on the urgent social issue of child care by having a child care program.

In a 1983 survey at Hoffmann-La Roche, Inc., 78 percent of those employees who took advantage of the company's on-site day-care facilities reported that their job performance had improved as a result, Dianne Keel, director of the firm's child care program, told an Oct. 25, 1985, conference on work and family issues. Forty-three percent of these employees also reported reduced absenteeism, Keel informed the conference, held in New York City and sponsored by the Oil, Chemical and Atomic Workers International Union.

On the question of equity, Keel said, 85 percent of those employees who were not raising children expressed support for the child-care benefit.

Keel also said that, before setting up its on-site facilities at corporate headquarters in Nutley, N.J., Hoffman-La Roche had experimented for two years with a site 10 miles away. "Having a facility at that distance, connected to the office by a major highway which may be clogged, didn't exactly reduce the stress that parents were subjected to," Keel said.

Some of the drawbacks to an on-site child care center include high start-up costs, unstable usage rates, liability issues, and the issue of equity for all employees. According to Catalyst, there are three main considerations related to the equity of a child care center. "First, an on-site center that benefits only the employees who use it may be perceived as an inequitable benefit by those employees who are not parents and never intend to be. This may be particularly true if the cost of care is subsidized. Second, parents who choose other forms of child care may consider it unfair if on-site center is the only form of child care that is subsidized. Third, if a company builds a center for one location, it might feel a need to serve other sites as well."

"Today, an astute employer can and must address child care concerns," said Dorothy Rich. "But employers need not be constrained in thinking that the only choice is to set up a child care center."

Child Care Approaches

On-site day care facilities are seldom the best solution to child problems in the work force for either the employer or employees, and employers can significantly contribute to employees' peace of mind, and thus to productivity and profits, by other responses, according to speakers at a Jan. 16, 1986, Conference Board-sponsored meeting in New York City on family and work issues.

Harold Heinze, president of ARCO Alaska, said that while his company wished to respond to the concerns of its working parents, "[w]e had no desire to be in the day care business. We felt that was a cop out, and we couldn't do it anyway."

Instead, Heinze said, ARCO spent about $100,000 in a variety of other ways. It gave a seed grant for a day care center at a YMCA in a part of Anchorage where no such facility existed. It also developed a database of all child care services in the city, sponsored the Alaska meeting of the White House's Advisory Council on Private Sector Initiatives on child care, and convinced the city to focus on setting up a program for latchkey children.

Peter Osenar, executive vice president for personnel and organization with AmeriTrust, a Cleveland-based bank with some 1,300 employees, said his company has been offering a Child Care and Assistance Program (CARE) since 1981. In surveying employees prior to launching CARE, AmeriTrust was most surprised to discover that the workers did not want a child care center at the bank's downtown headquarters.

CARE concentrates on being an effective information and referral service, and on closely monitoring the facilities it recommends. Osenar maintained that "cost savings to the bank from CARE, if we only look at retaining employees who take maternity leave and need child care to return to their jobs, has been 7,000 times the annual cost of the program." CARE and other of the bank's attempts to alleviate external stresses on employees have contributed to a high productivity level at AmeriTrust, according to Osenar.

Margaret Franklin, manager of benefit services for Levi Strauss & Co., said her company had, over a 10-year period, experimented with various modes of child care assistance, including an on-site project. But, she explained, Levi Strauss found it could be most productive in an advisory and facilitative role. Specifically, the company is focusing on identifying family day care homes in the various communities where it has offices and production plants, Franklin said.

Financial Support

Establishing on- or near-site day care centers for employees is only one of the many options open to corporations interested in helping employees successfully balance work and family responsibilities. Other options may involve some financial support from employers, unions, and others. Employers can help to fund the cost

---

"Children need more than child care — they need parents who can take care of them while still managing their work and family lives."

---

of child care by providing vouchers for a specific amount of money that can be used at any licensed child care center or family-day care home, or for a caregiver at the parent's home.

Employers also can reserve slots in an existing child care center, and subsidize a portion of the cost. By retaining slots, the employer insures the availability of care when supply is limited. When ample services are available in a community, an employer can pay for slots when care is needed.

Employers also can band together in groups to develop and support a child care center or other child care program to serve their employees.

Employers do not have to go into the child care business to be responsive to employee needs, Dorothy Rich maintained. Even if they did, this would not solve all problems because centers are helpful only to parents of preschool children and

only for a short period of time, she said. "Children need more than child care —
they need parents who can take care of them while still managing their work and
family lives."

What Should Be Done?

Employers, schools, the child care community, churches, and other civic groups
should become more sensitive to child care needs and ensure that an adequate
delivery system for child care and preschool programs is put into place.

This was one of a series recommendations contained in a report published by the
Family Policy Panel of the Economic Policy Council (EPC) of the United Nations
Association of the United States of America. The report was released at a meeting
of the EPC in Washington, D.C., in January 1986.

With the influx of women into the labor force, particularly mothers of young
children, the need for child care has grown dramatically in the last two decades,
the panel concluded. "In the area of child care, the scope is so broad that a wide
array of initiatives must be taken. Effectively meeting the child care needs of
children and parents will require the development of a variety of options that
support and facilitate individual choice in selecting suitable care arrangements,"
the panel said. Cooperative efforts of the public and the private sectors, the
existing child care community, and the public schools are required if existing child
care problems are to be overcome, the panel contended.

In late 1985, another blue ribbon panel which examined the subject of family
and work, the Yale Bush Center Advisory Committee on Infant Care Leave,
produced recommendations similar to those of the EPC panel. The Yale committee concluded that the problems encountered by working parents in providing care
for their infants have reached such great proportions that they require "immediate
national action."

Hobby Horse Day Nursery by Crystal Truslow, age 4.

*   *   *

ON-SITE DAY CARE

Organizations: **Boston City Hospital and SEIU Local 285**
                    Boston, Mass.

Summary: **In its 1982 contract with Boston City Hospital, Local 285 of the
                    Service Employees International Union won an on-site day care
                    center for the employees it represents at the hospital — clerical
                    and technical employees, registered nurses, licensed practical
                    nurses, and public health nurses. Demand has grown enough that
                    the union is now negotiating to expand the center.**

In 1982, Local 285 of the Service Employees International Union negotiated with Boston City Hospital for establishment of an on-site day care center for union-represented employees. At that time, 16 slots for infants and toddlers were arranged, but the demand is such that more slots are now needed, according to Peter Hardie, Local 285 representative.

Local 285 represents four bargaining units at the hospital — a group of 950 clerical and technical employees and three nursing units which include a total of 1,000 registered nurses, licensed practical nurses, and public health nurses. The local has 10,000 members statewide.

Local 285, along with two other unions that represent employees at Boston City Hospital — the House Officers Association and Council 93 of AFSCME — is now discussing expansion of the center with hospital management, Hardie said. Local 285 also is expanding its day care committee to include representatives of AFSCME and the Officers Association, he said. The principal problem is finding the room for on-site expansion since space is at a premium at the city-run hospital, he explained. The center now accommodates the maximum number of children allowed by state law.

In addition to considering the need for an expanded facility, the committee also will consider the possibility of lengthening the day care hours, according to Hardie. The center is open from 6 a.m. to 6 p.m. Monday through Friday. The committee, however, will have to examine closely the questions of whether it would be cost effective to have the center open late at night, he said, and whether there would be enough day care professionals to staff the center at those hours.

Local 285 also is working with the city to establish another committee which would investigate the possibility of a day care center for the 2,000 SEIU members who work for the city of Boston.

The hospital day care center "has expanded way beyond what we thought it would originally be," Hardie said. Of the 16 slots, 11 are subsidized by the city, and, Hardie pointed out, there is a big demand for these subsidized slots. Fees are established according to a sliding scale, with the maximum fee set at $135 per week. The maximum is excessive for the clericals represented by SEIU, Hardie said, but is more affordable for the nurses. However, the problem faced by the nurses who wish to take advantage of the on-site center is scheduling day care around rotating shifts.

The parents who use the center are pleased, Hardie said, because they are able to drop their children off in the morning, visit them during the day if they wish, and pick them up on the way out of the building in the evening.

Benefits to the hospital include improved productivity and a drop in absenteeism, according to Hardie, who said he believed that, in cases where companies have a problem with excessive tardiness, one of the main reasons for that absenteeism is lack of sympathy on the part of management to day care problems faced by employees.

ON-SITE DAY CARE, SUMMER CAMP

Organization: **Fel-Pro, Inc.**
                   Skokie, Ill.

Summary: **Fel-Pro has long considered itself an extension of its workers' families and as such provides a generous benefits package, including a summer camp for employees' children; college scholarships; a Better Neighborhood Fund, which makes donations to worthy neighborhood organizations in communities where Fel-Pro employees live; and counseling, income tax preparation, and tutoring services. Two years ago, the company opened its own on-site day care center, which now serves 40 children. An employee's per-child cost runs $60 per week and is about half of what the firm contributes.**

The idea of a company being an extension of the family has been the cornerstone of corporate practice at Fel-Pro, Inc., since its founding in 1918. A family-owned company headquartered in Skokie, Ill., Fel-Pro is one of the world's largest manufacturers and marketers of automotive and industrial gaskets. The company also makes adhesives, sealants, specialty lubricants, and elastomeric products.

"We have always felt that treating people decently and fairly is good business practice," said Vice President Kenneth Lehman, a member of the fourth generation of his family in active management. "We consider everything we do to be enlightened self-interest."

Fel-Pro's beneficent paternalism includes a generous fringe benefit package for its 1,500 employees. Relatives of current employees are given preferential treatment for vacancies and new positions, and nearly all temporary summer helpers are drawn from employees' children.

While the benefit plan at Fel-Pro is extremely comprehensive — ranging from traditional vacation time and health insurance to a tuition refund plan for job-related education — family-oriented benefits are the highlights of the plan.

Summer Day Camp

Fifteen years ago, realizing that during summer school vacation employee absenteeism went up because parents stayed home, the company established the Triple R Ranch, a summer camp program for children ages seven through 15. Bus service from plant to ranch coordinates with shift times. A 250-acre company-owned recreational facility, Triple R Ranch includes an olympic-sized pool and family garden plots. "We had kids out on the streets during the summer, and providing a camp took a big load off their parents' minds," Lehman said.

Two years ago, Fel-Pro opened its own on-site day care center, which now has 40 enrollees. "Because of our camp, we had a long history of children coming to work with their parents," says Ken Lehman, whose own children attended Triple R, "and we had been looking at day care for nearly a decade."

Other family-oriented benefits include:

• A scholarship program which pays up to $2,200 annually toward school costs.

• The Better Neighborhood Fund, which makes donations to worthy neighborhood organizations in communities where Fel-Pro employees live. During the past 10 years, the fund has poured more than $750,000 into grass roots community organizations like Scout troops and school PTAs.

• Counseling, income tax preparation, and tutoring services. Legal assistance is provided free of charge, and the company will pay a portion of the charges for diagnostic testing and individual tutoring for employees' children with learning problems.

• "Special" gifts. In addition to Christmas bonuses and a free birthday lunch, employees also receive $100 when they marry; a $1,000 U.S. Treasury security, redeemable at age 21, for each new baby; $1,000 toward legal expenses for the adoption of a child; $100 when each child graduates from high school; and a $200 check in the event a relative dies.

Fel-Pro also has a quality of worklife, or participative management, program, called Employee Forum. Hourly employees in each department elect a delegate for a one-year term to the Forum. Delegates meet monthly with management to discuss subjects of interest to the whole department. To reward the extra effort required, delegates receive one extra day of vacation for every four meetings they attend, or three extra days for a year of service.

Concerns: State Licensure, Equity

Despite its philosophy of "enlightened self-interest" and its extensive list of benefits, the prospect of a day care center was daunting, Lehman confessed. The state licensure issues "gave us pause" for a while, he said, adding that a more important sticking point was that on-site day care is "a significant benefit that only a minority of employees participate in." So far the issue of equity has not surfaced among employees, according to Robert O'Keefe, the firm's director of employee relations. Since Fel-Pro has been consistently profitable, no hard choices about benefits have had to be made. But the equity issue is certainly one which management is aware of, and which might surface in an industry downturn, O'Keefe said.

Employees pay $60 weekly, although the actual cost of the service is $180 per child, making the company subsidy $120 weekly, Lehman explained.

Another initial concern, according to Lehman, was that a company-run center might siphon off clients from other area day-care centers, but this was resolved early when the company hired an outside consultant who pointed out that currently the demand for good day care far exceeds the supply.

Expensive, But 'We'd Do It Again'

Eventually, Fel-Pro bit the bullet and went ahead, committed to a first-class facility. "It was more expensive than we thought it would be," said Lehman, who quickly added, "but we'd do it again."

The center is open from 6:40 a.m. until 5:45 p.m., a schedule which takes into account all day shifts. While it is located in a separate building on the plant site, parents may spend their lunch hour with their children, paying an additional $1 for a lunch brought over from the company cafeteria. The center accepts children ages two to six, and includes an accredited kindergarten, according to Scott Mies, the center director.

With eight full-time staff members for 40 children, the center now has an optimal staffing ratio. This permits children to be kept in relatively small groups. Mies said he believes this accounts for the fact that Fel-Pro has experienced "significantly fewer problems with illness" than most larger centers do.

Mies also said he believes that the proportion of company subsidy to the day care program will drop over time. Because of the company's commitment to quality, no expense was spared in initial investment, according to Mies, who explained, "We're making efforts now to trim costs,"

Staff retention, a serious problem at other Chicago-area day care centers, is no problem at Fel-Pro, according to Mies, because of its unequalled benefit package and competitive salaries. "People simply don't leave Fel-Pro until they die," he notes.

In an effort to use the center to capacity, the company recently made day care available to the grandchildren of full-time employees, either on a full or part-time basis.

Full to Capacity in the Long Run

Both Mies and O'Keefe believe that in the long run the center will be fully used. "We're getting a lot of excellent feedback from employees, who at first were apprehensive about leaving their children in a center," Mies reported.

Mies, who has previously taught at Triton College in River Grove, Ill., and as a kindergarten teacher in addition to serving as a child care center director, frequently receives calls from other companies considering day care, and speaks on the subject to organizations.

Most employers do not dispute the demographics pushing the issue, Mies said. "I sense, rather, that they haven't quite come to terms with caring for the children of employees as something which is an employer's responsibility," he said. "They ask, 'Is it really my job to look after his or her kids, too?' "

Fel-Pro has never conducted a cost-effectiveness study of the day care center's benefits, according to Lehman. "We believe," Lehman explained, "that the totality of our program creates a payback which can't be quantified. But we have competition, and by all the traditional business yardsticks of sales growth and profitability, we are highly successful."

NEAR-SITE DAY CARE

Organization:	Hill Holliday Connors Cosmopulos, Inc. Boston, Mass.
Summary:	Concern about attracting and retaining quality staff prompted Hill Holliday to open its own day care center just a few blocks from its offices in downtown Boston. The center is largely subsidized by the firm, with fees to employees determined by a sliding scale based on salary and the age of the child. The center provides

care for children from the age of two months. Only Hill Holliday employees may use the center.

When a senior vice president and a vice president at Hill Holliday Connors Cosmopulos, Inc., a Boston advertising and public relations firm, became pregnant, the firm's senior partners, Jay Hill and Jack Connors, grew concerned about retaining those two women and other key staff, Margaret Bowles Fitzgerald, vice president and director of community relations, told BNA.

Hill and Connors hired a day care consultant and used their own market research group to conduct a needs assessment and feasibility study for a day care center. Ultimately, the firm decided to open a company-sponsored, non-profit center.

HHCC Day Care, Inc., opened on Oct. 28, 1985. Because Massachusetts law and Boston city fire department regulations prohibit infant care anywhere but on the first floor of a building and no suitable affordable first floor space was available in the John Hancock Tower, site of the firm's offices, Hill Holliday's center is not on-site, but instead is located at a church about three blocks from its main office.

"We were lucky to have top management not only support, but initiate the idea," Fitzgerald said. "It's a wonderful place . . . a joy to visit," said Fizgerald, who added that even those who were initially against the idea have been "converted" after seeing the final product. The firm, which employs about 340 workers at its main office, has a tradition of high standards in everything it does, and the day care center is no exception, she maintained.

Renovations Boosted Start-up Costs

A Massachusetts Executive Office of Economic Affairs publication says $50,000 to $150,000 is the most likely range for start-up costs. Hill Holliday spent about $200,000 to renovate the space, and staff and equip the center for its first year of operation. But, Fitzgerald insisted, other companies should not turn away from the idea of corporate-sponsored day care because of Hill Holliday's start-up costs. Much of the firm's costs, she said, are attributable to the extensive renovations performed to bring the space into compliance with Massachusetts Office for Children standards. Rooms were gutted to get rid of old lead-painted walls, an elaborate sprinkler system was installed, and pipes had to be covered, she explained.

Of the company's 340 employees, 11 were using the new center as of mid-January. The center cares for infants two months old and older, as well as toddlers and preschoolers — a total of 12 children as of mid-January. By April, Fitzgerald predicted, all seven slots for infants would be taken and a waiting list will probably be started. Another teacher for infants will soon join the present staff of one director/teacher and three teachers, she said, adding that day care staff salaries are well above the national norm.

The center is largely subsidized by Hill Holliday, Fitzgerald continued. Fees are assessed on a sliding scale depending on income and the age of the child. At the high end, for example, Fitzgerald said, an employee earning $50,000 or more would pay $120 for five full days of infant care. At the other extreme, it would cost an employee who earns less than $20,000 a year $65 a week for care of a preschooler.

The center is a non-profit entity under Sec. 501(C)(3) of the IRS Code. It is open only to Hill Holliday employees and will not be open to outsiders, according to Fitzgerald. Employees have access to the day care center on a first-come, first-served basis, she said.

A 'Family' Tradition

Asked about the philosophy or events that inspired Hill Holliday to open its own center, Fitzgerald replied that the company itself is only 17 years old, has many young employees, and has always had a tradition of a "wonderful family atmosphere" characterized by, among other things, a very generous benefits package. Opening the center simply carries on that tradition, Fitzgerald stated, noting that one of the firm's senior partners had to be convinced not to offer the center as a 100 percent paid benefit.

Fitzgerald strongly recommended that a company considering opening a day care center for its employees first get some outside expert assistance. "Put some money up front and hire the best day care consultant available," she suggested. A consultant can help assess the company's needs, map out choices, and otherwise facilitate the process, she said.

Fitzgerald said the most difficult task, in Hill Holliday's experience, was to identify and negotiate for acceptable real estate in the city's Back Bay, an expensive downtown business and residential area. She suggested that, while state laws and city fire codes are necessarily strict concerning day care centers, they may be prohibiting some firms with downtown locations from opening their own day care centers.

PUBLIC-PRIVATE CONSORTIUM

Organization: California Child Care Initiative
                    San Francisco, Calif.

Summary: **The Child Care Initiative is a consortium of 17 private and public
                    entities, headed by BankAmerica Foundation, San Francisco. The
                    Initiative raised $700,000 in six months to bankroll six pilot
                    projects aimed at increasing the availability and quality of child
                    care statewide. Funds are channeled through existing child care
                    resource and referral agencies in local communities. Those agen-
                    cies decide which child care needs are most important for them
                    and design programs to meet those needs.**

Increasing the availability and quality of child care in California is the goal of the California Child Care Initiative, a joint effort by private and public sector backers spearheaded by the BankAmerica Foundation. The Initiative intends to accomplish its goal by building on an existing state resource and referral network.

In November 1985, backers of the Initiative announced funding for six pilot programs throughout the state that, if successful, will create more than 1,000 new child care spaces in California over the next year and train more than 300 new and existing family day care providers.

"The California Child Care Initiative is a collaborative, public-private partner-ship to increase the supply of child care in California by using resource and referral agencies to recruit and train new child care providers," explained

Rosemary Mans, vice president and associate director of BankAmerica Foundation, which administers the $700,000 raised for the Initiative from corporations, foundations, and from county and local governments.

The Initiative does not provide child care for any of the organizations that have contributed money, Mans said, but will serve as a catalyst, underwriting the efforts of community-based resource and referral agencies to deliver the kind of child care most needed in the communities.

Mans said the Initiative was born out of discussions in 1984 between Bank-America Foundation and Bank of America's Human Resources Division, which indicated that child care was a concern for the bank's employees as well as for the communities where the bank operates. In March 1985, the foundation unveiled both its plans for the Initiative and its intention to raise at least $700,000 to fund six pilot projects.

The $700,000 goal was reached quickly as BankAmerica Foundation, Chevron USA, Inc., and Mervyn's (a department store chain), contributed $100,000 each, American Express Foundation and Pacific Telesis Foundation chipped in $50,000 each, and $25,000 each came from Clorox Company Foundation, Pacific Gas & Electric Company, and the California Community Foundation. Other contributors include the State of California ($100,000), Wells Fargo Foundation ($35,000), the City and County of San Francisco ($25,000), Contra Costa County ($10,000), the City of Sacramento ($10,000) and the County of Sacramento ($10,000).

Through the six pilot projects, nearly 1,000 new child care spaces will be created statewide, Mans explained. The pilot projects are located in Contra Costa County, San Francisco, Sacramento, Los Angeles, Long Beach, and Bakersfield.

To dramatize the need for new child care services, California Lt. Gov. Leo McCarthy said at a press conference announcing the pilot projects in November 1985 that more than three million minor children in California require some kind of day care from people other than their parent and that, according to some estimates, more than half of those children do not receive adequate care now.

Nearly half of California's work force is female and two-thirds of the state's two-parent households will have both parents working by 1990, said McCarthy, who referred to the "dramatic change that is occurring in the work force and in the family structure." Putting the problem those parents face into economic terms, McCarthy said, "No child care facility means no job for a lot of parents."

Building on an Existing Network

Funds provided through the Initiative will help child care resource and referral agencies to:
- Conduct market analyses of the local demand for, and supply of, child care and identify the types of care most needed;
- Recruit and train potential new child care providers;
- Train new and existing providers in the delivery of quality care and effective small business management;
- Work with existing providers who could expand or adjust their capacity to better meet demand; and
- Provide technical assistance to new providers in meeting state licensing requirements and local codes.

The six pilot projects began Oct. 1, 1985, and will end in September 1986, Mans said. Technical advice will be provided to the six local project sponsors by the California Child Care Resource and Referral Network.

Pilot Project Goals

The pilot project receiving the largest funding — $80,000 — is one run by the Contra Costa Children's Council. The goal of that project is the creation of 300 new spaces in family day care homes in the county and the licensing of 60 new family day care homes. An estimated 130 new and existing family day care providers will receive training and workshops during the one-year pilot project.

Connections for Children, in the West Los Angeles area, received $62,500 to create an estimated 200 new family day care spaces and 40 new licensed family day care homes. Training for 80 new and existing family day care providers also is covered by the project. Similar goals are set for a project run by the Children's Home Society in Greater Long Beach, which has been given $57,500 to achieve those goals.

The San Francisco Children's Council is focusing its attention on care for school-age children. That pilot project, with a funding amount of $61,500, will help establish three new after-school programs for an estimated 125 school-age children and train 50 community organizers and child care program staff.

In Sacramento, Child Action, Inc., plans to spend $61,500 of its grant to create 12 new licensed family day care homes with 60 new spaces. The organization also will conduct training for new and existing providers as well as for planners, architects, and developers so they can incorporate child care considerations into new buildings and developments.

Bakersfield's Community Connection for Child Care plans to spend its $60,000 grant to establish 40 new family day care homes with an estimated 200 new spaces. Like its counterpart in Sacramento, the Bakersfield project also will provide training for planners, architects, and developers.

Mans said the pilot projects will be evaluated when they are completed in September of 1986. New commitments of funds are being sought in the expectation that programs will expand if the pilot projects are successful, she said.

CHILD CARE VOUCHER SYSTEM

Organization: **Polaroid Corporation**
                     Cambridge, Mass.

Summary: **Polaroid pays a direct subsidy to cover a percentage of an employee's day care bill. The percentage varies according to a sliding scale based on income, and the actual dollar amount depends on the percentage for which an employee qualifies as well as the day care provider's fee. On average, 100 employees a year have taken advantage of the benefit since it was instituted in 1971.**

When a survey 15 years ago revealed that employees wanted the company to help with child care, Polaroid launched the day care voucher program. Polaroid's pioneering voucher system for child care is still evolving after 15 years of success.

According to Public Relations Manager Harry Johnson, the Polaroid Corporation has two major corporate goals: to create unique products and to create a work environment for its 13,000 employees that "frees them to work to their fullest potential." Subsidizing day care for employees who have preschoolers is an outgrowth of Polaroid's corporate philosophy, Johnson added. Relieving a working mother of "some of the hassles of child-rearing" is just as much a benefit to the company as it is to the employee, he maintained, because it contributes to her productivity.

Polaroid pays a direct subsidy to cover a percentage of the employee's day care bill. The percentage varies according to a sliding scale based on income, and the actual dollar amount depends on the percentage for which an employee qualifies as well as the day care provider's fee.

Using guidelines from the National Day Care Council of America, the Massachusetts Office for Children, and the now-defunct U.S. Children's Bureau in the U.S. Department of Labor, Verna Brookins, formerly the human resources administrator in charge of implementing the program and now corporate community relations manager, developed Polaroid's sliding scale subsidy program. As of March 1, 1986, employees with total family income of $30,000 or less were eligible for the subsidy. This is an increase from the previous $25,000-income limit, Brookins noted. She commented that many employees who earn more than $30,000 would like to be eligible, but would not speculate on whether this might come to pass. Brookins said, however, that all employees are eligible to use Polaroid's day care referral service that complements the subsidy program.

Polaroid signs contracts with the day care provider chosen by the employee and pays a percentage of the total bill on a quarterly basis. Employees must use licensed day care centers or homes to be eligible for the assistance. Brookins offered the example of a single mother earning $20,000 with two children in day care. The company would contribute about $28 per week, which would probably represent about 20 percent of the employee's total cost, she said.

On average, 100 employees a year have taken advantage of the benefit since it was instituted in 1971, said Brookins.

Other companies considering a voucher system should first assess their employee population in terms of size and the employees' needs, advised Brookins. Other key factors are the number and location of worksites, she noted, saying the chief reason Polaroid opted for a voucher system is because its work force is spread out among manufacturing facilities in five eastern Massachusetts towns and distribution facilities in seven other states. If the majority of employees were centrally located, she explained, the company might well have built an on-site day care center instead.

DAY CARE SUBSIDY

Organization:	**Procter & Gamble** **Cincinnati, Ohio**
Summary:	**Relying on the results of a 1984 survey which showed that the lack of reliable child care services was a serious concern for some, P&G gave the Cincinnati Community Chest $35,000 to help establish a child care resource and referral system.**

Over the past 18 months, Procter & Gamble has subsidized the establishment of two day care centers and a community child care referral service, Steve Clayton, corporate manager of medical services, told BNA late in 1985. These actions underline its "commitment to aiding families," Clayton said.

After a survey of employees at its Cincinnati, Ohio, headquarters three years ago revealed "reliable child care wasn't just a women's problem," P&G decided "to help many people in several ways," Clayton said. In June 1984, P&G gave the Cincinnati Community Chest $35,000 to help establish a child care resource and referral system. The system provides Cincinnati parents, regardless of whether they work for P&G, with free telephone counseling and referrals, Clayton said. In 1985, its first year of operation, the system fielded 3,300 calls averaging 30 minutes each, according to Clayton.

In addition to screening providers, the system has helped the Community Chest to recruit "some 300 family day care homes," Clayton said. After training individuals how to care for children in their home, the Community Chest provides ongoing support and regular referrals "so that [the providers] have a means of keeping full," he said. This has been a boon to the community, he maintained, since most parents opt for family day care homes "which, traditionally, ha[ve] been the hardest to refer on and check on."

P&G followed up its Community Chest contribution with "substantial" day care center grants to two local non-profit agencies, said Clayton. In return, the centers — which opened in November 1984 and January 1985 — agreed to "prioritize" 75 percent of their slots for P&G employees, he said; this means, he said, that, as openings occur, the centers contact P&G workers first. P&G employees' enrollment is around 50 percent at one center and about 40 percent at the other, he said, predicting "it will take a couple more years to reach 75 percent."

The weekly child care rates at the centers run from $73 to $80 for pre-schoolers, from $81 to $90 for toddlers, and $90 for infants, Clayton said. Overall, P&G parents have had "an overwhelmingly positive response" to the centers, he said.

As part of its agreement with the day care centers, P&G covered each center's under-enrollment operating deficit its first year, Clayton said, adding that the corporation does not otherwise underwrite child care costs. P&G does provide, under its cafeteria-style benefits plan, funds that may be used for any purpose, including to offset child care costs, he explained.

INFORMATION AND REFERRAL NETWORK

Organization:	Metropolitan Washington Child Care Network Washington, D.C.
Summary:	Since 1983, the Network, funded by corporate and other contributions, has helped parents find out about child care information and services provided by the governmental jurisdictions in the Washington metropolitan area. The Network is now turning its attention to the recruitment and training of new child care providers.

In their 1982-84 contract, The Bureau of National Affairs, Inc., and the Washington-Baltimore Newspaper Guild, the union representing employees at

BNA, included a provision establishing a joint labor-management committee on child care. The first thing the committee did was search for child care information from the various governmental jurisdictions in the Washington, D.C., area. That search led the committee to conclude that information on child care was both sketchy and hard to come by, according to Jean Linehan, assistant to the president of BNA. Jurisdictions that were able to provide information were just beginning to put it together. In one case, it took the committee eight phone calls just to find out where to call for information, which, the committee ultimately learned, was eight months out of date.

According to the Metropolitan Washington Child Care Network, the Washington, D.C., metropolitan area leads the nation in the percentage of mothers in the work force, and child care is a major concern. In the area:

• Approximately 124,000 preschool-age children and 253,000 children of school age need child care services.

• There are more than 90,000 working mothers who have children under age six.

• There are more than 221,500 working mothers who have children age 6-17.

• 20 percent of all children in the area live in single-parent households.

Areawide Referral Service

The BNA joint committee's largely fruitless experience in seeking child care information led committee members to conclude that an areawide referral service would be an important contribution to helping workers — not just at BNA, but also at other metropolitan-area employers — to solve the child care dilemma, Linehan said. The committee decided to approach the Metropolitan Washington Council of Governments (COG) — the regional organization of the area's 18 local governments which works on problems such as transportation, public safety, and housing — with a proposal to begin an areawide referral service. The areawide approach, Linehan said, was important because many people in the Washington area work in a different jurisdiction than the one in which they reside — a couple living in Maryland might work in the District of Columbia or one of the numerous Virginia localities and the same kind of situation might hold true for workers residing in the District or Virginia.

The Council of Governments had begun considering such a service four years earlier, and, when contacted by members of the BNA/Newspaper Guild joint committee, was ready to proceed.

Area employers were solicited to join the Metropolitan Washington Child Care Network by contributing $1,000 or more, COG put up $15,000 of public funds, and the Network began in February 1983, with a budget of $40,000.

The Network located all the agencies in the jurisdiction dealing with child care and printed a booklet with those agencies' phone numbers and the services provided, along with some pointers on choosing child care. The booklets are available free of charge in the major grocery chains and in public libraries. There is also a recorded information line that provides current telephone numbers of the agencies. Agencies in its jurisdictions receive 31,000 calls a year, according to the Network. Because of its activity, the Network says, most communities have upgraded their information systems, often from card files or typed lists, to computerized records.

Using the Information

Parents seeking a child care provider can look on a chart in the brochures to find the locality where they want the care to be provided, according to Pat Marks, the Network's coordinator. In any locality, there may be several agencies dealing with child care; the chart and a written explanation detail what services are available from each agency. Parents may choose any location that they find most convenient. If financial aid is needed, however, parents usually must get it from the jurisdiction where they reside and must contract for care in that jurisdiction, Marks said.

Parents contact the agency and tell a counselor what kind of care they prefer — such as a child care center or a child care home — the age of the child, and the location desired, Marks explained. The counselor then sends a list of child care providers to the parents; most lists are broken down by zip code or political ward. Parents can then contact and interview the providers, make their decision, and make arrangements with the provider. No recommendations are made by the Network. Child care homes are used much more often than other types of care, Marks added.

Marks noted that, in accordance with state requirements, all providers on the lists comply with the local jurisdiction's requirements for registration or licensing and are screened through criminal records or checks through child protective services. In addition, all jurisdictions offer some type of orientation to providers, and some train the providers, she said. Child care training is offered also by other sources, such as the University of the District of Columbia, Marks said.

Complaints about providers tend to fall into two general categories and are handled in two different ways, Marks said. Regulatory complaints — an unsafe environment, too many children — are reported to the regulatory agency in the jurisdiction, which then monitors the provider and effects changes when necessary. Other types of complaints involve matters such as the provider's care philosophy differing from the parents', and questions about payment. The Network attempts to solve these problems by educating both parties about communication and about the rights of both the parents and the provider, Marks said.

Funding

Funds for the Network come from four sources, Marks told BNA:

• Employers. There are now 17 employer members, who pay from $250 to $1,000 for various levels of membership in the Network. Employers can also become sponsors by providing in-kind contributions, such as printing.

• Foundations. One foundation has made a grant to support the telephone information line.

• Public funds. These funds include COG money budgeted for the Network's headquarters operation and money spent by each jurisdiction for its own information agency.

• Contracts with employers for specialized services. Two employers thus far — IBM and the Mitre Corporation — have contracted with the Network for child care referrals. An employee at either of these companies can call the Network, which will find three appropriate providers with space available, and give the employee information about them. If the employee is not satisfied with the three, the process is repeated. The agency makes follow-up calls to make sure the employee has found care. Neither IBM nor Mitre requires employees to pay costs under the contracts with the Network.

The cost for specialized services is based on the size of the employee population 22-50 years of age, according to the Network. For example, in 1985 a company with 1,000 employees would have paid approximately $7,500 for the service.

In the first year, 95 percent of the IBM employees who called found child care that met their first-choice specifications, the Network reports. Such contracts have an advantage for all users of the Network, because the money provided helps keep the information more up-to-date and because the contracts specifically include funds for recruiting and training more child care providers. One locality where IBM has a facility did not have a child care information service; the IBM contract brought one into existence, and its services now are available to anyone looking for child care.

The Network's Future

The Network is now turning its attention to the recruitment and training of new providers, Marks said. The Washington, D.C., metropolitan area has a severe shortage of child care providers — only 14 percent of children needing child care are served by identified child care centers or homes, with some others receiving care from family members or some other informal arrangements. As more mothers join the work force, and the number of children living in single-parent homes increases, the shortage of child care services will become more severe, Marks said.

The Network is hoping to alleviate the shortage by promoting child care as a career, Marks explained, and has received a Gannett Foundation grant to fund recruitment and will use television, radio, flyers, and posters in the attempt to interest people in becoming child care providers.

Increasing employer interest will be a goal of the Network, too, Marks added. Although employer support is important to keep the program going, the Network wants to increase employers' awareness of the child care issue, so that the employers can decide what their position will be on child care. The Network will also continue to contract with employers for specialized services, she said.

PARENTING SEMINARS

Organization:	**PSFS Bank**
	Philadelphia, Pa.
Summary:	**Six-hour-long parenting seminars, conducted in small groups by an outside consultant, allow PSFS employees to express their feelings about problems such as finding high-quality day care and to discover solutions to those problems. Some 300 to 400 PSFS employees have participated so far, and consultant Stephen Segal said 12 groups have been scheduled for 1986.**

Hundreds of employees of PSFS, Philadelphia's largest bank, are learning how to be better parents on company time. In groups of 20, employees attend a six-hour seminar in which they express their worries about problems such as having to leave their children alone after school and the difficulty of finding reliable day care, and then discuss solutions with each other and with seminar leader Stephen Segal, president of the Philadelphia-based Resources for Parents at Work. Employees are scheduled for the seminar on a rotating basis.

PSFS contracts with Segal to help employees relieve the stress and learn how to resolve the conflicts that arise from the competing demands of work and family.

The cost to the bank figures out to approximately $60 per employee, said Segal, who holds a master's degree in health science from the Mental Hygiene Department of Johns Hopkins University. He and his wife Patricia, a school psychologist, have three children.

"Their general feeling is that they have too much to do and too little time to do it," said Segal, who has been working with PSFS employees on a regular basis since conducting a pilot program in 1982. The pilot program was instituted after a survey showed that several hundred PSFS employees liked the idea.

"I limit sessions to 20 people in groups with similar age children: preschoolers, younger schoolchildren, and teenagers," Segal says. "I'd say there have probably been 300 to 400 people to date who have participated at PSFS. [In the fall of 1985,] I had eight groups. There has been an enormous response this past go-round that is continuing. For [1986], I have already scheduled 12 groups," he says.

'There Are Some Risks'

"What we do in the program is not to tell people whether or not they should leave a child at home while they work, but that there are some possible risks when you leave a child home alone at age 9 or 10 or 11 and here are some ways to minimize the risks," Segal explained. "The parent makes the decision. They have a better sense of control. They also learn to tune in more to children's signals about how they are doing."

Segal divides the parents by the age of their children because children present parents with different problems at different ages. "Parents of infant toddlers are terribly concerned about turning over this really young child to someone else and whether they are losing their influence, losing their relationship with the child. With parents of school-age kids, the latchkey issue surfaces . . . . A fundamental concern is, can the child handle it? What is the impact on him or her being alone?" he said.

"The concern of teenagers' parents about lack of supervision is also a general parents' concern: discipline, limit-setting," Segal added.

'Not a Canned Program'

"It is not a canned program," Segal said of his seminars. "Every group is somewhat different. The parent of an infant might raise the issue of a kid waking up four times a night. We look at ways to deal with it. Another may be really concerned about a child falling apart at the end of day . . . . In a general sense, it is the separation issue — from the parents' and the child's point of view," he said.

"From the participant's standpoint, the most important things that come out of it are: one, the sense of support from other people who are faced with a similar situation. [Two,] it is about the only time that people have the opportunity to sit down and take a look at the two most important elements in their lives and figure out how to become better at them," Segal says. "People are so busy they can't really sit down and attack these issues by themselves. This is tremendously important. Also important is the awareness that develops about specific strategies that can help them improve on a daily basis and further their goals as parents as they work," he said.

"It is also tremendously important, from an individual basis, that the company is sanctioning this kind of activity. It says to the participants that the company feels it is important that they become effective in managing these two roles because it affects the company. It does a lot for the parents' dimension. It is easy for the work dimension to overwhelm the parents' dimension and [leave them with] very little left to give at home," Segal says. "But when your employer says to you, 'Here is a program designed to raise your effectiveness as a parent while you work,' people feel better about it. It is terribly significant that people walk out of there feeling more proud of their task."

Segal said some employees are initially reluctant to participate in seminars to discuss personal family concerns, but as the first groups report progress in resolving family-work conflicts, it stirs others to participate. The PSFS program, he says, is "a perfect example how, over time, the concept becomes more and more established and accepted," as employees recommend the program to others and managers either participate themselves or refer their employees to the program because "they have seen that it is good for the bank."

Segal said companies he works with do not attempt to measure results of his parenting seminars through productivity studies. He explained:

"There is a practical reason for that: It is very difficult to measure productivity. What we are doing is accumulating anecdotal evidence. Managers say they are hearing employees comment that 'Now I'm not fighting my kids to get dressed in the morning. Now I can focus more on my work.' Before that was under control, the supervisor really didn't know whether or not anything was going on. It took the individual to come forward and say there had been a problem. The company is satisfied to see results. They perceive it to be positive. They look at the employee relations aspect of it, they look at testimony that comes from participants. They are beginning to get managers who are able to spot certain things."

The program has proved so successful that M. Todd Cook, retiring PSFS chairman, praised the results in a 30-second public service announcement on a local television station. "PSFS has been a shining example of company support for the program," said Segal, who has some two dozen corporate clients around the country and has conducted seminars for a total of about 2,000 of their employees since beginning his consulting business in 1981.

A Vice President's View

James Nugent, vice president in the PSFS finance division, who attended one of Segal's sessions, called it "a good seminar" from both the employee's and the bank's point of view.

"It told me about the need for discipline, the need to spend the time I do have with my kids in the best way I can and not to feel discouraged," said Nugent, who had been concerned about not having time to spend with a daughter who has a birth defect. "From the seminar, I see how I should treat her. I treat her like everyone else," he said.

"You only have a little bit of time, so spend it the best way you can so you are able live with it," Nugent added.

Other employees who have attended the seminars voice similarly positive reactions, according to Nugent. "Everyone I have talked to always enjoyed it and got a lot out of it. We run a lot of seminars here and I think that is the best one I went to. It brings it home. It deals with your home and work. It's nice to have the bank offer something that is not just career-oriented," Nugent said.

Nugent, who attended a seminar two years ago, said most of those who attend are women. "I was one of two men. [The women] felt guilty; there is pressure on women to stay home on one end and on the other end to make some money," he said. The message of the seminars is how to "work and provide for your kids and spend that time at home the right way."

"I think a lot of men are embarrassed to go. It seems like a women's course to them. I felt it was good for me," Nugent said.

Although he said the number of men in his seminars is growing, Segal says that four-fifths of the participants are women. "This is true simply because women experience this issue more acutely than men," he says. "Men typically feel a conflict in terms of work and family roles when they lose their jobs; then they feel they are not fulfilling their role properly. Women feel that way when they take a job," he adds. "There is a gradual blurring, with more men interested. A significant but small increase among men is occurring."

Summing up his feelings about the seminar, Nugent said: "What it does for the company is provide a goodwill gesture for employees. It allows something that affects home life to be brought into the workplace. Performance [of employees] is better and it says that the company has an understanding that people have a life outside of the office. A lot of companies don't worry about the outside life."

A Bargaining Issue Soon?

So far, Segal said, none of his seminars has been conducted under a company-union contract nor has he seen any similar program as a negotiated benefit, but he thinks programs such as his may well become part of the union-management bargaining picture in the future.

"It has not come up, although some places where I have worked the participants have been members of a union . . . . I think employee expectations are growing in this area. Many companies may bargain now on flextime and child care facilities," but not parenting programs such as he offers, Segal says. "I think those expectations might become demands over the next five to seven years. The work force is very much in transition," he adds.

Segal also notes that the baby-boom generation is gradually assuming a role of corporate power. "People who were in college in the 60s are now moving into positions of power gradually. They are much more sensitive to the needs of the work force and how to manage it," he says. "Many kinds of things will come out of that, things that haven't even been dreamed of, when corporate America really starts thinking how it can manage this work force and remove impediments to productivity," Segal predicts.

DAY CARE FOR SICK CHILDREN

Organization:	**Chicken Soup**
	Minneapolis, Minn.
	3M Corp.
	St. Paul, Minn.
	Sniffles 'n' Sneezes
	Miami, Fla.
	Respite, Inc.
	San Antonio, Texas
Summary:	**Since September 1985, an organization called Chicken Soup has been providing child care exclusively to sick children in the**

Minneapolis area. The 3M Corp., also located in Minneapolis, has set up a program to help employees pay for care for sick children, and organizations similar to Chicken Soup have been started by a Miami, Fla., hospital and by the city of San Antonio, Texas.

"I don't feel well."

Four words any working parent dreads. It's 7 a.m. and you're due at work in one hour. Your child has just told you she doesn't feel very well. What do you do? Stay home? Call a friend?

In some communities, there is a growing awareness of the need for sick child care, and in those communities, some innovative solutions to the problem are now available.

The first choice of any parent, said child care provider Birdie Johnson, is to stay home "and 'mother' the child." Because that option is not always available, Johnson and partner Ruth Matson opened Chicken Soup, which Johnson described as "day care for kids who don't feel so good."

Kids didn't stop getting sick when mothers started to work, said Johnson, who noted that many states prohibit sick children from attending regular day care centers. Taking a day off work at a moment's notice can be problematical for parents, however. Chicken Soup was started as a way to help parents resolve this dilemma, Johnson said.

Children who are brought to Chicken Soup are examined by a nurse and then assigned to one of three rooms — the Polka Dot room for those with chicken pox, the Sniffles Room for those with colds, and the Popsicle Room for those with influenza or other stomach ailments. Johnson said parents are often surprised by the brightly decorated rooms and the absence of a single hospital bed. Cots are kept handy for tired tots, she explained, but children are often so charmed by the center that they "almost forget they don't feel so well." Cost for the care is $30 for a full day and $20 for four hours or less. Chicken Soup is open from 6 a.m. to 6 p.m.

"Parents are encouraged to call and check on their children if they like," Johnson said, "but most parents feel secure just knowing their child is safe in a loving environment."

Staffing: A Difficult Aspect

Chicken Soup co-founder Ruth Matson told BNA that "labor is one of the most difficult aspects" of their operation, and she gave two reasons for the difficulty: because they're never sure about the number of children that will need care on any day and because state licensing regulations set requirements for staffing. The uncertainty about daily staffing requirements, Matson said, is one reason care is fairly expensive.

Every day that children are at the Chicken Soup, a nurse and a teacher are present, Matson said. Other part-time staffers are called in as needed. One nurse works a 13-hour shift Mondays, Wednesdays, and Fridays, and two other part-time nurses alternate working on Tuesdays and Thursdays.

State licensing regulations require two staff people to be on duty even if only one child being cared for, Matson pointed out. She added that, if there are only three children at the center and each is in a different care room, she and Johnson require one individual to care for each child separately.

Matson said that she and Johnson consider their hours to be fairly flexible. Each works about 30 hours a week.

Funding Sources

Start-up costs for the care center — the Polka Dot room has a separate ventilation system and separate entrances — were fairly high, Matson said. The center is averaging four to five children per day, she said, adding that she expects Chicken Soup to break even in three years.

Funding for the center, which opened in September 1985, has been provided through a one-time grant of $100,000 from the U.S. Department of Health and Human Services. Additional funding of $160,000 in grants and in-kind services has been provided by major Twin Cities-area organizations, including the General Mills Foundation, Northwestern Bell, the Dayton-Hudson Foundation, and Northern States Power Company.

Johnson said the organization behind Chicken Soup, Alternative Services for Children, Inc., has worked with downtown Minneapolis firms to promote the program. Brightly colored flyers explaining Chicken Soup are available in the employee assistance offices of many companies, and some firms, such as Dayton-Hudson Corporation, have taken women on tours of the facility in hopes of spreading the word.

As of early 1986, Johnson said, no firm had a specific agreement with the day care center to reserve slots for employees or to promise to help pay part of the cost of care, but some firms are investigating such a possibility. Dayton-Hudson spokesperson Marcia Townley said the corporation is exploring additional means of strengthening its ties with center.

3M Corp. Program

Taking another tack in helping provide care for sick children of working parents, 3M Corp., based in St. Paul, Minn., has established a program designed to aid parents of sick children by sharing the cost of that care. 3M Corp. seeks to provide its workers "peace of mind" by assisting with their child care concerns, explained 3M Child Care Coordinator Sue Osten.

3M has established a program to provide in-home care for employees' sick children, Osten said. Under the program, operated in cooperation with Children's Hospital in St. Paul, health care workers are sent to the homes of parents whose children have contracted common childhood illnesses, such as chicken pox or influenza. The company pays a portion of the $8.25-per-hour fee, on a sliding scale based on a family's ability to contribute to the cost of care.

Osten said during the two years the program has been in operation, there have been approximately 200 users, with about 30 percent of those cases being repeat users. The program is still in its pilot stage, but has been "going quite well," she said. The pilot program will end in mid-1986, she indicated, and at that time a decision will be made whether to continue the program on a permanent basis.

Employee comments show that the system has been quite well received by working parents who are faced with the need to come to work even though their child is sick. On average, a child experiences six to seven viral infections per year, Osten said. 3M allows employees — at their supervisor's discretion — to use vacation or other paid absences to care for sick children, she explained, but some workers feel a internally generated pressure to come to work if there have been too many occasions when the employee has stayed home to care for an ill child. Professional personnel have been the primary users of the sick care program, said Osten, who explained, "Many professional people feel a self-imposed pressure to be at work. They are most likely to be the people facing deadlines, important meetings, or business trips that can't be postponed to care for a sick child."

Sniffles 'n' Sneezes Center

A third approach to child care for kids who don't feel so good is the Sniffles 'n' Sneezes center, a day care facility for ill children operated by the Southeastern Medical Center in Miami, Fla. The hospital provides on-site care for children who are afflicted with a common childhood illness.

The center's director, Mary Rosen, said the program has received "rave reviews" from parents who have made use of the facility. Costs for use of the center, which officially opened Jan. 10, 1986, are $20 per day and $30 if the child is seen by a physician. The center is available to any working parents, not just hospital employees.

Sniffles 'n' Sneezes, which is located in a previously unused wing of the Medical Center, operates in a more hospital-like atmosphere than the homey Chicken Soup center in Minneapolis, Rosen said, but many parents feel at ease knowing that there is a doctor "just down the hall." Although parents are encouraged to call if they are worried during the day, few parents make use of that option, she said. "They seem to be quite reassured by the hospital atmosphere of the center," which eventually will accommodate 32 children. Because some supervisors frown on personal calls by employees during the workday, "this reassurance is especially important," she said.

The center, which is a wholly owned operation of the Southeastern Medical Center, opened unofficially for business on Dec. 6 and was averaging three children per day in early 1986. Rosen said the center has no plans to seek subsidies from local firms, and said Sniffles 'n' Sneezes is being promoted primarily through local schools and day care centers.

"It is an option for parents who didn't have an option before," explained Rosen, who said some working parents within the hospital have remarked, " 'This is so logical. Why didn't they have a program like this when I was younger?' "

San Antonio's Response

When children of San Antonio, Texas, city employees are ill, they receive care at home from Respite, Inc., thanks, in part, to their parents' frugal use of health care benefits and participation in a comprehensive fitness program. Savings realized from San Antonio's health care cost containment and fitness programs introduced in 1983 have enabled the city to contract with Respite, a babysitting service for sick children employing home health aides.

Beginning in 1985, the city began paying Respite a subscription fee and, in return, Respite is on short-notice call to care for city employees' sick children. San Antonio's workers pay Respite "a nominal fee," said City Personnel Director Leroy Harvey, "that's far less than a day's pay, which they'd lose staying home with their child. And, their minds are at ease because they know their child is being well cared for."

Funds for subsidizing Respite were available because a number of health care cost containment efforts by the city were successful. In 1983, the city's bill for health care was $8.5 million, said Harvey, who told BNA that, by 1988, the city expected the bill to be $20 million. City officials concluded something must be done as soon as possible to halt that trend, and the city instituted a number of cost containment measures, including co-payments, higher deductibles, and a cafeteria benefits plan, and began an extensive employee fitness program. After two years of the cost containment and fitness programs, the city has made considerable progress in combatting high health care costs. Harvey reported that, in 1985, the total bill for health care was just under $8.5 million, less than it was in 1983.

LABOR-MANAGEMENT CHILD CARE PROGRAM

Organizations: Local 399, Service Employees International Union, and
                     Kaiser Permanente Medical Group
                     Los Angeles, Calif.

Summary: A joint labor/management Child Care Committee, established by
                     contract in 1980, meets regularly to examine child care and
                     attendant issues. The company's child care program is primarily a
                     resource and referral service, providing, among other services,
                     directories which outline for employees tuition prices, available
                     transportation, child care philosophy, special activities, parent
                     participation, and other information about child care centers.

Kaiser Permanente Medical Group and Local 399 of the Service Employees International Union took a more formal approach to child care in their contract negotiations than did BNA and the Washington-Baltimore Newspaper Guild. (See case study above.) In July 1980, the parties set up, as part of their contract, a joint labor/management Child Care Committee, Liz Barry, employee assistance coordinator for Kaiser Sunset Medical Clinic in Los Angeles, told BNA. The committee comprises three representatives appointed by the President of the Union and Kaiser's Child Care Coordinator. As explained in the contract, the committee "shall meet on a regular basis with the Employer's Child Care Coordinator in order to advise and assist the coordinator whenever possible."

Child Care Coordinator is a position which was created on recommendation of the committee. Barry explained that the Child Care Coordinator is responsible for assessing the child care needs of Kaiser's 22,000 employees in Southern California. Those workers are represented by 10 labor unions. Representatives from Kaiser's Regional Personnel Administration and the Child Care Advisory Committee of Local 399 meet with the child care coordinator "regularly," Barry said.

"The child care program is, for the most part, a resource and referral service that employees can take advantage of," Barry explained. Child care directories outlining, among other things, tuition prices, available transportation, philosophy, special activities, parent participation, availability of a bilingual staff, and miscellaneous other details, are provided to those employees seeking assistance.

The Child Care Coordinator sends out evaluation forms to employees after they have chosen a service through the employer's program. Barry says approximately 50 percent of those that utilize the program actually find what they are looking for.

Kaiser also publishes and distributes a handbook entitled "Child Care: Guidelines for Parents." The book counsels parents in evaluating programs, and discusses what to look for in good care; the provider's environment; child care resource and referral services; special services, including counseling for parents and children, resources for children with special needs, and child abuse reporting and counseling.

Technical assistance on improving a program or expanding a program to include infant and toddler care or evening care has been made available to community child care providers and parenting seminars are currently in the planning stages, Barry said.

Robert Leighton, research and negotiations associate for Local 399, told BNA that SEIU Local 399 also has established child care committees in contracts with CIGNA Health Plan and the Watts Health Foundation. "Equal union/management participation on these committees does serve to identify needs and problems, resulting in referral systems set up by employers. To secure on-site child care seems to require the force of negotiations, particularly in light of potential employer liabilities," he remarked.

Child Care Coordinator Elena Weeks said "one-twentieth" of Kaiser's 4,600 employees at the Medical Center and outlying regional offices make use of the child care referral service. The program is "perceived" by management as successful, she said. She suggested that management may expand the program to the other eight Kaiser medical centers in Southern California which are not presently involved in the program; no announcement about expansion of the program has been made, however, she added.

AFTER-SCHOOL PROGRAMS FOR CHILDREN

Organization: Houston Committee for Private Sector Initiatives
Houston, Texas

Summary: Supported by corporate funding, the Houston Committee sponsors after-school programs for children. Programs are operated in schools, churches, and community service organizations. Among its other activities, the committee has awarded start-up grants, and conducted training for program coordinators.

The "Hi mom, I'm home" phone calls start hitting office switchboards as school lets out across the country. The "Three O'Clock Syndrome" sets in, with employees hunched over their phones whispering admonitions about homework and directions for making dinner.

Mindful that employees' need to know their children are safe, and that minutes are lost each work day, employers nationwide have begun to support programs for so-called latchkey children. These children, numbering upwards of 6.5 million, return to an empty house after school because their parents work.

The ways that employers have chosen to deal with the latchkey child problem are myriad. A common theme, however, is that the programs they foster are aimed at helping whole communities, not just company employees. And many are based at schools themselves, because "that's where the kids are all day," according to Ellen Gannett, coordinator of training and education for the Wellesley College-based School-Age Child Care Project.

Houston Initiative Began in 1982

Perhaps one of the most comprehensive employer-supported programs for latchkey children is in Houston. The Houston Committee for Private Sector Initiatives, started in 1982 as an outgrowth of President Reagan's National Task Force on Private Sector Initiatives, sponsors after-school programs in three schools, three churches, one YMCA, and one YWCA store-front.

The committee, which received pledges totaling $454,000 from 26 corporations in 1985, provided $5,000 start-up grants to the programs. In 1985, the committee conducted a training workshop for program coordinators. Because such programs are new, the committee said in its 1985 annual report, "after-school caregivers require training and the exchange of ideas that will support one another's efforts."

Sliding Scale for Fees

The programs charge fees based on sliding scale. The highest cost is $17.50 per week, but some children attend the program for free or for as little as $12 a week. The original school program, at Cunningham Elementary School, and the next oldest program, at Sutton Elementary School, have a licensed capacity of 50 children. They operate at about 90 percent capacity, according to Kathleen McNemar, child care coordinator for the committee. The third school program at Piney Point Elementary School, got under way in the fall of 1985, and enrolls 12 to 15 children.

While the programs are operated with the blessing and cooperation of the Houston Independent School District, the district itself sponsors free after-school programs in some schools. The committee's programs differ because they have outside teachers who work elsewhere in the morning before their after-school jobs, McNemar said. Those teachers are employed by the YMCA; the programs are not directly administered by the YMCA, however.

The community at large and the sponsoring corporations have been intimately involved in the programs. "The Junior League of Houston has been instrumental in developing volunteer opportunities," says the committee's 1985 annual report. "Volunteers from Texaco come three times a week to tutor and lead recreational activities. The Houston Zoo and the Museum of Natural Science participate in Cunningham After School with regular programs and activities." High school students in service clubs in 1986 even plan to build some dividers for the school cafeterias where the after-school programs are held.

The committee is set to become even more involved over the next two years, according to McNemar. Houston Mayor Kathryn Whitmire set as a goal the creation of after-school programs for all of Houston's needy latchkey children in the next two years. A "small, select committee" organized by the overall committee will advise the mayor on the project.

The after-school programs are not the committee's only child care projects. The committee has sponsored a forum on child care for corporations, and by the end of September 1986 plans to hold 10 child care seminars in 10 corporations, according to Donna Rybiski, who directs committee staff as manager of private sector initiatives.

The committee also operates the Child Care Resource and Referral Service with the Houston Public Library. The service provides child care referrals and one-on-one consultation and guidance for parents, and trains and helps start support programs for child care providers.

Outside the child care realm, the committee runs a "loaned executive program" to put professionals in private enterprise to work on city problems. It also does considerable work in housing and neighborhood revitalization, and employment and training.

Aid to After-School Programs

Following are some other examples of ways employers are helping parents deal with care of children after school:

• The Dallas-based Brock Hotel Corporation sponsors after-school clubs for six to 12-year-olds in some of its Chuck E. Cheese Pizza Time Theater and Showbiz Pizza Palace franchises.

• The Pillsbury Co. sponsors research into the latchkey issue in the Minneapolis area, and also supports activities through service clubs and a community service project through the schools and the mayor's office.

• The Gannett Foundation, which is the philanthropic arm of the media chain, has funded 145 projects since 1981 to help school-age children and their families, according to the School-Age Child Care Project. The grantees, which are located in communities in which the company has local papers, TV and radio stations, or outdoor advertising organizations, include service organizations and, once again, schools.

In 1985, the Gannett Foundation identified family-and-work issues as the theme of its Communities Priorities Program, a series of grants awarded each year in 90 communities with Gannett broadcasting stations, newspapers, or advertising companies. In 1985, the McKennan Hospital in Sioux Falls, S.D., garnered a $35,000 award for a child care project for sick children, said Calvin Mayne, vice president of grants administration for the foundation. The hospital set aside space for "wee care," where children with minor illnesses can be brought during workdays.

In 1981, the YMCA, YWCA, and Boys' Club and Girls' Clubs of Sioux Falls were awarded a grant of $40,000 to provide transportation for children to after-school programs conducted jointly by the four organizations.

The Gannett Foundation has spent at least $610,000 in the last four years addressing traditional day care, school-age child care, or sick child care needs, Mayne said. The Foundation identifies issues crucial to the communities served by Gannett properties through Gannett executives located in those communities. "We think it's a unique program," said Mayne.

                      CARING FOR LATCHKEY CHILDREN

Organization: **Family Communications, Inc.**
                     Denver, Colo.
Summary: **FCI has developed, and is testing in a pilot project, a device called The Home Companion, which enables latchkey children to notify their parents that they are home safely from school. The Home Companion also enables children to notify authorities of medical, fire, or police emergencies.**

For children not part of an after-school program, the telephone may be the only form of adult supervision. Many parents, however, are not accessible even by phone.

Ellen Galinsky, project director of The Work and Family Life Study at Bank Street College of Education in New York City, said she believes stress is most acute among parents who aren't accessible by phone. "There's a big difference [between] those parents who are accessible to the phone, and those who are not," she said. "The most poignant stories come from those who work in factories" who've had family emergencies occur "and didn't get the message." She explained, "[T]here's a real feeling of helplessness, of being trapped. How antithetical to good work!"

At corporate seminars which she conducts, Galinsky said, she finds that "parents are clearly worried about their kids."

Family Communications, Inc., a Denver-based company, is just beginning to market a device which may help quell the fears of parents who are unable to supervise their children after school or who are inaccessible by phone. Larry Modesitt, president of Family Communications, Inc., explained that the device, called The Home Companion, is connected to the home phone. Parents set a timer on the device for a time during the day when a child is expected to be at home. If the child fails to press the "home" button on the device within 30 minutes of the time set — 3:30 p.m., for example — a response center run by FCI is notified. An operator at the response center then phones the child's home. If no one answers, the response center then phones the child's parents, or whoever is on a contact list. Modesitt noted that some families also use the timer to mark a child's departure time.

The Home Companion, invented by Modesitt's partner, Frank Zayle, contains a notification system for medical, fire, or police emergencies. A fire truck, police badge, and a medical cross head three columns of two buttons. To activate the notification system, a child simply presses the two buttons in one or more of the columns. Within 30 seconds, the response center calls to determine whether it's a false alarm. If it is not, the center then notifies authorities, and the parents or nearest relatives. Since August 1985, Family Communications, Inc., has been testing the device with 15 families in the Denver area and has experienced only two false alarms, which were caught by the response center. One of the false alarms was caused by a toddler who crawled over the device, activating its buttons.

The response center also keeps on hand data about the family, such as the number and ages of the children, medical information, or any other information the parents feel should be known in the event of an emergency.

FCI's Modesitt believes his device may help children make the transition from fear and helplessness to confidence and self-reliance. FCI also provides a self-care manual for latchkey children, an activities book designed to combat boredom, and a newsletter with tips for parents and children.

While he said he doesn't want his device to be seen "as an excuse to leave kids alone," Modesitt maintained that nearly all children are left alone regularly, if only for short periods. "For a child left at home some of the time, we're making it a safer experience," he said. "The length of time [a child is left alone] is not as relevant as just being left alone. The greatest fear is of not being able to control a situation." The Home Companion, he said, gives children control. "It's not an emergency if people know what to do," he maintained.

No Substitute for Adult Care

The device, Modesitt readily admitted, is no substitute for after-school programs or other adult care. But, he pointed out, constant supervision may not be an option for many families.

Modesitt said he was initially concerned that older children might resent having to check in through the device. Instead, he said, children who've helped test the device have reported feeling secure because they know that the machine is there to notify parents or other loved ones in the event they don't return home on time.

The emergency features of the device eliminate the need for children to be able to give their addresses in distress situations. These features turned out to be particularly important to one couple who tested the device, the parents of two boys, ages 13 and 15. The couple plans to purchase the device, which, they said, has "absolutely" helped alleviate their fears for the safety of their children.

Family Communications, Inc., offers a range of lease or purchase plans. One option is a lease arrangement with a one-time expense of $49 plus a monthly charge of $29.95. Or, parents may purchase The Home Companion for $419, with a monthly charge of $9.95.

'Warm Lines'

In some locations, organizations are operating "warm lines," phone services targeted to latchkey children.

One warm lines organization is PhoneFriend, which is run by the State College, Pa., branch of the American Association of University Women. PhoneFriend contends that it was the first such service, and says others have sprung up in communities throughout the nation.

PhoneFriend provides information and assistance to children home alone. Volunteers advise children on how to handle common situations such as taking care of wet clothing, or books forgotten at school, and also refer authorities to a child's home in the event of an emergency, or when the possibility of an emergency exists. The majority of the calls, however, require volunteers to simply listen to a child express fear or loneliness, according to the PhoneFriend organization.

PhoneFriend also has produced a manual advising other groups on how to set up such a hotline.

CHILD CARE ORDINANCE

Organization: City of San Francisco, Calif.

Summary: **In September 1985, San Francisco Mayor Dianne Feinstein approved an ordinance requiring office developers to provide space for an on-site child care facility or to contribute to the city's Affordable Child Care Fund. Some observers believe that most developers will opt for the easier of the two options — paying the fee — thereby leaving the city with the task of creating the child care facilities.**

On Aug. 26, 1985, the Board of Supervisors of the City of San Francisco passed an ordinance requiring developers within the city either to provide on-site child care space or to contribute to a city child care fund. The proposal was not the target of any organized opposition from developers, according to an aide to Supervisor Nancy G. Walker, who sponsored the ordinance. Approving the ordinance on Sept. 6, Mayor Dianne Feinstein said she believed the measure was a reasonable way to pay for child care in a city such as San Francisco. The measure took effect in mid-September.

Supervisor Walker said that San Francisco's working parents face child care costs of up to $450 per month per child. At those rates, many women and single parents may not be able to afford to work in San Francisco, she observed. "This rattles the very foundation of our city and concerns developers, employers, and parents alike," she said.

Walker noted in the ordinance that San Francisco has been undergoing an office building boom in recent years even as the availability of child care was shrinking, and that employers may find it increasingly difficult to attract and keep employees in the city. The city expects nearly 100,000 new jobs — most of them office jobs — to be created during the next 15 years under the Downtown Plan for development.

When it was approved, the San Francisco ordinance was believed to be the first of its kind in the nation. Walker said she believed the ordinance could become a model for other cities to follow in dealing with the child care issue.

Provisions of the Ordinance

Under the ordinance, office developers may opt to provide space for a child care facility on site or to contribute not more than $1 per gross square foot of office space to a city-sponsored Affordable Child Care Fund. Developers also may elect to provide some space for child care on site and to contribute some amount to the fund. If a developer does not comply with the child care ordinance, the city may refuse to grant the developer an occupancy permit for the building.

Under a formula prescribed by the ordinance, the amount of space to be allotted for an on-site child care facility is determined by multiplying the net addition of gross square footage of the building by 0.01. The minimum amount of space that must be allotted is 3,000 square feet.

If a developer opts to provide an on-site facility, the space devoted to child care is to be used by a non-profit child care provider without charge for rent, utilities, property taxes, or building services. The measure does not apply to offices owned by either the state or the federal government.

The measure covers new office projects or renovations that would create a net addition of 50,000 gross square feet of office space outside of San Francisco's downtown area. Developers of facilities in the downtown area will have to offer on-site child care or brokerage services.

The child care fund is expected to raise nearly $1 million per year, according to Erik Schapiro, Walker's administrative assistant. The city's present limit on growth, however, means that the fund will not exceed $1 million per year, he told BNA. Also, some 22 million square feet of office space previously approved or under construction will not be affected by the measure, he added.

The More Likely Response: To Pay the Fee

Downtown developers probably will pay the fee rather than provide the space, speakers told a panel discussion on child care sponsored by, and held at, the University of California Nov. 21, 1985.

Mark Solet, director of development for Embarcadero West, a huge office complex, revealed that before the ordinance was enacted, his firm negotiated an agreement to include space for child care in exchange for exclusion from the Downtown Plan's project size restrictions.

"As part of our building project of 600,000 square feet, we . . . provide 3,000 square feet for an on-site facility, and at least $30,000 over three years. We figure our total obligation will be $600,000. It would be tough to make this a profitable venture, but we figure we'll be setting some kind of standard for others to follow," he said.

Solet said other developers probably would prefer to pay the fee because it is easier than actually providing a facility. But he suggested that employers who lease space in the new projects could persuade some developers to include a child care facility rather than pass off the responsibility to the city. "If there is corporate sponsorship to make it economically viable, there would be an added incentive for developers," Solet said. He noted that The Prudential Insurance Co. of America, a major investor in Embarcadero West, agreed to provide insurance for the facility, something that otherwise might be difficult to obtain.

Other panelists said developers might be reluctant to provide child care facilities because they don't know how restrictive state and local codes will be. "There are a lot of hurdles," Supervisor Walker admitted during the panel discussion, "and the bureaucracy is just one of them. We're going to have to relax some provisions, like the fire code, to make this work." City fire regulations restrict child care facilities to the ground level of a building, which would reduce the amount of prime lease space, she noted.

Questions about how the fees will be used to develop near-site child care facilities, and how such facilities will be shared by employees, still need to be resolved, Moira So, of the Mayor's Office of Community Development, acknowledged. The Mayor's Office said it is working on clarification to the rules on fees and service providers, and hoped to propose them by the spring of 1986 for approval by the Planning Commission.

                                              ELDERLY DEPENDENT CARE

Organization: **The Travelers Corp.**
                    Hartford, Conn.

Program: **Travelers surveyed 20 percent of its employees — more than 1,400 individuals — to find out the extent of their responsibilities for elderly dependent care. The survey revealed that 20 percent of the respondents were providing some form of care for elderly relatives or friends. Travelers is just beginning to examine the survey data, but probably will adopt one of several options in dealing with the issue. Among those options: holding seminars on different aspects of caregiving, providing information on an ongoing basis, and developing criteria on how to make decisions regarding the dependents.**

As the median age of the population increases, more workers may be called upon to take care of elderly relatives. For many of those workers, caring for the elderly can become a second full-time job.

It is a "growing problem for working people," said Gayle Kataja, administrative supervisor at Connecticut Community Care, Inc. (CCC), a private, non-profit organization that coordinates services for the elderly. "Companies will have to reckon with [employees'] need" to provide for care for the elderly, she said.

One company which is acknowledging that need is The Travelers Corp.,

Hartford, Conn. To determine the extent of employees' responsibilities for providing dependent care for elderly individuals, the Travelers surveyed 1,412 employees — age 30 or older — and received responses from 739, or 52 percent. The 1,412 employees represent about one-fifth of its home office work force.

The survey, developed with the help of Connecticut Community Care, Inc., revealed that 20 percent of the respondents were providing some form of care for elderly relatives or friends. About 8 percent of the responding employees said that they devoted at least 35 hours a week to caring for the elderly.

By a wide margin (69 to 29 percent) — and consistent with the trend nationwide — women were found to be the primary caregivers, the survey showed. The average amount of time spent per week in providing care was 16.1 hours for females and 5.3 hours for males. Most employees who were caring for elderly dependents said they had been doing so for approximately five years.

The typical person receiving care, according to the survey results, was a 77-year-old woman. More than half of the dependents lived in their own home or apartment, 20 percent lived with the caregiver, and 15 percent lived in a nursing home.

A Stressful Situation

Not surprisingly, the Travelers survey found that the responsibilities of providing care, combined with job and other family demands, can be quite stressful. Eighty percent of the employees with caregiving responsibilities said that those responsibilities interfered with social and emotional needs and family responsibilities. Eighteen percent said they had not had a vacation away from caregiving responsibilities for more than two years.

When asked whether they could continue providing care for as long as necessary, 30 percent said they could if they had additional help, 20 percent weren't sure, and 5 percent said they could not, even with additional help.

The Corporation's Response

Jim Davis, vice president of personnel at Travelers, said that if stress levels can be alleviated, employees will be more productive. The company is just beginning to examine the survey data, but probably will channel its efforts into providing information, Davis explained. Some of the options being considered include:

• Staging a caregiving "fair" at the worksite, attended by representatives from community agencies and the company's employee assistance program;

• Holding seminars on different aspects of caregiving. Such seminars might include, he said, videotapes on particular problems, such as stroke or Alzheimer's disease;

• Making space available for support group meetings;

• Providing information on an ongoing basis;

• Developing criteria on how to make decisions regarding the dependents, such as choosing a nursing home; and

• Bringing in outside speakers.

Davis said that copies of the survey results had been sent to personnel departments in the Fortune 500 companies, and that Travelers has received lots of calls about the survey.

Georgina Lucas, a spokesperson for Travelers, said that the company is now working to develop an insurance product to cover the chronic long-term needs of the elderly. Asked whether it would be offered to Travelers employees as a benefit, she said, "I'm sure it will be."

What Caring for Elderly Means for Workers

There is "tremendous anxiety and guilt" among employees who provide care for elderly individuals, and the stress on them is "absolutely enormous," said Barbara Adolf, of Adolf and Rose Associates, a private consulting firm in New York City. Although she had no statistics, Adolf suggested that absenteeism, tardiness, and turnover were among the employer problems resulting from the caregiving responsibilities of employees.

"It's difficult to focus on the job when you have an Alzheimer's mother at home and you're wondering if she's going to start a fire."

According to a 1985 report on a Boston University study of employees in a large corporation, 18 percent of employees cited responsibility for an aging parent as a very serious problem. One-third of the employees studied gave financial assistance to their parents and spent considerable time making arrangements for their care, said the study, which concluded that the stress of balancing work and family responsibilities is the most significant factor contributing to depression among employees.

Elaine Brody, of the Philadelphia Geriatric Center (PGC), told BNA, "It's difficult to focus on the job when you have an Alzheimer's mother at home and you're wondering if she's going to start a fire." She noted that studies show that women not only are more likely to be affected by caregiving responsibilities, but are more likely to quit jobs to assume those responsibilities. A PGC study of 150 women who took care of their mothers found that 28 percent of non-working women interviewed had quit their jobs, and 26 percent of employed women had considered stopping work because of their responsibilities.

Diane Cohan, a research associate at the University of Bridgeport Center for Aging in Bridgeport, Conn., surveyed several corporations for information on employees' caregiving responsibilities. The survey revealed that worries about elderly dependents sometimes took time away from the job, and that the lack of transportation for dependents forced employees to miss work to take parents to medical appointments.

What Is Needed

An important finding of the Travelers survey, which was echoed by many other experts on aging in interviews with BNA, is that information on services for the elderly is difficult to find.

Kataja said that workers need a resource they can contact to find out what services are available. She said that a doctor may say a home nurse is needed — at $55 an hour — but a case management agency, such as CCC, might analyze the situation differently and determine that what really is needed is a companion — at minimum wage — to sit with the older person.

Elaine Brody suggested that companies should consider the different kinds of benefits for employees who take care of elderly dependents: respite care, an arrangement in which the primary caregiver is given a few hours or a weekend off; flextime work schedules; and sabbaticals for parent care. Brody also said that there is a need for counseling for women who suffer from guilt because they "can't do it all."

Diane Cohan suggested that job sharing and working at home could help workers who must care for elderly persons. Cohan said that 80-90 percent of care is provided by the family, rather than nursing homes, and that a telephone information line, respite care, personal time to use for caregiving, and support groups would be beneficial.

Private consultant Barbara Adolf remarked that providing information at the worksite would be a good way to help caregivers, who, she said, are "hungry for information." Support groups also are helpful, she said.

What Employers Are Doing

Benefits specialists contacted by BNA said that there was not much happening in terms of providing benefits to aid employees who take care of the elderly. Jamie Roberts at Hewitt Associates noted that reimbursement accounts that often are offered with flexible benefits sometimes are used for dependent care, but, she said, the dependent must live in the employee's home at least eight hours per day. Roberts also said that a survey of 120 employers offering flexible benefits found that 83 percent had reimbursement accounts, but only 3-5 percent of employees are using them for dependent care.

Cohan mentioned that employee assistance programs could be helpful in coping with the problem and in assisting with information, but added that the EAP director sometimes had a basic problem: finding the information. As a result of her research, which is funded by a federal grant, Cohan said that she is working with two employers who are contracting for respite care on a cost-matching basis with employees. The grant will also be used by other employers who will start support groups for caregivers, which will be managed by professionals, she said. The grant will provide the funding for the support groups and for an information and referral service.

Adolf said that her organization has been presenting programs to various employers on the problems of caregiving. Seventy-five employees attended a session at Johnson & Johnson, she said. There is "tremendous interest" in the issue on the part of workers, Adolf said, and the issue is "going to get hotter."

Employers may find it productive to invest in local programs, such as the visiting nurse program, and to provide such programs to employees, Adolf said. The bottom line for companies, she said, is that the adult dependent care problem is bigger than some executives realize, and companies may have to do something about it sooner than they think.

The Special Problem of Alzheimer's Disease

One of the difficult problems that adult caregivers sometimes face is dealing with a parent or spouse with Alzheimer's disease. The number of older adults suffering from this disease is growing, according to Helen Chambers, executive director of the Alzheimer's Disease and Related Disorders Association chapter in Montgomery County, Md.

Chambers' experience with Alzheimer's is a personal one: Her husband developed the disease in his early 60s. Because of the disease, he took early retirement from his civil service job, but, she added, the disease also prevented him from understanding why he took it.

An Alzheimer's patient can be left alone during working hours, Chambers said, but eventually the day will come when a neighbor may call to say that the relative is wandering around the neighborhood inappropriately dressed — in a nightgown, or without a coat in winter. At that point, the relative often can be placed — usually free of charge — in a community senior center. Someone will have to tell him to get in lines for meals, and put him on the right bus to go home, she said, but this option often works for several years.

When more supervision is needed, the individual may have to be moved to an adult day care center, which charges a fee. Chambers noted that Alzheimer's patients often wander, and try to leave the center. "They're living in the past," she said, and they often believe they must be somewhere else — that mother is waiting dinner for them. They're often difficult to deal with too, she added. If the Alzheimer's victim continually tries to leave the day care facility, or becomes incontinent, the center usually will not be able to take them.

The next step is a nursing home, Chambers said. Good nursing homes, which usually have a waiting list, charge $2,000-$3,000 a month, she said. Hiring someone to come in to care for the patient can cost upwards of $7.25 an hour, Chambers said. Medicare pays nothing towards these expenses, she added.

Chambers noted that, at home, the Alzheimer's victim is often unable to communicate, needs to be taken for walks, bathed, and taken to the bathroom. Some individuals wander at night, she added, or turn on the stove, or flush things down the toilet. Often the victim has other medical conditions like heart failure, and some are unable to walk. Caring for the relative is "an emotional and physical burden," said Chambers.

An additional burden Chambers faced was unemployment. When her husband required her care, Chambers said, she quit her job as a librarian. When it finally became necessary to place him in a nursing home, she faced the difficulty of being an older women trying to find a job — not an easy situation, she said. Her husband's civil service pension covered the cost of his care, but left nothing for her to live on.

*   *   *

B. ALTERNATIVE WORK SCHEDULES

Time-off from work will become an increasingly important benefit over the next decade as the percentage of single-parent and two-worker families increases.

That's the prediction offered by the Opinion Research Corporation of Princeton, N.J., in its 1985 survey on employee attitudes toward benefits.

Although satisfaction with benefits generally is higher than satisfaction with pay, the ORC report said, the last decade witnessed a significant drop in favorable ratings of employee benefits within every job category except managerial.

Women still bear the brunt of child care responsibilities, and, with the percentage of women in the work force still on the rise, the report said, future conflict is likely. "This conflict may be particularly fierce in the managerial and professional ranks where career commitment is high and more females are trying to balance dual-career families," said ORC Vice President William A. Schiemann. "We would also expect more of the child care responsibility to be shared by males and, consequently, it will also be males who will become increasingly dissatisfied."

"Beyond these child-raising responsibilities," Schiemann explained, "lifestyles have also changed. Individuals value more time away from work."

Alternative Work Schedules Encouraged

Alternative work schedules are being advanced in many quarters as one answer to employees' desire for more free time.

In an October 1985 address to the AFL-CIO's annual convention, Secretary of Labor William Brock urged private industry to consider adopting one type of alternative scheduling option — flextime. Brock said that flextime — already a successful program in the federal government — can help parents solve the dilemma of trying to reconcile "their simultaneous and often conflicting roles as workers and child tenders."

Reporting on its 1985 survey of white collar clerical workers in 300 firms, the American Management Association said that flextime improved productivity and morale. According to AMA, 24.8 percent of banks, 39.2 percent of insurance firms, and 20 percent of public utilities had flextime schedules.

The AMA also reported the following:

• Although the majority of the responding companies reported no change in work volume under flextime, all reported that the quality of work had improved.

• Flextime scheduling led to a decrease in lateness behavior in banks, insurance firms, and public utilities, and, although absenteeism did not decline to the same extent that lateness did, all of the three industries showed marked improvements in this area.

• The amount of overtime was significantly reduced after the introduction of flextime.

• An overwhelming majority of respondents noted greater levels of job satisfaction. Replies indicating negative effects of flextime were infrequent and atypical.

The Family Policy Panel of the Economic Policy Council of UNA-USA also has urged employers to create a more flexible work environment as a way of helping

---

"Working parents in particular need flexibility in working hours and working days so as to attend to sick children, family crises, and gaps in child care arrangements."

---

alleviate the stress on individuals who are trying to balance the roles of parent and worker. In *Work and Family in the United States: A Policy Initiative*, published early in 1986, the panel maintained that flexible work schedules are a relatively inexpensive way of accommodating the needs of working parents.

Employers, the EPC panel recommended, should become more sensitive to the time pressures experienced by their employees and should permit greater flexibility in the scheduling of work hours and leave time. "Working parents in particular need flexibility in working hours and working days so as to attend to sick children, family crises, and gaps in child care arrangements." The EPC panel warned, however, successful flexible work schedules are truly flexible, "not simply alternative, but equally rigid, work schedules."

Employers that are considering whether to offer alternative work schedules to their employees have a number of options from which to choose, including, in addition to flextime:

• Compressed workweeks — Employees can work less than five days per week, but maintain full-time hours by working longer days.

• Job sharing — One job is performed by more than one employee, with the total number of hours worked adding up to one full-time position.

• Permanent and temporary part-time employment.

• Voluntary reduced work-time programs (V-time) — Employees who are classified as full-time, with the approval of their supervisors, voluntarily work less than a full workweek.

• Telecommuting — A telephone hook-up with the office enables employees to use computers to perform work away from the office.

• Flexible use of vacation time and personal days to attend to child care or other parental responsibilities.

Many Employers Skeptical

Although an increasing number of public and private sector employers are adopting or experimenting with flexible scheduling, many other employers remain skeptical about such programs. Costs are a prime reason for that skepticism. Costs associated with flextime and compressed workweek schedules are minimal, but job sharing and part-time employment present potentially higher benefit costs, the EPC panel pointed out in its report. Benefits calculated on the basis of salary or work time can be prorated, but, the panel explained, some labor costs are fixed by statute, and, thus, part-time workers can increase per-hour labor costs. Higher productivity and reduced overtime payments help some employers that provide full-time benefits to part-time workers to make up for the expense of the benefits package, the EPC report said. Other employers offset the cost of benefits to part-time workers through cost sharing, with employees assuming some of the cost of the benefits package, according to the panel.

Some employers provide few or no fringe benefits to part-time workers, the EPC panel reported. "While these employers might obtain short-run savings in labor costs by not providing benefits, in the long run costs may be increased due to the effect on job performance, turnover, and employee development," the panel concluded.

Barbara Cook, head of the metropolitan Washington, D.C., chapter of the American Association of Part-Time Professionals, Inc., pointed out one other possible reason for employer reluctance. Cook said, "A lot depends on the individual manager's personality and what his thoughts are, whether they are older and have had a wife at home all along or have some of these problems and have had to deal with them."

Some Unions Skeptical, Too

Unions, like many employers, are somewhat skeptical about alternative work schedules, and have been slow to embrace them. Jack Golodner, who is director of the AFL-CIO's Department for Professional Employees, noted a number of the reasons unions have been wary of alternative work schedules, including the fear that the workday may be extended, that some programs are not truly voluntary, and that the opportunities for overtime pay may disappear. On the other hand, Golodner said, "when ground rules which address these concerns have been set forth in contracts, a number of programs developed jointly by management and unions have worked successfully."

Barbara Cook noted that unions increasingly are realizing that women are a major untapped vein of potential new members and that women are interested in part-time employment. These facts may influence some unions to rethink their position on part-time work.

The Association of Part-Time Professionals, which promotes alternative work patterns for professionals, has 1,500 members and the largest component, she said, comprises women who are trying to balance career and family responsibilities. Cook gave the example of a female attorney who "may desperately want to spend a year at home with a new baby." Realistically, if she does stay home, the woman is putting her career on hold. "It's not going to be easy [for the attorney] to get promotions" if she leaves the work force altogether, Cook noted. More and more professionals, however, think putting an end to rapid career movement — for a time — is worth the extra time at home, she said. By working on a part-time basis, she explained, the attorney can keep her professional skills up to date, which makes eventual return to full-time work easier, Cook said.

According to results of a poll of 4,900 women, conducted by Working Woman magazine and published in its February 1986 issue, 77 percent of those mothers who changed to part-time work said they were very satisfied with life. "Unfortunately," the magazine points out, "part-time jobs are very hard to get. Over 40 percent of the mothers indicate that they would like to work part-time after the end of their maternity leave, but only 8 percent of those with children age three or less are currently doing so."

On Employer Reluctance

Cook contended that the cost question for employers — at least as far as permanent part-timers are concerned — is not that complicated. Essentially, she said, in most cases benefits are pro-rated. Permanent part-time employees working 30 hours normally get benefits now, said Cook, and people working 20 hours can now expect pro-rated benefits.

Many benefits also flow to employers who employ permanent part-time employees, Cook insisted. Most often, employers first encounter the issue of part-time

---

"I've never met a part-timer who didn't say that 'they are definitely getting more out of me than when I was there [full time].' "

---

work when a valued employee considers dropping out of the work force to attend to family needs, such as a maternity situation, Cook said. Many firms are on tight budgets and recognize that someone working less than full time offers them a valuable alternative.

Some studies, Cook added, are showing that productivity levels are higher for part-timers because there is not as much slack time as occurs for workers in full-time positions. "I've never met a part-timer who didn't say that 'they are definitely getting more out of me than when I was there [full time],' " Cook maintained.

Absenteeism and employee turnover for part-timers also is lower, Cook said. Employee morale and employer-employee relations improve. In addition, the employer using permanent part-time workers is broadening the employee base, which is important when there is competition for professionals in a particular field, such as engineering. Part-time professional employees also help an employer better match the task to the skill, said Cook. The components of the professional's job that do not require a professional's skills can be accomplished by a less-skilled — and lower-paid — worker, Cook explained.

"In the long run, it's better business for corporations" to employ permanent part-time workers, Cook maintained. "I don't think it's a give-away. Our emphasis is on convincing employers that it is in their best interest to hire permanent part-time employees."

The case studies which follow examine a variety of alternative work schedule options offered by public and private sector employers.

FLEXTIME

Organization: **U.S. Government**
Summary: **Flexible work schedules, initiated on experimental basis in 1979,**

became a permanent feature of employment for federal government employees in 1985.

Alternative work arrangements — flexible work schedules and compressed work schedule programs — became a permanent element in the federal government's employment program when President Reagan signed P.L. 99-196 on Dec. 23, 1985.

Alternative work schedule programs in the federal government were originally authorized on an experimental basis in 1979 to permit employees to vary their work hours, with the restriction that hours worked totaled the number required within a specified time. The program later was re-authorized by the Federal Employees Flexible and Compressed Work Schedules Act of 1982. Legislation exempts the federal government from the Walsh-Healey Act, which requires overtime pay for employees working more than eight hours a day.

It is estimated that the program is now being used by between 300,000 and 500,000 employees who work in 41 federal agencies.

Since the early 1970s, more and more private businesses have adopted a variety of flexible schedules for employees. The House Committee on Post Office and Civil Service noted in its June 1985 report on the federal program that it is estimated that more than 10 million full-time workers enjoy flexible work schedules or compressed workweeks. The report also said:

"These variations from the standard eight-hour workday evolved as a means of coping with social change, particularly the dramatic increase of women in the work force, as well as the desire of all employees for a better accommodation between their working and personal lives. Employers found they benefited from better use of buildings and equipment, decreased traffic congestion, and improved attendance, punctuality, and morale. Because employees have more control over their working lives, flexible schedules also helped to reduce conflicts between work and personal needs, particularly for working mothers and others with household responsibilities."

According to a survey by BNA's Personnel Policies Forum published in July 1984, 32 percent of 195 employers surveyed had established flexible hours in the previous five years.

Flexible schedules can take several forms, but, in general, they permit employees to vary their arrival and departure times while requiring them to be on the job during a "core time." Compressed schedules permit employees to work longer than eight-hour days in order to complete their biweekly work requirement in less than 10 days. Individuals, as well as unions, work out flextime schedules in negotiation with management.

Types of Alternative Work Schedules

Following is an excerpt from the September 1981 Office of Personnel Management's *Interim Report on the Alternative Work Schedules Experimental Program*. The House committee used the report to describe the various types of alternative work schedules (AWS):

1. Flexible Work Schedules

Flexible work schedules, popularly called flexitime, refer to a variety of arrangements in which fixed times of arrival and departure are replaced by a working day composed of two different types of time — core time and flexible time. Core time is the designated period during which all employees must be present. Flexible time is designated as part of the schedule of working hours within which employees may choose their time of arrival at and departure from the work site within limits consistent with the duties and requirements of their positions. The only other requirement of flexitime is that employees must account for the basic work requirement. The basic work requirement is the number of hours, excluding overtime hours, which an employee is required to work or to otherwise account for by an appropriate form of leave. For example, a full-time employee is required to work 40 hours a week or 80 hours every two weeks. A part-time employee might be employed under an appointment which requires the employee to work 32 hours a week or perhaps 64 hours every two weeks.

Certain types of flexitime schedules in which employees work eight hours each day, but may vary their arrival and departure times with or without prior approval, have been used by Federal agencies since 1972. Public Law 95-390 made possible the testing of more sophisticated flexitime schedules by introducing the concept of "credit hours". Credit hours are any hours of work in excess of the basic work requirement that an employee elects to work on a given workday or in a given workweek in order to shorten the length of another workday or workweek. For instance, an employee could work 10 hours on one day in order to shorten the length of a subsequent workday, or an employee could choose to work 50 hours in a particular workweek so as to gain the advantage of a shorter workweek of 30 hours the next week.

The following flexible schedules have been used in the AWS experiment:

• *Flexitour:* Employee preselects starting time; may modify schedule with prior notification and approval of supervisor.

• *Gliding schedule:* Within flexible bands, employee may vary starting time without prior notification or approval of the supervisor.

• *Variable day:* Employee may vary the length of the workday as long as he or she is present for daily core time with limits established by the organization; must work or account for the basic work requirement, e.g., 40 hours per week for a full-time employee; credit hour carry-over between pay periods is limited to a maximum of 10 hours.

• *Variable week:* Employee may vary the length of the workday and the workweek as long as he or she is present for daily (five days a week) core time; must work or account for the basic work requirement, e.g. 80 hours in a bi-weekly pay period for a full-time employee; credit hour carry-over is limited to a maximum of 10 hours.

• *Maxiflex:* Employee may vary the length of the workweek and workday as long as he or she is present for core time which is scheduled on less than all five week days; must work or account for the basic work requirement, e.g. 80 hours in a bi-weekly pay period; credit hour carry-over is limited to a maximum of 10 hours.

Federal agencies can vary in the specifics of implementing a schedule. For example, two organizations might both have Maxiflex but differ in the total number of core hours, the number of days with core time, and the length of the flexible band.

2. Compressed Schedules

Compressed work schedules take a variety of forms. The most common compressed schedule is the week with four 10-hour days, referred to as the 4-10 schedule. A compressed schedule, however, is any schedule which enables the full-time employee to complete the basic bi-weekly work requirement of 80 hours in less than 10 full workdays. For employees working under compressed schedules overtime pay was continued for overtime hours which were officially ordered by an agency official and which exceeded the basic work requirement. While compressed schedules had not generally been used in Federal agencies prior to the AWS experiment, private sector firms have used such schedules, particularly in computer operations, where 10-hour days permit the most economical use of expensive equipment. In addition, compressed schedules permit increased service to customers. For example, by splitting the work force, with some employees working Monday through Thursday and others working Tuesday through Friday, an organization could be open to serve the public two additional hours every work day.

Like flexible schedules, compressed work schedules may also take a variety of forms, but provisions for earning and accumulating credit hours do not apply. While some organizations, typically those operating 24 hours a day or seven days a week, have used unique compressed schedules, the two most common types of compressed schedules are:

- *4-10:* Employees work 10 hours per day, four days per week, for a 40-hour workweek. Employees have both a daily and a weekly basic work requirement.

- *5-4/9:* Although there are variations of this plan, the most common approach is to have employees scheduled to work nine hours a day during eight days of a bi-weekly pay period and eight hours on the ninth day. Employees have both a daily and bi-weekly basic work requirement.

Benefit to Single Parents

The 1981 OPM report also contained an extensive study of flextime. The interim report on the federal program found that the ability to set their own schedules was considered "very to somewhat important" by 93 percent of the 325,000 federal employees surveyed, and by an even higher percentage of single parents. Single parents appeared to prefer schedules in which they worked longer days, but earned three-day weekends either every week or every other week. A total of 83 percent of single parents surveyed felt it was very important to have more time with their families.

OPM noted that the freedom to set work schedules enabled employees to spend less money for baby-sitting services, more time on household chores, more time with their families, and more time participating in children's school activities. Some 63 percent of employees on flexible schedules "feel this schedule is most compatible with quality care for children and other dependents," OPM found, noting that the data "strongly suggested that AWS allows employees workable alternatives to enhance the quality of family relationships and child care."

The alternative schedules reduced the need to use short-term leave for child care, the study found. About half of those surveyed reported that their use of short-term leave either decreased or decreased greatly under the alternative scheduling arrangements. Employees working compressed schedules "seldom or never change their work schedule for child care during school vacations or holidays," the report noted.

Alternative Work Schedules: A Good Track Record

Rep. Gary L. Ackerman (D-NY), who introduced the measure making flextime permanent, said that options such as flextime provide civil servants with a way to better manage their leisure and employment time.

Alternative work schedules, Ackerman said, have a proven record. "[AWS] has decreased absenteeism, increased worker productivity, improved employee morale, expanded agency contact with the public, and bettered the effectiveness of federal agencies — all at absolutely no cost to the American taxpayer."

Rep. Dan Burton (R-Ind) listed advantages as better morale, more personal freedom, fewer persons traveling during rush hour, longer office hours for service to the public, fewer conflicts with personal or family matters, more flexibility in scheduling for managers, and use as a benefit to attract and retain employees.

The General Accounting Office, in a 1985 report on flextime, concluded that the advantages of alternative work schedules appeared to outweigh the disadvantages. According to the GAO survey:

• 74 percent of some 2,000 federal employees who responded to the GAO questionnaire indicated they supported continuing the flextime program;

• 72 percent who used alternative work schedules felt the schedules gave them greater flexibility to meet family obligations, such as doctor's appointments, meetings, and taking children to school;

• 74 percent believe the program has had a favorable effect on their morale; and

• 89 percent of those on an alternative work schedule who have a need for dependent care were satisfied with the work schedules, compared with 62 percent of employees on a fixed schedule who were satisfied.

Flextime Common in Europe

The Final Bill Report on the Ackerman measure pointed out, as background, that flextime schedules are "very common in Europe." In Switzerland, approximately 30 percent of the work force is on flextime. In Austria the figure is 25 percent.

The recent report of the Family Policy Panel of the Economic Policy Council of United Nations Association of the United States of America reported that 45 percent of workers in West Germany are on flextime schedules.

In the United States, an estimated one million workers are on flextime schedules. Among the private sector employers using the concept are General Motors Corp., American Airlines, Exxon, Hewlett-Packard, Transamerica Occidental Life Insurance Company, and SmithKline Beckman Corp.

Either administratively or legislatively, 42 states allow at least some of their employees to work flexible schedules, according to the House committee's report.

There are disadvantages, however, the report pointed out. "Under flex-time scheduling and planning work flow can be more demanding; employees frequently will not be present when supervisors are on duty; managers will be challenged to plan the work and develop better ways to increase effectiveness of their work units; administrative problems with timekeeping occur; additional energy may be needed to heat and cool buildings for the additional hours of operation; flex-time bites into employee overtime pay; and under flex-time cross training is necessary."

FLEXTIME

Organization:	**Transamerica Occidental Life Insurance Company** **Los Angeles, Calif.**
Summary:	**Transamerica Occidental Life operated a pilot flextime program in 1973. It was so well received that the company adopted flextime**

as policy. According to Transamerica, 90 percent of the company's 3,800 Los Angeles-area workers now participate in flextime scheduling.

While many companies have only recently begun to respond to changes in the demographics of the American work force — and the corresponding developments in the area of workers' needs — Transamerica Occidental Life Insurance Company saw the changes on the horizon and began adjusting as early as 1973, according to Sandie Comrie, the company's vice president for human resources.

At the request of management, Occidental that year instituted a pilot flextime program. The pilot program operated in a variety of the company's home office departments as well as its Canadian headquarters.

Three issues prompted the establishment of the pilot program, Comrie said. Flextime was seen as:

• A recruiting incentive;
• A way to deal with traffic congestion and parking problems; and
• A way for employees to gain control over their work time and to solve their child care problems.

Feedback on the pilot program was positive, said Comrie, who noted that 90 percent of the company's 3,800 Los Angeles-area workers now participate in flextime scheduling. Two-thirds of the participants are women, she said.

The schedules are worked out between workers and department managers on a one-on-one, case-by-case basis. Specifically, the program allows employees to begin work at various times between 7:00 a.m and 9:00 a.m. Lunch breaks can be as short as 30 minutes or as long as 60 minutes, depending on how early an employee wants to leave. Between May 1 and Oct. 31, the company also allows for "early Fridays" — employees work only five and one-half hours on that day.

"While the program is flexible," said Comrie, "most people chose a personal schedule and stick to it. During the core hours of nine to three, everyone is here."

Flextime scheduling is a more difficult, the vice president said, in departments where operations are slightly more rigid in their time structuring due to the service functions they provide and the need for staffing at particular hours.

For some managers, Comrie said, flextime adds more pressure. There are a handful of problems, such as individuals who can't be accommodated because of their job requirements and others who make use of car and van pools that adhere to fixed time schedules. None of the problems were unforeseen at the program's outset, however, according to Comrie.

"We advertise flextime as a benefit to employees. We look at it as a statement about progressiveness — a statement of what we are," Comrie remarked.

Flextime and Child Care

"The flextime benefit helps many of our employees who are parents. For example, we have one employee in public relations who is able to adjust her work schedule to drop off and pick up her child before and after school. Without flextime, she would need to hire a babysitter for either the beginning or the end of the day. Flextime means cost savings for this employee, as well as peace of mind about her child's safety," explained Comrie.

To supplement and balance its flextime program, Occidental began a child care referral program in October 1984. The program, Comrie said, was put into place after a survey of employees revealed a large number of parents in the company, many of whom were single. Employees expressed frustration about both the lack of quality child care centers and the difficulty in finding them. Comrie said, "We found employees with dramatic problems, people who didn't know how to solve these problems."

The company set up a program to match employees with appropriate public agencies to help them find day care. Later, an on-site center was set up to provide counseling and information about child care topics.

In one case, Comrie said, an employee in pension plan administration "had spent months trying to find affordable day care facilities in her area." After she contacted the company's Child Care Resource and Referral Center, "she was able to find appropriate facilities within three days. Without day care, she would not have been able to work."

"Another employee in actuarial and reinsurance systems," Comrie related, "wanted to work full-time and breastfeed her newborn simultaneously. The Center was able to coordinate her responsibilities so she could do both."

The child care office is now open twice a week, but there are plans to include additional hours, Comrie said. Since the program's inception, some 200 employees have been assisted in the solving of a variety of child care problems, she told BNA.

To mark the first anniversary of the program, Comrie said, Occidental on Nov. 1, 1985, began a fingerprinting program for employees' children. The program is intended to help police and other investigators identify children. All Los Angeles-based employees, as well as some 2,000 Occidental workers nationwide, received fingerprinting kits. They were advised to store the prints along with other valuable documents in a safe or safety deposit box.

"With the attention that has been focused on the missing children's issue, we wanted to help our people feel more secure about their children's safety," Occidental Chairman and Chief Executive Officer David Carpenter said at the time.

                                                           FLEXITIME

Organization: **SmithKline Beckman Corp.**
                    Philadelphia, Pa.

Summary: **SmithKline Beckman has offered a flexible working schedule —
                    Flexitime — to the majority of its employees in Philadelphia area
                    for 10 years. Employees use the program to ease child care
                    burdens, to further their education, and for a variety of other
                    purposes. The company lists as benefits improved productivity and
                    employee morale.**

For more than a decade, SmithKline Beckman Corp. has offered a flexible working schedule to the majority of its employees in the area of Philadelphia, Pa., site of the worldwide pharmaceutical firm's headquarters. With approval from their supervisors, employees can start their seven-hour workday any time between 7:30 a.m. and 9:15 a.m. and leave any time between 3 p.m. and 6 p.m., with two restrictions: They must be on the job a minimum of five and one-half hours during the company's "core" workday, 9:15 a.m. to 3 p.m., and they must work a five-day week. The company calls the program "Flexitime."

"We have always been very pleased with the program," Jeremy Heymsfeld, director of corporate information at SmithKline Beckman, said. "Flexitime applies to most of [the 6,000 employees in the company's] Philadelphia-based operations," Heymsfeld said. Employees in manufacturing operations, which require that everybody be there at the same time, don't have the Flexitime option.

"We have found it helpful in terms of morale and reduced lateness and absenteeism," and also in terms of improved productivity, Heymsfeld said. "It has a positive effect in all those regards," in addition to helping employees work out time conflicts between work and family responsibilities, he explained.

"It sure does," agreed Mrs. Eileen Harding, who arranges her work schedule so she can get two-and-one-half-year-old daughter Ashley to a day care center by 7:30 a.m. and pick her up again before 5:30 p.m. "She can't get day care before 7:30 a.m. and she has to be picked up before 5:30 p.m.," Harding explained. "As long as you have your supervisor's agreement, you can set up hours that fit your supervisor's needs as well as your own," said Harding, a personnel department employee who has worked for the company for six years.

Harding said Flexitime is especially helpful to her because her husband, William, personnel manager for another Philadelphia company, has fixed working hours of 8 a.m. to 5 p.m. with no flextime option. That means that Eileen Harding frequently has to drop Ashley off at day care and pick her up.

The firm does not keep figures on how many employees take advantage of the Flexitime option, but, Harding said, in her department of 70 employees it is used extensively. "It's gotten to the point where the supervisor has to have somebody assigned to watch the phones after 4:30 p.m.," she said.

Harding has used Flexitime ever since returning to work after the birth of her daughter. She formerly used another SmithKline program, a van pool in which employees can come to work early and leave early under the Flexitime program. The company leases the vans, which run at various times between company facilities and various neighborhoods. Employees pay for the service through payroll deductions.

Other employees who live farther away from their jobs at SmithKline Beckman facilities use Flexitime to avoid rush-hour traffic or for other reasons. "A lot of poeple coordinate their schedule to avoid peak [traffic] hours," Harding reported. "One big reason is school. A lot of people go to school at night," she adds. "Some work later hours and go right from work to school, or they may arrange an early work schedule to give themselves some time to study before going to school in the evening."

Heymsfeld, who noted that Flexitime has been in effect well over a decade at SmithKline, said simply: "I think people are very pleased with it."

JOB SHARING

Organization: **The Rolscreen Co., Pella, Iowa**
Summary: **In 1975, an employee at Rolscreen asked if she could split her job with her sister-in-law. The company agreed, and the job-sharing "team program" was born. Participation in the program is limited to workers whose jobs consist of repetitive tasks — factory**

workers and some clericals. As many as 100 workers have participated in the team program at one time.

In 1975, an employee approached the management of The Rolscreen Company, an Iowa manufacturing firm, and asked if the company would allow her to share her job with her sister-in-law. The worker had young children and wanted to spend more time with her family. Rolscreen agreed to the plan and today approximately 100 workers participate in the firm's "team program," according to Personnel Manager Mel Petersma.

The city of Pella, Iowa, where Rolscreen is located, is a town of 8,500. In Pella, as in many Iowa communities, family life is important and parents want to spend as much time as possible with their children. Rolscreen's team program allows parents to spend more time with their children by providing set classifications of workers with the opportunity to share their jobs with other employees.

Petersma said the job-sharing program "works very well," and noted that the annual average absence rate for individuals participating in the program has dropped from 4.5 percent of scheduled work time to less than 0.4 percent.

The majority of Rolscreen's 2,000 workers are employed in its factory operations. There are in nine job classifications; employees in levels three and below are eligible for participation in the team program, according to Petersma. Persons in levels one through three are "generally assembly line workers whose jobs are repetitious," he explained. It is this repetition that makes those jobs "ideal" for sharing. Employees in levels four and above bid for job promotions, he said, and it is not possible for employees to "bid on half a job."

Employees who participate in the program are expected to work at least 1,000 hours per year, based on an average working year of 2,000 hours per year. But Rolscreen allows the job-sharing teams to decide how those hours will be divided up. Some workers, he said, alternate days, while other teams split the hours worked in a day. And some pairs even split the days so that one employee works Wednesday, Thursday, Friday, Monday and Tuesday, and then the next employee takes over allowing them in effect, seven-day weekends. Employees can even take weeks off at a time for a long leave of absence, and then take over a work full-time for their counterpart when they return.

"As long as the work gets done, we don't care how they divide it up," Petersma stressed.

Employees may split jobs only with employees on the same level, and they receive 50 percent of the annual wage for that job. Wages do not vary with seniority in levels one through three, Petersma explained. On paid holidays, each worker gets paid for half a day, and each employee is entitled to half the vacation due someone at his or her seniority level. For example, he explained, if a 10-year veteran and a 20-year veteran were sharing a job, the 10-year employee would get one-half of the three weeks a 10-year worker is granted, while the 20-year employee would get one-half of the four weeks a 20-year employee earns. The company pays in full the cost of dental and health insurance coverage for all employees.

Workers who are interested in enrolling in the team plan are asked to find a partner with whom to share the job. If they are unable to locate a counterpart, the company will try to match up that employee with a worker in a similar job. If no partner is available, the employee must wait until another worker expresses an interest in job sharing. Once an employee decides to go on job sharing, Petersma explained, they must remain in the program for at least six months. This is to prevent a lot of "hopping in and out," he said.

Employees appear to be "tickled to death with the team program," Petersma stressed, and Rolscreen officials are equally pleased. He noted that the productivity and morale of workers enrolled in the program is "better than among the other employees." He said part of the reason for this high level of morale "is because they come in with better spirits after having some time off." Employees with sick children also are able to rearrange their schedules with their partners to take time off, so the worker on the job does not have his or her mind on a child and not on the job.

While most of the program participants are young mothers, Petersma said a large number of the team players are women in their 50s and above. "They appear to have gotten to the point where they might need to work a little, but they are also beginning to slow down and spend their time on activities they enjoy." Presently, three men are participating in the program, he added. He acknowledged he was not exactly sure why the men are participating, but indicated his belief that "the men are working all the hours they want to work. They've made a decision to have more leisure time."

Clerical workers whose jobs are of a repetitive nature also are eligible for the program and currently five to seven teams are making use of the Rolscreen program, he said. The number of teams enrolled in the job-sharing program companywide has ranged from a high of 50 to a low of 27 teams.

The idea of listening to employee suggestions, and implementing them if they are "reasonable" is at the heart of the Rolscreen team plan — a program that benefits both management and employees, said Petersma, who concluded that the idea of listening to employees is probably the primary reason "that Rolscreen is not unionized today."

PEAK-TIME EMPLOYMENT STRATEGY

Organization: **Provident Bank of Cincinnati, Ohio**

Summary: **Under its Peak-Time program, the bank pays part-time workers who work the hours of peak customer traffic more than it pays other part-timers who work lighter-traffic hours. The bank says the higher pay rate is attracting better qualified workers and mothers who seek to re-enter the work force.**

"Paying people what they're worth when you need them most" is the rationale for Peak-Time, a pioneering part-time employment strategy introduced by the Provident Bank of Cincinnati in March 1983.

Under the Peak-Time strategy, which was conceived by Stuart Mahlin, then Provident's vice president for personnel, part-time employees who work during the bank's busiest hours are paid higher hourly rates than those who work during the remaining bank hours.

A substantial amount of take-home pay combined with limited working hours has attracted more mature, better-educated applicants — among them, many early retirees and mothers looking to re-enter the labor force — for Provident's teller openings, Mahlin told BNA.

Since it takes as much effort to go to work for two hours as it does for eight, said Mahlin, the premium wage incentive makes "real sense to people" who otherwise might not consider part-time work worthwhile. Mahlin, who is now a consultant to firms interested in adopting Peak-Time, said peak-time hourly pay rates range from $6.50 to $10.50 nationwide, but generally fall around $8. A conventional part-time employment scheme that pays minimum wage "doesn't make sense" to former professionals, who would prefer volunteering their time to working for such low pay, he explained.

Peak-Timers work only during high-volume periods, for a total of anywhere from 10 to 25 hours a week. By paying targeted-period workers a premium wage, employers can attract "people out-of-sync with the usual labor pool," Mahlin said, individuals looking to integrate part-time work with other commitments, like mothers who only want to work during the hours their children are in school.

Terming it "a full-time solution to the part-time problem," Mahlin said Peak-Time drastically reduces turnover among part-time employees, thereby cutting training costs while encouraging work force continuity. A 65-branch bank in Connecticut, for instance, saved $1.2 million its first Peak-Time year, he claimed. Businesses adopting this strategy also save money by not providing Peak-Timers' with discretionary benefits, he said, noting that most Peak-Timers are already covered by their spouse's plan, "so offering benefits would be redundant."

More Efficient Workers

The quality of Peak-Time work is high, said Mahlin. "[B]ecause they come to the job fresher," Peak-Time workers are often faster and more efficient. In addition, banks have found that customers in their 30s, 40s, and 50s respond positively to tellers closer to their own age who project a confident, polished air, he said.

At the Provident Bank, Peak-Time has been very successful, said Personnel Representative June Waddell, who hires all of the bank's tellers. Better qualified applicants and low turnover characterize Provident's experience, she said, with Peak-Time positions paying from $6.60 per hour for a 25-hour week to $8.72 per hour for a 13-hour week. Most of Provident's Peak-Timers are mothers re-entering the workforce, Waddell said. Peak-Time scheduling fits their lifestyle, but does not infringe upon familial duties, she explained, commenting, "It allows them to be in the adult world for a while."

The changing composition of society — in particular, the shrinking pool of very young workers and the growing surplus of workers in the 50- to 60-year-old age bracket — has made part-time work one of the megatrends of the 1980s, said Mahlin. Further, as the workweek's parameters continue to change, employers are realizing "there's a much larger potential part-time work force out there," he said.

While Peak-Time has been primarily embraced by the banking industry — "simply because that's where it started," said Mahlin — it is being introduced into the retailing, computer programming, accounting, collections, and airline industries, he explained, as more companies realize the benefits of scheduling additional workers during peak periods. Over the past year, Mahlin has worked with firms in 40 states and Canada interested in Peak-Time and has found that many of the problems employers face "are generic." Basically, most need to alter their perception of part-time employees, he explained: "They need to realize quality people can be attracted, and retained, in targeted-staffing positions, if the hours and the pay are right."

VOLUNTARY REDUCED WORKWEEK (V-TIME)

Organization:	Shaklee Corporation San Francisco, Calif.
Summary:	A suggestion from employees led to Shaklee's institution of V-time. Individual employees negotiate with their supervisors on the exact number of hours to be worked. Some benefits are pro-rated, but Shaklee continues to provide full medical, dental, and vision coverage for all workers on V-time. So far, the company says, the program is resulting in reduced costs.

Business conditions and expressions of interest from employees convinced Shaklee Corporation some two years ago to offer voluntary reduced time — V-time — on a limited basis to some employees. While only a small number of the company's workers actually use V-time, Shaklee Personnel Manager Alan Hubbard reported that both the company and the employees on V-time like the option.

In the winter of 1983-1984, a slight business downturn led San Francisco-based Shaklee Corporation to reconsider suggestions from some of its employees that the health products company offer voluntary reduced work time as an option.

At Shaklee, voluntary reduced time, or V-time, is negotiated between an employee and his or her manager, explained Hubbard, who described Shaklee's program as "an agreement between the manager and the employee that is less than the normal 37.5-hour-work week." The agreement is made in writing and spells out the number of hours the employee normally works, the number of hours in the reduced workweek, and how fringe benefits are to be computed.

When V-time was first offered, some 15 employees — about 2 to 3 percent of Shaklee's San Francisco work force — took advantage of it, Hubbard reported. Since its inception, the number of people on reduced workweeks has fluctuated, he added, and appears to be on the rise now.

Many of those using the voluntary reduced workweek option are working mothers, Hubbard said, but they're not the only users. The program also has benefited employees who want to pursue outside interests, such as hobbies, and others who wanted to devote more time to private business ventures. Typical V-time agreements at Shaklee call for three- or four-day workweeks, he said.

"Shaklee has gained more benefits than were perceived when this program started," Hubbard conceded. Employees on reduced workweek schedules "are at least as productive as they were before and in some cases more productive," he said. "Overall, we have found that the reduction in workweek provides some savings to the corporation, and although there is some administrative expense involved, it is minor compared to the overall dollar savings."

Sick leave and vacation pay accrual are prorated under a reduced workweek agreement. Paid holidays are reduced from 11 to 10 per year for those on reduced workweek agreements. If a holiday falls on a regularly scheduled day off, the employee must take a day off within five days of the holiday in order to receive holiday pay.

Shaklee has opted to grant those employees on voluntary reduced workweeks full medical, dental, and vision coverages, rather than prorating those benefits, Hubbard said. "It is a very difficult thing to break out the benefit cost for each individual," Hubbard explained, and because of the difficulties inherent in prorating medical benefits, Shaklee has opted for full coverage for all workers. Life insurance coverage is based on the prorated annual salary under the reduced workweek, however.

A big increase in the number of people using the reduced workweek option could cause Shaklee to rethink its practice of keeping those employees under full medical coverage, Hubbard said. "If this gets to be a serious problem, if we have a lot of people go on this program, or if it becomes a very expensive aspect of running the program, I think we would have to look at it and reevaluate it," he said.

Shaklee has had a few problems with job definitions under reduced workweek arrangements, Hubbard reported. In one case, an employee was taken off a reduced workweek "because the work wasn't being performed the way it had to be in order to be satisfactory for both the employee and the employer," he said.

Administrative expenses associated with V-time have been minimal, Hubbard said, and have consisted mainly of changing computerized payroll and personnel data.

Shaklee plans to continue offering the reduced workweek option as long as the company doesn't find major problems with the definition of the work to be performed, the costs of V-time to the company, or medical benefits issue, Hubbard said. "I think the company feels at this point that it is working very well for the people using it and it will continue to offer this particular program as long as there aren't any major concerns or serious problems that come from it."

TELECOMMUTING

BACKGROUND

The computer and the telephone are becoming the principal tools of a new generation of homeworkers — the telecommuters. With a computer to perform the work and a telephone to connect the worker with an office, telecommuters are able to accomplish at home work they ordinarily would do at the office.

So far, telecommuting seems to appeal primarily to those men and women who have family responsibilities, but who nevertheless want to be a part of the paid labor force. The Department of Labor estimates that telecommuters now number only about 15,000, but other sources figure the number is much higher. Some 350 business firms now use telecommuting, according to Monmouth Junction, N.J., consultant Gil Gordon. The estimate is "a highly educated guess," but nevertheless a conservative one, said Gordon, who figured the number was double that of five years ago. "I suspect the growth curve will begin picking up quite quickly and will more than double again in the next 10 years."

According to Electronic Services Unlimited, a New York-based telecommunications research and consulting company, there are about 450 to 500 corporations with formal or informal telecommuting programs and approximately 100,000 persons working in their homes or remote centers. An ESU spokesperson told BNA that there are a lot of people who are telecommuting on an informal basis and "not calling it anything." ESU estimates that there are 5 to 6 million persons in the latter category, she said.

In a separate study, ESU concluded that there are currently 7.2 million jobs in the work force that could be moved "tomorrow" to employees' homes — at least part time — with no problem.

Estimates of the number of telecommuters doing office work by 1990 range from 5 million to as many as 18 million.

Telecommuting, however, may never appeal to a majority of the work force. Honeywell Information Systems, Inc., reports that 56 percent of workers interviewed for one of its surveys reported they would rather go to their offices than work at home, while only 7 percent preferred working at home entirely. Thirty-six percent said they preferred to split their work time between home and the office.

Analysis by OTA

Late in 1985, the Congressional Office of Technology Assessment issued *Automation of America's Offices*, an extensive report on how technology is changing the office and what the future may hold for offices and office workers. The report dealt at length with telecommuting.

Because of the continuing declines in the cost and improvements in the capability of telecommunications, there may be significant increase in the next 10-15 years in the volume of clerical work done at home or sent offshore to be done in other countries where labor costs are lower, the report concluded. OTA also concluded, however, that the amount of both home-based work and offshore data entry work may decline again after that period, as automation decreases the costs of data processing in the United States, and the congressional research agency advised against taking legislative or other actions to limit offshore performance of clerical work.

OTA suggested that any intervention by the government to "forbid, restrict, or regulate such work would need to be carefully designed to avoid placing an unintended burden on other kinds of home-based work, such as occasional 'telecommuting' or small entrepreneurship."

Congress nevertheless may be asked to consider — possibly in 1986 — the following options: "1) encouraging home-based work through tax incentives or removing minor regulatory barriers, 2) banning home-based clerical work, and 3) providing more effective and systematic regulation of home-based clerical work."

Women Attracted to Working at Home

OTA said that women constitute the overwhelming majority of clerical homeworkers and the report indicated that most of those women homeworkers have one or more children under six years old.

The report pointed out that the likely increase in the employment of home-based clerical workers raises a number of thorny questions: "What is their legal status vis-a-vis employee rights and benefits? To what extent can they be protected under existing labor laws and regulations? What is the potential effect on conventional office employment opportunities?" The report also noted that "alternative child-care arrangements will be needed for those who prefer or need full-time employment."

OTA concluded that working at home is very attractive to women for a number of reasons:

• *Flexibility:* Telecommuting gives them the opportunity to control their own work hours and to schedule job tasks around household responsibilities.

• *The opportunity to be with young children and save on costly day care:* OTA cautioned, however, that the demands of working at home often are such that mothers must make day care arrangements of some sort.

• *Savings in work-related costs such as food, clothing, and transportation.*

• *Fewer work interruptions.*

Because many women seek work even though they continue to have the primary responsibility for home and family care, it is likely that women will continue to constitute a substantial proportion of the telecommuters in the future.

Some employers find work-at-home programs attractive because the programs provide access to a skilled work force of women who are unavailable for traditional employment because they have family responsibilities.

According to the federal Department of Labor, there is documented evidence of productivity increases ranging from 15 to 80 percent among homeworkers.

The Work-and-Family Conundrum

Although little research has been done to determine the effects of telecommuting on family life, the OTA report said indications are that the effects are generally positive:

"Mothers perceive several specific advantages for their children, in addition to the primary advantage of having a parent care for them, instead of strangers or a commercial facility. They believe it is good for their children to realize that 'mothers can do more than cook . . . and take care of them.' They want their children to see women performing a broader social role than that of housewife,

however they themselves value that role. Some say that their children become more independent because they are not the only focus of mother's attention. They say also that their children become familiar with computers and what they can do."

Some caveats, however, were also provided in the report:

"On the other hand, some mothers report that their children get less time and attention, and that the mother gets impatient when she is under pressure to get work done. For women struggling to earn an income and care for children at the same time, home-based work may be a golden opportunity, but it is not an unalloyed blessing. It involves significant stress, both physical and mental, and may create emotional strains within the family as well. One expert says, 'It appears that work at home cannot be called a "good solution" to child care.' "

The OTA report noted that mothers who work at home often have babysitters while they are working if they are not dependent on the income they are bringing in. OTA maintained that this situation shows that doing paid work and taking care of children at the same time is difficult and stressful, and that it is important to these women to have some other work besides taking care of a family. "The second point is repeatedly confirmed by home-based working mothers, who say that they need something to occupy their minds or that paid work gives them pride and self-respect (and respect from others) that is lacking otherwise."

Where the effects on marriage of home-based women workers have been studied, most husbands were supportive and helpful, the OTA report said. Most of the women, however, said that their husbands did not help them any more with housework than they had before. "The women had been, and still were predominantly responsible for the household work, and a few spontaneously expressed dissatisfaction or resentment of this. Most were unable to draw boundaries between household and work responsibilities, and move back and forth between them during the day."

Managerial vs. Clerical

Many companies are adopting homework programs for both professional and managerial employees in order to meet shortages of skilled personnel or to attract or retain skilled workers whose family situation constrains them from working full-time in an office. These workers usually receive salaries and benefits comparable to those granted their counterparts in the office, and they are subjected to a low to moderate amount of supervision. They usually are provided with all the necessary equipment they need by their employers.

Clericals on the other hand are likely to be paid piece rates or, if they receive an hourly salary, that salary is most likely below that of their counterparts. They are less likely to receive benefits and in some instances must pay for equipment they use at home. In addition, they may be supervised much more closely through on-line computer monitoring.

There are acknowledged disadvantages to telecommuting, however:

• Some managers feel an overpowering need to constantly check up on employees they cannot see, while others provide too little supervision.

• Homeworkers may have additional expenses such as renting equipment and higher electric bills resulting from the extensive use of electronic equipment.

• Most clerical homeworkers do not receive any benefits and are paid lower wages than comparable workers in an office setting.

• Some homeworkers must trade control they get over their working hours for the stress of managing home and work responsibilities at the same time at one site; interruption of work may be especially troublesome for clericals working against piecework demands or quotas under electronic monitoring.

Unions and Homework

The union movement is, in general, opposed to homework, and the AFL-CIO in October 1985 adopted a resolution calling for a ban by the Department of Labor on computer clerical homework as a way to protect those workers. According to the AFL-CIO resolution, homework "has historically led to worker exploitation and will likely have a devastating impact on the well-being, wages, hours and working conditions of clerical homeworkers."

A handout prepared by the American Federation of State, County and Municipal Employees for its members outlines the major issues associated with homework, especially for clerical workers:

• *Homework vs. housework:* "Homework is often portrayed as a panacea for the working mother. In reality, it is often a nightmare, as women are forced to juggle housework, child care and their homework. The cost of child care may be reduced, but only because the working mother has taken on two jobs simultaneously."

• *Piece rate pay:* Computer homework lends itself to piece rate or incentive pay. Although piece rate pay theoretically offers talented employees the opportunity to make more money, in reality "standards are often set to increase 'average output' without increasing pay. Once set, standards may be unilaterally adjusted to speed up the pace of work. Piece rate productivity increases are gained only by increasing employees' work efforts and stress."

• *Simplistic performance appraisal:* Because the homeworker is not in the office, performance must be monitored in some way that is measurable and quantifiable. "Many jobs do not, of course, lend themselves to such simplistic measures of work quantity. This may mean that computer homeworkers' jobs will be redesigned so they do become simpler and more easily monitored. Quality and variety of work may be sacrificed."

• *Dead-end jobs:* Because a homeworker is not visible to supervisors and co-workers, chances for promotion and transfer may be diminished.

• *Harm to union solidarity:* "Computer homeworkers are isolated and, thus, less able to engage in concerted activity than office workers. For well-established unions considering computer homework, innovative techniques may help to combat this isolation, e.g., electronic union bulletin boards displayed on the computer."

• *Cost to the employee:* "The employer may want the employee to bear many of the costs for installing and maintaining an office in the home. In addition to equipment costs, there are costs for electricity, appropriate lighting, an appropriate desk and chair and the rental value of the space itself."

Despite these warnings, AFSCME has admitted that computer homework "may prove beneficial to some workers in specific situations."

Work vs. Family Responsibilities

While at the University of Wisconsin-Madison, Cynthia Butler Costello interviewed several homeworkers employed by the Wisconsin Public Service Insurance Corporation (WPS) in Madison, Wis., for her thesis, "On the Front: Class, Gender, and Conflict in the Insurance Workplace."

Costello found a major difference between the homeworkers and the clerical workers employed at the company's home office was the relationship between work and family responsibilities. One homeworker described for Costello her way of managing the two sets of responsibilities:

"When I get the claims at night, I try to put in an hour at night while the kids are watching t.v. Then I get up at 4:30 a.m. to work before the kids get up for the possibility that I might have to deal with my [handicapped] daughter during the day. It all depends on what the kids are doing. I work between 5:30 and 7:30 a.m. . . . . It is easier when nobody is around so my mind isn't wandering. The oldest boy (a teenager) gets up at 6:15 and then I take a break and yell upstairs. Then I get the disabled child up. During the day, I turn on the t.v. and tell [my preschooler] to watch . . . . Then, when she takes a nap, I can work. There are days when she plays well . . . taking the dirt out from the pot for half an hour before she notices . . . . I haven't found it too hard to get the work done . . . . I'll see what happens in the future."

Another homeworker Costello interviewed described the frustration of trying to juggle homework, housework, and childcare:

"I would have preferred to work from 4 to 8 at WPS. This would be easier because the work is always on my mind at home. I think, 'Oh, I have that work; I have to get it done.' If I could go there, it would be done and I could come home and not think about it. I would just think about work around the home. Doing homework is real difficult for me because I think I should be doing homework when I'm doing the laundry and then I think, 'No, this comes first.' I'd prefer to work out just for myself to get out . . . . Also, I have to keep track of my time by the minute because I have to quit for feedings."

Costello noted that, for the first woman, the responsibility of caring for two children made homework a preferable option. The money saved on babysitters, gas, parking, and clothes partially compensated for the low wages. "In contrast to the woman who complained about the double burden of combining homework and family responsibilities, this homeworker appreciated the flexibility, 'I don't mind homework because I am home and I can have the laundry going when I am doing my homework.' "

Organization:	**Pacific Bell** **San Francisco, Calif.**
Summary:	**Pacific Bell instituted its telecommuting program in April 1985. By the end of that year, approximately 80 managerial employees were working at home or at remote work sites. Although in most cases the reason for telecommuting is family related, employees who want to work by telecommuting must demonstrate that their participation in telecommuting makes good business sense for the company.**

Pacific Bell, a Pacific Telesis Group Company headquartered in San Francisco, Calif., began a telecommuting program for its managers in April 1985. As of December 1985 about 80 programmers, analysts, engineers, marketing planners, project managers, external affairs managers, and forecasters were working at remote sites or at their homes throughout California.

According to Lynda Anapol, Pacific Bell's director of telecommuting, the company is considering allowing other employees to participate in the telecommuting program. Those employees include training developers and employees in the non-salaried classifications of technician and service representative. She added that there are many non-management employees that are well suited to telecommuting, but the company does not know whether the Communications Workers of America, their union representative, would be amenable to the program. She said that the company plans to approach CWA on the matter.

Pacific Bell began the program because it believed that telecommuting could benefit both employees and the employer in a number of ways, Anapol said. The company saw several advantages for employees:

• More flexibility to handle family situations. Anapol explained, however, that Pacific Bell is strongly opposed to telecommuting as a way to perform work and take care of children. "Child care is a full-time job and employees can't do two full-time jobs well," she said.

• Decreased expenses because no commuting would be involved.

• Increased participation in community activities.

Anapol said Pacific Bell believes that accommodating employees enables them to give more to their jobs. Telecommuting's advantages to the company, she said, include:

• Expanding the labor pool to include individuals who could not work in the office because they lived too far away or found commuting too difficult.

• Reducing overhead costs by doing away with an office or by setting up remote offices. Pacific Bell currently has two satellite centers — one in San Francisco and one in the Los Angeles area. Despite the popular belief that telecommuting takes jobs out of the city, in reality it takes jobs closer to where people live, Anapol said.

• Increasing production.

• Retaining valuable employees who might otherwise have left for personal demands, and thereby keeping down training costs.

• Eliminating relocation costs.

• Decreasing computer timeshare costs. Telecommuters don't have to work 8 a.m. to 5 p.m., but can stagger their hours.

In order to participate in the telecommuting program, employees must show why their participation makes good business sense for Pacific Bell. Even though in most cases the primary reason for wanting to work by telecommuting is family related, Anapol said, employees nevertheless must demonstrate that telecommuting is beneficial not only to themselves, but to the company.

Justifications for Telecommuting

Anapol gave several examples of reasons for telecommuting that are essentially family based, but that can be justified as helping Pacific Bell. She said that to relocate an employee in California costs, on the average, $40,000. Although the reason an employee may want to telecommute, rather than relocate, might be that a spouse does not want to transfer to another location or a child is a senior in high school and does not want to change schools, the business reason would be that the telecommuter would save the company $40,000 in relocation costs.

Anapol related that a highly skilled analyst had to leave the company because her daughter was frequently ill. She was able to return to the company as a telecommuter, however, and saved Pacific Bell about $100,000 in training costs.

Anapol emphasized that, as long as an employee can come up with a good business reason for telecommuting, the request will be approved. "The company can't afford to do it just because it's the nice thing to do," she admitted, but telecommuting almost always can be translated into a benefit for both parties. She added, however, that one of Pacific Bell's governing principles is that it values the individual and is willing to consider non-traditional alternatives.

Anapol said Pacific Bell considers it critical to minimize the differences between telecommuters and employees in the office. Pay is the same for telecommuters and office workers and the company makes sure that any equipment provided to office workers also is provided to telecommuters. Work-at-home participants are provided a business phone line specifically for telecommuting. All work-related expenses are paid for by Pacific Bell, including toll charges, as applicable.

Because the Pacific Bell telecommuters are management employees, their jobs are not monitored. They are not evaluated any differently than those workers in the office, Anapol said, and at the start of the program managers and telecommuters agree to goals and objectives for an evaluation period. Evaluations are based largely on qualitative rather than on quantitative measurements.

Pacific Bell is now marketing its telecommuting program to its clients, Anapol told BNA. She said her staff go out in the field and work with any company interested in starting a telecommuting program. "If companies can take advantage of the benefits of transporting information, not people, to and from the workplace," she said, Pacific Bell will benefit from increased utilization of its products and services.

The project has been under way for only a short time, so long-term results are not yet available, Anapol related. However, the initial response has been both positive and promising, she said.

FLEXIBLE TIME-OFF POLICY

Organization: Hewlett-Packard Company
                    Palo Alto, Calif.

Summary: **To end abuses of sick leave and to respond to enhanced benefits offered by competitors, Hewlett-Packard instituted a flexible leave policy which combines sick leave and annual leave. Leave is accrued on the basis of length of service, and may be carried over from one year to the next. Both full-time and part-time employees are eligible for leave time.**

Sick leave and annual leave are combined into a flexible leave time at electronics industry giant, the Hewlett-Packard Company, headquartered in Palo Alto, Calif. The flexible leave time dovetails with a liberal personal leave policy that allows unpaid leaves of absence for up to six months for a variety of reasons.

Hewlett-Packard Company adopted a flexible leave policy in 1980 that does away with the distinction between vacation leave and sick leave. Instead of accruing two kinds of leave, employees earn personal time off that can be taken for any purpose, according to Kathy Keehn, the company's policy coordinator. The amount of personal leave an employee is granted depends on length of service with the company.

Keehn said the policy was adopted in response to abuse of sick leave by a few employees who were using accrued sick leave for other purposes. Hewlett-Packard wanted to stop this abuse without penalizing those who did not engage in the abuse, she explained.

When Hewlett-Packard switched from the traditionally separate annual leave and sick leave about five years ago to a combined personal time off concept, some employees found their accrual rates dropped. For instance, an employee who had been accruing 12 days of sick leave and 10 days of annual leave per year under the old formula suddenly earned a total of only 15 days under the personal time off system. When the switch was made, Hewlett-Packard took each employee's annual leave accrual rate and added five days, explained Keehn.

Initially, some employees who had small children or suffered from chronic illnesses complained about the change, Keehn admitted, because they lost days that formerly accrued as sick leave. However, since the changeover, complaints have diminished, she said.

Hewlett-Packard also switched to the flexible leave time concept in response to enhanced leave benefits offered by competitors, Keehn said. Since Hewlett-Packard adopted its flexible leave policy five years ago, some other companies in the electronics industry have followed its lead, she added.

Keehn explained that, after five years of service, an employee earns 15 days of leave per year. One day of leave is added to the allotment each year after that until 25 days per year are reached after the 15th year of service, she said. After the employee reaches the 25-day limit, leave accrues at the rate of one-half day per year until the maximum accrual rate of 30 days per year is reached after 25 years of service. Hewlett-Packard has a liberal policy on carrying over to the next year leave that is earned in the previous year, she added.

When an employee is terminated, the unused leave time is paid off as salary, Keehn reported.

Personal Leave Policy

Hewlett-Packard also has a liberal policy regarding the use of unpaid personal leave time for a variety of purposes. Such leaves are available for up to six months for personal reasons, medical reasons, and military service, Keehn said. Employees who need more than 20 days off work are eligible for the leave benefit and it is renewable, she said.

Personal leave time is available for childbirth, adoption, travel, education, and other purposes, Keehn explained. Requests for such leave must be approved by the employee's supervisor, the company personnel office, the employee's department head, and functional supervisor, she said. The personal leave policy has been offered by the company for at least 20 years, she noted.

Both full-time and part-time employees may request personal leave, Keehn said. A minimum of one year of service with the company is required before an employee may request personal leave, she noted.

Hewlett-Packard has no firm numbers on which groups of employees use the benefit most, or what it is used for most often, Keehn said, but she noted that many female employees use it after their maternity leave is exhausted. Other uses include emotional disability, care for sick relatives, or travel for reasons such as religious missionary work, she said. On some occasions, when Hewlett-Packard employees have been stationed overseas, spouses who also are employees of the company have used personal leave to maintain their employment status, Keehn said.

Personal leave time also could be used as a bridge for an employee who has been in a rehabilitation program and is not quite ready to return to work on a full-time basis, Keehn said. In this situation, when a doctor has given an employee permission to return to work, personal leave time could be granted to allow the employee to return to work gradually, she said.

Keehn said Hewlett-Packard offers the personal leave benefit because it helps satisfy the needs of its employees and helps the company attract and keep good workers. The policy is not, however, a pivotal selling-point in recruiting, she added.

*   *   *

C. EMPLOYEE ASSISTANCE PROGRAMS

Many employers are becoming increasingly aware that workers' personal problems may have an adverse effect on their performance, and that absenteeism, low or reduced productivity, and low morale may, in part, be caused by those personal problems.

Boston University Study

In a study by Boston University, reported in late 1985, the stress of balancing work and family responsibilities was found to be the most significant factor contributing to depression among employees. More than one-third of all employees in the study reported significant difficulties with managing family responsibilities.

The study was conducted by the Boston University School of Social Work and C.O.P.E., a Boston-based licensed family counseling, education, and resource center.

Conflicts between job and homelife demands, and the level of stress associated with these demands, were examined in a study of all 651 employees in three divisions of a large Boston-based corporation. More than one-third of employees who were parents said that, while they were at work, they worried always or most of the time about their children.

The most frequently mentioned sources of conflict between job and homelife were:

- scheduling difficulties;
- an inability to leave problems at work or at home;
- an irregular work schedule that interfered with personal life; and
- interferences with personal time caused by job-related travel.

University researchers Bradley Googins and Dianne S. Burden would not identify the employer, but said only the firm was typical of many in the United States.

Programs developed and implemented by C.O.P.E. to reduce the stress of job/family role strain and to boost employees' morale, commitment, and productivity were evaluated by the Boston University researchers. A "Work and Family Resource Fair," a series of eight "Managing Work and Family Seminars," and a yearlong "Information and Referral Telephone Service" for employees were among those rated as "highly successful" by employees. Many employees reported that these services enabled them to more successfully manage and integrate the conflicting demands of their work and family lives.

Stress and Productivity

Personal problems can produce stress. Psychologists and counselors treating stress in the workplace told BNA that stress can cause illness, and can lower productivity and creativity, and may even reduce a company's ability to stay competitive. Unresolved personal, family, legal, or financial problems can drive employees to abuse alcohol or drugs, some experts maintain.

Employees can bring stress into the workplace, or they can find it there, Dr. Patricia Webbink, a psychologist in private practice said. Stress can be produced by environmental factors such as noise pollution; by problems with personal relationships; by illness; and by financial difficulties, among other causes, Webbink said. Stress also can be produced by a number of workplace-related factors, including changing societal views on the relative value of work, family, and leisure, according to Webbink and Dr. Bob Rosen, assistant clinical professor of psychology and behavioral sciences at the George Washington University School of Medicine in Washington, D.C.

Compounding the workplace-related stress on women are the responsibilities they have at home, Prof. Dale A. Masi of the University of Maryland School of Social Work and Community Planning, said. Although men are helping out at home, their contributions are not that significant, Masi maintained. In addition, she said, women are "the parent of worry." It is usually the mother who must act if the carpool doesn't work out or a child gets sick, Masi said.

Although female parent employees are under heavy pressure because of the job-family conflicts, the Boston University research indicated that the measures of well-being are most strongly associated with job-family role strain, not with gender. The explanation for different rates of depression between employed men and women may lie in the greater combined job and home responsibilities faced by women, the study suggested. Women, the study noted, work twice as many hours on homemaking and child care tasks as men. Men who have increased family responsibilities are as likely to experience a decreased sense of well-being as women, the study suggests.

EAPs: One Way to Deal with Stress

Some employers are turning to employee assistance programs (EAPs) to help employees deal with stress and with personal problems.

Every year, 20 percent of us experience personal problems that significantly affect our job performance . . . .

EAPs can help workers to identify problems, and then to deal with them before they reach a critical stage. Some EAPs are set up to deal with a wide variety of employee personal problems, including problems encountered by employee's family members.

Every year, 20 percent of us experience personal problems that significantly affect our job performance, according to Process Dynamics, a Minneapolis-based counseling, consulting, and referral group. "When we are concerned with personal problems, we make more mistakes, have more accidents at home and on the job, are less creative, are more likely to miss work, are more likely to become ill and are more likely to terminate our employment. Besides that, distressed employees can be unreliable and difficult for others. Employees and their family members who can be helped to effectively solve what is on their minds make more productive and efficient employees," Process Dynamics said in a report describing its services.

Human Resources Group, Inc., a New York-based firm that develops and administers EAPs, reports that, in 1984, the major problems referred to EAPs were:

- psychological — 29 percent;
- legal — 16 percent;
- drug and alcohol addictions — 15 percent;
- social/welfare troubles — 15 percent;
- financial — 10 percent;
- marital — 9 percent;
- job-related difficulties — 4 percent; and
- physical abuse or violence — 2 percent.

The Human Resources Group study involved 7,276 referrals in a total work force of more than 100,000 employees at 26 companies in 10 major metropolitan areas.

EAPs and Work-Family Problems

One problem that employee assistance programs are increasingly dealing with is the stress associated with conflicts between home and work responsibilities of working parents, according to Don Phillips, president of COPE, Inc., one of the leading EAP service providers in the Washington, D.C., area.

Although the area is not very well researched or documented, Phillips said, "My sense is that, if you talk about clusters of problems, family/marital represent the single largest group." Family/marital problems, which include those associated with the conflicts between home and job responsibilities, are in the range of 30 to 35 percent of EAP caseloads, Phillips suggested. The rate has leveled off, however, Phillips said, and is not liable to rise much higher.

"The more someone takes on in terms of responsibility — the more we get pulled in 18 directions — the higher the stress level," said Phillips, who added that the ability of individual to handle the stress varies greatly from person to person. The EAP's role is primarily to help the individual function at an optimum in the circumstances, Phillips explained. Sometimes, something like a schedule change adjustment might make the troubled worker's overall circumstances easier to deal with, he said. "Otherwise, beyond that, we have to accept the workplace as a given," and focus on improving the individual's coping skills, Phillips said.

Other professionals in the field say feedback to companies from such programs can facilitate change at the workplace. Pat Marks of the Metropolitan Washington Child Care Network information and referral service notes that the Network provides companies with feedback from employees. (See case study above.) Without naming names, the Network indicates areas of concern expressed by employees, she said. For instance, an employer might be told that long hours are a problem, Marks said.

"It's another channel of information and makes employers aware of employees' concerns," Marks said. "I would assume that EAP programs have similar feedback," she added. "I think that companies that are responsive enough to have an EAP in place are people-oriented and will respond to [those] employees' concerns that the programs brings to their attention," Marks said.

This section of the special report examines how four EAPs work. One is run primarily by a union, the second is a joint labor-management effort operated by a public sector employer, and other two are run by private corporations.

 STATE EMPLOYEE ASSISTANCE PROGRAM

Organization: New York State and public employee unions

Summary: New York's EAP helps employees with a variety of personal problems, including, among others, family difficulties and alcohol and substance abuse problems. The EAP is part of an overall program on family-work issues which includes on-site day care,

flexible scheduling, and voluntary furloughs. The program was implemented on a statewide basis in 1982, under collective bargaining agreements with unions representing state workers.

An employee assistance program which helps employees deal with a wide variety of personal problems appears to have become an effective tool in New York State for dealing with employees' problems, and, thereby, helping to integrate family life and work life.

The program is part of an overall effort by the state and the unions representing state employees to deal with family-work issues. Other programs include an on-site day care program, flexible scheduling, and voluntary furloughs. (See Chapter V, *Developments and Trends*, for more information on New York's furlough, flextime, and day care programs.)

"There is a fundamental recognition on our behalf and on the unions' behalf that it's in all our best interests to help employees in the workplace with problems they bring to the workplace," said Thomas F. Hartnett, director of the Governor's Office of Employee Relations (GOER).

The EAP program offers a referral service for some 200,000 state employees. There is no professional counseling or treatment directly involved. The program consists of more than 200 individual EAP programs at agencies and offices throughout the state. The individual EAPs are governed by a labor-management committee, which chooses an EAP coordinator to make referrals and to run the program.

The EAP program began in 1976 as a pilot program at two sites. It was implemented on a statewide basis in 1982, under collective bargaining agreements with four of the six unions representing state employees, according to J. Thomas Going, EAP program manager for the state. The four unions representing state employees currently involved in the program are: the Civil Service Employees Association; Public Employees Federation; Council 82 of the American Federation of State, County and Municipal Employees; and United University Professions.

About 50,000 employees used the program from September 1984 to September 1985, and 20,958 referrals were made, GOER reports. Of that total number of referrals, 3,025 were for family counseling services; 2,195 for inpatient and outpatient mental health services; 2,941 for legal or financial services; 2,598 for self-help groups; and 3,506 for alcohol or substance abuse.

All of the information discussed with an EAP coordinator is kept confidential, although the state collects data on the total number of referrals for a particular problem. Employees who participate in the program are not exempt from disciplinary action or from their responsibility to improve their job performance.

$4 to $10 Return for Each $1 Spent

James M. Murphy, director of employee assistance programs for the Civil Service Employees Association, estimated that the state is getting back the equivalent of $4 to $10 for every dollar it spends on EAP. The state is funding a study to determine the cost effectiveness of the program.

"We've all gotten a lot out of it — management and the union," said Murphy, whose union has the most members among state employees. "We've been able to help people who historically were dragged through a disciplinary process, which was very costly to both the union and the state."

Hartnett said, "What we've gotten out of it is we have turned troubled employees around, which has impacted on absenteeism, productivity, [and] morale."

The EAP has also led the state to focus on other problems. The discovery that a high percentage of absenteeism was due to child care problems served, in part, to prompt the development of a child care benefit, Murphy said. "People came to the employee assistance program with the problem that they were missing work because their babysitter canceled and they couldn't leave their three-year-old home alone," he said. "We've gotten together with the state and said, 'Hey look, people are missing work. Might it not be more cost effective to get some kind of day care at the worksite to help them through that?'"

The state also has made certain changes in its health insurance benefits as a result of the EAP program, Hartnett reported.

"What we do, and I think we do very well, is not to look at this program in the abstract, but to realize that this program is a component part, an early identification part, of a much broader program," he said.

FAMILY COUNSELING IN ALCOHOLISM PROGRAM

Organization: The International Longshoremen's Association
New York, N.Y.

Summary: As part of ILA's alcoholism treatment program, members of a recovering alcoholic's family are strongly encouraged to participate in the treatment program and to attend Al Anon, the branch of Alcoholics Anonymous for family members of alcoholics. The union believes that family involvement is essential to the rehabilitation process.

The International Longshoremen's Association Alcoholism Program began in October 1974 through the efforts of shop steward John J. Hennessy, a recovering alcoholic who wanted to help fellow members recover. He obtained a grant of $206,857 from the National Institute on Alcohol Abuse and Alcoholism of the Department of Health, Education, and Welfare (now, Health and Human Services) for the program, which operates under a memorandum of agreement that is part of the basic Agreement between the New York Shipping Association, Inc., and the International Longshoremen's Association of the Port of Greater New York. The program operates out of the Manhattan Clinic of the NYSA-ILA Medical Center, and also out of clinics in New York and New Jersey.

Family Involvement in Treatment

From its inception, the ILA program, which requires one year of attendance at Alcoholics Anonymous meetings, has included families in the treatment process. Family participation is often the key to recovery, according to Vince Dowling, the program's counselor and himself a recovering alcoholic. If the wife won't go to Al Anon, the branch of Alcoholics Anonymous for family members of alcoholics, the husband probably won't make it through the program, Dowling says. But if she does go, Dowling added, the husband knows she means business. Often it takes a little work to get families to participate in the worker's recovery — they are often relieved when he is hospitalized, and believe that the problem is solved, Dowling said.

Most program participants are referrals, but there are some volunteers, Dowling said. Co-workers who have been through the program sometimes encourage others who need help to volunteer for the program, or a wife who belongs to Al Anon convinces her husband that he needs help. The problem with volunteers, Dowling says, is that sometimes they think they don't have to go along with all facets of the program, such as mandatory meetings, because they are there voluntarily.

Referrals are made from the job for a number of reasons, for example, when job performance is affected because of absenteeism. Other referrals come from personnel at the NYSA-ILA medical center. Dowling said he has asked the doctors and nurses there to be aware of possible problems, such as members who come in for treatment with alcohol on their breath.

When a member has been referred, or volunteers for the program, Dowling explains the program, checks the employee's records, sends him for a medical examination, and makes an evaluation of the type of treatment needed. If the member balks at going through the program, Dowling said he can call he member's boss — who usually tells the worker to take the treatment if he wants to keep his job.

After arrangements have been made for the hospital stay, Dowling calls the member's family. He arranges transportation, if necessary, explains visitation and the need for family involvement in the treatment, and suggests that the family begin attending Al Anon.

The minimum hospital stay is 30 days, in addition to the time it takes for detoxification. For long-time drinkers, Dowling said, 30 days, however, is not nearly long enough.

While in the hospital, the member is urged to attend all the meetings, lectures, movies, and other programs that are available. Full participation can often shorten the hospital stay, Dowling said.

One Year of Counseling

After release from the hospital, the individual is required to remain in the program for one year. During that year, he must attend one counseling session a week with Dowling and attend three meetings of Alcoholics Anonymous each week. Dowling noted that there are lunchtime AA meetings on the piers. Additional meetings with Dowling can be arranged if the employee feels the need.

There are additional resources available to help the member and his family during this difficult period, Dowling added. When necessary, referrals are made for private therapy, marriage and family counseling, and medical care. The program also provides for financial counseling and legal assistance.

A man who has spent much of his free time drinking needs other outlets, Dowling said, so he tries to point out some things the man can do in his spare time, such as taking his wife out to dinner, going to art museums, and traveling. He also encourages participation in adult education programs and art programs. Many of the men take up painting or writing, Dowling said, or become avid readers. Others have bought houses and fixed them up.

The members in the program are good fathers and husbands, Dowling said. "No one starts out to be an alcoholic," he said, "they end up in it, in hopelessness and despair."

After the one-year follow up, the member is finished with the program. Usually, that's all it takes, Dowling said. When a man knows his job is at stake, he can be rehabilitated. His boss tells him not to come back if he can't shape up. Other recovering alcoholics help by following up on the newly released member, Dowling said.

The program also helps employees and their dependents who are on drugs, Dowling explained, although the drug abusers are referred to outside programs because the Center is not set up to handle drug rehabilitation. The younger men tend to have problems with drugs, the older ones with alcohol, he said.

CONTRACT EMPLOYEE ASSISTANCE PROGRAMS

Organization: Parkside Medical Services Corp.
                    Park Ridge, Ill.

Summary: The Employee Assistance Programs Division of Parkside Medical
                    Services provides contract EAP services to more than 55 client
                    organizations in 40 states. One of Parkside's primary tasks is to
                    train supervisors to evaluate an employee by focusing on those
                    performance aspects that are properly the employer's concern, "to
                    take the manager out of a diagnostic role." The firm believes that
                    helping employees deal with problems which affect their perform-
                    ance boosts morale and pays off on the bottom line.

The Employee Assistance Programs Division of Parkside Medical Services currently provides contract EAP services to more than 55 client organizations in 40 states, covering about 200,000 employees and family members, according to Dr. John C. Clarno, vice president of Parkside. Clients range from the Village of Wilmette, Ill., to Bank of Denver and Arthur Andersen & Co.

Parkside is part of the Lutheran General Health Care System, which in 1969 opened the first specialty hospital for alcoholism treatment in the United States. For nine years prior to joining Parkside, Clarno served as manager of special health services for Caterpillar Tractor Co.

Clarno maintained that, on a nationwide scale, alcohol is still the biggest cause of personal and work problems. "Don't focus on cocaine, because it's such a small segment of the problem," said Clarno; alcohol, he noted, is legal and is part of our culture. He said the mass media, in part, are at fault for the nationwide focus on drugs like heroin in the 1970s and cocaine now, while overlooking the extent of al-cohol-related problems.

But Parkside is also seeing an increase in referrals for emotional and mental disturbances. Clarno said the increasing role for EAPs in treatment of both types of problems is due, in part, to increased penetration of the health care market by health maintenance organizations, "which have generally poor mental health benefits," and to cutbacks in benefits by employers seeking to lower health care costs.

Nationwide, emotional and mental health problems constitute 27 percent of Parkside's case load, according to Clarno. Alcohol and drug abuse by either the employee or a family member, account for 23 percent of referrals, while marital relationships excluding alcohol are 17 percent of the case load. Legal problems account for 9 percent, and financial problems for 5 percent.

"We can't compartmentalize our lives any more," Clarno said in pointing out that the statistics were interesting, but not particularly revealing. "People often don't have single, but [rather] multiple problems."

One of Parkside's primary tasks is to train a client firm's supervisors to evaluate an employee's performance by focusing on those performance aspects that are properly the employer's concern. "We want to take the manager out of a diagnostic role," he said.

Referrals to Parkside can be performance-based or employee self-referrals. Once a program is established, the vast majority of participants are from the latter category, Clarno maintained.

The Payoff: Performance, Morale Boosts

If a client wishes, Parkside can provide computerized utilization data on health care benefits usage and other statistics. While many firms today offer EAPs as part of a competitive benefits package or because it's the "humanitarian" thing to do, in fact, "there's a direct payoff in performance," said Parkside EAP Coordinator Michael D. Houle.

One satisfied Parkside customer, an insurance and financial services firm in Chicago's Northwest suburbs, believes the biggest payoff is in company morale. "The biggest benefit is that you can talk to someone outside the company about your problems," the firm's employee benefits manager told BNA. With a diverse work force that is 60 percent female and with a lot of two-earner families, the insurance company has a "flexible, rehabilitative approach." The company has a one-year contract with Parkside, the manager said.

During the first six months of service, the benefits manager said, 97 percent of cases were self-referrals. Alcohol and drug abuse by the employee constituted 22 percent of referrals, while alcohol and drug abuse by others in the family accounted for an additional 16 percent. Emotional and mental problems represented 19 percent of referrals, stress 11 percent, and marital relationships 11 percent. Eighty-six percent of the individuals referred were employees, 5 percent spouses, 2 percent children, and 5 percent other relatives.

Purely family-related problems probably don't come up in the work setting unless they are very serious, according to the benefits manager. She related, for example, that when the firm relocated to the suburbs from its previous office in downtown Chicago, it expected about 30 percent turnover in clerical positions because of commuting problems of mothers of small children. In fact, turnover for that year was only 15 percent. She acknowledged, however, this lower-than-expected turnover rate might have been attributable the lingering effects of the recession on the Chicago job market.

An Industry Shakeout Coming?

The employee assistance program industry, which has grown incredibly in the last five years, will shake out by the end of the decade, leaving a few national firms providing the bulk of the service, according to Clarno. The "entrepreneurs" in the field and the "bed-fillers" — hospital-based programs using referral services — will be particularly susceptible to the weeding out, he believes.

Nationwide EAPs with ties to a respected clinical center have the advantage of being better able to serve as a resource to management, Clarno told BNA. The major advantage to a company's contracting out EAP services instead of running an in-house program is that an outside referral service can gain the credibility of employees, which is an all-important factor in an effective program, in Clarno's view.

"The old days of company alcohol and drug programs are long gone because their label became counterproductive to the program goals," Clarno said. Drug testing, he said, serves as an example of the important distinction in operations between internal and external programs. "While we support the need for urine screening in certain circumstances, we prefer that it remain independent of an EAP," Clarno explained.

'REACT' PROGRAM

Organization: AmeriTrust Bank
Cleveland, Ohio

Summary: The REACT employee assistance program, in operation for more than 10 years, deals with a wide range of employee problems, from substance abuse to marital complications. The bank also offers "How to Parent" and "Perfectly Pregnant" classes to provide peer support as well as counseling for workers. Ameri-Trust is convinced that the EAP has helped to substantially improve productivity.

For more than a decade, the AmeriTrust Company has helped employees balance family and work responsibilities through its REACT employee assistance program. Initiated in 1975, REACT provides employee counseling and assistance for any problem that could affect job performance, according to Peter Osenar, the Cleveland-based bank's executive vice president for personnel and organization.

The "broad brush program" encompasses everything from substance abuse to marital problems, Osenar said, and is credited with reducing absenteeism, on the average, from 3.2 days annually per employee to two days. AmeriTrust also believes the program has helped enhance productivity, he said.

A good employee assistance program is dynamic, Osenar said, changing in response to work force needs. Accordingly, the emphasis REACT places upon family concerns has increased markedly over the past few years, he said.

Problems facing working parents are a prime concern, said Osenar, therefore AmeriTrust's EAP offers day care referral and "How to Parent" classes broken down by age groups. Both offerings "are very pro-active," he explained, with an emphasis on practical problem-solving. If a parent does not know how to evaluate a day care facility, for instance, a REACT counselor will suggest criteria.

"We are addressing things that never would have been dealt with in the workplace before," said Osenar. "Our goal is to anticipate problems and resolve them before they become stressful or debilitating, before they impede job performance."

AmeriTrust knows that if an individual is worried about child care or is experiencing marital difficulties, "it's bad for the company and it's bad for them," Osenar said. To address as many potential problems as possible, the program takes "a broad brushstroke approach," he explained; a REACT counselor provides confidential advice to any employee requesting it. If specialized assistance is needed, however, workers are referred to outside sources, he explained.

"Many times it just helps to have someone to talk to," continued Osenar, noting much of the benefit from the How to Parent classes comes from people sharing their experiences. In that spirit, AmeriTrust has introduced weekly "Perfectly Pregnant" seminars where expectant mothers can receive information on diet, exercise, and childbirth while enjoying the emotional support of peers.

Osenar sees this humanistic approach to employee assistance "not only as the right thing to do, but as a good business practice." AmeriTrust contends "if you ignore personal problems, you'll ultimately get hit with them," he said, which makes the preventative value of this support system "inestimable."

"AmeriTrust has long supported the concept that corporations have a legitimate role in nurturing the family life and total well-being of their employees," Osenar told a Jan. 16, 1986, Conference Board seminar on work and family in New York City. "This is more than an altruistic concern. Studies repeatedly show that persons with stable family environments and good mental and physical health are the most productive employees, and let's face it — in our service-oriented industry, we can't afford anything less," said Osenar.

*   *   *

D. PARENTAL LEAVE

The growing number of parents in the work force and the corresponding change in attitude about work and parenting have started employers talking about the matter of parental leave from work for maternity, paternity, infant care, and adoption. Parental leave has become a public policy issue and is the subject of much current debate.

This section of the special report examines the evolution of corporate leave policies, and provides case studies of leave policies at specific employers.

Maternity Leave

By and large, maternity and parental leave policy in this country has been left to employers in the private sector and to the private fringe-benefit system, the Congressional Research Service reported in July 1985 in *Maternity and Parental Leave Policies: A Comparative Analysis.*

CRS noted that a federal law — the Pregnancy Discrimination Act of 1978, which amended Title VII of the Civil Rights Act of 1964 — prohibits discrimination in employment on the basis of pregnancy, childbirth, or related medical conditions, and requires that "women affected by pregnancy, childbirth, or related medical conditions shall be treated the same for all employment-related purposes, including receipt of benefits under fringe benefit programs, as other persons not so affected but similar in their ability or inability to work . . . " [42 USC §2000e(k)].

In its analysis, CRS found that the basic components of maternity-related leave policies, available in varying degrees to workers in the United States and overseas, include:

• job-protected leave for a specified time with protection of seniority, pension, and other benefit entitlements;

• full or partial wage replacement to cover all or a significant part of the job-protected leave; and

• health insurance covering hospitalization and physician care.

Another element of the parental leave question being considered by some employers is allowing new parents some time flexibility on return to work after childbirth — either some period of part-time work or some flexibility in hours, or both.

Maternity leave policies seem to be affected by company size, Bernard Hodes Advertising, a New York City-based firm, concluded in a 1985 report on 153 survey responses. Companies with 500 or more employees, "are noticeably more likely to offer full salary leave than smaller ones," concluded the advertising agency, which based its study on responses to questionnaires sent to the more than

8,500 subscribers to the firm's bimonthly human resources newsletter.

Nearly one-fourth of the companies responding to Bernard Hodes survey allowed employees to utilize any accrued vacation, sick, or personal leave as maternity leave. Some 10 percent of the sample indicated that they offered some

---

By and large, maternity and parental leave policy in this country has been left to employers in the private sector and to the private fringe-benefit system, the Congressional Research Service says.

---

type of reduced work schedule as part of their maternity policy. Seventy-five percent of the respondent companies offered a return to work guarantee for women on maternity leave; usually this return to work guarantee was conditioned on employees not being off the job longer that four months. Most of the respondent companies maintained some benefits during maternity leave, with 40 percent continuing all benefits.

Half of companies surveyed by Bernard Hodes paid employees on maternity leave their full salary. About one in four paid employees their salary for 16 weeks or less. Only two percent said they extended full salary maternity leave for more than four months. According to Bernard Hodes, the maternity benefits policies often included some combination of fully paid leave and either partial salary payment or unpaid leave.

A BNA's Personnel Policies Forum survey conducted in 1983 showed that approximately 90 percent of 253 employers responding made unpaid maternity leave available to employees. The most common length of maternity leave was six months, although more than one-fourth of employers responding said they had no limit on maternity leave.

Catalyst Study

In 1984, Catalyst launched a national study of corporate parental leave policies, asking some 400 senior human resources planners of leading U.S. companies what options they would consider in developing a new parental leave policy. In its 1986 final *Report on a National Study of Parental Leaves*, Catalyst, a resource for information on career and family trends in the workplace, detailed the responses:

For new mothers:
- 83 percent would provide short-term disability with a job guarantee.
- 66 percent would offer three to six months of unpaid leave (beyond disability).
- 59 percent would allow part-time work schedules for a limited period following the leave.

For new fathers:
- 50 percent would offer two weeks' unpaid non-vacation leave.

For all employees:
- 38 percent would include a two-to-12-month eligibility requirement for leave.

Survey of Law Firms

In its 1986 report on a *Survey on Work Time Options in the Legal Profession*, New Ways to Work (NWW), a non-profit organization which conducts research and serves as a clearinghouse for information on work time options, stated that in a growing number of law firms, corporate law departments, and other legal organizations, employees are requesting leaves to accommodate childbirth and child-rearing. The report was based on 143 responses by legal organizations in San Francisco and Alameda Counties in California.

NWW reported that 82 percent of the respondent corporate legal departments, government agencies, and public interest organizations had maternity leave policies for both attorneys and non-attorneys. In contrast, 35 percent of private law firms reported having a maternity leave policy for attorneys, and 43 percent for non-attorneys.

While most government agencies said they did not offer paid maternity leave to attorneys, NWW reported, those agencies were "quite generous" with regard to the total amount of time allowed — paid and unpaid — for maternity/child care purposes. All the responding government agencies allowed a total leave of at least 16 weeks, with 33 percent allowing more than 26 weeks leave. Twenty-five percent of the private law firms allowed 16-23 weeks, and 33 percent allowed 24-26 weeks. Some 43 percent of the corporations allowed 24-26 weeks total leave; 36 percent, however, allowed less than 12 weeks. Fourteen percent of the firms and 22 percent of the public interest organizations were "flexible" about the total length of maternity leaves, according to NWW.

NWW noted a direct correlation between the size of a private firm and the likelihood that it will have a maternity leave policy. Some 91 percent of the private firms with 75 or more attorneys had a maternity leave policy for attorneys, while 12 percent of those with three to five attorneys had one, NWW reported. Larger firms have had more maternity leaves taken and have a greater likelihood of having a policy, NWW said.

Unions and Maternity Leave

Organized labor generally has favored maternity leave benefits, and, more recently, some labor leaders have supported parental leave benefits, according to the CRS analysis. "However, actual union efforts in this area have not always been vigorous," CRS concluded.

Maternity leave is provided for in about 36 percent of U.S. collective bargaining agreements, according to CRS. Most U.S. collective bargaining agreements that provide maternity leave benefits require a worker to be employed with the company for some period of time, CRS noted.

In its 1986 study of basic patterns in union contracts, BNA's *Collective Bargaining Negotiations and Contracts* service (*CBNC*) reported that leave of absence is provided for maternity in 36 percent of the 400 sample agreements for all industries. Maternity leave was provided in 40 percent of manufacturing agreements and 30 percent of non-manufacturing contracts.

A length-of-service requirement must be met in 23 percent of the contract provisions on maternity leave: A one-year service requirement was imposed in 24 percent of service requirement provisions, three months in 27 percent, and six months in 15 percent. Twenty-five percent of contracts required a physical examination or medical certificate upon return from leave.

The Congressional Research Service report noted that length of maternity leave in collective bargaining agreements is "far from uniform." Under agreements in the *CBNC* study specifying leave duration, the most common period allowed was six months (38 percent). Leave for one year was allowed in 36 percent of such clauses, and leave for either nine and three months was granted in 5 percent. Length of maternity leave was determined by a physician in 34 percent of the contracts that discussed duration.

The effect of maternity leave on seniority was specified in 69 percent of the sample contracts with maternity leave provisions. Of these, 58 percent allowed accumulation of seniority; 38 percent allowed retention of seniority.

CRS concluded in its report that maternity leave did not differ markedly between unionized and non-union companies. CRS did note the conclusion of Richard Freeman and James Medoff in their book, *What Do Unions Do?*: "[N]onunion employers offer more maternity pay with leave while union employers are more likely to guarantee full reemployment rights after maternity."

Future drives by organized labor to unionize new members could center on millions of female workers who want maternity leave benefits, the CRS report suggested. This "would indicate that unions may press with added vigor for maternity leaves."

Organized labor generally has favored maternity leave benefits, but, weakened by economic and social conditions, "unions may find themselves forced to devote their energy and resources to other areas . . . besides maternity leave."

CRS also noted that much of labor has been weakened by economic and social conditions in the early 1980s. This factor "would indicate that unions may find themselves forced to devote their energy and resources to other areas (e.g., wages, work rules, federal labor legislation, and even dealing with the National Labor Relations board under the Reagan Administration) besides maternity leave," CRS concluded.

Unsettled Legal Questions

CRS noted in its report that some states have enacted legislation which goes beyond the Pregnancy Discrimination Act. Two of those laws are being challenged in court, however, and in early 1986, the Supreme Court agreed to decide whether states are free to grant pregnant workers special protections beyond those afforded under the federal law. The Court will review the 1985 ruling of the U.S. Court of Appeals for the Ninth Circuit in *California Savings and Loan Association v. Guerra* (No. 85-494) in which the appeals court decided that the federal and state laws could coexist (37 FEP Cases 849). The appeals court declared that Congress intended "to construct a floor beneath which pregnancy disability benefits may not drop — not a ceiling above which they may not rise."

The California law, passed in 1978, requires employers to grant up to four months of leave to a pregnant worker, and to reinstate her to the same or a similar job. The state law was challenged in 1983 after California Federal Savings and Loan Association denied receptionist Lillian Garland reinstatement to her same or a similar job after she returned from pregnancy leave. Cal Fed argued that the state law was preempted because it exceeded the requirements of the Civil Rights Act of 1964 and the Pregnancy Discrimination Act of 1978. The employer argued that the state law subjected management to reverse discrimination lawsuits by men who enjoy no special protection when they are temporarily disabled.

Also pending before the Supreme Court is a challenge to a Montana law requiring employers to grant reasonable maternity leave to female employees. In 1984 the Montana Supreme Court upheld the state law (36 FEP Cases 1010). The Justices have not yet announced whether they will review the case — *Miller-Wohl Co. v. Commissioner of Labor and Industry of Montana* (No. 84-1545).

In a brief filed with the Supreme Court in November 1985, the Justice

Department argued that both the Montana and the California laws are illegal. The government argued that state laws favoring pregnant workers run afoul of Title VII. In an unusual alliance, the National Organization for Women, the American Civil Liberties Union, the Women's Legal Defense Fund, and the U.S. Chamber of Commerce, among others, have voiced similar arguments in friend-of-the-court briefs. Although the groups differ radically on exactly what should be done about it, the women's groups recommend extending disability rights to everyone. Equal Rights Advocates, a San Francisco-based, public interest group, is representing California groups which have urged that the law be upheld.

Paternity Benefits — Trends

Paternity benefits are not very common, Bernard Hodes Advertising concluded in its 1985 survey. Nonetheless, the existence of paternity leave policies in one out of seven companies surveyed, the advertising agency said, "represents a tremendous leap forward in this area from a generation ago when the underlying concept was virtually nonexistent." The paternity benefit offered most frequently is unpaid leave, Bernard Hodes said.

Approximately two-fifths of the 253 firms surveyed by BNA in 1983 had one or more leave provisions allowing male employees to take time off from work for the birth of their children (PPF Survey No. 136). Among those firms, nearly half allowed employees to use paid vacation or annual leave for such purposes. BNA also reported that companies with more than 1,000 employees were more likely to grant annual leave to an employee for paternity reasons than companies with fewer employees. The provision of paid sick leave for paternity purposes was more common among small companies than large firms, BNA found. There was little difference in the percentage of large and small companies permitting employees to take an unpaid paternity leave.

The maximum amount of unpaid paternity leave granted in firms covered by the BNA survey ranged from five days to one year for plant workers, with a median of 90 days. For office staff, the range was from two days to one year, with a median of 90 days. For managers, the amount ranged from two days to one year, with a median of four months.

Paternity Leave

In its Report on a National Study of Parental Leaves, Catalyst said, "A growing number of companies are also beginning to offer unpaid leaves with job guarantees to natural fathers and adoptive parents." More than a third of the 384 Catalyst survey respondents reported that they offered an unpaid leave with a job guarantee to men. The unpaid leaves offered to men were similar in length to those offered to women — between one and six months.

"[I]t is fairly common for fathers to take a few days off at the time of the child's birth, but they rarely request this time as a separate paternity leave."

Despite the fact that more and more companies are offering leaves to new fathers, very few men are taking them, Catalyst reported. "Follow-up discussions with human resources policy makers indicate that it is fairly common for fathers to take a few days off at the time of the child's birth, but they rarely request this time as a separate paternity leave. More often, men use their vacation days or arrange to take the time off informally as paid or unpaid personal days."

Catalyst offered several explanations for the apparently limited use of leave by fathers. If paternity leave is covered under the general leave-of-absence policy, some employees may not be aware of the leave option, said Catalyst. It is also possible that, although companies have paternity leave policies, the corporate climate does not encourage men to take advantage of them. In some companies, it is clearly considered inappropriate for men to request leave even though a policy exists.

Corporations take a far more negative view of unpaid leaves for men than they do unpaid leaves for women, according to Catalyst. Almost two-thirds of its survey respondents did not consider it reasonable for men to take any parental leave whatsover. Another quarter of the companies reporting thought it reasonable for men to take six weeks' leave or less.

Even among companies that currently offer unpaid leaves to men, many thought it unreasonable for men to take them, Catalyst added. Some 41 percent of such companies did not sanction their using the unpaid leave policy, and only 18 percent considered it reasonable for men to take leaves of three months or longer.

"These results may explain at least in part why men are not taking advantage of the leaves that policies offer," Catalyst said.

Leave for Infant Care

"Parental leaves begin where maternity leaves leave off," the Family Policy Panel of the Economic Policy Council of UNA-USA commented in a report released in January 1986. Parental leave is usually unpaid, allows new mothers and fathers to stay at home to care for their child or children, and permits the employee to return to his original job or to an equivalent position.

"Parental leaves begin where maternity leaves leave off."

Although even fewer companies offer these parental leaves than offer maternity leave, the EPC panel noted that parental leave is becoming an increasingly popular benefit. "Job-protected maternity and parental leaves enable a woman to have a child without losing her job, offer parents a period of adjustment after the birth of a child, and may help provide an infant a good start in life by allowing parents to choose the mode of care they prefer for their new infant. The child care function of parental leaves is very important, especially because of the expense of infant care and the very limited availability of quality infant care arrangements," the EPC panel said.

The EPC panel maintained that parental leave generally is not costly or difficult for an employer to implement.

Employer Opposition

The Congressional Research Service noted in its report that, "[s]ince the idea of parental benefits is relatively new in the United States, there is little documented opposition." CRS continued: "However employers might be expected to raise questions about the added costs of such a benefit, which might be passed on to consumers in the form of higher prices by private sector companies. Guaranteeing the job of an employee on long-term parental leave might also be more burdensome for small businesses, with their limited personnel resources, than for larger businesses. Finally, there is likely to be opposition on philosophical grounds to any form of Government involvement in child care or family development, however benign it might appear, due to the belief that such involvement is an unnecessary and undesirable interference in private, family matters."

When asked to name three chief concerns in considering parental leave policy options, Catalyst noted in its 1986 final report that human resources executives identified the following:

- handling the leave-taker's work;
- losing valuable employees if the company does not meet the needs of a changing work force; and
- the equity of granting leaves to new parents but not to other employees.

Concerns of lesser importance, Catalyst said, were obtaining high productivity in departments where employees work on part-time schedules, the possibility that employees would not return after leaves, and containing the cost of parental benefits.

The Chamber of Commerce's Position

Opponents of the proposed parental leave bill (H.R. 2020, Rep. Patricia Schroeder (D-Colo)) which was pending in 1985 in the House of Representatives, such as the U.S. Chamber of Commerce, have focused their criticism on the mandatory nature of the proposal. "It's a great benefit when employers and employees negotiate for it, but it's a question of making it mandatory," Jim Klein, manager of pension and employee benefits for the Chamber, told BNA.

Right now, Klein said, companies are spending 37 percent of their payroll on some form of employee benefit. "By injecting a new mandatory one, we could crowd out some other benefits serving a broader base of employees," he contended. Retirement, workers' compensation, and unemployment insurance coverage are the only benefits that currently are mandated, he said. To inject a new, mandatory

---

"[Parental leave is] a great benefit when employers and employees negotiate for it, but it's a question of making it mandatory."

---

one meeting a national social objective not on the same level only serves a narrow category of people at the expense of these broader-based benefits. In addition, requiring parental leave would place a particularly heavy burden on small companies, Klein said.

Even if the United States is the only industrialized country which does not require the granting of parental leave, Klein said he doubted whether those countries putting a high value on parental leave compare as well to this country across the range of other benefits American workers enjoy. In its 1985 analysis of maternity and parental leave policies, however, the Congressional Research Service noted that, despite the dramatic increase in fringe benefits, "the relative level of U.S. fringe benefits still remains a smaller part of total compensation than it is in most other industrialized nations."

Klein acknowledged that worker interest in the benefit has grown significantly. "Employers may find that to stay competitive they will have to offer it more and more, and that's great. That's the marketplace responding as it should."

Klein applauded the growth in flexible or cafeteria benefit plans. If young employees want to take off time to care for children, they would have the choice of giving up some other benefit, such as a high retirement benefit, he said. "That's the kind of choice we ought to give employees, rather than the government getting in and saying all must provide this or that benefit," Klein added. (See Chapter VI, *Views of the Experts*, for additional comments by Klein on work and family.)

Precedents Being Set?

The problem of discrimination in relation to the granting of parental leave is dramatized by a recent legal proceeding in Chicago, Ill., and by a mediation board decision in Connecticut.

Under terms of a consent decree between Commonwealth Edison, a Chicago utility, and EEOC, the utility's male employees now have the same right as female workers to take unpaid personal leave to care for infant children (*EEOC v. Commonwealth Edison Co.*; USDC NIll, No. 85- C-5637, June 28, 1985). The decree resolved a suit filed on behalf of a male employee in which EEOC claimed that, by denying leave to the man but allowing non-disabled women to take leave following the birth of a child, Con Ed violated Title VII's ban on sex discrimination.

The leave provision at issue was contained in a collective bargaining contract between the International Brotherhood of Electrical Workers Local 1427 and the company. The provision stated that, "for justifiable reasons," a regular employee may be granted a leave of absence without pay, after reasonable notice to the company, and provided the employee's services can be spared. During the leave, seniority continues to be accumulated.

Under the provision, Commonwealth Edison had routinely granted women employees six months' unpaid leave to care for newborn children — and in one case, an adopted infant — after their normal, paid maternity leave had expired.

But when Stephen Ondera applied for permission to take six months' unpaid leave to care for his new baby, the company responded negatively.

Under the decree, the company agreed not to consider the sex of an employee "as a factor affecting the granting or denial of unpaid personal leave for care of an infant child during the first six months of its life."

In the Connecticut case, the state mediation board decided that Hartford City policemen whose wives have babies are entitled to paternity leave equivalent to the amount of maternity leave provided to female officers who give birth. The collective bargaining agreement at issue between the city and the International Brotherhood of Police Officers provided only for sick leave, not for maternity or paternity leave.

The State Board of Mediation and Arbitration said that when the city granted female officers maternity leave, it departed from the contract and relied on provisions of city personnel rules governing maternity/paternity leave for city employees to establish its policy for female officers. By failing to do the same for male officers, the city violated the "No Discrimination" clause of the union contract. The city appealed the ruling to the state superior court in Hartford.

A settlement of the legal dispute was reached between the city and union on Feb. 10, 1986. Under terms of the settlement, the City of Hartford will grant sick leave of up to eight work days following the birth of a legitimate child to male members of the police union. This leave will be charged to sick time. In the event that sick leave is exhausted, sick leave may be granted without pay. The leave must be taken on consecutive work days either immediately following birth or immediately following the baby's arrival home.

(*City of Hartford and International Brotherhood of Police Officers, Local 308*;

Conn. Dept. of Labor, State Board of Mediation and Arbitration, No. 8384-A-526, July 25, 1985)

Adoption

In the past decade, more and more companies have provided adoption benefits for their employees, according to the National Adoption Exchange (NAE), a Philadelphia-based organization which promotes adoption opportunities for children with special needs. Employees have begun to ask about the availability of adoption benefits, and employers have increasingly sought information on developing adoption benefit plans, said NAE.

An adoption benefits plan is a company-sponsored program that financially assists or reimburses employees for expenses related to the adoption of a child and/or provides for paid or unpaid leave for the adoptive parent employee. Adoption leave may be paid or unpaid and gives the adoptive parent time to help the child adjust after placement, according to NAE. Financial assistance may be a set allowance regardless of actual expenses or may be reimbursement for specific costs, NAE said. Some companies provide a combination of financial help and parental leave, NAE noted.

"For companies concerned with benefits cost containment, perhaps no other form of employee benefit offers the potential for high positive public exposure at such a low cost," NAE maintains.

Since 1980 there has been a notable increase in the number of companies offering adoption benefits, according to Catalyst. A 1984 Catalyst survey of the Fortune 1,500 companies showed that some 27.5 percent of the employers now offer such benefits, a significant increase over a 1980 Catalyst study which found

---

"For companies concerned with benefits cost containment, perhaps no other form of employee benefit offers the potential for high positive public exposure at such a low cost."

---

that only 10.3 percent offered adoption benefits. Adoption benefits also were reported by Catalyst to be among the options under consideration by companies planning to alter their parental leave policies.

One-fourth of firms responding to the 1983 BNA Personnel Policies Forum survey reported they provided leave to employees adopting children. Of those firms with some leave policy, 77 percent offered time off without pay; limits on such leave ranged from two weeks to a year, with a median of six months. The remaining firms offered paid leave for adoptive parents, usually the personal leave the employee has accrued.

While leaves for adoption are generally unpaid, about one-third of companies that have adoption policies reimburse employees for adoption expenses, Catalyst said. The amount of reimbursement varied from $1,000 to no limit.

Most companies offering adoption benefits set 18 years as the maximum age of the child for whom benefits would be allowed, according to Catalyst. Nearly 12 percent of the Catalyst respondents limited benefits to those adopting infants or babies up to one year old.

Transportation, communications, and public utilities companies were most generous in offering adoption benefits, Catalyst found. Manufacturing, construction, and agricultural companies tended to be the least likely to grant adoption benefits to parents. Thirty-nine percent of larger companies and 31 percent of medium-sized companies offered adoption policies, while only 13 percent of smaller companies did so, Catalyst reported.

The absence of provisions for time off from work upon adoption of a child has become a major issue with adoption groups and has been the subject of some legal controversy. In a recent arbitration case involving a local government employee in Pennsylvania, the arbitrator held that maternity leave language in a collective bargaining agreement covered all employees who became mothers, not simply employees who became pregnant. There are no differences in the duties of natural and adoptive mothers, the arbitrator found, and the employer's maternity leave provisions should apply to an adoptive parent because the leave is principally for the purpose of establishing a relationship between parent and child, not for medical recovery from childbirth (*Ambridge Borough*, 81 LA 915).

State legislatures also are beginning to address adoption leave benefits. (See, for example, state law provisions in Minnesota and Maryland in Chapter V.)

A Policy Evolution Under Way

Maternity, paternity, infant care, and adoption leave policies are still evolving, according to Catalyst. In its 1986 final report on parental leave policies, Catalyst noted that more than half of the corporate respondents had changed their policies in the past five years, primarily in response to passage of the Pregnancy Discrimination Act of 1978.

According to Catalyst, because of the Pregnancy Discrimination Act, a number of employers changed the length of leave offered. There was some tendency among companies (34.8 percent) to increase the length of *paid* disability leave. Some companies (23.2 percent), however, appeared to have decreased the length of *unpaid* leaves. "Follow-up interviews with human resources administrators indicated that some employers who had had flexible, liberal responses to maternity leave requests changed their policies to offer only what was legally required," said Catalyst. Others, however, made their *unpaid* leaves longer (13.4 percent) and most (63.4 percent) have maintained the same amount of leave as before passage of the Act.

Other corporate policy modifications which may be at least indirectly attributable to the Pregnancy Discrimination Act, Catalyst added, include increased standardization and clarification of policy, and the more consistent application of existing policy.

New Policy Initiatives

Several "blue ribbon" panels that have studied the problems facing working parents are calling for national policy reform initiatives in the public and private sector on the issues of parental leave.

In January 1986, when it released the results of its two-year study of the extent of ongoing changes that are affecting the family, the workplace, and the economy, the Family Policy Panel of the Economic Policy Council of UNA-USA made the following recommendations:

• Federal legislation should be enacted requiring public and private employers to provide temporary disability insurance to all employees.

• Disability leave for all employees should be fully job protected. Consideration should be given to raising the wage-replacement ceiling and to extending the standard length of disability leave for pregnancy from the current six to eight weeks.

• Employers should consider providing an unpaid parenting leave to all parent-workers with their job or a comparable job guaranteed. This leave should extend until the child is six months old.

More than 100 countries, including almost every industrial country, have laws that protect pregnant workers and allow new mothers a job-protected leave at the time of childbirth with full or partial wage replacement, but the United States does not, the EPC panel noted.

Noting comments it received from Columbia University Professor Sheila B. Kamerman, the EPC panel pointed out that in the United States only 40 percent of working women are entitled to a leave from work for childbirth that includes even partial income replacement and a job guarantee "for the six to eight weeks most doctors say is minimally required for physical recovery." Even fewer parents are entitled to an additional unpaid but job-protected leave for the purpose of caring for a newborn or an adopted infant.

While some employers voluntarily provide temporary disability insurance, many do not, the EPC panel noted. The panel maintained that, since temporary disability insurance is a low-cost, contributory benefit, it would not be prohibitively expensive for most companies — even small ones.

At least five states — California, Hawaii, New Jersey, New York, and Rhode Island — have laws that require employers to provide temporary disability insurance. In its report, the EPC panel focused on New Jersey, where private employers are required to provide disability insurance. In that state, the panel said, both employers and employees contribute one-half of 1 percent of the employee's first $10,100 in annual earnings to the program. The panel noted that the New Jersey program is currently running a surplus, and added that pregnancy-related disability claims accounted for 13 percent of all the state claims in 1981, the number of weeks during which disability was received averaged 11, and the average benefit paid out was $108 per week.

Infant Care Problem Is 'Urgent'

Problems encountered by working parents in providing care for their infants have reached such a magnitude that they require "immediate national action." That's the conclusion of the Advisory Committee on Infant Care Leave at the Yale Bush Center in Child Development and Social Policy.

The committee — composed of leaders in health care, academia, government, business, and labor — recommended in late 1985 that the federal government institute a policy directing employers to allow leaves of absence "for a period of

---

Problems encountered by working parents in providing care for their infants have reached such a magnitude that they require "immediate national action."

---

time sufficient to enable mothers to recover from pregnancy and childbirth and parents to care for their newborn or newly adopted infants." Such leave should provide "income replacement, benefit continuation and job protection," the panel said.

Infant care leave should be available for at least six months, with about 75 percent of salary paid for three months, the Yale committee suggested. Employers could set a "realistic maximum benefit, sufficient to assure adequate basic resources for the families who need them most," the panel said.

The cost of the plan would be about $1.5 billion a year, according to Edward Zigler, director of the Bush Center, who commented, "That figure is certainly not a break-the-bank figure."

The Yale group stressed that the United States is one of few industrialized nations that does not provide through federal law some protection for parents taking leave to care for infants. The group noted that the proportion of married mothers of infants who are in the U.S. labor force has risen from 24 percent in 1970 to 46.8 percent in 1984, and that 85 percent of working women are likely to become pregnant during their working lives.

"The majority of parents work because of economic necessity. The employed mother's salary is vital to the basic well-being of families," the Yale committee found. "A growing proportion of American families do not have the means to finance leaves of absence from work in order to care for their infants."

Under the parental leave bill pending in the House of Representatives, employers would be required to provide at least 18 weeks of leave within a two-year period for employees of either sex who choose to stay home to care for a newborn, newly adopted or seriously ill child. (For a discussion of the bill, which does not require wage replacement, see Chapter V. For text of the bill, see the Appendix. Dr. T. Berry Brazelton, Associate Professor of Pediatrics at Harvard Medical School, also discusses the legislation in a BNA interview in the Appendix.)

Insurance Fund Recommended

The most efficient method for financing parental care leave would be through a federally mandated insurance fund financed by contributions from employers and employees to cover "both short-term disability and infant care leave," the Yale report said. Options could include a federally managed insurance fund, state managed funds, or employer selection of private insurance to fund such leaves.

Until a national infant care policy can be adopted, employers should assist their employees with their own leave programs, something many firms already have done, the Yale group said. In addition to leave policies, employers can implement policies such as flexible work schedules, reduced work hours, job sharing, and child care information and referral services, it said.

Catalyst Recommendations

In its final report, Catalyst recommended adoption of the following policies by corporations:
- Disability leave with full or partial salary reimbursement.
- Additional unpaid parental leave of one to three months.
- A transition period of part-time work for one month to one year for returning leave-takers.
- Reinstatement to the same job or a comparable job at all stages of the leave.
- Parental leave policy should be explicitly communicated in writing, clearly identifiable, and distributed to all employees.

"These recommendations enable an employer to strike an effective balance between the priorities of a company and those of its employees. From the company's standpoint, the total policy is adequate but not excessive, particularly when a part-time transition period is utilized as an alternative to a lengthier (six months or more) unpaid leave," Catalyst said.

"From the employer's perspective, the policy takes the leave-taker's career commitment seriously. It allows a reasonable amount of time for physical recovery and adjustment to a new role, but does not encourage a leave length that works against employees' professional goals," Catalyst concluded.

MATERNITY AND PARENTING LEAVE

Organization: Foley, Hoag & Eliot
                    Boston, Mass.

Summary: Foley, Hoag & Eliot provides eight weeks of paid leave for any attorney unable to work because of pregnancy, childbirth, or other conditions related to pregnancy. Beyond the eighth week, the firm continues to pay an attorney's full salary should she be certified by her physician as unable to work. The firm also provides unpaid parenting leave to male or female attorneys.

Foley, Hoag & Eliot, a well-known Boston law firm, has, over the past few years, instituted maternity and parenting leave policies which one partner describes as "very flexible." Barry White, who sits on the managing committee responsible for personnel policy, reported that the firm formalized its leave policies in 1985. According to White, no one has expressed any dissatisfaction with the policy — either before or since it's been formalized — and at least one of the firm's attorneys called it "very generous."

While there is some room for negotiation on the policy, the firm basically provides eight weeks of paid leave for any attorney unable to work because of pregnancy, childbirth, or other conditions related to pregnancy. (While Massachusetts law stipulates that eight weeks be granted for disability leave for pregnancy, it leaves to the employer the decision whether this leave is paid or unpaid.) Beyond the eighth week, White explained, the firm continues to pay an attorney's full salary should she be certified by her physician as unable to work.

The firm, in addition, provides unpaid parenting leave to male or female attorneys. For women, it is normally an extension — for up to ten months — of maternity leave. For men, it is a distinct period of leave, lasting up to ten months. White reported that "a couple of male attorneys" have taken parenting leave, one for several months.

Absence longer than ten months is treated as resignation and one full year must intervene between successive maternity leaves or parental leave periods, White told BNA. The firm assumes, he said, that its attorneys are primarily interested in pursuing a law career, not full-time parenting. There is no minimum period of employment before an attorney is eligible for maternity or parenting leave, he said.

Asked how leave absences affect one's career progression at the firm, White replied that, in terms of promotion and benefits, a leave of up to six months is not considered a material break in service. During maternity leaves, and any parenting leave up to four additional months, all insurance coverage remains in effect, he noted.

Dinah Seiver, an attorney who was granted a four-month paid maternity leave in 1980, confirmed White's claim, saying she did not believe using maternity or parenting leave in any way interfered with career progression at Foley, Hoag &

Eliot. Her own leave, which preceded formalization of the firm's policy, was "individually negotiated," she pointed out.

Seiver said it was the "first case" of an associate taking maternity leave in recent years. "Following quickly on my heels," she added, were a few other attorneys who requested maternity leave. It was this experience that prompted the firm to formalize its policy. As Seiver suggested, "It would have been burdensome and unfair for each of us to negotiate separately."

Part-time Scheduling

The firm also allows a part-time work schedule to facilitate a parent's return to work after leave. Typical, according to White, is a four-day-a-week schedule. However, a few attorneys have eased back into their professional duties with a three-day schedule.

Seiver contended that liberal maternity and parenting leave policies benefit not only the employee, but the employer. "It's imperative for productivity in the workplace and for general morale that employers be conscientious in setting maternity/paternity leave policy," she said. "I think employers should be aware that a generous policy will redound to their benefit. My employer was very generous and I think that other employers would do well to do the same," Seiver said.

Women's Bar Association Survey

In terms of flexibility and what Seiver called "generosity," Foley, Hoag & Eliot performed better than most legal employers surveyed in 1982 by the Women's Bar Association of Massachusetts. The firm was one of seven granting paid maternity leave of eight weeks or longer; one of two granting unpaid leave to a year; one of four private law firms with a part-time employment policy; and one of the three with any paternity leave policy. The survey covered 26 legal employers in Massachusetts.

Foley, Hoag & Eliot has 53 partners and 48 associates in its Boston office, White said. Six partners are female, as are 16 associates, and all the female attorneys are of child-bearing age.

A less liberal leave policy applies to non-professional staff.

PARENTAL LEAVE

Organization: **Bank Street College of Education**
                   New York City

Summary: **Bank Street permits up to three months of paid leave for workers who are the primary caregivers for new children and other children in a family. Employees who adopt children younger than 36 months old are eligible for the same amount of leave. In addition to the paid leave, unpaid leave of six months to a year is available, depending on an employee's particular work situation. Initially, the parental leave policy applied only to professional workers at Bank Street, but on Jan. 1, 1986, the provisions were**

extended to the college's service employees, who are represented by AFSCME Local 1707.

Bank Street College of Education in 1980 adopted a policy of providing parental leave for fathers and mothers on an equal basis.

The policy permits up to three months of paid leave for those employees "committed as the principal or co-principal caregiver of the new child and other children in the family, providing at least 50 percent of the parental caregiving time." To be eligible, employees must have worked for Bank Street for at least a year, and need only work more than half-time to be eligible for the leave.

Employees who adopt children younger than 36 months old are eligible for the same amount of leave. Bank Street also allows a month's paid leave for employees who adopt children of between three and 12 years old, and for biological parents who are not "primary caregivers."

In addition to the paid leave, unpaid leave of six months to a year is available, depending on an employee's particular work situation.

A Commitment to Continued Employment

"Conditions for continued employment for those who take family leave," the policy states, "are the same as all other employees. The college is committed to continue employment subject to available funds and satisfactory performance. It expects staff to make a commitment in return."

When originally enacted, the parental leave policy applied only to professional workers at Bank Street. But on Jan. 1, 1986, Bank Street Personnel Director Florence Gerstenhaver said, the provisions were extended to the college's service

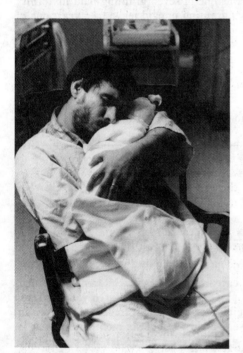

employees, who are represented by the Community and Social Agency Employees, AFSCME Local 1707. Bank Street employees about 300 people.

That Bank Street provides parental leave for employees is not surprising since it states that "its business is children and families." Founded in 1916, Bank Street College trains teachers, counselors, and school administrators, conducts research on teaching and learning, and produces classroom materials, books, and television programs for and about children and parents. Among the projects now under way at the college are:

• A study of work and family life in several nations that measures the productivity of workers in relation to the quality of their home life;

• A cable television series on parenting, titled "Family Matters";

• A project to help fathers become more active in raising children;

- Consultation by a team of specialists on the design of a model children's center in a U.S. industrial park;
- A series of books on parenting;
- A study of sibling relationships; and
- Research on how microcomputers influence children's learning.

One Father's View

Personnel Director Gerstenhaver noted that "not a lot" of fathers have taken advantage of paternity leave. A talk with Dr. Bret Halverson, one new father taking advantage of Bank Street's paid paternity leave, might be an incentive for more to do so, however.

Rather than leaving work entirely for three months, Halverson has opted to take every Friday off for 15 months. He directs Jobs for the Future, a Bank Street youth employment project, and says that, if he left the scene entirely for three months, "I wouldn't have a project left."

Halverson feels that the extra day at home substantially affects his relationship with his son, Paul. "I'm not just flitting in and flitting out," he says. He also says his Fridays off have "given me a fascinating look into what life is like for somebody who stays home. I have gained a lot of empathy for, and appreciation of, the role of the mother. A lot of those responsibilities aren't so fun; there's a lot more excitement, at least in certain ways, in being the breadwinner."

Halverson says he is not doing any less work in four days than he used to do in five. "I've gotten more efficient in some ways, and I also take work home."

Halverson is 37, and Paul, born in July 1985, is his first child. Halverson's wife Cecilia took three months' unpaid leave from her job at the City University of New York, returning to work in October. Aside from the financial imperative of Cecilia returning to work, she "felt the need to," Halverson explains.

Halverson began to take his Fridays off in September 1985 and will continue doing so through December 1986. Monday through Thursday, the couple hires a baby-sitter at the cost of $4 per hour. Halverson says, "I've been fortunate on two counts: I have an employer with a progressive outlook, and both my wife and I make reasonable incomes."

Other Fathers 'Envious'

In the suburban community of Nanuet, N.Y., where he and his wife live, Halverson says, there is "an epidemic" of babies among two-career couples in their thirties. Other fathers, he contends, are "very envious" of his ability to take paternity leave. "You hear a lot about the superwoman," Halverson says, "but there's a lot of pressure now to be superdads, and people get into that without really knowing what's involved."

Halverson feels that the equal sharing of child care duties by mother and father — a goal he sees as desirable — "is more likely to happen if there are incentives from employers." He adds that these incentives are "more important the further down a person is in the hierarchy" because higher-level employees naturally tend to have more flexibility about when they are physically in the office. He adds: "Employers need to understand that, if they are well organized and flexible enough, leave[s] can be a very productive thing."

"In an ideal situation," Halverson says, "I think I would enjoy staying home full time for a while. It would be good for Paul, although it would be hard for me. Your adrenaline doesn't get pumping a lot when you're at home, and that's one of the reasons I enjoy working."

Summing up what the first six months of fatherhood have taught him, Halverson said, "It's that what you put in with a child is what you get out. Paul's a happy kid because whoever's with him is able to spend a lot of time."

PARENTAL LEAVE

Organization: **Lotus Development Corp.**
                  Cambridge, Mass.

Summary: **Lotus Development provides up to four weeks of parenting leave for its employees who are biological or adoptive parents. The leave, which may be supplemented by vacation leave, may be taken at any time, but employees must negotiate with department managers on whether leave is possible, and on the length of leave.**

A parenting leave policy at Lotus Development Corp., a computer software company, has turned out to be "very popular," Janet Axelrod, vice president for human resources, told BNA. The policy, which is formalized in the employee manual, provides for up to four weeks of paid leave, primarily, the manual states, for "parenting and bonding," she said.

In the manual, Lotus, which has a fairly young work force, acknowledges its employees' concern about the impact parental responsibilities may have on their careers. The parenting leave program is available to the primary caregiver, whether mother or father, and to parents who adopt children, Axelrod said. Parenting leave is distinct from any disability leave for childbirth, she added, and is not restricted to caring for newborns, but can be taken at any time there is a need to be with a child for awhile.

Parenting leave is available to employees who work 28 or more hours per week and who have been with Lotus for at least a year, Axelrod said. The leave accrues at the rate of two and a half days per month beginning on the employee's first anniversary. The limit is 20 days, Axelrod said. Vacation time can be added to it, if necessary or desired, she said.

Details of parenting leave, Axelrod said, must be worked out in advance with the employee's manager to make sure the department can function without the employee.

In addition to parenting leave and using vacation days, Lotus employees may be able to take an additional four-week unpaid leave of absence or arrange for a flexible work schedule for up to three months. A flexible work schedule may consist of fewer hours or days per week, work at home, or longer hours and fewer days per week.

Lotus guarantees employees their jobs upon return to work; for those returning from an unpaid leave of absence, "Lotus will use its best efforts to find the employee a comparable job at the end of leave," according to the manual.

A Commitment to Employees

Lotus stresses in the manual that its progressive benefits package is a sign of its commitment to its employees and that it expects in return certain commitments from employees who use parenting leave: that they will discuss in advance and agree on leave arrangements with their managers; that they will provide timely notification of any changes in the arrangements; and that they will return to work following parenting leave. As a way of encouraging employees to return to work after parenting leave, Lotus does not pay employees for the leave until they have been back at work for four weeks. Those employees who find they are not able to return are asked to return on a temporary basis until a replacement can be found, Axelrod said.

Chris Bresnahan, a human resources specialist at Lotus who used the parenting leave after the birth of her first child in July 1985, said, "It was great." She said it gave the baby a chance to "get settled" and on a daily schedule before she returned to work.

When she came back to Lotus, Bresnahan said, she had five and a half weeks of vacation time accrued, so she arranged to return on a four-day schedule, giving herself a relaxed day with the baby on Monday. Bresnahan said she knew one Lotus employee who used the parenting leave to come back to work half-time for two months after the birth of her child.

In developing the plan, Axelrod said Lotus investigated every policy on parenting leave it could, but concluded it wanted to do more than any of the policies examined. She added that she didn't know of any other companies that were following Lotus' lead, but she characterized parenting leave as "the wave of the future." Axelrod said that, in her opinion, employers don't have any choice but to offer parenting leave if they want to run their companies and have women working for them.

ADOPTION ASSISTANCE

Organization:	**Bank of America** **San Francisco, Calif.**
Summary:	**Since 1983, Bank of America has provided reimbursement for adoption expenses of more than $250 and up to $2,000 to employees adopting foster children or stepchildren and children from overseas.**

Since 1983, Bank of America has eased the burden of adoption by providing financial aid to salaried employees who have decided to legally adopt a child.

"I feel strongly that if we pay maternity benefits, we should offer an alternative to those who want to adopt children," Bob Beck, executive vice president of corporate human resources, stated in a company newsletter. He added that the adoption assistance program follows the bank's concept of offering employees "as many alternatives as possible in their benefits package."

After an employee pays the first $250 in covered adoption expenses, the plan reimburses up to $2,000 of remaining expenses. Covered expenses include agency placement fees, court costs and legal fees, temporary foster child care, and maternity benefits not covered by the natural mother's insurance.

Assistance is available for adoptions arranged by both public and private agencies, and by private sources such as attorneys and physicians.

Nancy Bronstein, who monitors the adoption assistance plan, said that about one-half of the bank's employees who apply for adoption assistance go through public agencies, where fees can run up to $1,500. The rest of the employees use lawyers, whose expenses run between $5,000 and $10,000, which includes about $1,500 for the natural mother's medical expenses and the balance in legal fees.

Bronstein said the firm is responsible only for adoption reimbursement, "not for helping to locate babies." Finding the right agency or private source is up to the individual, she stressed.

Bank of America's adoption assistance plan also covers adoption of foster children or stepchildren and children from overseas. Adopted children must be under age 17 for an employee to receive assistance.

Through 1985, according to Bronstein, 40 employees have applied for and received adoption assistance. All but one were for newborns; one case involved a foster child. Three children were from foreign countries and one adoptive mother flew to Argentina to pick up the child.

Employees are eligible for the adoption assistance as long as the adoption is legalized after the employee has completed 90 days of salaried service, Bronstein said.

Bronstein explained that responses to a Bank of America survey of other employers on the issue of when employees become eligible for the plan are split evenly, with about half providing assistance upon legalization of the adoption and the other half making assistance available prior to actual legalization.

*   *   *

E. RELOCATION ASSISTANCE PROGRAMS

"Researchers have identified relocation as one of the major stress-inducing events in life, similar in its effects to the death of a loved one or to divorce."

So stated a 1983 report on relocation by Catalyst, a national non-profit organization that works with individuals and corporations to explore and develop career and family options. In *Human Factors in Relocation*, Catalyst also stated that relocation stress can also have a direct impact on job performance.

"Researchers have identified relocation as one of the major stress-inducing events in life, similar in its effects to the death of a loved one or to divorce."

In an information kit to assist employees with relocation, Catalyst notes, "Each year between 300,000 and half a million people are relocated by their employers. On the personal side of the story, the main considerations are family, friends, and fun. Sometimes family matters can get a bit complicated . . . . The relationship with your parents and those of your spouse may be an important consideration, especially if the parents are elderly or dependent upon you for special reasons. If you have children, you'd most likely begin considering how the move would affect them."

For employers, a major problem with relocation of employees is cost. "Fourteen billion corporate dollars were spent in 1984-85 to relocate close to half a million employees," according to Catalyst. On average, the relocation of an employee in 1984 cost $33,000 per transferee, said Anita Brienza, manager of public relations and advertising for the Employee Relocation Council, a Washington, D.C.-based membership association. Other relocation specialists place the cost as high as $35,000 to $40,000.

"Relocation," Catalyst concluded, "increasingly depends on merging family and business concerns."

No False Moves

Although relocation inevitably causes some pressure and anxiety for transferred employees, especially those with families, choosing to relocate doesn't have to be a complicated and stressful decision for employees, according to Catalyst, which has developed *No False Moves*, a program for dealing with problems attendant to relocation. The firm describes *No False Moves* as a "self-guided kit which gives employees a chance to explore their choices and to realistically anticipate the stresses of the move." The kit, containing two tapes and a workbook, explores the personal, family, and emotional aspects of a relocation and provides information employees need to make an informed decision about a transfer offer.

Particular attention is given to the problems of two-earner couples. Relocation services estimate that 30 to 40 percent of relocations involve two-earner couples, Catalyst said. "The difficulties of balancing a two-career partnership are heightened by relocation. Even when the couple has reached an explicit agreement that one person's career will have temporary priority, the employee who has accepted the offer often experiences a great deal of tension as a result of initiating the move and uprooting the spouse. Relocation often means an abrupt career interruption for the spouse, who may not find an equivalent career position in the new location," Catalyst stated.

"Many employers are beginning to offer special assistance to make a move easier for these couples," says *No False Moves*. "However, this assistance is generally informal. You probably won't find it written into the company policy. But rest assured it is becoming increasingly available."

Employer assistance can take several forms: family counseling, financial assistance to employees, and career assistance to the relocating employee's working spouse.

The number of spousal job-assistance programs more than doubled from 1984 (20 percent) to 1985 (44 percent) . . . .

Spouse job-finding assistance and homefinding are popular programs, according to a 1985 survey of 151 firms by Runzheimer International. The number of spousal job-assistance programs offered by the surveyed firms more than doubled from 1984 (20 percent) to 1985 (44 percent), according to the results of a study by the Rochester, Wis.-based management consulting firm. Most of the firms (85 percent) with spousal job-assistance programs, the study added, offer such aid only through informal programs.

Relocation and the Two-Career Family

Dual-career families present tremendous problems in relocation and are the reason so many companies are addressing the issue of spousal counseling, said relocation specialist Jan Dickson, a consultant who operates The Relocation Center in Beaverton, Ore. The employee is giving up his or her "comfort zone" and social network, and is concerned about the new pediatrician for the children, the new schools, housing, and churches.

Merrill Lynch Relocation Management, Inc., of White Plains, N.Y., cites survey findings showing that 60 percent of corporate moves involve dual-income couples and that by 1990 the proportion will be 75 percent.

Dickson, who worked with the Georgia-Pacific Corporation in its huge move to Atlanta, Ga., from Portland, Ore., in 1982, said there is now a great deal of interest in spousal counseling in relocation situations. She recalled that Georgia-Pacific told 500 employers in Atlanta that the company was coming to town and asked them to accept resumés. "All but two responded and most were positive. Many arranged interviews on site," she said. Georgia-Pacific also bent its anti-nepotism rule to permit qualified spouses to apply for jobs as long as they would not end up working for the same department head as the spouse-employee.

Some companies offer assistance ranging from three-day workshops for employees being relocated to paying one month of a spouse's former salary while the spouse looks for a job in the new area, said Dickson.

One of every 10 employees who relocate is a female, according to Dickson, and there are special problems when the husband is the "trailing spouse."

Relocation of professionals also requires special employer effort, said Dickson. At the least, an employer would have to link the "trailing spouse" together up with someone in his or her professional field to help the spouse discover what is available in the new area, she said.

In addition to spousal counseling, employers increasingly are offering counseling as part of employee assistance programs to provide a forum for employees to talk about their needs, Dickson said.

Formal Assistance Programs

A small but growing number of companies are developing formal spouse assistance programs, according to RESOURCE: Careers, a career development and referral service located in northeastern Ohio. In 1983, RESOURCE: Careers surveyed 156 northeastern Ohio corporations about their employee relocation policies. Only 10 percent of the respondents indicated that they had developed a formalized policy of assisting spouses of relocating employees, while 25 percent said they would help at the request of the employee.

Merrill Lynch, among others, has begun offering a "trailing spouse" service as part of its relocation package. Travenol Laboratories, Inc., in Deerfield, Ill., provides the relocating working spouse a step-by-step system designed to assist in the job search. Travenol's Job Search Organizer includes job search forms and information on identifying potential employers in the new community, as well as a filing system. Travenol also provides special travel kits for children of different ages involved in a relocation. The hard cardboard kits contain T-shirts, a coloring book, tote bag, stationery, an address book, and other items. The materials attempt to underscore the positive aspects of moving.

Formal spousal assistance programs, according to RESOURCE: Careers, usually involve all or some of the following:

• Counseling to deal with any resentment or negative emotions surrounding the disruption of the spouse's career path;

• An assessment of the spouse's skills, education, work experience, and career goals;

• Job search strategy counseling, including instruction on self-marketing techniques and on sharpening of interview skills;

• Help with preparation of a resumé that is directed toward achieving the spouse's career goals;

• Referrals to appropriate companies and key contact people in the spouse's specific occupation. This also includes access to up-to-date information on the spouse's new job market and the spouse's career field;

• Use of a telephone, desk, typewriter, and answering service; and

• Follow-up and encouragement throughout the job-search process.

Catalyst identified some programs and services corporations are offering to meet the individuals' needs in relocation:

• Spouse involvement programs, in which the spouse of the relocating employee is contacted by the company and offered assistance at the time the relocation offer is made. Some firms offer a guide developed by a task force consisting primarily of relocated spouses;

• Spouse sponsor programs offering social activities for newcomers; and

• Company reimbursement for workshops on stress reduction, decisionmaking, and personal adjustment skills.

Corporations are making increased use of third-party firms to manage relocations, Catalyst noted, although most of this assistance is related to housing. However, third parties can also be used to provide counseling and and other personal assistance to relocating employees, Catalyst said.

The Reluctance to Relocate

One major trend to which companies must adapt in the coming decade is employees' growing reluctance to relocate, according to Catalyst.

In a 1985 report, *Corporations and Families: Changing Practices and Perspectives*, the Conference Board observed that employees are increasingly resistant to company-initiated moves. The resistance is due, in part, to working-spouse considerations, but also is due to "the potential disruption of the whole family, changes in the standard of living, or a desire to be close to parents or other extended family members," the Conference Board stated.

Catalyst reported in 1983 that the executive transfer refusal rate was 24 percent. In responses to Catalyst's 1983 survey on their firms' relocation practices, 70 percent of the respondent human resources professionals said they felt that reluctance to interfere with a spouse's career plans would play a larger role in employee relocation decisions in the future.

"If [lack of] spousal assistance becomes a deterrent to relocation, you'll find corporations responding," declared Anita Brienza of the Employee Relocation Council. For instance, she noted, when extremely high interest rates became a problem in relocating employees who needed to buy a new home, many companies responded with assistance in the form of a mortgage interest differential allowance to offset the "shock" of the difference in rates between old and new mortgage payments.

A 1984 survey of Employee Relocation Council members revealed that only about one-third of them had programs that included career and job counseling for spouses. Many of the employers that do provide some sort of job location do it on an informal or ad hoc basis, said Brienza. Nevertheless, she said, "Spousal assistance is a question our members say is coming up more and more." The issue is raised more often in a recruiting setting, she said, because spousal assistance is something a lot of incumbent employees don't feel comfortable discussing.

In spite of expanded benefit packages designed to make employees' relocation as comfortable as possible, employees have identified some corporate relocation assistance as inadequate. One of the five most frequently expressed complaints is lack of adequate assistance for spouses. "Spouse assistance, if offered at all, is often inadequate, inappropriate, or offered in a manner that is patronizing and insensitive to the needs of the modern, career-oriented spouse," said Catalyst.

Catalyst recommends that corporations offer a flexible relocation package, which includes an option for quality job search assistance for spouses.

The following case studies examine a United Auto Workers relocation assistance program, the mortgage assistance program at Diamond Shamrock Corporation, and The Standard Oil Company (Sohio) spousal assistance program.

COMMUNITY SUPPORT NETWORK

Organizations: **United Auto Workers and General Motors**
                    Fort Wayne, Ind.

Summary: **UAW is providing a thorough orientation to workers who are relocating from cities in Missouri and Wisconsin to a soon-to-be-constructed truck plant in Fort Wayne. The program is being operated under an agreement with GM. The automaker is providing the funds, the union is providing the manpower.**

When the trauma of a plant closing is compounded by the prospect of relocation — of leaving behind relatives and friends to establish roots in a new area — many families have difficulty coping. Yet the pain of starting over can be eased, the United Auto Workers union believes, by a support network designed to acquaint newcomers with the community and one another.

In Fort Wayne, Ind., the union's belief is being tested on a large scale as UAW endeavors to facilitate the relocation of workers from General Motors' Janesville, Wis., and St. Louis, Mo., plants by providing counseling and information "on everything from lawyers to trash removal," according to Roger Anclam, president of Local 2209, which is located in Roanoke, Ind.

Paragraph 96 of the UAW's National Master Agreement with GM allows certain workers at plants which are closed to relocate. Anclam said 1,714 workers from Janesville and 316 workers from St. Louis are seeking jobs at the GM pickup truck factory under construction in Fort Wayne. The plant will have two shifts employing some 3,000 workers, he said, with production scheduled to begin in late 1986 at the earliest.

Workers are being brought to Fort Wayne in small groups for training and orientation, said Anclam. Local 2209 sends each worker a packet with information on Fort Wayne and about the community, such as, cost-of-living estimates; an overview of local government and taxes; employment breakdowns and labor outlook; a comparison of housing costs and a glossary of real estate terms; an apartment guide; and lists of schools, churches, hotels and motels, community agencies, hospitals, and retail outlets. A "Welcome to Indiana" letter from the UAW's region 3 director also is included, along with city and state maps, plus a toll-free number union members can call for further information.

Because workers are being introduced to the community in small groups, the local housing market should be able to accommodate them easily, said UAW Region 3 Assistant Director Elmer Blankenship. "When a large number of people come into a community at one time, it makes it more difficult to find homes and apartments," he noted.

Once workers arrive in Fort Wayne, additional assistance is available at the UAW's relocation trailer, said Anclam, which is parked at the plant site and staffed seven days a week. Although the trailer offers "thousands of pieces of literature," Anclam said that most UAW members want to know what workers who have preceded them think about Fort Wayne and how they are coping with the strain of re-establishing roots. "No matter what the concern, we're open and honest about our experiences," he said.

Under the joint agreement with the union, GM is providing project funding and UAW the manpower, Anclam said. "It's in both sides' common interest to make this transition as easy as possible," he said. "It's truly been a joint effort."

The Hardship of Starting Over

Both the company and the union realize "it's quite a hardship to pull up roots and start over," continued Anclam. The change is usually a large financial strain, he said, which exacerbates any existing interpersonal difficulties. In such situations, divorce is not uncommon, he said, noting that a 45 percent divorce rate was one result when UAW members relocated to an Oklahoma production facility a few years ago.

Because relocated spouses often feel more acutely isolated, Local 2209 will initiate a women's group where frustrations can be aired, acquaintances made, and ways to cope shared, said Anclam. Aside from personal bonding, practical information will be offered, particularly financial counseling, he said.

In addition to the women's group, a coordinated recreational effort is planned, Anclam said, to encourage social interaction among newcomers. Softball and bowling leagues, holiday parties, and involvement with community causes will be part of this effort, which, he said, should, in the long term, "make the transition easier for everyone."

Right now, however, providing individuals with information about Fort Wayne is the main thrust of the relocation assistance program. The union also has helped relocating families find schools for dependents with special disabilities and clinics for treatment of chronic illness, said Anclam. "It's been an extremely large gamut, but if someone has a special need, we'll go to any length to find the answer for it," he said.

As one of the first to come from Janesville, Anclam knows how sought after basic community information is: "When I arrived, I went to the Chamber of Commerce for maps and pamphlets, which everyone wanted when I went back. Interest was so great, I ended up without any [information] for myself." The idea of the UAW's effort may be simple, "but it's what people need."

Blankenship said the UAW "is very proud of its efforts to make the transition easier for its members," noting that the hardship of relocation "is infinitely easier if someone's there to help you."

MORTGAGE ASSISTANCE

Organization: **Diamond Shamrock Corp.**
                    Dallas, Texas

Summary: **Diamond Shamrock's extensive corporate relocation program annually helps between 250 and 300 of the company's employees and their families to relocate. By serving in several capacities — from real estate broker to home seller — the company tries to bring the employee's cost of moving "as close to zero as possible."**

When it transfers an employee, Diamond Shamrock Corp. serves the employee as real estate broker, advisor, lender, mortgage banker, and home seller.

"We've had the mortgage assistance program for 10 years," said Midge Gilmer, manager of relocations for Diamond Shamrock, a manufacturer of agricultural and industrial chemicals.

Until 1982, under its assistance program, the company paid a mortgage interest differential. Money was given to employees to cover the difference between the mortgage payment they used to have and the payment they were going to be making at their new location.

"When, in the early 1980s, those differences rose to as much as eight points, the company re-evaluated its program," Gilmer said. The mortgage assistance program was revised in 1982. The idea of the new plan is stated in the packet of information provided to each employee who is planning a move: "It is the intention of the corporation to provide employees with an approximate 1.75% spread between a five year subsidized interest rate and a bought down 30 year fixed note rate."

"We're basically buying points," Gilmer explained.

And Making Money

Acting as a mortgage banker, Diamond Shamrock has been able to make enough money to justify the whole relocation program, according to Gilmer. "We held some of [the mortgages], the rates came down and we sold and came out looking like big heroes. We've been doing that since 1982. So far, we've been able to sell loans and make enough money to pay the way. We do it all with two people on the corporate level."

Because Diamond Shamrock sells mortgages to the Federal National Mortgage Association (Fannie Mae), it is careful in the way it writes its loans. For any mortgage over $115,300, the company requires a 20 percent down payment — smaller mortgages require 5 percent — and approval from the treasurer's office. The company won't make a loan for more than 225 percent of an employee's yearly salary, or for more than 130 percent of the mortgage balance on the employee's old home.

One major problem in moving employees is the "area differential," Gilmer said. Identical homes in different places may have vastly different prices, and that can present hardships to transferred employees. Diamond Shamrock addresses this only peripherally, she said: "We don't have area differentials. We tried a five-year balloon loan, but that didn't work, so we try to provide those employees [moving to a more expensive home] with a deeper discount." The amount of discount varies by market. When it transfers employees to its Morristown, N.J., facility, for example, the company offers a "3-2-1" plan that brings the mortgage interest rate down three points from the prevailing conventional rate the first year, two points the second, and one point in the third year. After the third year, the employee pays the full rate. In San Francisco, a similar program lasts five years instead of three.

House-Buying Trips and Child Care Help

Diamond Shamrock also helps relocating employees and their families in other ways. The company pays for one house-hunting trip in the new location, and the employees are encouraged to stay there until they've got something picked out. In addition to paying for travel, meals, and lodging, the company pays up to $100 for child care while the search is being conducted.

Employees selling houses have three options, Gilmer said. They can take the conventional route, and sell it through a broker. They can sell it themselves, in which case Diamond Shamrock will pay them 2.5 percent of the selling price as a brokerage fee. Or they can sell it to Diamond Shamrock for the average of three appraisals. If the company sells the house in 30 days for more than it paid the employee, it will pay the employee the difference, less costs.

Diamond Shamrock also will sell a house to an employee coming into a new town, if the company owns something there. And it typically discounts those sales by 2 or 3 percent, said Gilmer. In most cases, the company helps the transferred employee find a realtor in the new city.

Moving expenses are paid by the company, as are the costs of temporary quarters if the new house isn't ready when the transferee gets to the new city, or when the employee has to move before the rest of the family. In the latter case, Diamond Shamrock also will foot the bill for weekend trips so the family can be together.

Incidental expenses are covered by an allowance of either one month's salary or $2,000, whichever is higher. The company will pay up to $600 in penalties when it forces an employee to break a lease. When it moves a renter, the company will pay the difference between the old rent and the new rent, up to $1,000, for six months.

Diamond Shamrock does all of this in-house because there are so many people to move, and because it keeps the company on top of the relocation business, according to Gilmer. There's a package of materials sent to employees to explain everything, and there's even a videotaped presentation for transferees and their families. "[The video program] runs 12 minutes, and we did it because most people won't read fat manuals," said Gilmer.

"The focus is to make it as easy as possible," Gilmer said. "The cost to an employee is as close to zero as possible."

SPOUSAL RELOCATION ASSISTANCE

Organization: **The Standard Oil Company**
                    Cleveland, Ohio

Summary: **Sohio guarantees relocation assistance — including resettlement and career continuance help — for spouses of employees it recruits. Once the family is settled, Sohio recruiters offer the spouse career assistance for up to 12 months. After reviewing the spouse's credentials, recruiters act as career counselors assisting with resumé preparation, interview coaching, and feedback on job search experiences.**

When The Standard Oil Company (Sohio) recruits a new employee, it guarantees relocation assistance — including resettlement and career continuance help — for the employee's spouse.

"We want both members of a 'career team' to benefit from the move," explained Edward Miller, manager of professional recruitment for the Cleveland-based petroleum corporation. "With the number of dual-career families today, it's pointless to pursue a candidate if you're not considering the needs of his spouse."

Although spousal relocation assistance had been "an ad hoc part of Sohio's recruiting effort for years," the corporation formally committed to the idea in 1978, said Miller. Under the assistance plan, individual recruiters first address resettlement concerns, he explained, by providing information on schools, taxes, churches, community agencies, and suburban areas. Sohio works with two Cleveland realty firms, he said, and pays closing costs on the relocating couple's new home.

If asked, Sohio recruiters can refer couples to a financial counselor, but generally "we try to steer clear of the employee's private business," said Miller. The company, however, does advise families to get a market appraisal of a house before buying, he said, "since in the corporate realm, you have to be realistic about transfers." Often relocating couples fail to do this, he said, then find they cannot sell their house following a transfer, "which causes problems."

Once the family is settled, Sohio recruiters offer the spouse career assistance for up to 12 months, said Miller. Roughly 85 percent of Sohio's career-assisted spouses are wives, whose occupations range from secretary to Ph.D. in anthropology, he said. After reviewing the spouse's credentials, Miller explained, recruiters act as career counselors — "nobody knows the job market better" — assisting with resumé preparation, interview coaching, and feedback on job search experiences.

Job Search Begins within the Company

Sohio communicates with 25 major corporations in the Cleveland area regarding job openings, said Miller, and works with RESOURCE: Careers. Before taking the job search outside, however, Sohio reviews each spouse's credentials to see if the spouse qualifies for any openings within the company. "Sohio is fairly forward thinking in its posture toward couples working for the corporation," he said. Both husband and wife may work for Sohio if neither supervises the other and if each reports to a different supervisor.

"Sometimes the spouse turns out to be a better hire," said Miller, noting it costs Sohio nothing additional to hire spouses. "With the cost of moving being what it is today, it makes sense," he said.

When the job search for the spouse expands beyond Sohio, recruiters expect spouses to actively stalk career leads, said Miller: "Job placement has to be a two-way effort."

The program has a high success rate, Miller said, noting that its only failures "have been in cases where the spouse expected us to do it all." In 1985, he said, the program had 46 job placements out of 50 participants. In 1984 there were 40 placements out of 46 participants. As of late 1985, 26 spouses were receiving career assistance.

Miller disagrees with those who consider spousal relocation assistance "a frill." He stressed that in recruitment "one of the most frustrating things is to have your top candidate turn you down because of the spouse's job situation." By offering spousal assistance, Sohio's job acceptance rate runs around 85 percent, he said, concluding, "We feel the fact that we have shown ourselves sensitive to the needs of the spouse accounts for this high level."

V. DEVELOPMENTS AND TRENDS

This chapter reviews trends and recent developments involving:
- *Federal legislation on parental leave and child care;*
- *State legislative and executive programs and policies for working parents;*
- *Flexible benefit plans, with a focus on the advantages of "cafeteria plans" for employers, single parents, and two-earner couples; and*
- *Child care and leave practices in other countries.*

[**NOTE:** As this report went to press, a revised version of the parental leave bill (HR 2020) was introduced in the House of Representatives. The new proposal (HR 4300), which was introduced on March 4, 1986, is similar in most respects to the original proposal, but restricts coverage to private-sector employers of five or more persons, and provides administrative, as well as civil, remedies. Hearings on HR 4300 were tentatively set to begin in the spring of 1986. A companion meaure was expected to be introduced in the Senate. HR 2020 is discussed in Section A of this Chapter and full text of the bill is contained in Appendix A.]

A. FEDERAL LEGISLATIVE DEVELOPMENTS

A number of legislative proposals directed at work and family issues, particularly parental leave and child care, are under consideration in 1986 by the 99th Congress. Following are summaries of the main features of these proposals.

The Parental and Disability Leave Act of 1985

The Parental and Disability Leave Act of 1985 would guarantee the jobs of workers who are temporarily disabled or who choose to take leave to care for newborn, newly adopted, or seriously ill children. The bill was introduced in the House of Representatives by Rep. Patricia Schroeder (D-Colo) on April 4, 1985. The bill (HR 2020) is the first proposal of its kind to be considered by Congress. As of February 1986, the bill had 46 co-sponsors.

Under HR 2020, employers would be required to provide at least 18 weeks of leave within a two-year period for employees of either sex who choose to stay home to care for a newborn, newly adopted, or seriously ill child.

The measure would require employers to grant "temporary disability leave in cases involving inability to work due to nonoccupational medical reasons with adequate protection of the employee's employment and benefit rights."

Under HR 2020, employers would be required to provide at least 18 weeks of leave within a two-year period for employees of either sex who chose to stay home to care for a newborn, newly adopted, or seriously ill child. Employees would be allowed to return to work on a part-time schedule after the 18-week period and work part time until their total parental leave — including the part-time period — totaled 39 weeks. Employees taking advantage of such leave would be guaranteed continuation of health insurance benefits and reinstatement to their original jobs or equivalent positions upon return, with no loss of seniority or pension benefits.

HR 2020 does not provide for wage replacement during parental or temporary disability leave, but calls for establishment of a commission to study and recommend ways to implement such a policy. The Paid Parental Leave and Disability Commission, which would be authorized for two years, would include 21 members who would be appointed by Congress and the Administration. The commission would look for ways employers could compensate employees, at least in part, for parental and temporary disability leave.

Hearings on the bill were held before four House subcommittees on Oct. 17, 1985. The hearing was sponsored by Schroeder, who chairs the Subcommittee on Civil Service of the Post Office and Civil Service Committee, and by Rep. Mary Rose Oakar (D-Ohio), who chairs the Civil Service Subcommittee on Compensation and Employee Benefits; Rep. William Clay (D-Mo), who chairs the Education and Labor Subcommittee on Labor-Management Relations; and Rep. Austin Murphy (D-Pa), who chairs the Education and Labor Subcommittee on Labor Standards. Witnesses testifying in support of the bill included representatives from the United Mine Workers and The Association of Junior Leagues, Inc. Among those testifying at the hearing were Sheila B. Kamerman and Alfred J. Kahn, professors at the Columbia University School of Social Work; Wendy Williams, an associate professor of law at the Georgetown University Law Center; and Dr. T. Berry Brazelton, Associate Professor of Pediatrics at Harvard Medical School. (An interview with Brazelton appears in the Appendix.)

Additional hearings were anticipated in the spring of 1986.

Full text of the bill appears in the Appendix. For further discussion of the issue of parental leave in general and some specific corporate initiatives, see Chapter IV, Section D.

Sen. Daniel Patrick Moynihan (D-NY) indicated that he would be an original co-sponsor in the Senate of legislation similar to Rep. Schroeder's, according to a Moynihan aide, who said the Senator planned to introduce the legislation by the end of March 1986.

Child Care Opportunities for Families Act of 1985

On June 25, 1985, Rep. George Miller (D-Calif), chairman of the House Select Committee on Children, Youth, and Families introduced HR 2867, a bill to increase the supply, and upgrade the quality, of child care by encouraging joint federal, state, and private sector efforts.

HR 2867 was referred to the Ways and Means, and Education and Labor Committees. As of February 1986, the measure had some 60 co-sponsors.

The Select Committee held extensive hearings in 1984 on the availability and quality of child care in the United States. For millions of American families, child care is unavailable, too expensive, or too crowded, the committee concluded in its report, which was endorsed by every member of the Select Committee. For infants, and for families whose children have special needs, the situation is even worse, the Select Committee said.

Key features of the legislation are set forth below.

Upgrading State Standards

Child care regulatory and monitoring systems vary considerably from state to state and are in many cases outdated, the Select Committee found. The committee suggested that licensing and monitoring — of health and safety standards, staff-child ratios, staff qualifications and training, and group size — be addressed.

Section 201 of the bill would require states to establish advisory committees to review state laws, regulations, and procedures for licensing, regulating, and monitoring child care services in both family day care and center-based settings. A National Advisory Committee also would be established to develop and propose model child care standards.

The section would make available $50 million in incentive grants to assist states in improving child care regulatory and monitoring systems.

Expanding Private Sector Initiatives

Section 301 would provide $10 million for a demonstration program of grants to local private non-profit organizations, on a matching basis, to expand child care services in the community by establishing a Community Child Care Fund, in partnership with private for-profit businesses. Non-profit organizations receiving federal funds would have to provide assurances that not less than 50 percent of the required match would come from the for-profit business sector. The funds would help low-income families pay for child care, and would serve as seed money for new child care facilities.

Training Child Care Personnel

Knowing that well-trained providers are caring for their children is most important to working parents, maintained Select Committee Chairman George

Miller (D-Calif). "Yet, only 24 states require the director of a day care center to have had specific course work in child development and only eight states require caregivers in group day care homes and day care centers to have had training in child care," Miller said in a statement.

Section 401 of the bill would continue current financial assistance to states for child development and child abuse prevention training, and for training of child care providers, state licensing and enforcement officials, and parents. Current funding, begun in 1984, would be expanded from $25 million to $50 million.

> "[O]nly 24 states require the director of a day care center to have had specific course work in child development and only eight states require caregivers in group day care homes and day care centers to have had training in child care."

"By conservative estimates, there are between seven and eight million children who are cared for in child care centers or family day care homes. Clearly, more trained professionals are needed," Miller said.

Section 403 would authorize $10 million in grants to institutions of higher education to be used to prepare students for careers in early childhood education and development.

Family day care accounts for at least two-thirds of all out-of-home child care in this country, Rep. Miller noted. Only 11 states require any training for family day care workers, and funding reductions have severely limited the little training and outreach that is available. Section 404 would direct $10 million to states to train family day care providers, to train those who train providers, and to make available the necessary technical assistance to improve the quality level of care offered in family day care homes.

The proposed legislation also would increase the incentive for Aid for Dependent Children recipients to seek work or training and would provide more choices for better child care.

Senate Child Care Initiatives

A package of bills (S 805-810), similar to Rep. Miller's, was introduced in the Senate March 28, 1985, by Sens. Alan Cranston (D-Calif), Dennis DeConcini (D-Ariz), Christopher Dodd (D-Conn), Gary Hart (D-Colo), Edward Kennedy (D-Mass), and Donald Riegle (D-Mich):

• S 803 would provide for an additional $300 million for child care services and training programs through the Social Services Block Grant Program under Title XX of the Social Security Act.

• S 804 would establish a $1.5 million scholarship fund to assist low-income individuals seeking to acquire a Child Development Associate (CDA) credential.

• S 805 would authorize $15 million a year for a child care demonstration program for public housing projects.

• S 806 would increase from $20 million to $30 million a year the appropriation for the dependent care block grant program and remove the prohibition against using funds from that program for operating expenses for school-age child care programs and child care information.

• S 807 would authorize $10 million to establish a resource program to provide training, technical assistance, and other support services to family day care providers.

• S 808 would authorize $50 million to establish a new grant program under the Elementary and Secondary Education Act to support child-care programs for four-

and five-year-old children in public school settings.

• S 809 would authorize $75 million to provide for students, particularly low-income students, through the Higher Education Act.

• S 810 was passed by the Senate, but died in conference. According to Sen. Cranston, who introduced S 810, the measure derives from provisions of the Child Care Assistance Act of 1985 (S 4), which he first introduced in 1979. Cranston noted that his support for S 803-810 "does not represent any lessening of conviction on my part that the comprehensive approach represented by S 4 is much needed . . . . Rather, I am proceeding with smaller initiatives in recognition of the reality of the budget problem confronting us and in order to help widen the base of support for legislation dealing with child care issues."

New Senate Family Committee

Contending that the problems of American families and children need to be more systematically addressed, Sens. Moynihan and Jeremiah Denton (R-Ala) introduced legislation on Feb. 3, 1986, to create a Senate Special Committee on Families, Youth, and Children. SRes 330 was referred to the Committee on Rules.

Like the House Special Committee, which has monitored family and children issues since 1982, the proposed Senate committee would have no legislative authority.

According to Moynihan's office, the committee would analyze the effect of government policies on the nation's families and children through hearings and research; evaluate the economic status of families and children; and issue an annual report. Currently, these responsibilities are divided among several Senate committees and subcommittees. The senators feel, said a Moynihan staff aide, that this division of responsibility prevents the Senate from giving these important issues the attention they deserve. The aide added the committee should be formed because so many government policies have an impact on families and children.

"The Senate needs an official focal point to study, evaluate, and provide oversight for the entire range of problems and government policies that affect families and children," Moynihan said. "This special committee will not solve the problems of childhood poverty and the growth of single-parent families, but it will help us better understand them."

The Senate Special Committee would have 11 members, six from the majority party and five from the minority. The chairman and members would be appointed on recommendation by the Senate Majority and Minority Leaders.

Title XX of the Social Security Act

HR 798, introduced by Rep. Barbara B. Kennelly (D-Conn), would provide for greater access to affordable child care though direct federal grants to the states and the establishment of a national resource center on child care, according to the Congressional Caucus for Women's Issues.

Title XX of the Social Security Act, established in 1974 to provide social services funding to states, is the principal source of dependent care funding, according to the Caucus. In 1981, Title XX funds were reduced from $2.9 billion to $2.4 billion for FY 1982 and the program was converted to a block grant, the Caucus noted in a May 14, 1985, report. Under a block grant program, states receive funds which then are allocated among the various authorized social service programs, the Caucus explained.

"In spite of the increasing need for child care services, 25 states spent less for child care in 1984 than they did in 1981, and 27 states served fewer children in 1984 than in 1981," the Caucus said.

HR 798 would increase the Title XX social services block grant authorization level from $2.7 billion to $3.42 billion, the approximate level at which Title XX would have been funded in 1985 had cutbacks not been instituted in 1981, according to the Caucus. Of these funds, $300 million is set aside for child care, the Caucus said.

The bill also provides $70 million for child care training and training for other human services staff, and $50 million for incentive grants to states to encourage implementation and enforcement of day care regulations published by the Department of Health, Education, and Welfare in 1980, the Caucus explained.

HR 798 is pending before the Ways and Means Committee.

*   *   *

B. STATE DEVELOPMENTS

This section contains a compendium of legislative proposals, administrative rules, laws, and collective bargaining agreements on work-and-family-related issues under consideration or enacted by 15 states: Arizona, California, Delaware, Hawaii, Illinois, Iowa, Maine, Maryland, Massachusetts, Michigan, Minnesota, New Jersey, New York, Pennsylvania, and Wisconsin. In this section are items relating to child care, maternity/paternity leave, parental leave, and alternative work patterns in both the public and private sector. State task force recommendations also are included.

Following are highlights of state developments:

• *Arizona:* A law passed in 1985 makes explicit that School District Governing Boards may contract for the operation of extended day resource programs on school property before or after school.

• *California:* A bill requiring employers to grant an unpaid leave of up to one year for child-rearing has been introduced.

• *Delaware:* A task force has made recommendations to deal with the problem of latchkey children.

• *Hawaii:* A Senate resolution orders a study on the effects of allowing working parents to take unpaid leave up to six months to care for newborn children.

• *Illinois:* A labor agreement covering state employees allows a year-long, unpaid family responsibility leave. A benefits program is intended to encourage the adoption of non-related children.

• *Iowa:* A report to the General Assembly makes 13 recommendations regarding assistance on child care and other work-and-family matters for parents of young children.

• *Maine:* Two bills introduced in early 1986 would encourage employers either to provide on-site child care or to subsidize child care benefits.

• *Maryland:* A law enacted in 1984 allows up to 30 days of earned sick leave as adoption leave for state employees. Another law enacted the same year allows a parent of school-age children to be absent from state service during the summer months.

• *Massachusetts:* A task force report leads to establishment of five child care resource and referral agencies serving parents, providers, and potential providers in the public and private sector, and establishment of at least 12 new child care facilities.

• *Michigan:* A task force makes recommendations on child care, and on a pilot child care center.

• *Minnesota:* A labor-management committee focuses on coordination of information regarding child care referral and educational services, and continues an examination into possible on-site child care.

• *New Jersey:* A 1985 allocation supports a statewide clearinghouse for child care information and referral.

• *New York:* In recent years, programs for state employees in flexible schedules, voluntary reduced work schedules, and worksite day care facilities have been expanded.

• *Pennsylvania:* Childbearing or adoption leave is available for up to six months for Commonwealth employees.

• *Wisconsin:* A 1985 Executive Order expands the employee assistance program to provide direct child care information and referral services.

ARIZONA

Legislation Enacted

After-School Programs

Introduced by a member of Governor Bruce Babbitt's 1984 School-Age Child Care Task Force, legislation enacted in 1985 (H.B. 2314), amended Arizona law to make explicit that School District Governing Boards may contract for the operation of extended day resource programs on school property before or after school for children of kindergarten age through grade eight. In his 1986 State of the State message, Babbitt noted that Arizona now has more than 100 new after-school programs.

Legislation Proposed

Maternity Leave

Babbitt's 1986 message proposed a legislated standard of at least 60 days maternity leave for every employee, public and private, in the state.

Child Care Tax Credit

As part of his 1986-87 budget, Babbitt proposed a $15 million child care tax credit — averaging $200 per family — as "an expression of Arizona's commitment to bring about quality day care for the children of working parents."

Latchkey Children Programs

The School-Age Child Care Task Force, established as a response to the "hidden problem of latch-key children," reviewed and assessed current school-age child care programs and encouraged the development of additional programs through public and private partnerships.

In his 1986 message, Babbitt endorsed the Department of Education's request of $100,000 to provide technical assistance and seed money for rural communities which do not currently have programs for latchkey children who return to empty homes after school.

Flexible Benefits

"Employers," the Governor said in his 1986 message, "need to recognize the growing number of working parents and design flexible benefit packages which allow employees more choices and include child care benefits among the options. To assert the State's leadership role, I am asking the Department of Administration to develop optional benefit packages for State personnel which can be presented to employees for comments in the fall of 1986."

Task Force Recommendation

Child Care Regulations

Babbitt's 1985 State of the State message focused on the condition of Arizona's children. That year, he established a task force to examine current child care licensing procedures and regulations, and to produce recommendations for reform that would upgrade programs. The final report of the task force was submitted to the Governor in December 1985. The task force's recommendations, endorsed by Babbitt in his 1986 message, include increasing the ratio of child care staff to children, more explicit program and personnel requirements, and training of child care providers.

Family Group Homes

Babbitt also agreed with the task force recommendation to establish a new category of child care facility — family group homes — to provide services for five to 10 children. He also called for a study of the feasibility of a resource and referral system for family day care homes. "This system will match voluntarily registered child care providers with those who desire child care in a family home setting. Providers who register will receive a variety of technical assistance for their programs," he said.

CALIFORNIA

Legislation Proposed

Parental Leave Bill

The Parents' Rights Act of 1985 (AB 613), introduced Feb. 7, 1985, by Assemblywoman Gwen Moore, would make it an unlawful employment practice for any employer of 15 or more individuals to refuse to grant an employee's reasonable request to take an unpaid leave of up to one year for child-rearing.

The employee would be permitted to utilize any accrued vacation or sick leave during this period. Leave could be granted to care for any minor dependent child of the employee, or any child for whom the employee is the legal guardian.

The proposed legislation provides that employees taking child-rearing leaves would continue to be eligible for health plans, retirement and pension plans, and supplemental unemployment benefit plans during the period of the leave. An employer may, however, require the employee to pay health and welfare benefit plan premiums during the period of leave.

The bill also would make it an unlawful employment practice to discharge, fire, suspend, expel, or discriminate against any individual who exercises the right to take such leave or who testifies in any inquiry related to the leave or the leave of another employee.

Following passage by the assembly in June, the proposal was referred to the State Senate Committee on Industrial Relations. No action had been taken by the time this report was published.

Resource and Referral

California is the only state that mandates its agencies to provide child care resource and referral services for the general public and state employees in each of the States 56 counties, according to Bess Manchester, referral coordinator for the California Child Care Resource and Referral Network. At least five other states have provided some funding for provision of the same services on a more limited basis., Manchester noted. In California, she added, the process began in 1976, but all the agencies were not operational until 1985.

State as Employer

Child Care

The 1984 collective bargaining agreements between the State of California and three unions representing state workers — the California State Employees' Association (CSEA), Communications Workers of America (CWA) and the California Association of Professional Scientists (CAPS) — called for establishment of a State Labor-Management Child Care Committee. The purpose of the committee was to encourage state employees to form non-profit corporations to provide child care services for their dependent children. A $1,000,000 Child Care Revolving Fund, administered by the Department of Personnel Administration (DPA), was established to assist the non-profit corporations in providing child care. The State Labor-Management Child Care Committee is responsible for development and proposal of criteria and processes for the operation of the program. In early 1985 DPA staff and the committee developed grant criteria, procedures for establishing non-profit corporations, and other information needed by employees wishing to establish child care centers.

To be eligible for funding, a group of interested employees must conduct a marketing/needs assessment and/or analysis which supports the establishment, expansion, or improvement of child care of the type proposed by their application.

As of Jan. 1, 1986, 46 applications had been sent out by the state to interested groups, according to the Department of Personnel Administration. Five have been approved and grants issued. Three of the grants are for new centers and would create 151 new spaces. Two of the grants were made under provisions aimed at improving standards (emergency restroom restoration and upgrading of playground equipment).

DELAWARE

Executive Action

Delaware's Commission on Work and the Family was created by House Joint Resolution No. 6 which was signed by the Governor on April 18, 1985. At its first meeting in July 1985, the Commission established task forces on:
(1) employee benefits/personnel policies;
(2) the state's role in child day care;
(3) tax and finance;
(4) information and referral;
(5) latchkey children;
(6) special needs.

The employee benefits/personnel policies task force is working on:
• A survey of state employees — similar to that conducted by E.I. Du Pont de Nemours, Inc., of its employees — regarding the need for employer support for working families;
• A survey of current employee benefits provided by all Delaware employers. This survey, which was sent to all large employers plus a sample of small businesses, also will measure business attitudes about adding various employee benefits in the future.
• A matrix of various options, in addition to on-site child care, that employers in Delaware and elsewhere now have to help working families to include all known programs currently existing in Delaware as well as national models.

The task force on the state's role in child day care will be reviewing proposed new day care center regulations and proposed legislation on licensing of day care centers.

The tax and finance task force has been investigating how the state's Development Office might educate businesses about incentives to offer child care options and might help businesses take advantage of those incentives, and whether full-day kindergarten should be implemented. The task force also is examining the issues of business licenses, and zoning and deed restrictions. Quality of care and insurance costs also will be studied.

The information and referral task force has decided that child care information and referral should be provided on a statewide basis, and is considering the implementation of this decision in Kent and Sussex Counties. Recently the service become available in New Castle County under the auspices of the United Way. The major funding source for this new service — called the Child Care Connection —is the Du Pont Company, although other organizations and businesses are being asked to contribute.

Latchkey Children

The task force on latchkey children has drafted the following 10 recommendations:

• All local school districts should consider furnishing transportation to children to get to child care programs after school at child care programs.

• Phone numbers and addresses of child care providers should be given to school district personnel and to elementary schools.

• Local school districts should determine through their PTAs and other appropriate committees the need for before- and after-school programs.

• Some $200,00 to $300,000 should be made available through grant-in-aid funds to each of the 16 school districts statewide for the development of latchkey programs in their respective districts.

• A partnership between corporations and private non-profit agencies should be encouraged to sponsor before- and after-school programs.

• A statewide, computerized information network needs to be developed on before- and after-school child care programs.

• The task force should review the need for guidelines/regulations for before- and after-school programs.

• A before- and after-school statewide conference sponsored by the Department of Public Instruction (DPI) and the Department of Services to Children, Youth and Their Families should be held in May 1986 to begin a dialogue and draw public attention to latchkey issues.

• A statewide feasibility study needs to be funded to examine the extent of need for latchkey services by the DPI.

• A mandatory full-day kindergarten program should be introduced legislatively.

The task force will examine the problems of children with special needs with regard to day care and the workplace. To assess the situation, the task force is surveying some 2,000 parents of such children in the state's special schools in early 1986.

HAWAII

Legislation Proposed

Parental Leave

In 1985, a bill was proposed in the Hawaii Senate to allow parents time off from work to build closer bonds with their infants. Although the bill did not make it out of committee, the Senate passed a resolution (SR 102) requiring the Department of Labor and Industrial Relations and the Office of Collective Bargaining to study the effects of legislation that would allow working parents to take unpaid leave of up to six months to care for newborn children.

State as Employer

In Hawaii there are no existing statutes that require employers to provide parenting leaves to employees. State government employees, by administrative rule, may be granted up to one year of child care leave without pay.

ILLINOIS

State as Employer

Parental Leave

A variety of parental leave programs are available. Under both the Rules of Personnel and the labor agreements with the American Federation of State, County and Municipal Employees, there is a provision for a year-long, unpaid family responsibility leave.

Family responsibility leave may be granted:

• to provide nursing and/or custodial care for the employee's infant, whether natural born or adopted;

• to care for a temporarily disabled, incapacitated or bedridden resident of the employee's household or member of the employee's family;

• to furnish special guidance, care or supervision of a resident of the employee's household or a member of the employee's family in extraordinary need thereof;

• to respond to the temporary dislocation of the family due to a natural disaster, crime, insurrection, war or other disruptive event;

• to settle the estate of a deceased member of the employee's family or to act as conservator if so appointed, providing the exercise of such functions precludes the employee from working; or

• to perform family responsibilities not otherwise specified.

Illinois also provides disability leave for employees in connection with maternity, if requested.

Child Care

In October 1985, Gov. James R. Thompson signed House Bill 2002, which allows state agencies to contract with day care providers for services on state property. The day care services will be paid for by the employees who use them. The state will subsidize the effort by providing free rental, utilities, and equipment. The Illinois Department of Central Management Services (CMS) says it is in the process of formulating rules for implementation of the program.

The first contract for day care has been let, with service scheduled to begin Feb. 18, 1986, CMS says. This facility is located in the new Illinois Department of Revenue Building in Springfield and will care for approximately 60 children between the ages of two and five. Selection of children eligible for day care will be done by lottery among the employees of the Department of Revenue.

A survey has been completed in Chicago on the need for day care services of employees based in the new State of Illinois Center. Illinois hopes to make this project a joint venture with the private sector.

Adoption Benefit Program

In a Dec. 12, 1985, memo to state employees, the Illinois CMS stated, "The goal of the Adoption Benefit Program is to provide an incentive for State of Illinois employees to adopt non-related children."

The program, which will not apply to the adoption of stepchildren or children related to either parent, includes a $1,500 reimbursement for the adoption of a difficult to place "special needs" child. This includes certain minority children, children with mental, physical or emotional disabilities, and brothers and sisters who need to be adopted together.

There is a $1,000 reimbursement for the adoption of other children.

The program provides an opportunity to cover the adopted child under the state's Group Health Insurance Program once the employee has custody of the child. Effective Nov. 15, 1985, pre-existing conditions will be waived as of the date the employee assumes custody of the child awaiting formal adoption as long as the state employee already has family coverage. New families who switch to family coverage when they assume custody will also be covered, but the insurance provider's liability for pre-existing conditions of the adopted children will be a maximum of $50,000 for the first six months.

Following are some of the expenses for which employees may be reimbursed under the program: legal fees; court fees; adoption agency fees, including foreign adoption fees, fees for initial immunization for the child, and transportation costs to bring the child to the adopting parents.

For an employee to file for reimbursement under this program, the adoption must be final. A certified adoption decree from a court in the United States, along with all itemized bills and receipts for eligible expenses, must be provided to the Illinois Department of Central Management Services, Group Insurance Division to complete the filing process.

Alternative Work Patterns

Illinois, for almost ten years, has fostered various programs to provide alternative work patterns for state employees.

IOWA

State as Employer

In a report to the Iowa General Assembly completed in November 1985, the state Merit Employment Department (MED) reviewed the state's various employment policies regarding assistance on child care and other forms of assistance for parents of young children.

Maternity/Paternity Leave

Sick leave with pay may be used by an employee who is medically disabled due to childbirth and recovery. In most situations this amounts to six weeks of paid sick leave.

Employees who are covered by collective bargaining contracts are subject to a sick leave policy issued by the Office of Employment Relations in 1984. This policy considers an employee "disabled up to 15 working days after the birth of the child" and a physician's statement is necessary to continue the use of sick leave beyond this. There are no similar policies for non-contractual employees. In addition to the use of sick leave, all employees can request use of accrued vacation leave or an unpaid leave of absence for maternity/paternity leave.

Leaves of absence are administered somewhat differently for contractual and non-contractual employees. Women covered by a collective bargaining agreement can use six months of leave without pay, with a potential six-month extension, for maternity purposes only. Employees may also request up to one year of leave without pay for any purpose, including parenting matters. Non-contractual employees are eligible for a one-year leave of absence with a potential one-year extension. These employees may take a leave of absence for any reason, as long as the employer agrees. Any employee on leave of absence has a right to return to a vacant position in the same job class they were in before leave, and, if this is not available, to a job class at the same pay grade. If none is available, then layoff policies and procedures go into effect.

Child Care

According to the MED report, the Iowa Department of Transportation (DOT) has been successful in providing on-site child care for its employees and recommends expansion of the program. The department's experience provides a model for other state agencies.

In 1983, a DOT committee studied the possibility of an on-site child day care center for its employees (i.e., the care providers would be state employees, and state facilities would be used), but rejected the idea because of high costs. Subsequently, a committee of DOT volunteers suggested, and implemented, a simpler program: provide the space and contract with a non-profit child care provider for services. DOT gives rent-free space to the child care provider, and is responsible for finding the space and paying for utility costs, janitorial services, and routine building maintenance. The cost to DOT is approximately $8,000 a year. Another $9,000 was spent initially to bring the selected building into compliance as a child care center. (Wiring, plumbing, and other work in the 1930s building had to be brought up to current fire code standards.) This expense was subsidized with 4,000 hours of volunteer labor and donated materials.

In 1984, DOT's on-site child care center opened with a program for school-age children. Pre-school and infant programs were phased in next, and a toddler program was begun March 1985. The child care provider charges parents fees according to a sliding scale based on the income of the parent(s).

The DOT's experience with on-site child care provides a case study for state government, the report concluded.

Adoption Leave

The state's collective bargaining contracts with the American Federation of State, County and Municipal Employees (AFSCME) allow up to five days of paid sick leave to be used during adoption. Non-contract employees are not provided similar leave, but can take annual leave and request a leave of absence (non-paid) for adoption purposes.

Using accrued annual leave to take care of matters associated with adoption prior to the child being received is also permitted.

Temporary Care

Iowa Code Ch. 79 establishes the sick leave usage policy for state employees. It does not provide for the use of sick leave when temporary care of a family members is needed, the report noted. "Therefore, current policies, collective bargaining agreements, and rules concerning this application of sick leave may have gone beyond the scope of law," the report noted in urging revision of the Code.

Research, the MED report said, shows that, in 21 other states, government employers allow the use of accrued sick leave to care for ill children. Of these, 11 states do not limit the use of sick leave for this purpose. The remaining 10 states limit this leave to five or six days per year.

Alternative Work Schedules

The state permits workers to establish alternative work schedules. Two types of arrangements are possible:

• Job Sharing: While job-sharing arrangements are currently an option in Iowa State government, very few have been created. Research, the report said, shows that while, nationwide, the trend seems to be to provide such a workplace alternative (28 states, a growing number of school districts and private employers, particularly banks, offer this option), Iowa employees have exhibited little interest.

• Flextime: The flextime policy for all executive branch state employees was established by Executive Order No. 25, signed by Gov. Robert D. Ray (R) in 1977. Basically, flextime allows employees to schedule an eight-hour workday between the hours of 6:00 a.m. and 6:00 p.m., with approval of the supervisor. Each agency must determine for itself where flextime is not appropriate within the organization. Most departments allow flextime for employees as long as operations are not adversely affected.

Compressed workweeks also may be arranged.

Recommendations

The Iowa Merit Employment Department concluded its report with the following recommendations for state action:

(1) Take no action at this time to create on-site child care centers because of the state's current economic condition.

(2) Continue the work of the committee currently researching benefits alternatives for the Governor's Management Advisory Council, and for the Merit Employment Department to use that research to develop a flexible benefits plan for state employees.

(3) Modify the current payroll system to accommodate a flexible benefits approach. When this is completed, a flexible plan with child care options should be implemented for all state employees.

(4) Establish a benefits manager position in the Merit Employment Department to provide continuing benefits planning, coordination, and evaluation.

(5) Revise Iowa Code Chapter 79.1 to include temporary care of family members as a use of paid sick leave.

(6) Revise Iowa Code Chapter 79.1 to allow adoptive parents to use up to six weeks of accrued sick leave following the adoption of a child.

(7) Revise Iowa Code Chapter 79.1 to allow fathers to use up to six weeks of accrued sick leave following the birth of a child.

(8) Promote awareness of alternative work arrangements through the *Personnel In Perspective* newsletter, the development of informational pamphlets, and supervisory and management training courses offered by the Iowa Management Training System, all to be coordinated by the Merit Employment Department.

(9) Publicize, through the *Personnel In Perspective* newsletter, the availability of information concerning existing child care homes and centers.

(10) Conduct a needs assessment to determine employee interest in lunchtime parenting education seminars, and, if sufficient interest is shown, determine a method of providing this service to employees.

(11) Conduct a needs assessment during FY87 to evaluate the need for resource and referral services, and if sufficient interest is shown, develop a package to be funded by the Seventy-second General Assembly.

MAINE

Legislation Proposed

Child Care

Two bills under consideration by the Maine legislature in 1986 would encourage employers either to provide on-site child care or to subsidize child care benefits.

State Sen. Nancy Clark, a sponsor of both bills, told BNA in February 1986 that, although the bills will be rewritten, their basic provisions are likely to survive intact.

One bill (LD 1864) would provide credits against state corporate income taxes to employers that provide on-site child care services to employees or that subsidize off-site care. The credit granted to employers would be the lowest of $2,000, or 20 percent of the costs incurred in providing day care services, or $50 per child enrolled.

Another bill (LD 1907) would mandate employers using public funds for certain purposes to build on-site child care facilities. Any worksite receiving at least $200,000 in state funds or state-administered federal funds for new construction, expansion, or renovation would be required to submit a policy for on-site child care facilities to the state Office of Child Care Coordination.

The bill also would establish a grant program through which the state child care office would award municipalities, school departments, government agencies, or non-profit organizations funds to set up pilot programs "to address the needs of before-school and after-school care of children between the ages of 4 and 15 years."

Executive Action

Child Care Task Force

A November 1984 report from the Maine Child Care Task Force predicted that by 1990 more than 57 percent of all mothers of children under six years old in Maine would be employed, and that 67 percent of all two-parent families in the state would have both parents in the work force by 1990.

Some 25,000 Maine children five to 12 years old spend some time caring for themselves each week, according to the task force report. As of November 1984, the task force noted, there were 16,063 child care slots in registered and licensed homes, but 54,000 of Maine's children under 13 live in households in which all adults work full time.

MARYLAND

State as Employer

Family-Oriented Personnel Policies Task Force

In 1983 the Maryland Commission for Women created a Task Force on Family-Oriented Personnel Policies. The Task Force was chartered to examine the state's personnel policies to determine the effects of the state's laws and policies on state employees and their families. Areas addressed by the task force are part-time employment, flexible scheduling, job sharing, sick leave/family leave, parental/adoption leave, telephone access, break-in-service policies, dependent care, and flexible benefit packages.

Analysis of a survey of state employees in 1985 yielded the following preliminary data:

• Nearly one-quarter of the surveyed employees said they have flextime programs in their offices.

• Seven percent had requested part-time work. Of those, 54 percent had their request approved.

• Sixteen percent had used leave at the time of the birth or adoption of a child in the past five years.

Adoption Leave

The Task force also monitored implementation of the Adoption Leave Law, which went into effect in July 1984. This law allows an employee who is the primarily care giver of an adopted child to request approval to use up to 30 days of earned sick leave as adoption leave.

The Task Force also supported legislation in the 1985 Maryland General Assembly to provide parental leave for state employees. That legislation, however, was rejected.

Seasonal Leave

In 1984 Maryland enacted procedures under which state employees may be granted an extended leave of absence without pay. "While a principal purpose of this program is to allow a parent of school age children to be absent from state service during the summer months, the program is in no way restricted as to the time of year or the employee's reason for making the request," the law provides. Seasonal leave may be granted for up to 12 weeks.

Executive Action

Private Sector Day Care Initiatives Task Force

The Governor's Private Sector Day Care Initiatives Task Force is reviewing and, as appropriate, will recommend creative, private sector-based policies to increase the availability of day care for families in need of such services.

MASSACHUSETTS

Executive Action

Child Care

"We have made corporate child care, in addition to publicly supported and financed child care, an essential part of what this state is all about," declared Massachusetts Gov. Michael S. Dukakis in a November 1985 conference in Boston on Women at the Workplace.

In February 1984, Dukakis recruited day care providers, employers, government leaders, and others to serve on the Governor's Day Care Partnership Project. The group's mission was to develop policy recommendations aimed at improving the state's day care delivery system.

In its final report, delivered in January 1985, the Partnership Project concluded that the state's unmet need for child care had reached crisis proportions due to rapid changes in household and work force composition, and recommended:

• establishing a statewide network of resource and referral centers;

• having state government serve as a model employer through establishment of on-site day care centers for state workers; and

• creating a program to stimulate private sector sponsorship of day care and to provide technical assistance to corporate sponsors.

During 1985, under leadership of the Executive Office of Economic Affairs, all of these recommendations took shape. Five Child Care Resource and Referral agencies across the state now serve parents, providers, and potential providers from the public and private sectors.

According to Patricia Cronin, special assistant to Secretary of Economic Affairs

Evelyn Murphy, a new day care center for state workers will open in 1986. One previously was opened in late 1983. Four more centers for state employees outside of Boston are planned for the future, she added.

But it is the Corporate Day Care Program which the Dukakis administration seems to consider its greatest accomplishment in the day care arena. At the gathering last November, Dukakis credited the program with playing a role in establishment in 1985 of at least 12 new child care facilities serving more than 400 children "which are being financed, supported and managed by businesses."

The Corporate Day Care Program's role varies considerably from project to project. It has become, in a little more than one year, a force stimulating and informing corporate decisionmaking on child care as an employee benefit.

Cronin explained that the program acts as liaison between business and state regulatory agencies, primarily the Office for Children, which sets standards for day care licensure. It provides technical assistance in selection and implementation of day care options. It also develops seminars designed to inform human resource managers about employer-sponsored day care. And it collects data on child care options, employer incentives, and child care availability in Massachusetts.

Typically, reported Cronin, the initial step is to send an interested employer an information packet that presents the case for corporate day care assistance; outlines costs, advantages, and tax implications of child care as an employee benefit; provides examples of options such as on-site and near-site centers, voucher systems, resource and referral services, and parenting seminars; and offers an extensive bibliography and directory of day care resources in the state. The packet includes case studies of union-sponsored, company-sponsored, and combined labor-management day care projects.

Boston Bar Association Program

On a limited basis, the program will also provide consulting services to organizations that have already identified specific needs. For example, a consultant is "on loan" to the Day Care Committee of the Boston Bar Association, Cronin said.

The committee was formed in 1983 to explore the possibility of establishing a downtown day care center to serve the needs of attorneys working in law firms, corporate legal departments, and federal and state offices. Committee members represent several professional legal groups, in addition to the Boston Bar Association.

Emily Maitin, an attorney with Sullivan & Worcester and mother of a two-year-old, is the Massachusetts Women's Bar Association representative on the committee. She said the consultant from the Corporate Day Care Program has become vital to the committee's effort since she began working with them in the fall of 1985. The consultant has met with committee members about four times, Maitin noted.

With the consultant's assistance in preparing a proposal, Maitin said, the committee will begin preliminary fund-raising efforts this spring. The attorneys' immediate goal is to obtain at least $12,000 from their respective professional groups — the Massachusetts Association of Women Lawyers, the Massachusetts Bar Foundation, the Boston Bar Association, the Massachusetts Women's Bar Association, and others — to finance a site search and major fund-raising campaign.

Maitin said the committee anticipates it will need about $190,000 to finance start-up costs for a center that will serve around 35 children initially and have the potential to expand later. It has identified a few potential sites and expects to further use the Corporate Day Care Program consultant's service in completing its site search, she said.

Parental Leave Study

A study commission on parental leave was approved by the legislature in 1985, according to Joan Quinlan, the governor's advisor on women's issues. The study will focus on both the private and public sectors, she said. If the measure receives the necessary technical reauthorization from the legislature in 1986, the commission would be expected to report on its recommendations in December 1986, said Quinlan.

MICHIGAN

Legislation Proposed

Parental Leave

Parental leave legislation is currently in the draft stage and was scheduled to be ready for introduction to the state legislature in early February 1986. The draft calls for a 60-day period of paid leave for the birth, adoption, or serious illness of a child, and calls for up to 120 working days of unpaid leave during which individuals would be able to return to their current jobs or comparable jobs, and would continue to accrue seniority for the purposes of retirement and other benefits. Such a leave could not be taken more than once every two years.

Executive Action

Child Care Provisions

The Michigan Women's Commission, according to the State Executive Office, made the following recommendations following a five-year task force study:

(1) Identify all agencies, departments, and committees that are presently involved in child care and assist them in coordinating their efforts.

(2) Bring to the child care industry uniformity in licensing provisions.

(3) Address the issue of availability.

(4) Promote coordinated employer, union and other private sector of involvement in the provision of child care services.

(5) Investigate tax incentives and other means of directing resources into the industry.

(6) Develop training and other support services for child care providers/givers.

(7) Research and publish child care information and provide referral materials.

(8) Develop an outreach program to eligible people in order to utilize existing subsidies.

At Governor James J. Blanchard's instigation, a pilot day care program has been established for children of state employees, the Michigan Legislature, and the Lansing school system. A contract was signed with the Lansing Public Schools to establish the child care center, which opened Nov. 15, 1985.

The center, EC3-Educational Child Care Center, is housed on the grounds of the Michigan School for the Blind in the Nandy Cottage in Lansing. The staff has been hired and the Center is accepting applications for admission for youngsters two and one-half to five years of age. The Center also is accepting names of families with infants so that when the second "classroom" is opened it can serve children younger than two and one-half years old. The Center is able to serve up to 100 children, but the numbers and services will depend on demand.

State as Employer

Alternative Work Patterns

Alternative work patterns have long been a part of state employment. Because of the U.S. Supreme Court's ruling in *Garcia v. San Antonio Metropolitan Transit Authority*, in which the Court held that the minimum wage and overtime requirements of the Fair Labor Standards Act (FLSA) applied to state and local government, the state changed its policy on flextime for individuals working more than a 40-hour week. Many state employees were surprised when they received notice in mid-July that their flextime arrangements were canceled as of July 28, 1985. Specifically, work schedules which permit employees working more than 40 hours of work one week to earn one day off the following week were suspended indefinitely.

Those employees covered by FLSA now must be provided premium pay for all hours worked in excess of 40 in a week. Most employees working a flextime schedule worked a schedule of 44 hours in one week and 36 in the next to get 4 hours off the second week. Under that schedule, the employer would owe the employee four hours of overtime pay for the first week. After *Garcia*, flextime simply proved to be too expensive for most departments.

With the November 1985 signing by President Reagan of legislation amending the federal law with regard to FLSA coverage of state and local government workers, states were off the hook — for the most part — from *Garcia*. Each department now has the discretion of settings its own arrangements. The state has shown its support for flexible work hours and some departments still permit flextime. It is important to point out that departments are bound by negotiated agreements with unions for employees that are covered by these agreements.

Job Sharing

There is a joint policy issued by the Department of Management and Budget and the Department of Civil Service that permits job sharing in agencies where two or more employees can work part-time and share one full-time position. This policy is presently being debated throughout state government as to effectiveness, productivity, and cost.

MINNESOTA

Legislation Enacted

Adoption Leave

In 1983 Minnesota required employers to grant the same leave benefit to adoptive fathers and mothers as that granted to biological fathers and mothers. "The minimum period of this time off shall be four weeks, or, if the employer has an established policy of time off for a biological parent which sets a period of time off of less than four weeks, that period of time shall be the minimum period for an adoptive parent," the law reads. Employers may not penalize an employee for requesting the adoption leave (Minn. Stats., Ch. 181.92).

Minnesota law also requires that insurance companies provide the same health and life insurance coverage for adopted and biological children.

Legislation Proposed

In April 1985, a bill (HF No. 1620, SF No. 1777) requiring employers to grant one year of unpaid leave to biological and adoptive parents requesting such leave was introduced in the state legislature.

State as Employer

Parental Leave

Parental leave is a term and condition of employment addressed in each of the collective bargaining agreements and in policies covering non-represented employees. All, however, contain similar provisions:

(1) A female employee must be granted sick leave, up to the amount she has accrued, for the period of time that the employee is physically unable to work because of pregnancy or childbirth.

(2) Up to three days of sick leave may be used during the birth or adoption of an employee's child — basically, paid paternity and adoptive leave.

(3) Unpaid leaves of absence up to six months in duration are required to be granted when requested by a parent in conjunction with birth or adoption. This leave may be extended up to one year upon mutual consent.

Thus, pregnancy is treated the same as any other health-related "disability" for purposes of sick leave use while the employee is unable to work. Adoptive and birth parents, as well as male and female parents, are treated alike for the other provisions.

Child Care

Under the auspices of a Labor-Management Committee on Child Care, a survey was conducted in 1985 to gather employee views about additional child care services and/or benefits, according to Minnesota's Department of Employee Relations.

No specific programs or benefits resulted during the recently concluded labor negotiations. However, a labor-management committee continues to be active during this contract period, which covers July 1, 1985, through June 30, 1987. A major focus will be coordination of information regarding child care referral and educational services and continuing an investigation into possible on-site child care.

Alternative Work Patterns

Minnesota offers flexible scheduling when it is mutually agreeable between the individual and his/her appointing authority. The flextime program was originally created by Executive Order of the Governor. "It is now continued in our union contracts," explained Department of Employee Relations Commissioner Nina Rothchild.

Minnesota's job-sharing program was enacted legislatively; it provides that 50 positions may be allocated as job-share positions. Originally a pilot program, it is now a permanent part of state government.

Some of the impetus for job sharing has lessened, as Minnesota now provides pro-rata benefits to permanent part-time employees. Until 1983, employees who worked less than three-quarters time did not receive any state contribution towards health or life insurance benefits. Now, benefits are provided on a pro-rata basis if the employee works at least one-half time and for at least nine months of the year, said Rothchild.

Executive Action

Family Task Force

A Governor's Council on Children, Youth, and Families has been created and is reviewing many areas affecting families.

NEW JERSEY

Executive Action

Employer-Supported Child Care

New Jersey has conducted since 1982 a vigorous program to encourage public-private partnerships in an effort to expand employer-supported child care programs and resources in the state, according to the New Jersey Department of Human Services, Division of Youth and Family Services.

In November 1982, Governor Thomas H. Kean convened a conference of business executives to encourage new employer-supported child care resources and to emphasize the important role of the corporate sector in the provision of child care as a means of helping New Jersey's economy.

At the same time, Gov. Kean named Division of Youth and Family Services (DYFS) Assistant Director Nicholas R. Scalera as the Governor's Liaison on Employer-Supported Child Care. Scalera functions as a one-stop information resource to New Jersey employers.

Since then, Scalera, staff of the Division of Youth and Family Services and the Division on Women, and volunteers from the child care community have traveled the state, promoting the role of employers in child care services and providing information and technical assistance on employers' various child care program options.

The Governor's Liaison has developed and distributed informational packets on employer-supported child care. The packets outline the various child care options available and describe in detail the services of the state government to help employers establish child care programs.

In 1982, there were some seven employer-sponsored or -supported child care programs in New Jersey; as of Dec. 9, 1985, that number had grown to 55 —an increase of almost 700 percent since 1982.

In New Jersey, a number of businesses/employers offer child care programs at the site of the workplace and open those programs only to the children of employees. Others provide programs off-site, near (but not on the grounds of) the worksite. Where a sufficient number of slots are available, other employers open their programs to families from the community as well as to employees. One center in downtown Newark, serving 100 children, is supported by five major Newark corporations which provided start-up costs for the center.

The Governor's Liaison maintains and makes available regularly updated listings of licensed employer-sponsored or -supported child care centers statewide.

The DYFS Bureau of Licensing, which licenses and regulates child care centers, conducts preliminary courtesy inspections to look at the prospective facilities and to give employers estimates on what may be required to meet state life-safety, physical facility, and licensing requirements.

Statewide Child Care Initiatives

The Department of Human Services allocated $1.5 million in fiscal year 1985 for child care expansion and improvement. Of this, $400,000 has been targeted for the development of a statewide clearinghouse for child care information and three regional child care resource centers for information and referral. The purpose of the new child care initiatives is to develop a comprehensive statewide system for providing information and referral on child care services to individuals and/or public and private agencies seeking such services, and to provide technical assistance to child care providers and other interested parties in developing child care programs.

The Statewide Clearinghouse for Child Care Information will function as a comprehensive, up-to-date computerized data bank of all available child care in New Jersey, including center- and home-based care for infants, preschoolers, and school age children, with listings for before and/or after school and summer camp.

The Regional Resource Centers for Information and Referral will utilize the information provided by the Statewide Clearinghouse to advise consumers of available child care to meet their needs. In addition, the Resource Centers will:

• provide information to parents on how to choose a child care program;

• collect and make available to child care providers and other interested parties information on all available child care training; and

• provide technical assistance to potential child care providers to assist them through the licensing process and/or the initial stages of their program development.

State as Employer

Child Care Project

In his Annual Message to the New Jersey Legislature in January 1985, Gov. Kean directed the Department of Human Services to establish a state-sponsored pilot child care center on site at one of the Department's facilities to serve the State employees at that facility. The center, which is expected to begin operating in 1986, will be located on the grounds of the North Princeton Developmental Center, an institutional facility in Skillman, N.J., that is run by the Department's Division of Developmental Disabilities and has about 1,000 state employees.

The center will serve a maximum of 30 children, including both infants/toddlers (children younger than 2½ years of age) and pre-schoolers (children between two and one-half and five years of age). The project will be financed primarily by Department of Human Services funds and by employee fees, which will be based on a sliding scale tied to employee salaries and the number of children in an employee's family who are enrolled in the program. The program is initially planned to accommodate employees who work primarily during the daytime hours, with possible extension to include other shifts.

The pilot center is the first such child care benefit for state employees in New Jersey (except for employees in state universities and colleges, most of which sponsor or support child care centers for their employees' children). The pilot project was developed by the Department of Human Services working in conjunction with the Governor's Office of Employee Relations, the Division on Women, the Department of Treasury, the three employee unions representing state employees at that facility, and advocates and professionals from the child care community, including the State Child Care Advisory Council.

If the program is successful, it could prompt the development of similar and other options to benefit the employees of other state departments and agencies, the Department of Human Services says.

NEW YORK

State as Employer

New York is becoming a leader among employers nationwide in the testing and development of innovative human resource concepts affecting employees and their families, according to state officials.

"When compared with the private sector's far more conservative attempts, New York State's accomplishments are indeed unique," Ronald L. Tarwater, assistant director of the Governor's Office of Employee Relations, told BNA. "Measured against the efforts of comparable public sector employers," he said, "the state is still a standout for the extent to which it has been willing and able to break new ground."

In addition to flextime, furlough, and day care programs, New York has a phased retirement program for state employees and a "take-the-summer-off" program to ease child care costs and create more summer jobs for area residents.

New York's innovations in employee relations policies and programs assume added significance in light of Gov. Mario M. Cuomo's widely publicized emphasis on the "Family of New York." In the employee system over which he presides, the analogy Cuomo draws between family ties and those that bind the body politic seems to have found its most eloquent expression, Tarwater explained. "The fact that New York State is the 12th-largest employer nationwide and that its policies affect some 200,000 employees and their families further enhances the importance and impact of these policies and programs," he added.

In recent years, Tarwater told BNA, New York has moved to test new theories and to expand proven programs in the following three key areas:

• *Flexible Schedules:* New York is the only public employer to date that has backed with money and manpower its stated commitment to expand part-time employment opportunities at all levels within state government. The state's part-time/shared job project and registry provided a model for public and private organizations wishing to build more flexibility into their employment systems.

• *Voluntary Furloughs:* New York State is currently experimenting with reduced work schedules for managers and professionals. This initiative is especially important to women who often require structures that permit them to work in responsible, career-path positions while still remaining at home with their children at crucial times during the week and year.

• *Worksite Day Care:* New York State is the first and still the sole employer in the nation to promote and sponsor worksite day care facilities on a massive scale. There are currently 25 such centers across the state that accommodate some 1,200 children; an additional eight centers are expected to open by mid-1986. In his Jan. 8, 1986, State of the State message, Gov. Cuomo said that an additional 51 would be added by 1988.

Worksite Day Care

In conjunction with its six unions, the state launched this ground-breaking program in 1981 with a start-up grant for a pilot program in Albany for 30 children, the Office of Employee Relations (OER) said.

All of the centers are prepared to handle children from eight weeks old to five years of age. Some also provide certified, year-round kindergarten programs as well as summer and after-school day care for six- to nine-year-olds.

Beyond the initial grant of $19,550 provided by the New York State Labor-Management Day Care Advisory Committee and drawn from funds now negotiated within each state contract, the day care centers are financially self-sufficient, operating primarily with fees paid by the parents. The sliding scale of $35 to $70 per child per week makes the program competitive with most other day care arrangements and puts the service within the financial reach of all state employees.

Besides providing an almost essential service and filling a serious marketplace gap for quality day care service, the New York on-site day care program has reaped important organizational dividends, OER said. These include an enhanced ability to recruit and retain highly qualified and experienced employees at all levels of government, fewer of the disruptions normally caused by extended maternity leaves and inadequate day care provisions for pre-school and school-aged children, reduced training and retraining costs, and increased employee morale and productivity.

The program's benefits to employees are obvious, OER noted. Workers whose children attend the worksite centers report an increased sense of security about their children's daytime welfare and a greater ability to concentrate on their jobs and perform at optimum levels. Often, parents can visit their children during lunchtime and coffee breaks, it added, and some mothers have been able to maintain normal breastfeeding schedules after returning to full-time work.

Tarwater summarized the state reaction to the programs: "Since most New York programs have been jointly conceived and implemented by both management and labor, they present a compelling case for creative, collaborative problem-solving in the workplace. Indeed, some have shown the potential for revolutionizing the structures within which we live and work, extending the hope that it may indeed be possible to achieve equally cherished personal and professional goals simultaneously."

Part-Time and Shared Jobs

New York State has long offered employees in several departments the option of setting their own hours within established parameters, often referred to as flextime. Other public and private sector employers have also adopted some form of this system, but few, according to Tarwater's office, have taken the concept of alternative, non-conventional scheduling as far as New York State.

Sparked by the results of a 1983 survey of state worker attitudes toward part-time employment, the state launched a major effort that same year to support and expand part-time and shared job options throughout government. With a $400,000 grant from Office of Employee Relations (OER) negotiated under contracts with the Civil Service Employees Association and the Public Employees Federation, the state established in the civil service department a special nine-member unit solely devoted to expanding part-time options in state service.

The Office of Employee Relations stressed that the term "part-time jobs" refers to permanent, part-time positions with all the benefits enjoyed by full-time employees, prorated to reflect the percent of full-time worked and that "part-time employment" is sometimes used to encompass the notion of shared jobs — another form of part-time employment.

Increase of 16 Percent for Part-Timers

The part-time/shared job project increased the number of part-time and shared jobs in state government by 16 percent from 1983 to 1984, and to date it has achieved the following goals:

• Through policy reviews, meetings, seminars, and a dozen publications, the project has raised the awareness of state personnel administrators, line managers, and employees to the possibilities, challenges, and benefits of part-time and shared job employment.

• The project has clarified existing civil service policies and procedures as they apply to part-time and shared jobs and thus removed what many perceived to be formidable, "artificial" barriers to fuller utilization of part-time options.

• The project has developed a central registry of workers interested in part-time employment and made it available to all state agencies and departments.

In April 1984, according to OER, New York took a giant step forward in humanizing the workplace by extending to its 64,000 professional and managerial employees the chance to trade a percentage of their incomes for an equivalent amount of time off.

Called the Voluntary Work Reduction Schedule Program or Voluntary Furlough Program, it offers the opportunity on a two-year pilot basis to members of the Professional Employees Federation and management, confidential, or "exempt" personnel, with the purpose of giving employees useful alternatives to traditional full-time or part-time work arrangements and giving state agencies a flexible mechanism for allocating staff resources to priority areas.

While the furlough concept was originally borrowed from a small-scale program in one department of California state government, New York is the first organization in the country to implement such a program on a massive scale, OER said. Unlike traditional part-time employment provisions, the voluntary furlough program maintains all existing health, leave, and pension benefits, regardless of the percent by which an employee's work schedule is reduced.

Job Security Strengthened

Furloughed workers can reduce their schedules by 5 to 30 percent, in 5 percent increments and can distribute this "banked" time in a variety of ways, such as on a fixed schedule like a shorter working day or one day off every week, or all at one time like a month off in the summer or a week off around the holidays.

Another significant feature of the New York program is its requirement of a written contract stipulating the terms of the furlough agreement. Signed by both supervisor and employee, the contract cannot be changed by either party without the consent of both.

OER pointed out that there are benefits to the employer, too, for agencies can redeploy manpower resources to areas of greatest priority or need. Agencies can maintain program levels and standards without compromising manpower quotas or other fiscal objectives; and, because the need for layoffs is reduced, agencies can enjoy improved employee morale and a strengthened sense of job security.

In the 14 months since the program's inception, nearly 1,000 persons in 97 agencies have participated in the furlough program. More than half the participants are women (58 percent), and a majority of men and women report they use the time for home and family-related activities. At least one employee has taken advantage of the furlough to devote more time to his art, and another is using it to pursue a graduate degree.

Most furlough participants earn between $20,000 and $40,000, and the majority have reduced their work schedules by either 10 or 20 percent.

At the time the program was introduced, payroll savings were projected at $2.3 million based on an assumption that 5 percent of professional employees would use the program. Actual savings for the program's first year of operation have not been calculated, but, based on figures available now, they will fall somewhat below actual projections, OER indicated.

PENNSYLVANIA

State as Employer

Parental Leave

All permanent employees of the Commonwealth of Pennsylvania who become parents through childbirth or formal adoption may be granted childbirth leave upon request for up to six months. State personnel rules provide that, "[u]pon the request of the employe and at the discretion of the agency head, childbirth leave may be extended or renewed for a period not to exceed six months. In no case shall the total amount of leave exceed 12 months."

Employees have the right to return to their jobs, or to an equivalent position, and they retain all seniority and pension rights that accrued up to the time of leave.

A pregnant employee who is on childbirth leave without pay is entitled to use accrued sick leave for the period that she is unable to work. Employees on childbirth leave without pay may use all accrued annual and personal leave. All other periods of leave related to childbirth leave are leave without pay.

Child Care

Two bills pending the General Assembly in 1986 would provide statutory authority to establish pilot day care programs for the children of state employees. "[H]owever, the probability of passage of this legislation is unknown," Deputy Secretary for Employe Relations Charles T. Sciotto told BNA.

"The long-term costs of providing day care services in government have yet to be determined and liability issues have become a major concern to all employers and an issue which will become increasingly complex in the near future," Sciotto said. "In weighing the potential benefits of providing day care facilities for state employees, considerations must be given to the total compensation currently provided to state workers. Generally, their salaries and employee benefits, particularly at the lower end of the pay schedule, are already higher than the average worker employed in Pennsylvania in the private sector," the state official said.

"At the same time," Sciotto added, the administration of Gov. Dick Thornburgh "has supported the provision of day care services for income-eligible families who are employed or enrolled in formal work training programs."

Alternative Work Schedules

"While the Commonwealth has not adopted true flexitime scheduling of work hours," Sciotto said, Pennsylvania does have a variety of work schedules "that are geared to maximize contact and communication with the clientele served by an agency while allowing employees some latitude in adjusting their work day." Outside of an institutional setting, the majority of Commonwealth employees work from 8:30 a.m. to 5:00 p.m., with staggered schedules from 7:30 a.m. to 4:00 p.m., and 8:00 a.m. to 4:30 p.m.

WISCONSIN

State as Employer

Maternity Leave

In 1981, the Department of Employment Relations revised the Wisconsin Administrative Code to provide — for non-represented classified employees — a leave of absence without pay for maternity of six months upon request of the employee. Extensions of this leave of absence are permitted upon approval of the agency head. A leave of absence is also permitted for paternity. Similar provisions for maternity and paternity leave are contained in contracts covering represented employees.

Child Care

Also in 1984, the Day Care Task Force, which was convened by the Department of Employment Relations, recommended and the Governor approved Executive Order #77 (dated Nov. 19, 1985) expanding the state's Employee Assistance

Program to provide direct assistance to employees in meeting child care needs through referral and information services.

The 1985 Wisconsin Act 29 contains provisions implementing other recommendations of the Day Care Task Force and the Department of Employment Relations. This Act:

(1) Authorizes the spending of state money to establish a day care center for the children of state employees with two goals in mind. One goal is to help fill gaps in the supply of specific types of day care services (e.g., infant care, adjacent site care) and the other goal is to serve as a model for other employers. The center is scheduled to open in the spring of 1986 and will be located adjacent to the major state office buildings in downtown Madison. Start-up costs and rent are subsidized with this money. State employees served by the center will pay operating costs for the child care services. The center will be open from 7:00 a.m. to 6:00 p.m. and will accommodate 50 children.

(2) Expands the scope of the state's mandatory supervisory training program to include a segment on understanding the concerns of state employees with children.

(3) Requires that the state building commission consider written reports prepared biennially regarding the desirability of including plans for day care facility space in the plans for any construction or major remodeling of state buildings.

Use of Sick Leave

For more than 40 years, the state Department of Employment Relations has had an administrative rule permitting use of sick leave by non-represented classified employees for periods of absence from employment which are due to attendance upon members of the immediate family where the employee's presence is required. Use of sick leave for this purpose is normally limited to five work days for any one illness or injury, the Department says. Contracts governing the use of sick leave by represented classified employees contain similar provisions.

Alternative Work Options

In 1984, the Department of Employment Relations created chapter ER 42 of the Wisconsin Administrative Code. That chapter requires agencies to prepare and file plans to provide alternative work options, including, but not limited to, part-time, shared-time, and flexible-time schedules. This chapter outlines the required components of these plans and the plan review and approval process.

*   *   *

C. FLEXIBLE BENEFITS PLANS

Employers traditionally tailored their benefits plans to the needs of the male worker who was the sole support of his family. That type of benefit plan, however, often is inappropriate for, and sometimes of limited use to, women, single parents, and two-earner couples, who represent an ever-growing percentage of the total work force.

A number of companies are adopting flexible benefits plans — also called cafeteria benefits plans — as a way of adapting to the needs of the new work force. Under a flexible benefits scheme, an employer provides a range of benefits, and permits employees to select, up to a specified limit or total dollar amount, those benefits they desire most.

A typical flexible benefits plan provides several "core" benefits, usually including basic medical coverage, and a number of optional benefits. Among those optional benefits might be:

• dependent care;
• vacation time;
• life insurance;
• dependent life insurance;
• accidental death and dismemberment insurance;
• dental insurance;
• deferred compensation plans under §401(k) of the Internal Revenue Code; and
• legal aid.

If the benefits selected cost more than the employee is allotted, the employee often is permitted to make up the difference from salary, with that amount being untaxed.

Employees like the plans because they can change their benefits as their needs change.

Most plans provide for a yearly election of benefits, although many will allow an employee to change some benefits if family status changes during the year.

Employers sometimes offer a flexible spending account as part of the flexible benefits plan. With a flexible spending account, an employee elects at the beginning of the year to give up a percentage of salary in exchange for the same amount of tax-free employer contributions for particular benefits, usually dependent care or health care. Such accounts require precise planning, however, because money provided must be used on the benefit specified, and any amount left in the account at the end of the year is forfeited by the employee.

Employers offer flexible benefits plans for many reasons, according to benefits specialists. In many cases, an employer chooses to adopt or create a cafeteria plan because the plan gives the employer the ability to control costs, especially those associated with medical benefits. Frequently, cafeteria plans offer several choices of medical plans, with different levels of coverage. Employees who wish to spend more of their benefits credits on health care can often choose lower deductibles, for instance. But some employers have initiated such plans because they see a need to give employees more choices and tax advantages, and to respond to their employees' desires for a range of benefits. With a flexible benefits plan, employers can spend the same amount of money while offering a wider variety of benefits, increasing employee satisfaction greatly. Flexible benefits plans also enable employers to meet the needs of some of their workers by offering a relatively expensive benefit such as child care, which not all employees need, without taking benefits dollars away from their other employees. Another advantage to employers is that increases in the cost of benefits are often borne by the employees. Employees have the chance, usually once a year, to make changes in their plans, but while the cost of an option might have increased, their benefits allowance may not have changed.

Employees like the plans because they can change their benefits as their needs change and can select those benefits they need most. If both members in a dual-earner couple have medical coverage, the one who is offered the flexible benefits plan can opt for less expensive, low-option care, and can choose dependent care subsidies or extra vacation time. As dependent care becomes less necessary, it can be dropped in favor of other benefits.

Tax Break for Employers

On May 2, 1984, the Internal Revenue Service proposed regulations in question-and-answer form for cafeteria plans (49 *FR* 19321). On Dec. 31, 1984, IRS published a proposed amendment to proposed cafeteria plan regulations that would grant general and special transition relief to employees and employers participating in certain plans from withholding taxes under those plans (49 *FR* 50733). While proposed regulations don't have the same force as a regulation, employers have to have a pretty good reason for not complying with proposed regulations, and thus most do comply, according to Lance Tane of the Wyatt Company, a benefits consulting firm.

Dependent Care Assistance Plans

Relying on these proposed regulations, a number of employers are offering dependent care assistance plans to their employees, even if they do not have a more comprehensive flexible benefits plan. While proposed regulations don't have the same force as a final regulation, employers have to have a pretty good reason for not complying with proposed regulations, and thus most do comply, according to Lance Tane of the Wyatt Company, a benefits consulting firm.

Under dependent care assistance plans, employees can usually use pre-tax dollars to pay for dependent care. The employer reimburses the employee's expenses for child care — or care of a dependent spouse or other relative who is physically or mentally incapable of self-care — up to an amount which is determined in advance and taken out of the employee's salary. (IRS rules and restrictions for dependent care assistance plans are explained in detail in the Appendix.)

BNA spot-checked a number of dependent care assistance plans and found that application of the IRS rules varies considerably from one plan to another. Plans ranged from those that paid quarterly to those that paid every payday. Some plans required original receipts or cancelled checks, but several required only the employee's signature. Some allowed salary reductions of varying amounts, from $2,000 per year to as much as a single employee's entire salary or the salary of a lower-paid spouse in a dual-earner couple.

Plans also varied in the extent to which they allowed adjustments during the year; the proposed IRS regulations allow employees to make changes during the year if "family status" changes. All such plans require employees to forfeit any allocated funds that are unused at the end of the year.

Flexible Plans Seen Becoming More Widespread

According to a survey of medium-sized and large companies conducted by Louis Harris & Associates, Inc., for The Equitable Life Assurance Society, conducted in February and March 1985, less than 20 percent of companies offer flexible benefits plans, but significant growth in the number of plans is expected in the next two years.

The survey of corporate initiatives and employee attitudes on flexible benefits revealed that 46 percent of management personnel expected their companies to introduce flexible benefits plans in the next two years. Surveyed were 1,253 employees, 1,250 benefit officers, 200 senior executives, and 200 senior human resource managers at a cross-section of companies with 500 or more employees. Also surveyed were 110 insurance brokers and consultants who work with corporate clients in the group health plan field.

Most of the surveyed employees said they enjoyed having a choice of benefits: Sixty-five percent said they liked it a lot, 21 percent said they liked it a little, 10 percent said they didn't care, and only 2 percent responded that they did not like it.

Forty-nine percent of the employees who had some choice of benefits said they were very satisfied with their benefits, compared with only 40 percent of those who had no choice of benefits. Interestingly, 55 percent of the employees who could choose benefits said they were very satisfied with their jobs, while only 45 percent of those with no options said they were very satisfied.

Eighty percent of the responding employees said their plans included at least some choice of benefits, regardless of whether the benefits plans were identified as cafeteria plans.

The Administrative Management Society, Willow Grove, Pa., in a separate benefits survey of 283 companies in 1985, found that flexible benefits plans were offered by 17 percent of the companies, and that another 9 percent were considering, or were in the process of implementing, flexible plans.

Of the firms that offer such plans, two-thirds or more offer dependent-care coverage.

Communication Is the Key

The communication of the plan to employees is the most crucial aspect in the successful adoption of flexible benefits plans, benefits experts have agreed.

One thing employers must do, as part of the communication process, is to determine in advance whether employees want a flexible plan and the benefits in which they would be most interested.

Once a flexible benefits plan is in place, information about the plan can be communicated in several ways, through articles in company newsletters, information packets to employees, hotlines, and training sessions. Experts say it is important to explain the program thoroughly at the outset, and to do yearly updates as benefits change. Many companies with flexible benefits issue workbooks to their employees, so employees can figure out the costs and advantages of the various benefits. Many employers with dependent care assistance plans, for instance, help employees figure out whether, with regard to taxes, they are better off using the salary reduction or the tax credit, or a combination of both.

When AmeriTrust, one of Ohio's largest banks, introduced its "cafeteria plan," the advantages and disadvantages of each option were described in detail at seminars which employees were required to attend. This formal educational effort was supplemented by home mailer campaigns "to heighten family awareness" of the various plans, said Peter Osenar, executive vice president for personnel and organization at the Cleveland-based bank. This process helped employees make option decisions based on need, not on the basis of out-of-pocket expenses, he said.

Feedback is another critical part of the communication process. When employers survey employees after instituting a flexible benefits plan, it has been found that the responses received usually lead management to change the plan design.

Recruiters are finding that prospective employees — especially those applying or recruited for hard-to-fill positions — are beginning to look more carefully at the benefits employers are offering. Child care is one benefit being sought more and more often. Women — who, despite their growing participation in the working world, are still primarily responsible for child care — will see more need for child care benefits and time-off benefits. And as men take on more of the responsibility for child care, those benefits also will become important to them, observers say.

As they see employees making wise choices and the cost of their benefits plans stabilizing, companies are becoming more comfortable with the idea of flexible plans. Some companies are ready to switch, according to Lance Tane of the Wyatt Company, but are waiting to see what action Congress will take in regard to benefits. Doreen Grove, manager of corporate employee benefits for U.S. Bancorp, a bank holding company, said, "Some companies say they should wait and see what the regulations will be. Our position is that there is always change. If you waited, you'd never do anything."

Administering the Plans

One disadvantage of the plans is that they are more difficult to administer than regular benefits plans, Tane said. He qualified that statement, however, by explaining that the disadvantage is decreasing in importance as employers become more experienced with the plans, and as more computer software is being developed to help administer the plans.

The Employee Benefit Research Institute says that benefits administrators find no real difference between the difficulty in handling flexible plans and the difficulty in handling traditional plans. EBRI also reports that employees using flexible plans have a better understanding of their benefits.

A study of 120 flexible plans conducted by Hewitt Associates, a human resources consulting firm, showed that 76 percent of the surveyed companies used internal resources for at least some of the computer work required to administer a flexible program. Of these, 58 percent accomplished the initial conversion of payroll programs or software development. Most — 62 percent — of the companies said they were able to administer their flexible benefits program with existing staff, Hewitt reported.

The study also revealed that, among the 24 employers that provided a financial analysis of their plans, 21 said that the flexible program had either reduced or limited benefit cost increases, two reported no change, and one indicated that costs had risen faster under the flexible plan than under the former arrangement.

U.S. Bancorp's Flexible Plan

U.S. Bancorp's benefits plan is typical of a plan offering a combination of flexible benefits and a reimbursement account. U.S. Bancorp is the holding company of U.S. National Bank of Oregon, which instituted flexible benefits early in 1985.

U.S. Bancorp went to a flexible plan for several reasons: Benefits costs were going up in the early 1980s, and the work force — more single parents and dual-income families — and its needs were changing, according to Doreen Grove. "Flexible benefits are a way to address these varying needs," she said.

Benefits costs for medical, dental, life, and disability insurance at U.S. Bancorp had climbed from 4.8 percent of payroll costs in 1978 to 6.9 percent of payroll in 1983, and were projected to hit 7.5 percent of payroll by the end of 1985, Grove said. Under the flexible plan, benefits were projected to account for 6.6 percent of payroll by the end of 1985.

Prior to the installation of the new plan, employees at U.S. National Bank of Oregon had little choice of benefits. Now, they are told what their benefits dollar amount is and are offered a menu of benefits outlined in an 85-page book, Grove said. Employees choose from medical and dental plans, and disability and life insurance, and after selection the costs are totaled. If the employee's selection is less than the amount budgeted for, the difference is added to his pay. If the amount is more than budgeted for, the difference is made up from the employee's pay, in pre-tax dollars.

The bank also offers a reimbursement plan for health and child care costs. After the employee estimates what he will pay, deductions are made from pre-tax earnings. The employee submits claims for reimbursement after the expenses are incurred, until the full annual contribution has been reached.

Rank-and-file employees — 75 percent of whom are female — have welcomed the new plan, said Grove, who attributed the widespread acceptance to an extensive communication process.

Eaton Corp. Rejects Flexible Plans

One company that has looked very hard at flexible plans, and rejected them, is Eaton Corporation.

Janice Jones, manager of special benefits projects, told BNA that when Eaton acquires a company, it becomes a division, and its benefits plan is usually left pretty much as it was prior to the purchase. Eaton, however, is striving for some unity among the benefits plans, Jones said.

The benefits plans of the various Eaton divisions are so diverse that if they installed a cafeteria plan it would have to be so large that it would be an administrative problem, or so narrow that it would cut out some of the benefits that have been found necessary in some areas, Jones said. When the company investigated the effects of a flexible benefits plan, no cost savings were found, Jones said, and even when it looked at cost containment features of flexible plans, the company concluded that administration of the plans would end up costing Eaton money.

What has worked for Eaton is flexibility in benefits, rather than flexible plans.

Another reason Eaton has, so far, rejected flexible plans, Jones said, is that some divisions have sophisticated and complex benefits structures, and they don't want to take benefits away from the employees.

What has worked for Eaton, Jones said, is flexibility in benefits, rather than flexible plans. At some Eaton facilities, employees may be unable, because of the nature of their work, to take holidays when they are scheduled. An individual plan is worked out for the employee, or group of employees, to make up for the lost holidays. Flexibility is worked out on a case-by-case basis, she said. Most Eaton locations have flexible hours, she added, and leaves of absence can also be arranged.

Iowa Report on Flexible Benefits

Flexible benefits offer an obvious solution to the question of equity when dealing with the monetary aspect of employees' child care needs, the Iowa Merit Employment Department concluded in a 1985 study. The study was in preparation for the development of a model employment policy for state employees. (See *State Developments* in Chapter V for details on policy.)

The department also concluded that flexible benefits were one way of containing overall compensation costs while allowing employees a selection of non-taxable benefits that could be tailored to individual needs.

Future Looks Bright

The number of flexible benefits plans is increasing significantly, according to Lance Tane, who said there are some 600 such plans in companies around the nation and that approximately 15 percent of Fortune 500 companies have them. Tane added that, to his knowledge, no company had instituted such a plan and then reverted back to a more traditional plan.

The Conference Board in New York put the number of flexible benefits plans somewhat higher than Tane, at 950 plans, and Hewitt Associates, in its January 1986 newsletter, *on Flexible Compensation*, said that more than 500 companies were expected to have flexible benefits plans by the end of 1986, with 384 already in operation and some 50 more scheduled to become active in the next six months. Hewitt credited recent growth in the number of plans to medium-size companies, those with 1,000-10,000 employees. Of the programs already in effect, Hewitt reported that 30 percent were in manufacturing, 17 in percent in banking/finance, 12 percent in health care, 9 percent in education, 5 percent each in insurance and communications, 3 percent in both utility and trade, 2 percent each in government and services, and 9 percent in other industries.

EBRI predicted that flexible benefits would become more popular as benefits costs increased, and as companies increasingly looked for ways to control costs and felt the competitive pressure to be responsive to employee needs.

The Economic Policy Council of the UNA-USA, in its report on work and family in the United States, recommended that employers and unions explore the possibility of implementing flexible benefits packages in response to the new needs of the contemporary labor force and to the rising cost of benefits as a percentage of total labor costs. The Council noted that fringe benefits represented 41 percent of payroll costs in 1981, and that most traditional plans were designed for the employee who was a male head of household — plans that often do not meet the needs or expectations of today's work force and which, thus, are not cost effective.

The report also recommended the following changes in benefits legislation:

• Removing the "constructive receipt" obstacle, which requires that an individual pay taxes on a plan that offers cash as an option, whether or not cash is selected;

• Allowing longer time periods for benefits legislation, so that creative programs can be developed with the assurance that they will not have to change again soon; and

• Carrying over unused credits/benefits at the end of the year.

*   *   *

D. CHILD CARE, LEAVE PRACTICES IN OTHER COUNTRIES

In its set of recommendations intended to serve as the foundation for a family policy in the United States, the Economic Policy Council of the United Nations Association of the United States of America noted that "most other industrialized countries have long considered family policy an integral component of all domestic economic and social policy formulation." In Western Europe, for example, the Council noted, family policies and support structures have grown in tandem with changes in family structure and increases in women's labor force participation.

Included in this section are examinations of the child care and leave policies of some other nations. The first two parts of this subsection deal specifically with child care and leave policies in Sweden, the country which is generally acknowledged as the trendsetter on work and family matters. The third part contains a survey of parental leave in West European counties by the *European Industrial Relations Review*, and the final part contains a global review of maternity benefits published by the International Labour Office.

WORK AND FAMILY LIFE IN SWEDEN
By Rita Ann Reimer

[Rita Ann Reimer, J.D., George Washington University, 1974, received a grant from the Bicentennial Swedish-American Exchange Fund and spent six weeks in Sweden in 1985 studying Swedish family law and women's economic rights.]

Swedish laws and social policy reflect fundamental assumptions that are not widely accepted in the United States. The most important of these in the context of work and family life is that each non-handicapped adult is responsible for his or her own economic well-being. This means, among other things, that both parents, including mothers of young children, are expected to work for pay, usually outside the home. Two necessary corollaries to this assumption are that both parents are equally responsible for the economic support of their children, and that children function best when their emotional needs are satisfied outside of the family unit as well as within.

1971 Tax Reform Act

Although the roots of this policy go back much further, the law which did the most to advance its implementation was a 1971 tax reform act which continued Sweden's stiff system of graduated income taxes but eliminated joint tax returns for married couples. As opposed to the United States' tax laws, which generally penalize two-income marriages, the Swedish system encourages them to the extent that most couples would find it difficult to survive financially if they were not both gainfully employed. Today, nearly 90% of all Swedish women work; and, since most of those who do not are older women, the percentage of working mothers with young children is even higher.

Since Sweden so strongly encourages both parents to work, it is seen as both proper and necessary that the government make it as easy as possible for them to do so. The country has thus adopted a comprehensive child care program and a wide range of social insurance benefits to insure both that children are well cared for while their parents are at work and that parents and children can be together during each child's infancy, in the event of illness, when adapting to day care, and at other times of need.

The following is a brief overview of these social insurance benefits. They are all mandated by law and are thus not subject to union negotiation or other modification.

Abundant Leave

In addition to regularly available sick leave, there is a special pregnancy allowance for a maximum of 50 days within the last two months of childbirth, if a pregnant woman's work is too strenuous or otherwise dangerous to the health of the fetus, and she cannot be given lighter work. As with most allowances for time off, the employee receives 90% of her usual salary during this period.

Each father receives two weeks' leave with pay at the time of childbirth. In addition, there is a 360-day parent's allowance for each child which can be taken at any time until the child reaches the age of four. Parents are required to use this leave until the child is six months old, as that is the earliest age at which the child can be placed in a day care facility. The remainder can be used when and for whatever purpose they find appropriate. Parents are paid 90% of their salary for the first 270 days of the parent's allowance, and a small sum for the remaining 90 days.

It is interesting that these benefits are available to adoptive as well as to birth parents. In contrast to the American view of pregnancy and childbirth as a medical disability, the Swedish approach recognizes the importance of parent-child bonding as an important component of maternity/paternity leave and thus does not distinguish between birth and adoptive parents in this context.

Parents of children under the age of 12 (16, in the case of handicapped children) are entitled to a joint total of 60 days' paid leave per child per year, to look after a sick child at home. Visiting nurses and other health professionals are available to help care for these children, and may be able to stay with a child in place of the parent so the parent can continue to work, or simply take a needed break from nursing responsibilities. Allowances are decreased if a child must be hospitalized, but are reinstated for any periods the child can spend at home. They are increased for disabled or extremely ill children. In addition, the comprehensive national health insurance program covers all medical expenses after a low annual deductible has been met.

Other parental benefits include two weeks with pay at the time a child is placed in day care or changes day care facilities. This leave is required both to help the parents become familiar with the center's operation and to ease the child's transition into the new environment. Parents may also take up to two "contact days" per child per year until the child reaches the age of 12, to visit the child's school or day care facility.

Except for the father's childbirth allowance, parents can split permissible days off in any manner they find appropriate. One parent can use the full amount; they can alternate days or weeks; or each parent can work part of the day.

Six-Hour Workday Possible

Another important component of the work/family life equation is a law which permits either or both parents of a child under the age of eight to work a six-hour day, with commensurate loss of pay but no other penalty. This recognizes that certain parents of young children want or need to spend more time with their youngsters and provides them with this option without unduly hampering their present or future employment prospects. If both parents choose to exercise this option, the child need be cared for outside the home only four working hours per day.

The Swedish child care system is justifiably world-renowned. Day care centers are typically open from 6:00 or 6:30 a.m. until 6:30 or 7:00 p.m. They are run by municipalities but regulated by the central government, and are financed through local tax revenues, parents' fees, and state subsidies financed via employer payroll taxes. In addition, there is a system of family day nurseries in which a "day parent" cares for a small group of children in his or her home. The Social Democratic Party, which was returned to office for three years in the September 1985 elections and heads a razor-thin majority coalition in Sweden's one-house parliament, favors the day care center approach and has embarked on an ambitious five-year plan to insure that by 1991 each child of working parents will have a place available in a day care center. Younger school age children (up to age 12) can attend recreation centers, open the same hours as day care centers, for those hours outside the school day when their parents are not at home. Fees for day care facilities are set by the municipalities and vary according to the parents' ability to pay.

Municipalities are trying a number of flexible approaches to provide day care under more difficult circumstances, such as when parents work non-traditional hours; when the children don't speak Swedish (an increasingly common situation due to large numbers of recent immigrants); and when parents live in rural, less-populated areas where distances between settled communities is great and when hours of work may be long and irregular. Special programs already exist in most areas for children who need special support in their development, e.g., handicapped children, late developers, or children with similar problems.

All of this means that Swedish parents can concentrate on their work, knowing that their children are well cared for at reasonable rates. Also, they can stay home with sick children or in other special circumstances. Thus, Swedes cannot readily identify with American parents, especially mothers, who may be precluded from entering the work force because they cannot afford satisfactory child care; or, if they must work, must often make unsatisfactory arrangements which can lessen job performance because of concern over the children (not to mention the potentially serious problems which can develop if young children are left unattended).

The Importance of Leisure Time

Leisure time is very important to the Swedes, and another component of work and family life is the amount of vacation time earned. By law, each Swedish worker is entitled to five weeks' paid vacation per year; and most employers extend the workday by 10 to 20 minutes each day so that employees can also have a week off at Christmas or for a winter vacation.

A side point is that the Swedish government would also like to shape somewhat how this leisure time is utilized. It views the ideal marriage as consisting of two equal wage earners; two equal citizens; two equal parents; and, most importantly in this context, two people with equal amounts of leisure time. Other than citizenship, these goals are proving elusive, although Sweden is closer to achieving them than most other countries. For example, Swedish women now average over 80% of the average earnings of Swedish men; and in industrial positions this rises to over 90%. Also, while women are still more likely than men to take maternity/paternity leave and stay home with sick children, more men are beginning to take advantage of these options. It is hoped and anticipated that this trend will continue, to the mutual benefit of fathers and their children, who will hopefully grow up with the view that parenting is not primarily woman's work and continue this trend with their own children.

Also, studies show that home and housework in Sweden remain primarily the woman's responsibility, although not to the extent that this is true in the United States. For example, in families with young children where both parents are employed full time, mothers have a total working week (housework and paid employment) of 74 hours, while the corresponding figure for fathers is 65 hours. Also, Swedish men are much more likely than Swedish women to participate in organized leisure time activities outside the home.

These patterns are difficult to change legislatively, even if this is thought advisable; and few view it as desirable for the government to mandate that fathers do more housework or more mothers participate in organized sports. Also, parents who hold professional positions may be reluctant to take advantage of leave policies, even those set by law, because they fear this could hamper their career development. However, informal efforts appear to be meeting with some degree of success. One effective poster which has been widely distributed shows a heavyweight wrestler, a Swedish national hero, taking obvious delight in caring for his infant son.

Unions and Employers Work Together

Since all of the preceding programs and benefits are set by law, there is no need for negotiation between unions and employers on these points. Rather, both unions and employer associations work with the government and political parties to enact additional legislation where needed in these areas. Sweden's largest union, the Swedish Trade Union Confederation [LO], is affiliated with the ruling Social Democratic Party. Others do not have these direct political ties but are also politically active.

Both Swedish workers and employers are highly organized. Out of a labor force of 4.3 million, LO, the leading blue collar union, has 2.2 million members, while the Swedish Central Organization of Salaried Employees [TCO] has over 1.1 million members. Thus together they represent over three-fourths of the working population; other, smaller unions represent much of the remainder. Also, Sweden has a number of employers' confederations which have no direct counterpart in the United States. The main such organization is the Swedish Employers' Confederation [SAF], which has 36 affiliated employer associations representing over 30% of all Swedish workers; another 30% work for employers who have joined smaller confederations. The unions and employers' confederations maintain continuing contact, and both sides agree that their non-confrontational approach helps to avoid or resolve most major controversies without extended problems.

Reading position papers put out by LO, TCO, and SAF indicates that there is little disagreement on eventual goals on work and family life, including the possibility of an eventual six-hour work day. (There *is* disagreement on how soon this might be possible!) The main concerns of both employers and employees at the present time are inflation, which has eroded workers' purchasing power even though incomes have risen; and unemployment, which, while still low by world standards, has recently crept upward and now stands at approximately 3 percent.

Politics and Policies

The five Swedish political parties are also in agreement on most of these basic policies, which over the years have become firmly entrenched throughout the country. Many of the programs run on the honor system and could easily collapse if people did not cooperate in their implementation. Even though costs continue to increase, and the tax burden is probably already too high to contemplate further increases, no person or party is currently proposing significant cutbacks. Most reform suggestions qualify more as fine-tuning than a major overhaul.

The only pertinent controversy in the September 1985 general election involved the question of child care, with the Moderate and Center Parties favoring increased use of day parents in place of day care centers, or a voucher system whereby parents could make whatever child care arrangements thought appropriate — including having one parent stay home with the child(ren). The Social Democrats, however, who ran the country continuously from 1932 until 1976 and have been in power since 1982, albeit with only a small parliamentary majority which they maintain by aligning themselves with the Communist Party, is firmly committed to the concept of child care centers and, as already noted, is working to insure that each child has a place in such a center by 1991.

The next opportunity for Swedes to formally voice their opinions on these matters will come in the 1988 elections. Given their history of commitment to the present policies, however, it is unlikely the country will change direction, barring some exceptional turn of events which cannot be foreseen at this time.

*   *   *

REPORT ON SEMINAR ON SWEDEN'S CHILD CARE SYSTEM

[The following account of a seminar on the working family in Sweden appeared in BNA's *White Collar Report* on May 23, 1984, p. 605, and reflects the parental leave laws and other policies and programs in effect at the time.]

Greater participation by women in labor organizations — especially as union leaders — is needed to stimulate changes in work patterns and attitudes toward mothers as family breadwinners.

This was the conclusion reached by speakers at a seminar in Washington, D.C., billed as *The Working Family: Perspectives and Prospects in Sweden and the U.S.*

The seminar was co-sponsored by the Swedish Embassy in conjunction with the Coalition of Labor Union Women (CLUW). Participants included U.S. labor, government, and corporate officials, and the advances in child care recently achieved in Sweden were the primary topic of discussion.

Swedish Undersecretary for Labor Berit Rollen said the labor movement in Sweden, where 80-90 percent of the work force is organized, has been instrumental in securing legislation that gives men and women equal opportunities to participate in community life and combine gainful employment with good child care. Laws that permit parents to work a six-hour day and that provide for adult education, day nurseries, free school meals, separate taxation of husband and wife, and parental insurance have all facilitated women's entry into employment, she added. Slightly more than eight of 10 Swedish women today have paid jobs, according to Rollen, who added that paid employment is more common among younger than older women. This means, he pointed out, that the highest employment participation rate is among mothers of infant children.

Three Principal Allowances

Parental insurance and various forms of child care have particularly helped working mothers and fathers to combine job with family responsibilities, Swedish Ministry of Social Affairs Director Soren Kindlund said. Parental insurance, introduced in Sweden in 1974, supercedes the maternity insurance scheme and established the principle that fathers also are entitled to leave of absence, with compensation for loss of earnings, in conjunction with the birth of a child. The costs of parental insurance are defrayed with government subsidy and social security charges levied on employers and calculated in proportion to the wage bill for employees in each company. There are three chief elements in the parental insurance system:

● Childbirth allowance — A leave of absence in conjunction with childbirth, payable to mother or father, is provided for 180 days but must be used before the child is 270 days old. Anyone eligible for sickness allowance can received this benefit, which normally is 90 percent of income.

● Extended care allowance — Both fathers and mothers may elect to stay at home and care for the newborn on a full-time, half-time, or quarter-time basis (i.e., six-hour working day) for an additional 180 full working days. The income allowance is 90 percent of pay during 90 of these days and a reduced amount for the remainder. Parents may take advantage of the special benefit whenever they wish, up to and including the child's first year at school.

● Temporary care allowance — This benefit has been expanded to enable one parent to stay at home to care for a child when the person normally providing care is ill. This allowance also entitles families to 60 days of sick leave per year per child. In the case of newborns, fathers may take 10 days' temporary care leave to stay at home and look after the other children and the mother and infant when they return from the hospital.

Kindlund said Swedish child care is governed by the Child Care Act, which requires municipal authorities to provide:

• Day nurseries which operate between 6:30 a.m. and 6:30 p.m. and care for children, age six months to seven years, while their parents are gainfully employed or studying;

• Part-time groups, which accept six-year-olds and, where space permits, five-year-olds for daily three-hour activity sessions;

• Before-and-after-school recreation centers, for children age seven to 12;

• Home day-nurseries, which operate in the homes of women employed by the municipal authorities and care for as many as four children of parents who are employed or studying; and

• Open preschools, which are run by trained personnel and are intended to give parents and children at home an opportunity to meet in groups.

*   *   *

PARENTAL LEAVE IN WESTERN EUROPE
Survey by *European Industrial Relations Review*

[Following is a survey on leave for family responsibilities for employees in Western Europe. The results of the survey on time off for family responsibilities appeared in Number 142 of the *European Industrial Relations Review*, November 1985. It is reproduced with the permission of the publishers, Eclipse Publications Ltd., London, England.]

Employees in most West European countries now have the statutory right to parental leave though in a few cases this is restricted to the public sector. Parental leave, which is almost always unpaid, is usually available to both men and women and may last between 10 weeks and three years. On expiry of their leave, employees normally have the right to their former job back. Most countries also give employees the statutory right to time off for family reasons, though the details are often filled in by collective agreement or custom and practice.

These are the principal conclusions of the second part of our two-part survey on time off for family responsibilities.

In the last issue — EIRR 141 p. 17 — we looked at maternity and paternity leave in 13 West European countries. This month we investigate parental leave and leave for family reasons in the same countries: Belgium, Denmark, France, West Germany, Greece, Ireland, Italy, Luxembourg, the Netherlands, Portugal, Spain, Sweden and the UK. The survey covers employed men and women (though not necessarily the self-employed) who have been contributing to social security for a specified minimum period.

This survey is based on the terms of the amended EEC draft Directive on parental leave and leave for family reasons which was submitted to the Council of Ministers in November 1984 (EIRR 132 p. 2 and p. 29). This draft will receive priority treatment at the next Council meeting of Labour and Social Affairs Ministers due in December, according to the Luxembourg Minister of Labour, Mr. Jean-Claude Juncker, who chairs the Council until the end of the year. According to Mr. Juncker — who was addressing the European Parliament's committee on social affairs and employment in September — the parental leave draft is the only draft Directive outstanding which can be "realistically" concluded.

Parental Leave

Parental leave is defined in Article 1 of the EEC draft Directive as:

" . . . entitlement to leave of a given duration for wage-earners including staff working in the public sector, consequential upon the birth of a child during the period following, but not necessarily consecutive with, maternity leave . . . ".

Article 4 adds:

"Parental leave shall be granted to enable any person entitled . . . to stay at home to look after the child concerned".

In other words, parental leave differs from maternity or paternity leave in that it is available to *either* parent some time not necessarily immediately following the expiry of maternity leave.

As can be seen from the table (which excludes Ireland where there appear to be no provisions at all), employees in most countries covered in our survey already enjoy statutory rights to parental leave. Employees in the private and public sectors in Denmark, France, Italy, Portugal, Spain and Sweden are covered, as are private sector employees only in Greece and public sector employees only in West Germany and Luxembourg. The law on sabbatical leave in Belgium includes provision for parental leave. Only the Irish Republic, the Netherlands and the UK make no statutory provision.

Article 6 of the draft Directive leaves the matter of payment entirely to the member states. In fact parental leave, where it exists, is unpaid except in Italy, where 30% of the claimant's salary is paid, and Denmark and Sweden, where 90% is paid. France grants a special allowance to larger families. In these cases, the social security fund is responsible for the financing. The draft Directive specifically lays down that allowances, where paid, should be made from public funds.

Leave Periods

Article 4.4 of the draft Directive stipulates a minimum parental leave period of three months per employee per child. In a two-parent family, therefore, where both the mother and father are at work, the total entitlement would be six months divided between the couple in whatever way they wished.

Our survey shows wide variation in the length of parental leave entitlements. It ranges from 10 weeks in Denmark and three months in Greece up to two years in France and three years in Spain. In some cases, parental leave may be taken on a part-time basis: Belgium, France, Portugal, Spain and Sweden all allow this. The Swedish system is particularly flexible and comprises all the following forms of leave:

— 180 days within 270 days of the child's birth;

— 180 days to be taken up before the child's eighth birthday (90 days are paid at the same rate as sickness leave, that is, 90% normal earnings, while the following 90 days are paid at a flat rate of 48kr (approx. £4.25) a day);

— 60 days per year per child until its twelfth birthday (in theory, a parent with six children could take the entire year off).

The draft Directive would not allow both parents to be on leave at the same time; in fact, none of the countries in our survey does allow this. However, Article 4.7 of the draft would also prevent the transfer of leave from one parent to another. Greece already conforms to this provision, but in France and Italy the father has the right to parental leave only if the mother chooses to transfer it to him.

Under the terms of the draft, parental leave may be taken at any time before the child reaches the age of two. Existing practice in this respect varies widely throughout West Europe. In Italy, parental leave must be taken before the child is one, in Spain before it is six. Two countries — Portugal and Sweden — make a distinction between full-time and part-time leave. Full-time leave in Sweden must be taken before the child reaches 18 months, in Portugal before it reaches two years. But in both countries, part-time leave may be taken until it reaches the age of 12. In Belgium — where the entitlement is awarded under arrangements for sabbatical leave — there is no age requirement.

Eligibility

A number of countries stipulate eligibility requirements. In Belgium, sabbatical leave may be taken after six months, while Denmark, France and Greece already correspond to the maximum period specified in the draft of one year's service (Article 5.3). Some countries stipulate further conditions. France allows companies employing fewer than 100 workers to turn down the request in certain circumstances, while Greece specifically exempts companies of that size, adding that not more than 8% of the workforce may be absent at any one time on parental leave.

None of the countries in the survey allows the extension of parental leave, though Article 4.5 of the draft suggests that member states may extend it for single-parent families or in the case of a disabled child living at home. All countries allow adoptive parents to take parental leave, though only Italy and Sweden explicitly grant the right to step-parents and guardians acting in place of parents (in line with Article 1).

All countries allow employees to return to their former job once their parental leave has expired. Greece specifies "the same or not inferior job" while Spain — which, allowing up to three years' parental leave, has one of the longest entitlements in West Europe — grants "only preferential rights to vacancies for the same or a similar category of job in the firm".

A number of countries treat parental leave as paid holiday for the purposes of maintaining social security contributions: Belgium, France, Denmark, Italy and Sweden.

Take-up of Provisions

Finally, Greece and Sweden have both mounted campaigns to bring parental leave to the attention of the working population. In Sweden — where the provisions for parental leave are the most advanced in West Europe — only 3% of fathers took advantage when they were introduced in 1974 (according to a paper prepared by Peter Moss of the Thomas Coram Research Unit in February 1985). By 1978-81, this had risen to 22% of fathers, who took an average of 47 days' leave during their child's first year. All mothers took advantage, averaging 288 days' leave. Each family took an average 300 days out of the 360 available under parental leave. Well educated fathers in the public sector are most likely to exercise their rights (and are sometimes referred to as "velvet daddies" by working fathers).

Meanwhile, figures from Denmark show that only 6% of all new mothers share parental leave with their partners (EIRR 141 p. 3).

Leave for Family Reasons

Most countries in our survey give statutory rights to time off for family reasons (for example, illness of a spouse, death of a near relative, marriage and so on). Ireland and the UK, however, do not. In Ireland, time off for family reasons appears to be regulated entirely through custom and practice, while in the UK collective agreements may allow up to five days off for, for example, bereavement, at management's discretion. Optical Fibres recognises in its agreement that "individuals' reactions to bereavement vary greatly" and so provides for individuals' circumstances to be discussed case by case. On the other hand, Cadbury Schweppes allows one day; British Rail, Burton Tailoring and Ford allow three; and the British Airports Authority and the Post Office give five.

Other West European countries provide a statutory basis for such time off in both private and public sectors. This may be found either in a special law covering the issue (for example, Belgium, France, Greece, Luxembourg, Spain and Sweden) or in the country's civil code, as in west Germany or the Netherlands. However, the terms of the law are virtually always improved through collective bargaining or custom and practice.

Reasons for Family Leave

The draft Directive specifies four reasons — amongst others — which should be considered as reasons for time off:
— illness of a spouse;
— death of a near relative;
— wedding of a child;
— illness of a child, or the person caring for the child.

Most countries already allow time off under most of these headings. However, Belgium (private sector), Denmark, France, Italy (private sector) and Luxembourg do not, for example, explicitly allow time off for the illness of a husband or wife. Portugal, on the other hand, gives up to 30 days on this account.

Amongst other reasons for time off not listed in the draft Directive are the employee's own wedding (France, Belgium, Luxembourg and Spain), moving house (Luxembourg, Spain), ordination of a close relative (Belgium, Netherlands), visits to the child's school (Greece), and wedding anniversaries (West Germany). In most cases, time off is allowed on each appropriate occasion but Greece imposes an upper limit for all causes of six days a year (raised to eight days if the employee has two children and to 10 days if there are more than two).

Leave for family reasons is almost always treated as holiday leave: full pay is explicitly guaranteed under Luxembourg law, but in Sweden leave may be unpaid if not for serious reasons.

Conclusions

The EEC draft Directive on parental leave and leave for family reasons would, if implemented, have the greatest impact on the UK, Ireland and the Netherlands, but especially the UK and Ireland where collective bargaining and custom and practice alone regulate these areas. The UK Government is deeply opposed to the draft.

Elsewhere in West Europe, greatest progress in introducing parental leave has been made recently in Southern Europe: Spain introduced its provisions in 1980, while Greece and Portugal both introduced theirs in 1984. However, Danish law dates from 1980 and a Bill covering the private sector has been with the Luxembourg cabinet since June 1983.

These recent moves — and, indeed, the EEC draft itself — are evidence of continuing concern to promote equal opportunities in employment for women. The distribution of family responsibilities between parents, it is claimed, not only improves family welfare by allowing fathers greater involvement with their children but also helps women to avoid discontinuity in their employment when they have children.

Belgium	Denmark	France
Statutory rights to parental leave		
No parental leave provisions as such, but under Articles 88-95 of the law of social recovery of 9 January 1985, employees may request sabbatical leave provided that it is covered by a collective agreement for, amongst other reasons, parental leave.	Parental leave provisions were introduced in July 1984 to become fully operative from July 1985 (under law no.234 on maternity leave of 4 June 1980, amended by law no.573 of 7 December 1983).	Parental leave is guaranteed under a law of 4 January 1984, enshrined in Articles L.122-28-1 and following of the Labour Code.
Entitlements		
Sabbatical leave may last between six and 12 months provided that the employee has at least six months' service and that he or she is replaced by an unemployed person. Such sabbaticals are unpaid, but under the terms of a Royal Decree of 21 March 1985 it is considered as time worked for the purposes of social security. These provisions cover both the private and public sectors. Sabbatical leave may be taken part-time and is not dependent on the age of the child. The employee has the right to return to the same job. Some collective agreements in the private sector allow men and women to take unpaid leave for up to two years, though in these cases there is no guaranteed right to return to the same job. Employers and employees have always had the right, on an individual basis, to suspend the employment contract by mutual agreement.	10 weeks' leave for either parent – but not both simultaneously – can be taken following the existing 14 weeks' maternity leave. Pay is made up to 90% of normal earnings. These provisions cover all workers in both private and public sectors, and there are no length of service requirements. Adoptive parents are also covered.	Parental leave may take the form of *either* unpaid leave (in the public sector or in private companies with over 100 employees) *or* half-time leave, in each case for a maximum of two years (though a parent opting to work part-time has the chance to take full unpaid leave after an initial period if desired). However, since 1 January 1985, a parent who looks after a child under the age of three and who is already responsible for three or more children is entitled to a special allowance for a maximum of 24 months. These rights cover private and public sectors and apply also to adoptive parents. In companies with fewer than 100 workers, the employer may turn down the request in certain circumstances. There are no central or major sector-level agreements covering parental leave. One year's service is required for eligibility, and benefits linked to length of service are halved during parental leave. The employee has the right to return to his or her job.
Statutory rights to leave for family reasons		
Royal Decree of 28 August 1963 grants statutory rights for leave for family reasons. Extra unpaid leave is provided for under a national collective agreement of 10 February 1975.	There are no statutory rights, though a number of collective agreements do provide for leave for family reasons.	Article L.226-1 of the Labour Code guarantees time off for family reasons once three months have been served. These rights are supplemented by a national agreement of 10 December 1977 and sector- and company-level agreements.
Entitlements		
Death of a close relative: 1-3 days Own wedding: 2 days Wedding of son/daughter: 1 day Ordination, Holy Communion: 1 day Time off is allowed on each relevant occasion Entitlements may be increased under collective agreement: the national agreement of 10 February 1975 provided for unpaid leave for family reasons with the details to be negotiated at a sector or company level: for example, metalworking: max. 5 days a year off unpaid.	Some agreements allow time off for the death of a near relative. Most agreements (though not, for example, construction) allow one day off with sickness benefit for either the father or mother when their child is ill. There is normally a one-year length of service requirement. The age of the child at which entitlement ends varies according to agreement. There is not normally a right to unpaid leave.	Death of spouse or child: 2 days Death of parent, parent-in-law, sibling or other close relative: 1 day Wedding of son/daughter: 1 day Own wedding: 4 days Time off is allowed on each occasion. The entitlements may be increased through collective agreement, and are counted as holiday leave for the purposes of social security.

West Germany	Greece	Italy
Statutory rights to parental leave		
There are no statutory rights to parental leave in the private sector though they do exist in the public sector.	Parental leave is guaranteed under law 1483/84 dated 8 October 1984 on the protection of workers with family responsibilities. It covers only the private sector (and excludes shipping and companies employing fewer than 100 workers).	Parental leave is guaranteed under law 1204 of 30 December 1971 (for mothers) and law 903 of 9 December 1977 (for fathers).
Entitlements		
The public sector allows three years' unpaid leave.	A working mother and a working father in a two-parent family are entitled to three months' unpaid leave each, and a parent in a one-parent family to six months' unpaid leave, until the child is 2½ years old. The parent must have at least one year's service. This leave, which is permitted for each birth provided that at least one year has elapsed since the previous time off, may also be taken by adoptive parents. It is to be taken after maternity leave. The percentage of workers away on parental leave may not exceed 8% of the total workforce and is allocated on a "first come, first served" basis. Workers must pay all social security contributions during their absence – their own plus the employer's – if they wish to maintain contributions. They have the right, however, to return to the same or a not inferior job. These provisions have been widely publicised by the Ministry of Labour in the media. There are no collective agreements covering these areas.	The mother or the father may take up to six months' leave during the first year of the child's life. Length of service requirements are unspecified. The parent receives 30% of normal earnings from INPS, the National Institute for Social Security. These rights, which apply to both private and public sectors, apply also to adoptive parents, step-parents and guardians acting in place of parents. There are no central agreements on this issue, but certain sector-level agreements may improve on the legal provisions. Part time leave is now allowed, but entitlement may be extended until the child is three if it is sick. There is also the right to unpaid leave. Parents have the right to return to their job. Parental leave is treated as holiday leave for the purposes of social security.
Statutory rights to leave for family reasons		
Statutory rights to leave for **family reasons** are guaranteed under Article **616 of the** Civil Code (Bürgerliches Gesetzbuch) and Article 165c of the Social Security Regulations (Reichsversicherungsordnung). Collective agreements may improve on these rights.	Law 1483/84, which deals with parental leave, also deals with leave for family reasons.	Employees in the public sector have the statutory right to leave for family reasons. In the private sector, rights are negotiated through collective agreements.
Entitlements		
Article 616 of the Civil Code allows male and female employees leave on full pay for "relatively insubstantial periods of time". The details are often settled through collective agreement. Under Article 165c of the Social Security Regulations, working mothers and fathers who take time off to look after a child below the age of eight who is ill may claim sick pay when there is no-one else at home. A maximum of five days' sick pay may be claimed in the calendar year.	Time off is allowed in cases of serious illness of husband, wife, dependent relative or child (aged under 16), or in cases of the child's mental illness. Time off is also allowed to visit the child's school. Maximum entitlement over the year, for whatever purpose, is six days, raised to eight and 10 days if there are two or more than two children in the family respectively. Custom and practice in Greece also often predates the law in allowing time off for a range of family reasons, including bereavement, weddings and so on.	Most employees are entitled to paid leave usually between 10 and 30 days – when they get married. Short periods of time off are allowed in cases of, for example, the death of a close relative: three days over the year is normal. Other leave for personal reasons is often regulated through custom and practice.

Luxembourg	Netherlands	Portugal
Statutory rights to parental leave		
Parental leave is guaranteed in the *public sector* under a law of 14 December 1983 (which modified the law of 16 April 1979). A bill on parental leave in the *private sector* was given its first reading in June 1983 but has since made no progress.	There are no statutory rights to parental leave. However Mr De Koning, Minister of Social Affairs and Employment, stated on 8 May 1985 that parental leave could help to reduce working time, which might indicate that there are thoughts about introducing it	Parental leave is guaranteed under the Maternity and Paternity Protection Law (law 4/84 dated 5 April 1984)
Entitlements		
The Bill referred to above would allow all workers in the private sector to take a maximum of two years' unpaid parental leave to look after a child under the age of three. Such workers would have preferential access to their old job - or a similar one - without loss of benefits on expiry of their parental leave entitlement. As it is, there are no major collective agreements covering parental leave. In the public sector, employees already have the right to one year's unpaid parental leave or to transfer to part-time work in order to look after a child under the age of four.	None. There are no collective agreements covering parental leave either.	The mother or father may take unpaid leave of between six months and two years to look after the child until it reaches the age of two. There are no length of service requirements. These rights, which apply to both private and public sectors, apply also to adoptive parents. Part-time leave is also possible, in which case entitlement lasts until the child reaches the age of 12. These periods of leave may not be extended, and there are no major collective agreements at either central or sector level covering the issue. Employees have the right to return to their old job on the expiry of their leave entitlement.
Statutory rights to leave for family reasons		
Leave for family reasons is guaranteed under Article 16 of the law of 22 April 1966.	Statutory rights to leave for family reasons are guaranteed under Article 1638c of the Civil Code (Burgerlijk Wetboek). A survey also recently showed that nine out of 24 collective agreements analysed contained, in April 1984, provisions for leave in cases of serious family illness.	Leave for family reasons is guaranteed under Decree Law no 674/76 of 1976 as well as law 4/84 on maternity and paternity protection.
Entitlements		
Entitlements are as follows: Death of parent or spouse: 3 days Death of an in-law: 1 day Wedding of a child: 2 days Own wedding: 6 days Birth of a child (for father): 2 days Moving house: 2 days Leave may be taken on each relevant occasion and must be taken at the time of the event. Entitlements may be improved by collective agreement or custom and practice. Full pay is guaranteed by law.	The Civil Code allows one day's paid leave for family obligations, two days for birth of a child or marriage and up to four days for bereavement. The engineering industry allows one day for - amongst other events - the employee's 25th or 40th wedding anniversary, marriage of a relative and ordination of a son or brother; two days for marriage and death of a parent or non-dependent child; and four days for death of a spouse or dependent child	Leave is allowed as follows: Illness of spouse: 30 days Death of close relative: 2-5 days Illness of child: 30 days These periods state a maximum annual entitlement under each category. Leave in cases of sickness is paid by social security; in cases of bereavement, it is treated as normal holiday leave.

Spain	Sweden	United Kingdom
Statutory rights to parental leave		
Parental leave is guaranteed under Articles 37(5) and 46(3) of the 1980 Workers' Statute.	Parental leave is guaranteed under the terms of the Act on Parental Leave for the Care of Children, 1978 (Lagen om rätt till ledighet för vard av barn).	No statutory rights.
Entitlements		
Article 37(5) of the Workers' Statute allows male and female workers to reduce their working day when looking after a child up to the age of six; Article 46(3) allows leave for up to three years in the same circumstances. In all cases, such leave is unpaid. Length of service requirements are unspecified. These rights, which apply to both private and public sectors, apply also to adoptive parents. These periods of leave may not be extended. There are no major collective agreements at either central or sector level covering the issue. Workers retain "only preferential rights to vacancies for the same or a similar category of job in the firm" once their leave entitlements have expired.	The following forms of paid parental leave may all be taken: – 180 days (within 270 days of the child's birth); – 180 days to be used before the child reaches the age of eight; the parent receives "parent's pay" for the first 90 days, and 48 kr (approx. £4.25) a day for the next 90; – 60 days per year per child for temporary care of the child until it reaches the age of 12; "parent's pay" is equal to sick pay (that is, 90% normal earnings). These rights cover both private and public sectors. Sector-level agreements may make minor improvements to the law, which also covers adoptive parents, step-parents and guardians acting in place of parents. Basic entitlements, which cannot normally be increased, may be taken until the child reaches 18 months if the parent works full time or until it reaches 12 years if the parent works part time. The parent has the right to return to same job.	Parental leave in the UK is regulated only through negotiation or custom and practice. Personal leave in exceptional domestic circumstances – which covers parental leave – may be allowed, for example, at British Rail (one day), the BBC (two days) and the British Airports Authority (three to five days). At the BBC, it is possible to split full days into half days. These periods of leave are treated like paid holiday for the purposes of social security.
Statutory rights to leave for family reasons		
Leave for family reasons is guaranteed under Article 37(3) of the 1980 Workers' Statute.	Parental leave is also guaranteed under the Act on Parental Leave for Care of Children 1978.	No statutory rights.
Entitlements		
Paid leave is allowed as follows: Illness of spouse: 2-4 days; Death of close relative: 2-4 days; Illness of child: 2-4 days; Own wedding: 14 days; Birth of a child: 2 days; Moving house: 1 day. Time off is allowed on each appropriate occasion and may be improved under collective agreement or custom and practice. It is considered as ordinary holiday entitlement for the purposes of social security.	Entitlements may be improved through collective agreement and custom and practice. Illness or death of a close relative and marriage are reasons for personal leave – the time off itself varies. Under the central agreement between the SAF and white-collar PTK, short periods of paid time off are allowed at the discretion of management for urgent family reasons. Similar rights also exist under other blue-collar sector level agreements such as metalworking. Unpaid leave may also be requested by the employee.	Companies adopt a wide variety of approaches to special leave. National agreements rarely contain clauses on special leave other than for bereavement. Most agreements provide for special leave to be paid and for it to be awarded at management discretion. Examples of such arrangements include Optical Fibres and Black and Decker, which allow unspecified paid time off for bereavement, and Marleys and Ford, which allow up to three days off for the same reason.

MATERNITY BENEFITS — ILO GLOBAL SURVEY

[Following is selected material from an International Labour Office survey on maternity benefits in countries around the world. The 35-page survey, *Maternity Benefits in the Eighties: An ILO Global Survey (1964-84)*, was published under 1985 copyright by the ILO, Geneva, Switzerland, and is reproduced, in part, with the permission of the publisher.]

An analysis of the national legislation of 127 countries for which information is available, shows that the average length of maternity leave in the world is between 12 and 14 weeks. Over half the countries (69) stipulate maternity leave of this duration. The next group (31 countries) provides less than the average, while the rest exceed this average. The shorter period of leave is prevalent mostly in developing countries, while longer maternity leave has been the national policy of socialist countries for a long time. In market economy countries, since 1975, there has been a trend towards increasing the period of maternity leave.

As far as working relations are concerned, maternity protection covers all laws, regulations and agreements that provide for specific benefits for women workers during or after pregnancy and protect their jobs during absence from work. The principal object of these measures is to protect the health of the future mother and child and to guarantee a continuing source of income and security of employment.

Although almost all the countries have laws and regulations on the subject, their nature and scope take various forms: laws relating exclusively to maternity protection, laws on female labour, labour codes, laws on conditions of employment in certain sectors of the economy, social security laws, labour ordinances or regulations, workers' charters, etc. A very large number of countries also have collective agreements to reinforce and supplement existing legislation or to fill the gap where there is no such legislation. Because these measures take so many different forms, it is difficult to assess their scope with any degree of accuracy, as the relevant texts do not always cover the same occupational categories. A comparative analysis is further complicated by the virtual absence in some developing countries of any information on enforcement of maternity protection legislation, particularly in medium-sized and small undertakings. The problem with women — especially those who are not members of a trade union — is that they often do not take full advantage of maternity protection laws and regulations as they themselves are not aware of their rights.

[The following tables summarize, for selected countries, the legislative provisions related to maternity protection in force as at 30 June 1984.]

ASIA AND THE PACIFIC: Summary of laws and regulations governing maternity protection (as at 30 June 1984)

Country	Qualifying conditions	Length of leave	Cash benefits paid by (a) social security or insurance (b) employer	Prohibition of dismissal	Nursing breaks (a) frequency (b) authorised period
Australia	Government employment [5]	12 weeks (6 + 6); possibility of unpaid additional leave (until child is 1 year old)	Full pay during maternity leave; accumulated annual leave, sick leave and seniority leave may be used in place of unpaid additional leave	Entitled to return to former or comparable post	—
Indonesia	6 months of contributions during past 12 months	12 weeks (6 + 6)	(b) 50% of wages during maternity leave [7]	—	—
Japan	Employment with social insurance coverage	12 weeks (6 + 6) [8]	(a) 60% of insured wages, as per wage scale, during maternity leave	During maternity leave and 30 subsequent days	(a) 2 of half an hour (unpaid) (b) Until child is 1 year old
Philippines	3 months of contributions during past 12 months	45 days, including at least 2 weeks before confinement; possible unpaid extension in case of illness due to pregnancy, confinement, abortion or miscarriage	(a) Full pay during maternity leave based on normal or average weekly wage; [13] possibility of using accumulated leave in lieu of unpaid leave	During pregnancy, maternity leave and illness due to pregnancy or confinement	—
Thailand	180 days with same employer (prior to pregnancy)	60 days	(b) 100% of normal wages for up to 30 days	During maternity leave	—

AFRICA: Summary of laws and regulations governing maternity protection (as at 30 June 1984)

Country	Qualifying conditions	Length of leave	Cash benefits paid by (a) social security or insurance (b) employer	Prohibition of dismissal	Nursing breaks (a) frequency (b) authorised period
Algeria	10 months' social security coverage and 120 hours in employment during past 3 months	12 weeks, including at least 6 after confinement	(a) 50% of basic wage	During maternity leave	(a) 1 hour (b) Until child is 1 year old

Country	Qualifying conditions	Length of leave	Cash benefits paid by (a) social security or insurance (b) employer	Prohibition of dismissal	Nursing breaks (a) frequency (b) authorised period
Egypt	Social insurance coverage for past 10 months	50 days, of which 40 days must be taken after confinement; possibility of 6 months additional leave in case of illness due to pregnancy or confinement	(a) 75% of wages during maternity leave	During maternity leave	(a) 2 of half an hour (b) Until child is 18 months' old
Kenya	—	2 months (but loss of annual leave)[7]	(b) Full pay	—	—
Nigeria	6 months with same employer	12 weeks (6 + 6 (compulsory): extension in case of illness due to pregnancy or confinement	(b) At least 50% of wages during maternity leave	During maternity and any absence for illness due to pregnancy or confinement	(a) 2 of half an hour (unpaid)

THE AMERICAS: Summary of laws and regulations governing maternity protection (as at 30 June 1984)

Country	Qualifying conditions	Length of leave	Cash benefits paid by (a) social security or insurance (b) employer	Prohibition of dismissal	Nursing breaks (a) frequency (b) authorised period
Argentina	Employment with social security coverage and at least 10 months' uninterrupted contributions prior to confinement	90 days (at least (30 + 45)	(a) 100% of wages during maternity leave	Guaranteed security of employment from the time pregnancy is declared to the end of maternity leave (extension in case of illness due to confinement)	(a) 2 of half an hour (b) Until child is 1 year old (under the national agricultural labour scheme, nursing mothers are entitled to appropriate breaks)
Brazil	Social insurance coverage	12 weeks (4 + 8)[4]	100% of wages (paid by employer) or fixed amount equal to regional minimum wage (paid by social welfare), during maternity leave	Even the sending of notice of dismissal is prohibited during maternity leave (pregnancy and confinement are not reasonable grounds for dismissal). Worker entitled to return to former post	(a) 2 of half an hour (unpaid)

Country	Qualifying conditions	Length of leave	Cash benefits paid by (a) social security or insurance (b) employer	Prohibition of dismissal	Nursing breaks (a) frequency (b) authorised period
Canada	6 months of continuous service with same employer, and 20 weeks with unemployment insurance coverage during previous year	17 weeks[7] (up to 11 + up to 17); 24 weeks of parental leave (start of leave left to discretion of person concerned)	At least 60% of average weekly insurable wage over previous 20 weeks, for 15 weeks (paid by unemployment insurance)	Maintains all benefits accruing to previous employment and is entitled to return to regular job or comparable post	—
Chile	Social insurance coverage and 13 weeks of contributions during last 6 months preceding request for leave	18 weeks (6 + 12)	Previous earnings with allowances, less social welfare contributions and deductions provided for by law, during maternity leave and additional leave	During pregnancy and for 1 year after completion of maternity leave	(a) 2, not exceeding 1 hour in all
Mexico	Social insurance coverage and 30 weeks of contributions during 12 months preceding entitlement to benefit	12 weeks (6 + 6); 9 additional weeks in case of illness due to pregnancy or confinement	100% of average earnings during maternity leave (paid by social insurance or employer) and 50% during additional leave (paid by social insurance)	Entitled to return to former post provided work is resumed within one year following confinement	(a) 2 of half an hour (unpaid)
Venezuela	Social insurance coverage	12 weeks (6 + 6)	(a) 66% of earnings during maternity leave	Entitled to retain former post until end of maternity leave	(a) 2 of half an hour (unpaid)

THE MIDDLE EAST: Summary of laws and regulations governing maternity protection (as at 30 June 1984)

Country	Qualifying conditions	Length of leave	Cash benefits paid by (a) social security or insurance (b) employer	Prohibition of dismissal	Nursing breaks (a) frequency (b) authorised period
Iraq	26 weeks of contributions during 12 months preceding probable date of confinement[7]	10 weeks, including at least 6 after confinement; up to 9 months' extension in case of illness due to pregnancy or confinement; additional 6 months to be taken during the first 4 years of the child's life (up to 4 times)	(a) 100% of wages during maternity leave; 75% of wages during extended leave; 50% of wages during the additional 6 months (up to 4 times)	During pregnancy, maternity leave and illness due to pregnancy or confinement	2 of half an hour

Country	Qualifying conditions	Length of leave	Cash benefits paid by (a) social security or insurance (b) employer	Prohibition of dismissal	Nursing breaks
Israel	10 months of contributions during past 14 months	12 weeks, including at least 3 after confinement: possible 4-week extension	75% of wages during maternity leave and additional leave (paid by national insurance)	During pregnancy and maternity leave	1 hour (over and above normal breaks)
Jordan	180 days work during past 12 months	6 weeks (3 + 3)	(b) 50% of average daily wage	—	—
Saudi Arabia	At least 12 months with same employer	10 weeks (4 + 6); 6 months' extension in case of illness due to pregnancy or confinement	(b) 50 or 100% of wages during maternity leave[12]	6 months before confinement, during maternity leave and illness due to pregnancy or confinement	One or more, of one hour in all
Syrian Arab Republic	6 months' employment in agricultural sector, 7 months in other sectors (prior to interruption of work)	50 days in all, including 30 after confinement, in agricultural sector; 60 days in all, including 40 after confinement, in other sectors	50% of wages in agricultural sector, 70% in other sectors, during maternity leave	During maternity leave and for 6 months after confinement (if absent for illness due to pregnancy or confinement)	1 hour for 6 months, in agricultural sector; 2 of half an hour for 18 months following confinement, in other sectors
Turkey	120 days of contributions during year preceding confinement	12 weeks (6 + 6); possible extension before and after confinement, depending on state of health and nature of occupation of worker	(a) Two-thirds of average daily earnings	During maternity leave	2 of half an hour

EUROPEAN MARKET ECONOMY COUNTRIES: Summary of laws and regulations governing maternity protection (as at 30 June 1984)

Country	Qualifying conditions	Length of leave	Cash benefits paid by (a) social security or insurance (b) employer	Prohibition of dismissal	Nursing breaks (a) frequency (b) authorised period
Austria	Employment with social insurance coverage ; for confinement allowance, worker must have been the dependent of an insured person for 10 months during past 2 years, including 6 months during year preceding pregnancy	16 weeks (8 (compulsory) + 8); 4 additional weeks in case of premature, multiple or Caesarean birth; if pre-natal leave has been reduced, post-natal leave is extended to up to 12 weeks; possibility of unpaid additional leave (until child is 1 year old)	(a) During maternity leave, daily allowance equal to average rate, per calendar day, of remuneration during past 13 weeks (or past 3 months), after deductions provided for by law	During pregnancy and until end of 4th month following confinement and 4th week following the end of unpaid leave	Two of 45 minutes or one of 90 minutes if working day is 8 hours or more; one of 45 minutes if working day is over 4½ hours but less than 8 hours
Belgium	6 months' social insurance coverage, including 3 months preceding confinement, and 120 days of actual or credited work	14 weeks (6 + 8) (compulsory)) ; possibility of unpaid leave for 3 years	For manual workers, 100% of wage for 7 days (paid by employer); for other workers, 100% of wages for 1 month; for all categories, 79.5% of earnings during rest of maternity leave (paid by social security)	During pregnancy and for 1 month after post-natal leave[a]	—
Denmark	Insured and working for 6 months during 1 year preceding confinement, including at least 40 hours in 4 weeks preceding leave	24 weeks (4 + 20), 10 of which can be taken by either parent; 2 weeks' paternity leave at birth	For manual workers, 90% of average weekly earnings for 18 weeks (first 3 weeks paid by employer, subsequent weeks by social security); for other categories, at least 50% of normal wages for up to 5 months (paid by employer)	During maternity leave and on account of pregnancy, confinement or adoption of a child	—

Country	Qualifying conditions	Duration of leave	Cash benefits	Employment protection	Nursing breaks
Finland	For cash benefits, past 3 months in employment with health insurance coverage; for medical care, residence in the country	258 working days, including 24 before confinement	45% of wages during maternity leave (paid by health insurance)[4,7]	During pregnancy and maternity leave (provided employer has been duly notified)	—
France	At least 10 months social security coverage prior to confinement and 200 hours employment during 3 months preceding pregnancy	16 weeks (6 + 10); 2 additional weeks in case of multiple birth possibility of unpaid parental leave of half-time work up to 2 years	90% of earnings (paid by maternity insurance)	As soon as pregnancy is diagnosed and for 14 weeks following confinement (16 weeks in the case of multiple birth) priority for reinstatement during 1 year following unpaid leave	(a) 1 hour, in 2 breaks (b) Until child is 1 year old
Federal Republic of Germany	Compulsory insurance coverage or employment relationship for at least 12 weeks between 10th and 4th month preceding confinement	14 weeks (6 (compulsory) + 8); 4 additional weeks in case of premature or multiple birth ; entitlement to additional leave (until child is 6 months old)	100% of wages guaranteed during maternity leave (health funds cover cost up to a ceiling, the difference between this benefit and the average wage being paid by employer); monthly allowance of 750 DM (approx. US$207) during additional leave (paid by social insurance)	During pregnancy and until end of 4th month following confinement (if employer has been duly notified); entitled to return to former post	(a) 2 of half an hour or one of 1 hour; if working day is more than 8 consecutive hours, two of 45 minutes or one of 90 minutes
Greece	200 days of contributions during 2 years preceding entitlement to benefit	12 weeks (6 + at least 6); possible extension in case of illness due to pregnancy or confinement	(a) Single lump-sum allowance for confinement expenses; for women with social insurance coverage, additional benefits up to equivalent of normal earnings during maternity leave	On account of pregnancy, during maternity leave, or longer period in case of illness due to pregnancy or confinement	(a) Up to 1 hour (b) Until child is 1 year old
Iceland	For daily allowance, social security coverage; for maternity allowance, residence in the country	3 months (1 + 2)	(a) Daily allowance not exceeding 75% of average wage during past 2 months during maternity leave; maternity allowance for residents	During pregnancy and post-natal leave	—

Country	Qualifying conditions [1]	Length of leave [2]	Cash benefits paid by (a) social security or insurance (b) employer	Prohibition of dismissal	Nursing breaks [3] (a) frequency (b) authorised period
Ireland	26 weeks of contributions during year preceding first day of maternity leave	At least 14 weeks (at least 4 + at least 4); if confinement is after expected date, pre-natal leave may be extended by up to 4 weeks; possibility of up to 4 weeks' unpaid additional leave	80% of average weekly net wage during maternity leave (paid by social welfare)	Guaranteed employment security during maternity leave and additional leave; entitled to return to former post	—
Italy	Must be employed and insured at start of pregnancy	5 months (2 (3 in case of arduous work) + 3); optional 6 months' leave at the end of compulsory leave during 1st year of child's life; 6 or 3 months in case of adoption (according to child's age); possibility of unpaid parental leave if child is sick (until child is 3 years old)	80% of earnings during maternity leave (paid by social welfare); 30% of wages during optional leave; 80% or 30% of earnings in case of adoption (according to child's age)	During pregnancy and until child is 1 year old	(a) 2 of half an hour (two of 1 hour if child cannot be nursed at place of work) (b) Until child is 1 year old
Luxembourg	Social insurance coverage for at least 6 months during year immediately preceding confinement	16 weeks, including up to 8 before and at least 8 after confinement; 4 additional weeks in case of premature or multiple birth or if mother nurses child	100% of earnings during maternity leave [16]	During pregnancy and up to 12th week after confinement	(a) 2 of 45 minutes or one of 90 minutes
Malta	50 weeks of contributions and 50 weeks of employment during preceding year	At least 13 weeks, including 5 weeks after confinement [17]	(b) 100% of wages for 13 weeks for full-time workers, provided employer has been duly notified at least 3 weeks before start of leave	During maternity leave (and 5 subsequent weeks if mother cannot return to work because of illness due to confinement); entitled to return to former or comparable post	—

Netherlands	Social insurance coverage	12 weeks, including at least 4 before and 6 after confinement	(a) 100% of earnings during maternity leave	During pregnancy, post-natal leave and 6 subsequent weeks	(a) Free time as necessary
Norway	6 months' national insurance coverage during 10 months preceding confinement	18 weeks, including at least 6 after confinement; at time of confinement, father is entitled to 2 weeks' leave to look after family and home	100% of earnings during maternity leave and leave taken by father to look after family and home (paid by national insurance)	During pregnancy and up to the 6th week following confinement	(a) 2 of half an hour or up to one hour's reduction in daily hours of work
Portugal	5 months' social security coverage, including 8 days of contributions during 3 months preceding entitlement to benefit	90 days, including 60 days of uninterrupted leave (10 to 30 in case of miscarriage, stillbirth or death of newborn child); 30 additional days before in case of complications; 60 days' parental leave in case of adoption, to be taken by mother or father	(a) 100% of earnings during maternity leave	From time person stops work because of pregnancy and for 1 year after confinement; entitled to return to work after parental leave, with all acquired rights	(a) 2 of half an hour (b) Until child is 1 year old
Spain	9 months' social security coverage before confinement and 180 days of contributions during year preceding confinement	Up to 14 weeks to be taken at the person's discretion; possibility of unpaid leave of 1 to 3 years for each child	(a) 75% of basic wage for calculating social security contributions, during maternity leave	Employment relationship may be suspended on account of maternity; at end of period of suspension, worker is entitled to return to former post (at end of unpaid leave, priority for reinstatement in vacant post in same or comparable category)	(a) 2 of half an hour or one of 1 hour, or possibility of reducing normal hours of work by half an hour per day (b) Until child is 9 months old
Sweden	6 months' employment prior to confinement or 12 months during past 2 years	12 weeks (at least 6 + 6); possible extension of post-natal leave up to 360 days, to be taken by mother or father	90% of wages for both parents for up to 290 days (paid by public insurance)[20]	During maternity leave and parental leave (mother or father)	(a) Free time as necessary

Country	Qualifying conditions	Length of leave[1]	Cash benefits	Prohibition of dismissal	Nursing breaks[2] (a) frequency (b) authorised period
Switzerland	—	14 weeks, including 8 after confinement (6 weeks, if requested by worker concerned); no provision for post-natal leave under federal law	—	For 8 weeks before and up to 8 after confinement	(a) Free time as necessary

EUROPEAN SOCIALIST COUNTRIES: Summary of laws and regulations governing maternity protection (as at 30 June 1984)

Country	Qualifying conditions	Length of leave[1]	Cash benefits	Prohibition of dismissal	Nursing breaks[2] (a) frequency (b) authorised period
Albania	Uninterrupted work with same employer for past 6 months; for entitlement to confinement allowance, income not exceeding 900 leks (approx. US$130) per month	12 to 15 weeks (5 + 7 to 10)	75% of earnings during maternity leave (95% in the case of an uninterrupted employment relationship of at least 5 years); confinement allowance (for child's layette and food) of 280 leks per child	During maternity leave	(a) 1 half-hour per 3- or 4-hour period
Bulgaria	None	120 calendar days for first child, 150 for second, 180 for third and 120 for each subsequent child, including 45 days before confinement; 6 to 8 months' additional leave (according to the number of children); possibility of unpaid additional leave (until child is 3 years old)	100% of earnings during maternity leave; benefits equal to national minimum wage during paid additional leave; monthly allowance of 10 leva (approx. US$10) during unpaid additional leave; confinement allowance of 100 leva for first child, 250 leva for second, 500 for third, and 100 leva for each subsequent child	During pregnancy and 8 months following confinement	Two of 1 hour (until child is 8 months old); thereafter, one of 1 hour (in case of multiple birth, breaks are increased by one hour)
Byelorussian SSR	None	112 days (56 + 56); additional 14 days post-natal leave in case of multiple birth or complications;[3] possibility of partly paid additional leave (until child is 1 year old) and unpaid (until child is 18 months old)	100% of earnings during maternity leave; monthly allowance of 35-50 roubles (approx. US$41-60) during partly paid additional leave	During pregnancy, nursing period and partly paid and unpaid leave	(a) One of at least half an hour per 3-hour period (b) Until child is 1 year old (break is twice as long for mothers nursing more than one child)

Country	Qualifying conditions[1]	Length of leave[1]	Cash benefits	Prohibition of dismissal	Nursing breaks[2] (a) frequency (b) authorised period
Czechoslovakia	270 days' social insurance coverage during past 2 years (still eligible for 6 months after stopping work)	26 weeks, including 4 to 8 weeks before confinement; 9 additional weeks in case of multiple birth and for single mothers; possibility of unpaid additional leave (until child is 2 years old)	90% of wages during maternity leave and additional leave; confinement allowance of 2,000 crowns (approx. US$150) per child	During pregnancy and so long as mother is looking after her child permanently (up to the age of 3)	2 of half an hour in respect of each child under 6 months old; 1 of half an hour during subsequent 3 months
German Democratic Republic	6 months' social insurance coverage during past year and 10 months during past 2 years; none for students	26 weeks, including 6 before confinement; additional 2 weeks post-natal leave in case of multiple birth or complications; as from second child, paid additional leave (until child is 1 year old); possibility of unpaid additional leave (until child is 3 years old)	Average net income during maternity leave; during paid additional leave, benefit paid at rate of sickness benefit as from birth of second child of 300 marks (approx. US$100) for 2 children, of 350 marks for 3 or more children; confinement allowance of 1,000 marks per child	During pregnancy, nursing period and leave following maternity leave	(a) Two of 45 minutes (b) Until child is 6 months old
Poland	None	16 weeks for first child, 18 for second (26 weeks in case of multiple birth)[a]; possibility of unpaid additional leave (until child is 4 years old) which can be extended up to 3 years if child is handicapped or suffers from a chronic disease (until child is 10 years old)	100% of earnings during maternity leave; confinement allowance of 2,000 zlotys (approx. US$16) per child	During pregnancy and maternity leave	(a) 2 of half an hour (two of 45 minutes for mothers nursing more than one child)
USSR	None	112 days (56 + 56); additional 14 days post-natal leave in case of multiple birth or complications;[3] possibility of partly paid additional leave (until child is 1 year old) and unpaid (until child is 18 months old)	100% of earnings during maternity leave; monthly allowance of 35-50 roubles (approx. US$41-60) during partly paid additional leave	During pregnancy, nursing period and partly paid and unpaid leave	(a) One of at least half an hour per 3-hour period (b) Until child is 1 year old (break is twice as long for mothers nursing more than one child)

VI. LABOR-MANAGEMENT APPROACHES

As this report demonstrates, both employers and labor unions are beginning to respond to problems arising out of the interrelationship between family and work.

Management and labor are learning that work issues can create family problems, and family problems can create work issues. In the public and private sectors, and in all areas of the United States, labor-management attempts to resolve these problems are evident. Case studies appearing earlier in this report illustrate some of these joint problem-solving efforts.

Yet such cooperative efforts are not yet the norm. Historically, the chief concerns of labor unions have been wages, benefits, and working conditions. For unions, and for companies, too, workers' private lives were considered to be just that — private. As one local union leader, Mark Dudzic of the Oil, Chemical and Atomic Workers Union, put it, "Unions traditionally have grown up addressing just the worker as an individual, not as a member of a family."

However, the trend toward the inclusion of work-and-family issues in collective bargaining has intensified, both because of the growing concern of rank-and-file union members and because of, and in reaction to, management's establishment of such programs as employee assistance plans and alternative work schedules. Unions and management have begun to extend the boundaries of the family-work dialogue and are continuing to define their positions on specific family-and-work issues.

Cooperation or Conflict?

Whether unions and companies will be able to work together in a cooperative fashion to resolve family-and-work problems or will reach agreement only after heated negotiations at the bargaining table depends on how the individual unions and companies approach each other. The styles of resolving problems are as different as the individuals involved.

Douglas Fraser, former president of the United Auto Workers, observed in a BNA interview in January 1986 that, in general, there is more cooperation between labor and management at this time in history than ever before.

Will this mood of cooperation extend to family-and-work issues?

John J. Sweeney, president of the Service Employees International Union, told BNA, "The labor movement is ready for any cooperative ventures that might be in the works."

"In addressing these [work and family] kinds of issues related to workers, we will be reaching out for whatever opportunities there are to develop labor-management programs," Sweeney said, adding, "It remains to be seen how much support is going to come from the management area on these issues."

And, according to Joyce Miller, president of the Coalition of Labor Union Women, the labor movement has begun to see family-related issues in a larger context than "women's issues." Miller told BNA: "I think the key thing is that work-and-family issues are now looked at in the labor movement as key worker issues, not women's issues."

One thing is certain, however: More and more, family issues are becoming part of the labor-management agenda. And as the number of women in the work force continues to grow, and as more and more women enter leadership roles in labor unions, family issues are likely to move to the top of that agenda.

Fraser told BNA: "I would predict that the development of these areas is almost inevitable, basically because the need is there. There are more women in the work force, in addition more women are becoming active in the unions, and when collective bargaining time comes around, the women's needs are going to be reflected in the collective bargaining process."

The importance labor is placing on family and work is underscored by the AFL-CIO Executive Council's adoption in 1986 of a resolution on "Work and Family." The resolution, adopted at the Council's midwinter meeting, states that the AFL-CIO continues to urge affiliates to seek "family strengthening programs through the collective bargaining process, including joint employer-union sponsored day care centers, information and referral services, allowances for care in existing centers, time off when the child or dependent is sick, and establishing flexible working hours to accommodate caring for children or other dependents." (Text of the resolution is contained in the Appendix.)

In addition, the AFL-CIO and some individual unions have lobbied Congress on family-and-work issues. The federation supports legislation (HR 2020) introduced by Rep. Patricia Schroeder (D-Colo) that would require employers to provide at least 18 weeks of leave to a father or mother of a newborn, newly adopted, or seriously ill child. The bill would guarantee that a worker could return to his or her same job or an equivalent position with like seniority, status, employment benefits, pay, and other terms and conditions of employment. (See Chapter IV for discussion of parental leave, Chapter V for discussion of proposed federal legislation, and the Appendix for text of HR 2020.)

The labor-management dialogue on family and work has taken several forms, including the establishment of joint labor-management committees to explore specific problems, as well as bargaining table negotiations over contract issues that affect family and work.

The primary focus of this labor-management dialogue has been on:
• Alternative work schedules;
• Child care;
• Parental leave; and
• Employee assistance plans.

Differences of Opinion

Although both are starting to recognize the importance of family/work problems, unions and employers do have some significant differences in how they think these problems should be tackled. On just about any work-and-family issue, the union position may differ at least slightly from that of management.

Alternative work schedules are a particularly thorny issue for labor unions. The labor movement worked hard to establish the eight-hour day, 40-hour workweek as the norm, beyond which overtime rates would be paid. In the view of some unions, alternative work schedules encroach upon this norm and carry with them the risk that the employer could use them as a way to avoid paying premium wage rates to workers. Unions often fear that a schedule which could benefit some individuals with special needs could also be used to harm the bargaining unit as a whole.

However, some union members want the option to work more flexible schedules and have asked that alternative work schedules be included in contract negotiations.

Advice to Negotiators

Advice from the American Federation of State, County and Municipal Employees to its local unions reflects some of the general concerns of labor toward alternative work schedules. Essentially, AFSCME has told its locals to "proceed with caution" in negotiating on the issue.

In its April 1983 publication "Alternative Work Schedules," AFSCME noted that there has been a growing interest in schedules that deviate from the traditional 9-to-5 day and five-day workweek. Warning that there are "pitfalls and potential for abuse," AFSCME suggested that locals "carefully weigh the pros and cons" before agreeing to deviate from traditional scheduling.

AFSCME conceded there are some advantages to alternative work schedules, specifically noting that flextime allows employees to:
- Schedule personal business into their day;
- Have the option of working either early or late; and
- Ease commuting.

There are drawbacks to flextime, however, according to AFSCME:
- "It threatens the concept of premium pay for time worked over 8 hours per day or 40 hours per week.
- "Employees who did not have to punch a clock before the institution of a flexitime system may resent the need to begin time-keeping.
- "The institution of flexitime may open up jobs for more part-timers who may not be covered by the union contract.
- "It is actually a fairly minor alteration of the work environment. Although it allows employees to slightly rearrange their schedules, it does not provide them with more free time for family responsibilities or leisure."

AFSCME noted that sometimes management resists flextime on the ground that the workplace may not be adequately staffed at times. However, according to AFSCME, flextime offers advantages to employers, too, including reduced absenteeism, less use of sick leave to take care of personal business, and improved employee morale, among others.

The AFSCME publication also provided sample contract language for negotiating flextime and other alternative work schedule provisions.

CLUW Suggests Careful Planning

The Coalition of Labor Union Women (CLUW) advocates bargaining for alternative work schedules, but like AFSCME, warns that such provisions can have disadvantages.

In "Bargaining for Child Care," published in 1985, CLUW said alternative work schedules "should be set up under the auspices of collective bargaining and/or a labor-management committee," and added that the union "should insist on careful planning of even a pilot program."

CLUW listed as advantages reduced absenteeism, reduced lateness, improved employee morale, reduced turnover, and increased productivity. Disadvantages, according to CLUW, are reduction in opportunities to earn overtime and premium pay; institution of different time-keeping measures; and longer workdays which may increase stress and other problems.

CLUW advised unions that, before negotiating alternative work schedules:

" — employee attitudes and expectations should be thoroughly canvassed;

" — employee participation should be voluntary;

" — the possible impact on personnel regulations and contractual requirements, including opportunity for overtime earnings, should be taken into account.

" — the potential effect on numbers of jobs should be analyzed."

The formation of joint labor-management committees "that encourage mutual cooperation and creativity in the development, administration, and implementation of more flexible workplace policies" is recommended in the report "Work and Family in the United States: A Policy Initiative," issued in 1986 by the Economic Policy Council of the UNA-USA. The EPC report noted that "work councils have played a crucial role in the adoption and management of flexitime policies in West Germany," where almost half of all workers are on flextime schedules.

The EPC family policy panel comprised leaders from the business, labor, and academic communities, including former President Gerald R. Ford, and was co-chaired by Service Employees International Union President Sweeney. Five other union presidents were among the two dozen panel members.

Collective Bargaining on Child Care

In general, unions are more positive, and less cautious, on the issues of child care and parental leave than they are on the issue of alternative work schedules. Many unions support actions on child care, whether those actions take the form of labor-management committees to investigate possible solutions to child care problems or programs to provide specific kinds of child care assistance.

Some unions are seeking gains primarily through collective bargaining and believe that companies should bear the responsibility of helping employees with child care and other parental concerns, while other unions believe that communities or government — more so than employers or unions — should be responsible for seeing that the nation's child care needs are met.

A few unions, particularly in the garment industry, have even opened their own child care centers to serve their members' needs. The International Ladies' Garment Workers' Union opened a child care center in New York City's Chinatown to serve members' needs.

Joyce Miller, vice president of American Clothing and Textile Workers Union and president of CLUW, said that ACTWU also has opened child care centers to serve members' needs. However, she described ACTWU's experience — particularly in Baltimore and Chicago — as "difficult" because the companies may go out of business, leaving the center with no one to serve. The union may be "left with a very beautiful child care center and none of the workers who it was set up for are able to use it."

"Basically, I would like to see child care in the community so that you are not dependent on one factory or one place for children to use the child care center," Miller said.

In collective bargaining, the costs of dealing with issues such as child care and parental leave are major union concerns. An employer's agreement to fund a child care center, or contract for a child care information and referral service for employees, might likely mean there would be less money available for salaries and more widely sought benefits. Nevertheless, in many places demands are being raised at the bargaining table and, more and more often, particularly since the late 1970s, child care provisions are appearing in labor contracts.

Some of the specific child care programs that have been negotiated at the bargaining table include:

• A child care subsidy of $500 per year for employees covered by the collective bargaining agreement between the *Village Voice* and District 65, United Auto Workers.

• An on-site day care center at Boston City Hospital, a result of the contract between the hospital and Service Employees International Union Local 285. (See case study in Chapter IV.)

• Development of experimental, model day care centers at both Ford Motor Company and General Motors Corporation, provided for in the companies' contracts with United Auto Workers.

• An information and referral program provided to employees of the Library of Congress, under terms of the agreement with AFSCME.

• An unusual overtime subsidy provision in the contract between Local 30 of the Office and Professional Employees International Union and Margolis, McTernan, Scope & Sacks, a Los Angeles law firm. The clause provides that a subsidy of 75 cents per hour, in addition to overtime pay, be paid when employees whose children are being cared for at day care centers or by babysitters work overtime. That provision was first negotiated in 1979.

Both CLUW in "Bargaining for Child Care" and AFSCME in its June 1984 "Negotiating About Child Care: Issues and Options" offer guidance to unions negotiating child care provisions. "Bargaining for Child Care" contains advice to labor unions interested in bargaining child care provisions, and includes model language on child care and samples of specific contract provisions negotiated by labor unions.

"Negotiating About Child Care: Issues and Options" also includes sample contract language, information about how to establish a child care center, and lists of reference materials. (See Appendix for text of several sample contract provisions.)

New York State Child Care Network

Probably the largest collectively bargained child care program can be found in New York. Initially a product of collective bargaining between the Civil Service Employees Association (CSEA) and the State of New York, Empire State Day Care Services now boasts 30 child care centers serving state employees represented by four of the six labor unions that bargain with the state.

Child care was first raised by CSEA as a bargaining table demand in 1976 labor negotiations, according to Michelle McCormick, employee program assistant with Empire State Day Care Services. At that point, "nobody knew what to do" about providing child care assistance, she said. However, a state official's experience in establishing a child care center proved valuable when the program was negotiated in 1979. A pilot program was established in 1979, with "seed money" provided by the federal government, she said.

The pilot proved successful, and led to the formation of Empire State Day Care Services, which McCormick described as a separate, private, not-for-profit corporation. Unions that currently participate are CSEA, the Public Employees Federation, United University Professors, and AFSCME Council 82, according to McCormick.

Separate labor-management committees oversee operation of the centers, McCormick said, and are involved at each level of the operation, from the local level to a state-level joint labor-management day care advisory committee. At the local level, each program is developed by a local labor-management committee, which establishes a board of directors, and incorporates as a subsidiary of the umbrella Empire State Day Care Services. The centers then apply for tax-exempt status.

McCormick said seed money covers start-up costs for each center, while New York State provides space and contributes funds for renovation. Once a center is operating, it is obliged to repay the state for renovation costs. The centers are self-supporting through parent fees, which are set on a sliding scale based on income.

Centers now operating are well utilized, and additional centers are being planned. McCormick said "every site" has a waiting list for infant and toddler care.

Family Responsibility Leave

An unusual "family responsibility leave" provision is contained in current contracts between AFSCME and the State of Illinois Department of Central Management Services. (See Appendix for text of provision.)

This provision establishes that leave may be granted to meet an employee's responsibilities "arising from the employee's role in his or her family or as head of the household." Leave of up to one year may be granted under this provision and requests "shall not be unreasonably denied." Among the reasons such leave may be granted are to care for a newborn or adopted child; to care for a temporarily disabled member of the family; to settle the estate of a deceased family member; or to respond to temporary dislocation of the family due to natural disaster, crime, insurrection, war, or other disruptive event.

Parental Leave

In "Bargaining for Child Care," CLUW asserted, "Pregnancy and the birth of a new child should be the occasion for the utmost assurance of continued employment and financial security for a working parent. Nothing could be further from reality."

CLUW noted that today there is greater variation in the kinds of leave available for childbearing or child-rearing, particularly following the passage of Title VII of the Civil Rights Act of 1964. (See *Parental Leave* in Chapter IV.)

Because of this variation in leave provisions, many unions — the United Mine Workers of America, for example — are placing a priority on gaining protection for pregnant women and new parents at the bargaining table. In "Bargaining for Child Care," CLUW included samples of actual contract language and offered the following suggested language on parental leave:

"The employer shall grant leave to an employee because of childbirth or adoption on the following basis:

"a. Leave with full pay and benefits, including accrual of service credit, for any period of time during pregnancy during which the employee's physician certifies that she is disabled from working.

"b. Six months leave with full pay and benefits, including accrual of service credit, for either parent of a newborn or newly adopted child.

"c. Leave without pay for up to two years for child care purposes for either parent, upon submission of a written request. The employee may take any accrued vacation during such leave, and shall have the right to continue medical coverage and all other employer-paid fringe benefits at his or her own expense during said leave. Upon return to work, the employee shall be restored to his or her former position, location and shift or, if that job no longer exists, to the most nearly comparable position. Such period of unpaid leave shall not be deemed a break in service for any employment-related purpose."

Parental leave, like child care, has become an important objective for some labor unions that are seeking contract language allowing workers time off to care for a newborn or newly adopted children and guaranteeing that their jobs will be available to them upon their return to the work force.

"Pregnancy and the birth of a new child should be the occasion for the utmost assurance of continued employment and financial security for a working parent. Nothing could be further from reality."

In testimony in the fall of 1985 before several congressional subcommittees that were considering parental leave and disability legislation, a representative of the United Mine Workers of America explained the union's bargaining table position on parental leave. Stephen F. Webber, member of the UMWA executive board, said parental leave "has made a great deal of sense to the Mine Workers as a bargaining demand." Webber stated:

"We have focused on a demand for an automatic right to six months of unpaid parental leave for a working mother following the period of disability associated with birth, parental leave for a male miner to care for his newly born, and parental leave for either working parent in the case of adoption or a seriously ill child."

The union's proposal also would require the employer to maintain full insurance coverage during the leave and would entitle workers to return to their old job and to accumulate seniority while on leave.

In explaining the Mine Workers' position, Webber said parental leave is a priority for the union because it "was identified by the rank-and-file of our union as an important priority." Before the union's 1983 convention, local union resolutions calling for parental leave to be part of the bargaining agenda "poured into the union headquarters," Webber said.

During 1984 bargaining with the multiemployer association of major coal producers, Webber said, the issue was "aggressively pursued." The parental leave proposal met with stiff resistance from management, he said, but the union was able, "at the last minute," to secure language establishing a special joint study committee on parental leave, which was instructed to issue a report on the feasibility and specifics of such a program.

Employee Assistance Plans

Employee assistance plans designed to help workers deal with family problems are being collectively bargained by unions and companies.

An example of such an EAP can be found in a contract negotiated in 1985 between Buffalo General and Deaconess Hospitals in Buffalo, N.Y., and Nurses United, Local 1168 of the Communications Workers of America. The Buffalo contract — which provides for the establishment of an on-site child care center — also establishes an employee assistance program to deal with problems relating to family life, including drug and alcohol abuse.

In the public sector, New York State and its employees' unions negotiated an employee assistance program with a focus on family as well as substance abuse problems. (See *Employee Assistance Programs* in Chapter IV.)

One Union's Approach to Family and Work

Some within the labor movement believe that whatever the work and family issue, the best way to attack the problems is at the local-union level.

Mark Dudzic, president of Local 8-149 of the Oil, Chemical and Atomic Workers Union, suggested that organized labor, like employers, has been slow to act upon work and family concerns. "At the top [offices] of organized labor, the average age is 60 or so, and it's all male. They probably never had to deal with [child care concerns]," Dudzic said, "so it's no surprise" that those issues haven't received more attention by labor. "But, I think," he said, "it's important that we start to deal with those issues now."

In 1983, Local 8-149 held a conference on work-and-family issues for its members. "People became really excited," Dudzic said. "The biggest response was that 'No one ever told me that the union could do anything about these problems.'" He continued, "Once [the members] knew the union could [do something about them], it sort of took off on its own."

"At the top [offices] of organized labor, the average age is 60 or so, and it's all male. They probably never had to deal with [child care concerns]."

Dudzic is working to establish work/family committees at each of local's work sites. He hopes the committees will function the same way health and safety committees do. "We're looking at a way that could institutionalize the ability of the union to address these types of issues," he said.

While the specific family-and-work problems vary from workplace to workplace, Dudzic reported that the major problem faced by the Local 8-149's members is the rotating shift. "It's almost impossible to do something about child care [because of rotating shifts]," he noted. Mandatory overtime, "especially on short notice," is also a problem, as is a "lack of flexible leave time," Dudzic said. "People can't get off from work when a child is sick, or to go see a teacher, or something like that."

In addition, Dudzic said, parents of latchkey children suffer from "a lack of ability to communicate with the outside world. In one shop, workers on the assembly line aren't allowed to receive phone calls. People want to know their kids got home from school safely."

Dudzic said that the leaders of Local 8-149 did not expect much of a response when child care issues were discussed because two-thirds of the local members are men. However, he explained, "in something like 70 percent of the families with children, both spouses are working [and] men have assumed a high degree of responsibility in the home."

Leave in Four-hour Blocks

Because Local 8-149 negotiates "21 different contracts at 21 different times," so far "the only thing we've really been able to do something about is the leave policy," Dudzic said. "We've been able, in a few contracts, to change sick days to paid personal days, payable in 4-hour blocks," he said. This allows workers to take time off for sick children, or take half days off to attend to school conferences, without "the punitive aspect of taking unexcused personal time."

Contract negotiations "may not be the best way" for the union to address certain family issues, such as phone accessibility, Dudzic opined. "Rather than get a company to do something, we may have to set up a hotline system" where adults field calls from children returning home from school. Some sort of fee system might be set up, noted Dudzic, who said the amount of the fee would be minimized if a large number of workers participated. Should a child not check in with the hotline, "we'd probably be able to get the company to put the call through, which we can ensure is an emergency call." The union will increasingly look to those kind of "self-help" projects, he said.

Another way to address day care concerns, the local union president said, would be to set up child care centers "geared to our members' needs" in cities where there are with three or four worksites where the local represents workers.

Mandatory overtime, however, will be addressed at the bargaining table, according to Dudzic. "We'd like to change to a voluntary overtime system, which would make the bookkeeping more complicated for the company, but I think it can work," he said.

BNA asked several individuals who have extensive knowledge about, or experience in dealing with, family and work issues to respond briefly to the following question: "What are the responsibilities of labor, business, and government toward family concerns of workers and how should those organizations respond to the workers' concerns?"

Responses were submitted by the following individuals: **Helen Axel,** *Director, Work and Family Information Center, The Conference Board;* **Lenora Cole Alexander,** *Director, Women's Bureau, U.S. Department of Labor;* **Jack Golodner,** *Director, Department for Professional Employees (DPE), AFL-CIO, and* **Judith Gregory,** *Research Associate, DPE;* **James A. Klein,** *Manager of Pension & Employee Benefits, and* **Mark A. de Bernardo,** *Manager of Labor Law, U.S. Chamber of Commerce;* **Phyllis Moen,** *Associate Professor, Human Development & Family Studies, and Sociology, Cornell University;* **Stanley D. Nollen,** *Associate Professor, School of Business Administration, Georgetown University;* **Karen Nussbaum,** *Executive Director, 9to5, National Association of Working Women, and President, District 925, Service Employees International Union;* **Barney Olmsted** *and* **Suzanne Smith,** *Co-directors, New Ways to Work; and* **Jerome M. Rosow,** *President, Work in America Institute.*

Helen Axel, Director,
Work and Family Information Center,
The Conference Board

WORK AND FAMILY: SEEKING A NEW BALANCE

[My response addresses the question posed from a somewhat different perspective. Because the Conference Board is proscribed from making recommendations and issuing judgments, the question becomes: "What might be some of the specific responsibilities and responses of labor, business, and government toward family concerns and workers?" The following brief essay explores these issues.]

Finding ways to achieve a better balance between work and family life may be looked upon as the ultimate public-private partnership. Government cannot provide all the solutions, nor is it equipped to do so: Individual choice is too highly valued in our society. And while business and labor have primary responsibility for determining conditions at the workplace, their efforts are not isolated from the social infrastructure of the community and the nation. Working families, who inevitably bear the decisions and burdens of meshing work and family responsibilities, must also depend on both the public and the private sectors as critical participants in the balancing process.

Business has often been accused of being unresponsive to the needs of working families. This "unresponsiveness," however, may be attributed to an unawareness of the changing demographics of the work force; to an unfamiliarity with the range of options that can be described as family supportive; to a lack of sympathy for "soft" issues that are difficult to relate to corporate profits; or to a narrowly defined corporate social role, characterized by a reluctance to intrude into the personal lives of employees. For these reasons, family-supportive responses are likely to spread slowly and unevenly throughout the business community.

For their part, too, labor organizations have been cautious about endorsing family-supportive positions and initiatives, although there have been several notable exceptions and programs. The often adversarial climate between labor and management has contributed to organizational rigidities that are pervasive in many industries. Moreover, organized labor's historical strongholds in old-line industries (where "traditional," male-intensive work forces predominate) have tended to mute unions' response to these issues. However, as unions move to expand their influence in high-growth industrial and service businesses — and to recruit more women, minorities, and non-production workers into their ranks — work-family issues are likely to play a more important role.

Finding ways to achieve a better balance between work and family life may be looked upon as the ultimate public-private partnership.

Workplace initiatives that recognize the diverse needs and capabilities of today's work force tend to be more flexible than the traditional practices of the past. Policies and programs that encourage more worker involvement in the decisionmaking process give employees greater responsibility for and control over their working environment, while allowing them to manage job and home responsibilities more effectively. Such practices — that place a high value on human resources — acknowledge the interdependence of work and family life, and its effect on worker productivity.

Union-Management Innovations

Employers and employees find that a number of useful initiatives are beginning to take hold at the work site at a time when the dynamics of work-force demographics are necessitating significant changes in workplace practices. These developments, coupled with an atmosphere of improving cooperation between union officials and business leaders, seem to indicate that business and labor are already taking innovative steps that will be beneficial to employees and their families. Examples of such steps currently include:

• Providing or encouraging greater flexibility in work scheduling, time away from the job, and work location;

• Giving or encouraging employees choice in the selection and use of company-subsidized benefits — by offering "cafeteria-style" benefits that permit trade-offs on such options as dependent-care assistance, parental and child care leaves, adoption benefits, special medical care coverage, special financial or legal services, or extra vacation time;

• Developing effective, non-adversarial communications systems that relay employee concerns to management and local union officials — and vice versa;

• Promoting employee health and well-being by offering counseling and assistance services for troubled employees, and by providing health promotion and/or fitness programs and educational seminars for a broader employee population;

• Seeking long-term solutions for problems resulting from plant closings and major work-force reductions — through career development, training and retraining programs, and by addressing personal, family, and community needs when work dislocations are unavoidable;

• Recognizing and assisting in major life transactions of employees — through leave policies for child care, relocation services, and retirement planning programs; and

• Encouraging employee involvement in community services by providing release time for such activities, and supporting them through financial, technical, or in-kind assistance.

What Government Can Do

Government — at the federal, state, and community levels — is often perceived as an equalizing force and the provider of last resort. Once thought of as a bottomless resource for a wide range of social programs, the government is now severely constrained by unparalleled deficits in the federal budget. Matched against the comprehensive social programs of many industrialized countries in Western Europe, it seems unlikely that U.S. social policies will ever be more than a complicated and changing mosaic of separate programs for specially identified populations, most notably youth and the elderly, the poor, and the disadvantaged. Government policies that serve working families are ones that:

• Cast government as an active participant in public-private partnerships;

• Encourage the development and dissemination of new family-supportive initiatives by providing funding for demonstration projects, start-up operations, and innovative research about model programs that the private sector can augment or replicate;

• Encourage individuals and families to be self-reliant — e.g., by sponsoring training programs for dislocated and disadvantaged workers; and

• Show government to be a model employer by providing family-supportive policies and benefits for its own employees.

Lenora Cole Alexander, Director,
Women's Bureau,
U.S. Department of Labor

WORK AND FAMILY: THE ROLE OF GOVERNMENT

The challenge of juggling work and family responsibilities is not new to women. From pioneer days, through the industrial revolution, to the present technological era, women in the U.S. labor force have felt the press of conflicting demands on their time and energy.

What is new is the persistent and dramatic increase in the number of married couples who are dual earners (now 54%) and the number of employees who are single parents. This trend is combined with fewer "extended" families to absorb child-rearing tasks and an increase in the average lifespan. It is likely today that many workers who have fulfilled their child care responsibilities face a future of care for an elderly or disabled adult. Most noteworthy is the number of very young children (9.6 million children under six years old) whose mothers are in the labor force, as well as 15 million children in the latchkey category, six to 13 years old. These numbers and the fact that many male workers also share dual responsibilities mean that work-and-family issues cannot be ignored in the modern economy.

Affordable, quality child and dependent care, pregnancy disability and parental leave policies, greater flexibility in work schedules and possibly workplace, and more flexible benefit packages are the concerns most frequently mentioned by workers with family responsibility. Whose role is it to meet problems which are sure to be stress producing if unattended? Responsibility is as widely shared as those who will be impacted if the health, well-being, and productivity of large numbers of families are imperiled. Individual families have major responsibility, but employers, local communities and community organizations, and state and federal policymakers can all play constructive roles.

What is the role of federal government, and particularly the responsibility of an agency like the Women's Bureau, created by Congress in 1920 to "formulate standards and policies which shall promote the welfare of wage-earning women, improve their working conditions, increase their efficiency, and advance their opportunities for profitable employment"?

The first task is to get information on what is actually happening to women workers, to identify needs and problems that limit their chance to contribute to the nation's economy and improve their own livelihood. Where information is inadequate, the Bureau can stimulate research. For example, for decades the Women's Bureau has worked in close collaboration with the Bureau of Labor Statistics, a federal agency of Census, and private researchers to identify the child care needs of women workers and the extent and kinds of child care available.

Once the information has been compiled, government has a major role in its dissemination. Encouraging private initiatives to meet problems, developing demonstration projects to test approaches, and providing technical assistance are other government roles. For example, in fiscal 1985, federal and private agencies worked together with employers to integrate the provisions of child care services with employment and training services; to increase awareness of the effect of parenting responsibilities on the productivity of employees; to develop information and referral systems on child care in a multi-jurisdictional metropolitan area; to develop a voucher system for dependent care or to develop a child care center at the worksite; to address other child-rearing concerns with the provision of child care, i.e., a used clothes bank, a parent resource center with books, a course on enhancing parenting skills in cooperation with a local institution of higher education; and to spread knowledge about various tax incentives available. "The Business of Caring," the Bureau's videotape on employer-sponsored child care, has been widely circulated and is available on a free-loan basis from the National Office and each of the 10 regional offices.

> *The [federal government's] first task is to get information on what is actually happening to women workers, to identify needs and problems that limit their chance to contribute to the nation's economy and improve their own livelihood.*

Other governmental roles are to develop policy, sometimes to set and enforce standards, to provide incentives, or to serve as a model employer. In an earlier era when workplace standards were almost nonexistent, the Women's Bureau assisted state legislators in developing state protective legislation for women and better policies for all workers. As general standards improved and special protection clashed with equal employment opportunity, the Bureau promoted broader, more flexible policies. While focusing on problems most often faced by women through the years, the Bureau has proposed and worked diligently for measures that have benefited men equally and taken into account changing family patterns.

With respect to policy on dependent care, federal laws provide tax credits for working parents, tax incentives for employers, food subsidies, and financial support for centers for low-income families under a variety of state-operated programs. States have taken major responsibility for setting child care standards. A number of federal agencies have demonstrated the feasibility of on-site child care, and the 99th Congress officially authorized federal agencies to utilize space rent-free for day care centers.

In 1984 Congressional and Department of Labor initiatives resulted in changes in pension law that have been important to working parents. The Retirement Equity Act of 1984 makes it easier for women and men to build up pension credits before and after time away from the job for child-rearing. It also provides better pension protection for the surviving spouse of a wage earner.

Vital Need for Flexible Benefits Plans

The whole area of flexibility in benefit packages is a critical one for families.

For example, if one earner opts for family health insurance coverage, the spouse, not needing to duplicate the health coverage, may opt for child care or an educational benefit for older children if flexible packages are available. Federal policy can set a climate that supports or inhibits such flexibility.

Flexibility in scheduling is also very helpful to families in meeting hours and work demands. After six years of experimentation with the concept and temporary authorization of flexible and compressed work schedules to virtually every federal agency, federal legislation has authorized their use on a permanent basis.

The widespread availability of computers has opened wider options for flexibility in the workplace, including the home. The great challenge to policymakers will be to find ways to combine the new opportunities with adequate safeguards for workers' health and labor standards.

An area commanding attention from federal policymakers in recent years is that of pregnancy disability and parental leave. While the Pregnancy Discrimination Act of 1978, as an amendment to Title VII of the Civil Rights Act of 1964, outlawed outright discrimination against expectant mothers, it did not attempt to set a minimum standard for disability policies for all workers, nor did it address the question of time that either parent might need for care of a newborn or newly adopted child. State laws and proposed federal legislation to meet these needs deserve serious consideration. Revised pension legislation in 1978 created more flexible break-in-service rules and provisions to make it easier for women and men to build up pension credits before and after time away from the job for childbirth, adoption, and infant care.

It is important to remember that for many families, the best solution will be for one parent, often the mother, to spend full time with the family for several years. To keep that option open, it is necessary to maintain continuing education, training, and retraining opportunities to prepare the homemaker to reenter the labor force. It is also because of the value of the homemaker to the family and often to the income-producing potential of the principal earner, that pension legislation was revised to recognize pension rights of both partners of the marriage. That is, where annuities are provided, survivor's benefits cannot now be waived without the signature of both the wage earner and the spouse.

Each family is unique. The particular ways of combining earning and nurturing differ among families and vary within a single family at different stages of life and because of the different obstacles and responsibilities families face. Employers who explore work-and-family issues with employees and are able to develop flexible policies not only add to the well-being of families, but give workers an opportunity to become more productive and to remain on the job.

Jack Golodner, Director,
Department for Professional Employees (DPE),
AFL-CIO

Judith Gregory, Research Associate, DPE

UNIONS AND THE WORKING FAMILY

Unions traditionally have been concerned with workers' problems outside the job — in the family and community — as well as on the job. In recent years, work-and-family issues — child care, flextime, alternate work schedules, parental leave — have risen higher among priorities for a diverse range of unions. The United Mine Workers of America (UMWA), whose membership is 98% male, fought for parental leave policies in 1985 contract negotiations in spite of concession demands made by the coal companies. The Association of Flight Attendants (AFA), whose membership is 85% female, represents women who were once fired automatically when they became pregnant, married, or reached the age of 32. Using the 1964 Civil Rights Act and collective bargaining, the union overturned these practices and recently won parental leave for both natural and adoptive parents.

In grappling with the problems of working families, unions are developing a new set of collective bargaining benchmarks to serve their members. Many of the unions' strategies also address the desires of today's workers for more flexibility, more autonomy, more control over their schedules, and more individually tailored solutions to their problems.

With the development of model contract language, incorporation of these work-and-family issues into bargaining programs, adoption of new policies at national conventions and in locals, and the accumulation of successful, practical experience, the breadth and pace of union action on work-and-family issues have accelerated and borne fruit, especially in the last five years. To highlight and to further such activity, the Coalition of Labor Union Women (CLUW) proclaimed 1985 the Year of the Family and held a series of three conferences on the theme of Work and the Family as union issues.

Union Activity Spurred by Changes

In the 1970s and 1980s, a number of forces came into play which prompted unions to devise bargaining programs to address the needs of working families.

Women entered the work force at the rate of more than a million a year in the 1970s and early 1980s. From 1975 to 1984, women represented more than 62% of total U.S. employment growth. More than 40% of all professionals are women, and women are the backbone of the white collar and service sectors of the economy, employed as secretaries, registered nurses, school teachers, bookkeepers and bank tellers, cashiers, and retail clerks. Women are in many of the jobs which have experienced the greatest growth, where workers receive the lowest pay and suffer the most arbitrary treatment. They work for companies which are major targets for unions today.

Women now constitute 41% of all union members, up from 19% in 1956. Of unionized white collar workers, 58% are women. The number of women trade union members has grown to seven million in a total female work force of 50 million, up from four million in a total female work force of 37 million 10 years ago. In the past 20 years, women accounted for half of all new union members; there is some evidence that unions now have greater union election success in female-intensive workplaces than in workplaces where men predominate. These new members are having an impact on union concerns.

While women are positioned to provide leadership in these areas, women in unions organize to include the concerns of men co-workers and to win the support of non-parents. Because of this, work-and-family issues are less likely to be marginalized as "women's issues."

Intersection with Traditional Union Issues

Some union responses to work-and-family issues intersect with traditional aspects of collective bargaining, for example, disability and other kinds of leaves, the right to a reasonable number of paid sick days, and paid personal days. Union contracts typically contain language on overtime, incidental absence, travel, transfers, and hours of work. Therefore, unions have a solid foundation to build on by adjusting provisions to accommodate working parents. Most contracts already provide for some kind of leave for pregnancy, childbirth, or child-rearing. Unions are now taking even more care to develop contract provisions that provide leave for male as well as female employees.

Unions recognize the diverse nature of families and thus the need to pursue diverse forms of assistance, based on sensitivity to their members' needs and preferences. For example, Shirley Underwood, an official for the United Auto Workers (UAW), which represents workers at the Douglas Aircraft Company in Long Beach, Calif., reported that her members are primarily concerned with availability of child care during evening shifts, and with company assistance in identifying care providers, rather than operating a worksite center. "People will not bring their child to the workplace; they want their child to stay in the community," Underwood said.

Unions are very concerned with the quality of child care not only as representatives of members who are parents, but also as representatives of organized child care workers. Perhaps nowhere else are pay inequities so painful as in the human and social services: The average child care center worker earns only $9,200 a year, and the middle 50% earn between $6,800 and $12,500. Alexis Herman, chair of the National Commission on Working Women, recently wrote, "The undervaluation and low wages of these workers have long been neglected as a subject of research .... higher wages and better working conditions for them are a necessary part of any solution to the child care crisis." Approximately 20,000 child care workers are unionized and thus receive higher wages, health insurance coverage, paid vacations, sick leave benefits, and provisions for regular breaks, and are protected by guidelines regarding overtime. Improving staffing ratios of children to care providers is a priority to the unions. Contracts achieved by unions improve the quality of care by making these jobs more attractive to qualified personnel.

AFL-CIO Survey: Responses on Child Care

Unpublished data from a 1984 survey conducted by Louis Harris and Associates for the AFL-CIO show that 37% of unorganized workers and 49% of unionized workers would like to have assistance in finding day care for their children while they are working. Among the unorganized respondents, identical percentages of men and women desired child care assistance. Among the unionized respondents, men were slightly more likely than women to say they would like assistance, 51% and 46% respectively.

Question: "... would you be interested in getting assistance in finding day care for your children while you are working?" Percent of unorganized workers answering "yes."

Years of Age

18–24	25–34	35–44	45–54	55 or older
51%	48%	31%	15%	22%

Source: Unpublished data from "A Study on the Outlook for Trade Union Organizing," conducted by Louis Harris and Associates for the Future of Work Committee of the AFL-CIO, November 1984. The sample was comprised of 1,202 adults in non-union jobs (610 men and 588 women) and 250 current union members (160 men and 90 women) of all ages, marital and parental status. A breakdown of the desire for assistance by age is not available for the union sample at this time.

The survey shows that desire for assistance is strongest among younger workers, those in the 18-24 and 25-35 age groups, followed by workers in the 35-44 age group. A somewhat surprising finding is that more workers 55 or older expressed interest in child care assistance than did the workers 45 to 54 years old.

Half of the unorganized workers with incomes less than $15,000 answered yes, compared with about one in three men and women in higher income levels. Black workers were most likely to say they would welcome help (62%), followed by Hispanic workers (56%) and white workers (34%).

Among unionized respondents, desire for child care assistance by occupation breaks down as follows: service (65% of respondents answered yes); unskilled blue collar (57%); skilled blue collar (45%); clerical (34%); other white collar combined — including professional, managerial/administrative and sales workers — (40%). In non-union workplaces, desire for assistance was expressed by 33% of clericals, 39% of professionals, 40% of unskilled blue collar workers, and 43% of service workers.

Union Programs on Child Care

In 75% of all married-couple households with school age children, both parents work. More than 12 million families are maintained by a single parent. In recognition of these facts, the AFL-CIO, at its 1983 convention, reaffirmed its vigorous support for enactment of a broad federal child care program. But the AFL-CIO also recognized how unlikely such an accomplishment is in the near future, and pledged itself to greater emphasis on the use of collective bargaining to meet the child care needs of parents and children, calling on its affiliates to "[s]urvey the needs of their members to determine the adequacy of their current child care arrangements and their preferred alternative(s)" and to "[c]onsider such options in bargaining on the issue as labor-management committees on child care, employer-sponsored centers, information and referral services for parents, allowances for care or subsidizing placement in existing centers or licensed family day-care homes, expanding sick leave, establishing flexible working schedules to accommodate caring for children or other dependents, and forming consortiums with other unions and other employers to provide care — possibly on a community wide basis."

Unpublished data from a 1984 survey conducted by Louis Harris and Associates for the AFL-CIO show that 37% of unorganized workers and 49% of unionized workers would like to have assistance in finding day care for their children while they are working.

A few union child care programs date back to the 1960s and 1970s. The pace of union activity on child care has picked up considerably in the last few years:

• In 1968, the Amalgamated Clothing and Textile Workers Union pioneered union-sponsored day care centers when it established the first center financed jointly by management and employees.

• In 1983, the International Ladies' Garment Workers' Union (ILGWU) established a child care center sponsored by a consortium of employers at the Greater Blouse, Skirt and Undergarment Manufacturers Association in New York City's Chinatown.

• Service Employees International Union (SEIU) Local 399 negotiated with the Kaiser-Permanente Medical Care Program of Los Angeles in 1980 to do a feasibility study of child care. The study led to the publication of a booklet on available child care services in Los Angeles. Joint labor-management committees have been established in a number of SEIU locals.

• The Newspaper Guild has negotiated several contracts with provisions for feasibility studies concerning on-site care or other types of assistance. The Guild's bargaining with The Bureau of National Affairs, Inc., a Washington, D.C., publisher, led to a joint union-management study committee which spearheaded the formation of the Metropolitan Washington Child Care Network, a coordinating umbrella for child care information and a referral agencies in nearly a dozen area locations, supported by several area employers.

• The United Auto Workers (UAW) negotiated with American Motors Company to provide for child care at a plant in Ontario, Canada, in what the union sees as a potential model for future U.S. contracts. Between 1980 and 1983, letters of agreement to set up joint labor-management child care study committees were included with contracts between the UAW and Rockwell International Corporation and Douglas Aircraft Company. Although no formal studies have been conducted to date, the joint committee for Rockwell's automotive group has been appointed and was to begin meeting in February 1986.

• American Federation of Government Employees (AFGE) Local 12 reached an agreement with the U.S. Department of Labor requiring maintenance of an on-site child care center. Each parent is allowed up to two hours of administrative leave per month to attend child care center meetings.

• At its 1984 convention, AFGE decided to set up a pilot union-sponsored, community-based day care center. According to Barbara Hutchinson, AFL-CIO vice president and director of AFGE's Women's Department, several ideas led to the decision: (1) While AFGE locals could bargain for child care programs in principle, they had a very difficult time getting subsequent commitments of funds from employers (in this case, mainly federal agencies). (2) A survey of the membership found that preschool programs (typically the fewest in number and the most expensive) are the most needed. The union felt that it could not wait for universal federal programs or help from the agencies which employ its members. (3) The union wants to reach out beyond the union itself to local communities.

Parental Leave, Dependent Care

In 1984, 60% of all working women had no paid maternity leave. Yet, 80% of women currently in the work force are of childbearing age and an estimated 93% of them will become pregnant during their careers.

Federal law does not require that leave be provided for disabilities resulting from pregnancy if it is not provided for other conditions. California and Montana state laws requiring that employers provide maternity leave are being challenged in federal courts. The members of the New York chapter of the Coalition of Labor Union Women write in *Bargaining for Child Care*: "It is less likely in 1985 than it was in 1975 that a woman worker will be able to take time off during a 'normal' pregnancy without losing her job."

Collective bargaining gains by The Newspaper Guild (TNG) from early 1984 to 1985 illustrate trends in union contract provisions for parental leave: The Wire Service Guild at Associated Press expanded maternity leave from 12 to 18 months; leaves of absence were extended to adoptive parents in the Guild's contracts with the *San Jose Mercury and News*, with the jointly owned and operated *Cincinnati Post* and the *Kentucky Post*, and the *Washington Post*; the Guild contract at the AFL-CIO Food and Allied Services Trades Department provides for three weeks paid maternity leave after hospitalization and unpaid leave up to six months; the new contract with the *State Worker*, a Communications Workers of America publication in Pennsylvania, grants the right to unpaid leave up to two years for maternity or paternity.

In the 1983-1986 agreement between the Association of Flight Attendants (AFA) and United Airlines, an attendant must notify the airline when she knows she is pregnant, at which time she may either continue to fly or go on leave for a maximum of 90 days after delivery. A flight attendant who adopts a child is similarly entitled to three months' leave from the date of adoption. A male attendant is entitled to a maximum of 30 days' paternal leave from the date of birth of a newborn child. In all cases, employees continue to accrue seniority.

In its 1984 negotiations with the Bituminous Coal Operators Association

(BCOA), the United Mine Workers of America (UMWA) proposed that: "Upon request, an Employee shall be granted an unpaid leave of absence, not to exceed six (6) consecutive months, surrounding a birth, adoption or serious illness of a family member . . . . " Despite owner opposition, the union persisted and at the last minute got the BCOA to agree to set up a special joint committee on parental leave which conducted a feasibility study, now being finalized. The union has requested that the BCOA/UMWA Joint Interests Committee consider a one-year pilot project in one location to be monitored by the Parental Leave Committee. Among the areas which would be monitored are: utilization rates; precise circumstances for use of leave to care for a seriously ill child; productivity costs of replacing workers while on leave; possible positive or negative effects on occupational safety.

Expanding parental leave to include the care of a seriously ill child was a priority for the UMWA in its 1985 negotiations with coal operators. At the CLUW conference on Work and the Family in October 1985, UMWA President Richard Trumka said that, in the course of the union's committee work on parental leave, "it became clear that the need for this leave program extends beyond the seriously ill child to all family members . . especially . . . our elderly parents who built not only our unions but also our communities . . . . "

The New York City CLUW Child Care Committee recently recommended that unions consider expanding dependent care to include not only children of all ages, but also dependent adults — elderly and infirm parents and relatives and handicapped spouses.

Alternate Work Schedules

Alternate work schedules include: reduced hours of work or part-time work; flextime; a compressed workweek; and job-sharing. Unions have been wary of such programs for a number of reasons: concern that hours of the day may get extended; concern that programs are not truly voluntary; concern over the possible loss of opportunities for overtime or premium pay, and potential reductions in the number of jobs.

When ground rules which address these concerns have been set forth in contracts, a number of programs developed jointly by management and unions have worked successfully. Model contract language developed by the American Federation of State, County and Municipal Employees (AFSCME) stresses that the employer and the union "agree to negotiate the implementation of flextime in appropriate work environments . . . by mutual agreement . . . . " AFSCME urges that a local interested in alternate work schedule programs first create a labor-management committee to carefully analyze employees' needs and interests, ensure that participation by employees is voluntary, develop and evaluate a pilot project, and allow either management or the union to "request termination of the program upon 30 days written notice."

Part-time work is probably the "solution" most commonly sought by working parents — one in four women workers works part-time. But part-time jobs provide fewer benefits, little or no job security, and too little income. The United Food and Commercial Workers (UFCW) has a number of contracts which provide fair treatment and positive conditions for long-term or "permanent" part-time employees, demonstrating ways that part-time work could be improved as a option for working parents. In the 1983-86 contract between the Northern California grocery chains — including, among others, Safeway and Lucky Stores — and UFCW Local 373, part-time employees receive overtime pay if they are required to work outside their agreed-upon schedules, which are for either four, five, or eight hours a day. Sick leave and pensions are based on hours worked per year, including paid vacations. The contract provides that all employees who work four hours or more per week and have been with the company for at least a year are entitled to a minimum of two weeks' vacation with pay.

The most popular approach among alternate work schedule options is full-time work with flextime or flexitime, in which employees work a "core time" of hours when everyone must be present, with flexible start and quit times each day. The contract between District 65/UAW and Barnard College provides that: "Flexible hours shall be arranged for any employee who has need, provided the operation of the department continues to function. Reasons for such flexibility may be but are not limited to school needs for children, medical needs, or daytime classes which are not available outside of regular working hours."

Conclusion

Unions will continue to broaden leave policies and other provisions for both men and women to include dependent care, as they have broadened provisions to include paternity leave and leave for adoptive parents. Unions will continue to pursue a number of pilot projects to establish child care centers, and to undertake joint labor-management studies to assess needs and determine the feasibility of a number of assistance options. Unions will continue to develop and evaluate alternate work schedules.

Unions will continue to unionize care-providers and insist on professional standards for quality care on behalf of employees as well as parents. Unions will continue to join forces in coalitions locally and nationally to engage in political action needed to increase the available supply of child care services which today's work force and working parents so urgently need.

In doing so, unions are continuing to fulfill their social mission, as described by Samuel Gompers in 1893: to strive for " . . . more of the opportunities to cultivate our better natures, [and] to make . . . childhood more happy and bright."

James A. Klein, Manager of Pension & Employee Benefits

Mark A. de Bernardo, Manager of Labor Law, U.S. Chamber of Commerce

WORK AND FAMILY: FLEXIBILITY IS THE KEY

The decades since World War II have often been noted for the rapidity with which our patterns of work and family life have changed. In all its aspects, the relationship of work and family life has been presented with new challenges that can only be met if government limits itself to articulating the basic outlines of needed national policies while leaving to workers and their employers the flexibility to shape programs and policies that serve their needs and interests.

An important example of the degree to which business, employees, and government have met the demands of changing needs is through the unfolding of the comprehensive employee benefits umbrella of protection.

The U.S. Chamber of Commerce recently conducted an extensive survey of employee benefits and found that employers devoted 36.6% of their total payroll dollars to employee benefits which serve the needs of workers and their families — a truly substantial percentage. Only 9% of the 36.6% is government mandated; this is the portion attributable to Social Security, unemployment insurance, and workers' compensation. These benefits are required to ensure that we meet certain national social goals of income protection for retired, unemployed, and injured workers.

The rest of the benefits umbrella is comprised of benefits for which workers and employers have bargained freely. These range from very common benefits — health and life insurance and pensions — to the true "fringes," such as employer-subsidized meals or tuition assistance for employees' continued education.

Surely government has encouraged the growth of this private employee benefits system by making employer-paid benefits either tax exempt or tax deferred to workers. This has allowed employers and employees to negotiate for the types of benefits packages that meet their specialized needs.

The growing popularity of flexible benefit plans or "cafeteria plans," which permit workers to choose the types of benefits their families need, is one way in which business is meeting the challenge of the changing profiles, demographics, and preferences of American workers.

Mandated Benefits: No Help

Both government and employee groups should be wary of championing new types of *mandated* benefits under the banner of meeting family needs. Such efforts could actually limit rather than expand employee choice.

An example would be the requirement of several months of guaranteed parental leave for both the mother and father of newborn or newly adopted children. No one denies that parental leave is a popular benefit. A recent Bureau of National Affairs survey found that voluntarily about 90% of employers were providing maternity leave and about 40% were granting parental leave for fathers. However, proposals to mandate such benefits would actually be requiring a new benefit that serves the interests of a limited category of employees (i.e., new parents) at the expense of all other employees who seek health and life insurance protection, larger contributions to retirement savings plans, and other benefits.

Given that employers already devote more than a third of the payroll pie to employee benefits, an additional mandated benefit would not expand the portion of the pie, but only make smaller the slices that are dedicated to other types of benefits. Furthermore, overly generous mandated leave requirements that provide months of guaranteed leave would be an undue burden on smaller businesses that can ill afford further costs.

Fewer government regulations will reduce the administrative cost of operating a plan and will not only encourage the growth of these plans, but will ensure that precious benefits dollars are directed to workers and their families who are their intended recipients.

If workers and employers have the freedom and flexibility to shape benefits packages that meet their needs, the needs of families will be well-served. The role of government should be limited to encouraging the proliferation of plans and to ensuring that they are provided fairly. Fewer government regulations will reduce the administrative cost of operating a plan and will not only encourage the growth of these plans, but will ensure that precious benefits dollars are directed to workers and their families who are their intended recipients.

Business Growth: The Broadest Solution

Of course, the most vital "benefit" from the workplace to the family is a paycheck. Isn't that why we work? The more than 90 million jobs — and 90 million paychecks — in the private sector provide for the ultimate family need — income. It is fundamental that a strong national economy and further growth out of our recent recession are essential to the well-being of the American worker and the American family. Thus, national policies which will encourage business growth are of paramount importance and are the *broadest* response to the needs of the family.

However, *specific* legislative initiatives also should be taken to help address the needs of the family with regard to the workplace. One action which already has been taken was recent Congressional enactment of Walsh-Healey reform lifting the requirement of *daily* overtime pay for government contractors. This will encourage flexible and compressed work schedules. Such alternative work schedules benefit working mothers and others with commitments in the home, such as those who must care for the aged or handicapped. In fact, compressed work schedules (such as a four-day, 10-hour-per-day workweek) are increasing in popularity — another example of how employers and employees together can work out mutually beneficial accommodations when given flexibility.

Industrial homework is another example. Work in the home is an increasingly popular and efficient work practice. Nonetheless, a series of outdated 40-year-old amendments to the Fair Labor Standards Act have effectively banned the home manufacture of women's apparel and accessories. Congress or the Labor Department should lift this ban on work in the home because such a ban is anti-worker, anti-family, and anti-business. For a working parent, industrial homework reduces child care costs and provides more time for the family to be together and for parents to attend to family needs. Homeworkers enjoy considerably more freedom than other employees since they choose when, where, and how long they work, and their level of productivity. Studies have shown industrial homework increases productivity and morale. Such a practice benefits not just working parents, but the handicapped, caretakers, those with restricted mobility, and retired persons seeking supplemental income.

Enactment of a youth differential wage also would be pro-family because it would provide as many as 400,000 new jobs for teenagers who would not have had the chance otherwise. Such jobs build self-respect and confidence, develop workplace skills, and may lead to additional job opportunities — jobs which benefit the family and get young people started on a productive future. The alternative may be no job, no hope, no chance to get to the second rung of the employment ladder because a young person was denied the opportunity to get to the first rung. The result can be crime and other anti-social behavior. One need not wonder why the Fraternal Order of Police supports the youth differential.

Cooperation Is the Key

Aside from such legislative initiatives, the key remains cooperation: employers communicating with and responding to the needs of employees, and providing an attractive package of wages and benefits in order to recruit top candidates and retain and reward good employees; employees working with employers, understanding the trade-off involved in various benefits, cooperating on sensible programs that benefit the most in the best way for the least cost; and government encouraging cooperation but not denying the flexibility which is in the interest of all parties.

Absent cooperation and flexibility, initiatives intending to benefit the family can be administrative nightmares, costly, inefficient, and detrimental to more workers than they help.

But with the proper approach, such programs as compressed work schedules, flextime, industrial homework, parental leave, job sharing, child care, and "cafeteria" benefit plans can be positive and effective personnel measures which benefit everyone involved.

Phyllis Moen, Associate Professor,
Human Development & Family Studies, and Sociology,
Cornell University

NEW PATTERNS OF WORK

Working parents are involved in two vital enterprises: the production of goods and services and the "production" of human beings. Each requires a substantial investment of time, energy, and personal commitment. The critical challenge confronting government, employers, and unions in the 1980s and beyond will be the development of strategies to foster both activities so that neither flourishes at the expense of the other.

There can be no doubt that the problems being experienced by working parents will not disappear of their own accord. By now, more than half of the mothers of preschoolers have joined the labor force, with the most rapid increase in labor force participation occurring among mothers of children under one year of age. The myth of "separate worlds" — one of work and the other of family life — long harbored by employers, unions, and even workers themselves has been effectively laid to rest. Their inseparability is undeniable, particularly as two-earner families have become the norm where they once were the exception and as a distressing number of single parents are required to raise children on their own. The import of work-family conflicts — for the family, for the workplace, and, indeed, for the whole of society — will grow as these demographic and social transformations in the roles of men and women come to be more fully clarified and appreciated.

New Work/Family Arrangements Needed

What is required are new arrangements that permit men and women to function effectively in both their employment and their families. But in fashioning these it should be kept in mind that the period of childbearing and child-rearing is not long-lasting; parenthood has come to occupy only a relatively short span of time in contemporary adulthood as a result of both reduced fertility and increased longevity. Indeed, today's parents will have young preschoolers in the home for perhaps a total of eight years, while the average working life exceeds 40 years. Thus, provisions for meshing working and parenting should be both flexible and limited in duration — options to be elected as required by individual and family circumstance.

A variety of innovative policies and practices have been devised to facilitate work-family integration, some seeking to reduce the demands of the job in order to provide the time and energy required for child care (e.g., part-time work, flexible hours, parental leaves) and others serving to ease the demands of family responsibilities (e.g., child care centers, referral, and subsidies) so as to permit fuller participation in the work role. From the perspective of employers and unions, these practices can also be viewed as strategies for maintaining the continuity of labor force participation and employment stability.

Most families currently "solve" the work-family dilemma by having one parent (almost always the mother) withdraw from the labor force and/or abandon full-time employment for a period when the children are young. Although the duration of labor force withdrawal has become increasingly brief, few mothers of preschoolers remain continuously in the labor force on a full-time basis. Those seeking to maintain employment during this stage of the family life cycle are often required to relinquish their full-time jobs for part-time employment that is less secure, lower paying, and otherwise less rewarding — but offers a reduced workweek. These discontinuities and sacrifices in women's work careers do enable fathers to continue their own full-time employment and parents to fulfill their child care obligations. However, the costs borne by women workers in their own career development and by employers in the loss of work force stability are substantial.

Leaves of Absence and Part-Time Work

Sufficient and quality child care is, of course, essential to resolving the dilemma faced by working parents. But no less crucial, in my view, are arrangements whereby mothers and fathers can temporarily reduce their work obligations while maintaining a continuous attachment to their jobs. Parental leaves of absence for an interval following the birth of a child are one such device, as is the cutback of full-time employment to part-time schedules for a reasonable period of time during the child's early years.

Would such policies gain the acceptance of workers? My own research, as well as a review of the literature on the subject, suggests that indeed they would. More than two-thirds of the full-time working mothers of young children interviewed in the Labor Department's 1977 Quality of Employment Survey said that they would prefer to reduce their working hours (and pay) in order to have more time to spend with their families. Noteworthy, too, is the fact that nearly two-fifths of the fathers would also opt for reduced work time. Moreover, those workers voluntarily on part-time schedules are less likely to report work-family strains and feelings of fatigue and more likely to express high levels of satisfaction with both marriage and family.

> *Permitting workers to tailor their working hours to their family circumstances would both reinforce their work commitment and contribute to the development of a more productive and satisfied labor force.*

Do liberal leave and reduced work-hour policies contribute to labor force stability? Evidence from Sweden, where such policies have been in place for more than 10 years, suggests that they do. Currently, 83% of the Swedish mothers of preschoolers are in the labor force, albeit with the majority (four-fifths) of them either on parental leave or employed part time. As a consequence, very few are required to leave the labor force during childbearing and the early years of child-rearing.

Most workers — women as well as men — have a strong work commitment, typically asserting that they would continue to work even if it were financially unnecessary to do so. But this psychological commitment to work is not always reflected in the work histories of women, who move in and out of the labor force and between full-time and part-time jobs as a consequence of their changing family responsibilities. Permitting workers to tailor their working hours to their family circumstances would both reinforce their work commitment and contribute to the development of a more productive and satisfied labor force.

Much of the stress experienced by parents — mothers and fathers — is a consequence of the existing structure of work. But the five-day, 40-hour workweek need not be considered immutable. Indeed, this "normal" work schedule is itself a fairly recent phenomenon, dating back only to the 1930s. Employment policies offering greater flexibility in working hours through both temporary leaves and a reduction in work hours could substantially alleviate the conflicts and strains working parents now face.

The Costs of Change

Current deliberations over the need for alterations in existing employment arrangements must balance (1) the costs of policy innovations against (2) the costs of continuing with the status quo. While providing paid leaves of absence for mothers or fathers of newborns is obviously expensive, it might well be considered a cost that is properly apportioned and shared by the federal government, accomplished through tax incentives or other changes in the tax structure. Such government involvement could serve well to underscore the value society places on the optimal care and development of young children. However, in the absence of government intervention, a policy of unpaid parental leaves of absence might be a more realistic option for employers to consider.

Permitting full-time employees to reduce their hours to part-time schedules for a period of months or even years may pose problems of logistics as well as costs. Particularly knotty, however, is the issue of prorating benefits according to hours worked, a practice that most employers have not been inclined to adopt. Still, whatever additional expense may be entailed, it may be more than compensated for by gains in worker morale, productivity, and work-force stability.

But what of the costs of continuing to operate in the traditional fashion now practiced by organizations? While both the potential costs and benefits of new policies are admittedly unclear, the price of not adopting any remedies is hardly obscure. Women will continue to resolve their particular work-family dilemmas by accommodating work to family as best they can. As the labor force comes to be more equally divided between men and women, this means that nearly half its participants will, at some stage of their work careers, be forced either to (1) leave the labor force, or (2) abandon full-time jobs for others offering part-time hours, or (3) simultaneously juggle two full-time jobs: work and parenting. The resultant costs, measured by worker turnover, absenteeism, and lost productivity, based on experiences to date, can be substantial and serve as a major impediment to the development and utilization of the nation's human resources.

Conclusions

Two-earner and single-parent families are acknowledged facts of contemporary American life. Yet employment policies have largely failed to take account of these realities. A majority of working mothers and significant numbers of working fathers of young children would prefer to work fewer hours in order to spend more time with their families. But for most workers the structure and constraints of their jobs make alterations of their working hours virtually impossible. What is required is a variety of adjustments — parental leaves, a reduced workweek for a period of months or years, flexible schedules, and time off for the care of sick children — for those periods of the life cycle when family demands are particularly acute.

The dilemma working parents face resides neither in the family nor in the workplace, but in the articulation of the two. A more enlightened approach to the time spent at work could substantially reduce the conflicts parents face in integrating their work and family lives.

Photo: E. Plaut

**Stanley D. Nollen, Associate Professor,
School of Business Administration,
Georgetown University**

ROLES FOR BUSINESS, LABOR, AND GOVERNMENT IN THE WORK-FAMILY RELATIONSHIP

[This article draws from the author's paper, "The Work-Family Nexus: Issues for Business," published in 1986 by the Work and Family Information Center of the Conference Board. (See that paper for references and sources.) It also benefits from meetings of the Work and Family Research Council of the Conference Board.]

The relationship between work life and family life is an issue that now commands growing attention in both the public and private sectors. What exactly is the work-family issue all about? What is the problem and what are the opportunities? What can business, labor, and government do about this issue?

What the Work-Family Issue Is All About

Work life and family life are two domains of human activity in which all employed people spend about one-third of their time. Work usually means the job you do for money. (Of course, we should also include housework, child care, and volunteer work as well.) Family traditionally means the spouse and kids you live with and care for. A modern definition would also include households of unrelated adults who live together.

The essence of the relationship between work life and family life today is that the two domains overlap and interact. What happens in one domain affects what happens in the other. (See Fig. 1, next page.) The interactions are growing, mainly because the work force is changing and the family is changing.

The most notable change in the work force is that it is now 45% female. Over half of all married women with children under age six are working outside their homes. And they are professionals and managers as well as secretaries, teachers, and nurses.

The most notable change in the family is that the classic nuclear family of Dick-and-Jane fame is a vanishing species. Over half of all families have two income-earners; single parents with dependent children amount to nearly 10 percent of all families.

The overlap between the work and family domains means that conflicts often result. One of the conflicts involves time, the only absolutely fixed resource. Workers and family members cannot be in both domains at once. More than one-third of all workers who have a spouse or children say that their job and their family life interfere with each other somewhat or a lot.

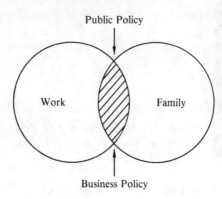

Fig. 1. Work and family are two overlapping domains affected by public policy and business policy.

A second conflict involves roles. The workplace and the family have opposite functions, which require opposite roles and behaviors. Workers must be objective and reliable; family members must be nurturing and compassionate. Switching back and forth from one to the other set of behaviors is hard to do.

Conflict generates stress and impaired performance both at work and at home, and that is a problem for both employers and families. But wherever there is a problem, there is an opportunity. What can business, labor, and government do to turn the problem of work-family conflict into the opportunity of better labor performance and healthier families?

What Can Business Do?

Businesses are concerned about the work-family nexus because good work-family relationships are likely to mean improved labor performance. Self-interest and profits motivate business action, not just social interest. A number of actions can be undertaken.

First, employers can adopt family-supportive human resource management. This is simply enlightened, quality human resource management. It includes putting people-planning into business-planning, recognizing changes in families as well as in the workplace, and treating workers as human capital — long-lived assets that increase the net worth of the employer. It also means examining the corporate culture for work-family biases, and empowering employees to help themselves. This means giving them flexibility, options, and a measure of control over their jobs and work lives.

Second, employers can implement programs whose objective is to improve the work-family nexus. Employment security programs can cushion the family-damaging effects of job change caused by plant closings, cyclical layoffs, reductions inthe work force, and job transfers and moves. Work schedule alternatives to rigid hours can enable workers to accommodate family needs to work needs; examples of alternative programs include flextime, permanent part-time employment and job sharing, and telecommuting. Child care programs such as information and referral services, vouchers, or on-site child care address one of many working families' most urgent needs. Employee assistance programs, which might include limited physical and mental health care, financial planning, and interpersonal relationship counseling, can improve employees' state of well-being. Flexible fringe benefits (cafeteria-style) that include parental leaves of absence help workers without costing extra. Training on topics such as executive stress, time management, or the work-family nexus itself can be added to ongoing technical and management training programs.

What Workers Can Do

Whether they are organized in a labor union or not, workers have one key task — to be self-reliant. Workers need to take responsibility for some of the work-family conflict they experience. Self-reliance means initiating changes in their employer's practices and in community organizations, acquiring training and maintaining health and fitness, and forging the family, friendship, and neighborhood bonds to support and nurture efforts to accommodate work-family pressures.

The overlap between work and family domains means that conflicts often result .... Conflict generates stress and impaired performance both at work and at home, and that is a problem for both employers and families.

Workers can also value and respect family and work equally, and try to achieve balance between work and family domains. For men, this means genuinely increasing their participation in all family tasks. For women, it means taking on some traditional male roles in families as well as at work.

What Governments Can Do

Government policy encompasses both legislation and regulation. Governments affect the work-family relationship via their own actions and via the requirements they impose on employers and workers. Governments' own actions are either spending or taxing actions. The first role for governments to take is to examine the inadvertent impact on families of their policies. For example, labor and benefits laws that regulate overtime pay, pension funds, and social security contributions restrict the use of flexible and part-time work schedules. Tax treatment of single vs. married people and assistance payments for poor children both have some anti-family effects.

A second role for governments is to adopt family-supportive programs and policies. Governments can improve the quantity and quality of child care if the marketplace does not function well, and parental leaves can be advanced. These are examples of social concerns that businesses and workers may not be able to adequately solve. Training and placement of adult workers in productive careers is another example. In all these cases, European models are instructive. Government programs often require new funding; however, in some cases, partnerships with businesses and community organizations that cost little can be forged.

**Karen Nussbaum, Executive Director, 9to5,
National Association of Working Women, and
President, District 925, SEIU**

WORK AND FAMILY: THE ISSUES OF TIME AND MONEY

Issues for Working Families

Every year, the 9to5 chapter in Cleveland gives the Heart of Gold award to a deserving company on Valentine's Day.

But sometimes we have a hard time, as we did one year when we surveyed every major downtown employer for the best policy on child care. When we couldn't find a *good* one, we had to settle for the best available. So the award for child care went to AmeriTrust Bank because it had someone in a couple of days a week to give advice to 5,000 or 6,000 employees on child care. No on-site child care facility; no vouchers as payment for child care of your choice; no special nurse program for sick children; no contribution to a publicly sponsored child care program in Cleveland. And Cleveland is typical. Somehow employers haven't caught on. They haven't seemed to notice some elementary facts. Men and women have children, and children need to be cared for.

Child care is a problem for all categories of workers — blue collar and clerical, professionals, and managers. They worry about finding good child care and having back-up for it. They worry about whether they will have enough flexibility in their jobs to handle an emergency, and what the response of their peers and superiors will be if they need help in handling emergencies. Low-income women find it hard to pay for extra baby-sitting. Upper-income women may have few resources among family and non-working friends to help out.

The *Personnel Journal* states: "As long as women need to work, society is obliged to make it a viable option." 9to5 agrees.

There are two major issues for women workers with families — time and money. Company policies on time and money bear little relation to the real lives of working women.

Let's take money first. A single mother with two pre-teenage children was working as a secretary at Syracuse University. She told me she had to place one of her kids with another family from her church because she couldn't afford to keep two kids at home on her salary.

Most women don't earn enough money to support themselves and their families. Just look at clerical work, a job held by over one-third of all working women. Average pay for female clericals is a little over $12,000 a year. Three million full-time female clericals earn less than the government poverty threshold — around $9,000.

The *solutions* are two — pay equity and unionizing. Women in female-dominated jobs — and 80% of women work in "women's jobs" — earn less than men in jobs that don't require as much in the way of skill, effort, and responsibility. Day care workers earn less than liquor store clerks. Nurses earn less than tree-trimmers. And secretaries earn less than parking lot attendants and grocery baggers at the supermarket. If our society is committed to ending discrimination, the only serious approach is to institute pay equity.

The argument for unionizing is even more straightforward. Unionized clericals earn 30% more than non-unionized clericals. The message is clear: If you want enough money to be able to pay for child care and keep your kids, organize.

Child Care: A Money Issue

Child care is a money issue. Child care policies in the United States are worse than any other Western nation and worse even than a number of underdeveloped countries.

In the United States, maternity leave with full pay is rare, yet this would be considered backward in Brazil where workers are entitled to 12 weeks of maternity leave with full pay. Kenya mandates eight weeks of paid leave. Nearly every European country offers more generous maternity leave than the United States. Many countries also re-quire employers to provide half-hour nursing breaks for mothers of infants and grant extended periods of unpaid leave without loss of job rights.

Company policies on time and money bear little relation to the real lives of working women.

Virtually anything here would be an improvement. Some specific corporate policy possibilities include:
- On-site child care facilities, underwritten by the company;
- Cash contributions, either to parents or centers;
- "Cafeteria Plan" benefits in which employees can choose child care from an array of benefits. For low-income workers, however, it's no solution to choose between child care and health insurance, or some other necessity;
- Information and referral services;
- Summer day camps on company-owned recreation property. This actually exists in one place where it is administered by the YWCA;
- Child care programs for sick children, in which a qualified person is available for pay on an emergency basis to care for a sick child.

The Issue of Time

Time is the other major issue. A secretary in Chicago told me of the time her child was sick and she had to stay home to take care of him. When she called in, her boss was furious. "You'll just have to decide what's more important to you," he threatened, "your child or your job." She was fired.

Let me ask each of you readers to consider: What's more important to you, your child or your job? That's a stupid question, isn't it? Why should anyone have to make that decision in the normal course of daily events?

Companies have to become more flexible if women (or parents) are to work and children are to be taken care of. Here's how they can do it:

• Sick leave for the employee should be available for use for a child's illness. As one clerical told me, "It's no vacation to be home with a sick child."

• Flextime is a system where established core hours are worked (say 10 a.m. to 3 p.m.), but the employee chooses to work any eight hours around that time.

• Job sharing is when two people share one job, each with pro-rated benefits. This is particularly attractive to mothers of infants.

• Part-time work is an option some women choose, but often with reluctance. Blue Shield in Boston recently switched over its clerical workforce from working full-time 40-hour weeks to part-time 30-hour weeks. Even their beneficent name for the new schedule — "mothers' hours" — couldn't fool the women there — they were performing nearly the same work, but now with no benefits whatsoever, *not even health insurance*. Part-time work without benefits is a step backward in anybody's book.

• Parental leave should be available with pay for at least eight weeks after the birth or adoption of a child. Currently under consideration in the U.S. Congress is an excellent proposal by Rep. Patricia Schroeder for 18 weeks of mandated full-time parental leave, followed by 21 additional weeks of part-time work, covering childbirth, infant care, and care for a seriously ill child.

A More Humane, Prudent View Is Needed

Management would gain from taking a more humane, prudent view. Implementing these policies is the realistic thing to do. We are living in the 1980s, not the 1950s. Women work and have children.

And these policies are also good for business. Several studies show that these kind of policies increase productivity, recruitment, morale, and stability, and reduce absenteeism, tardiness, and turnover rates.

Many of these good policies are coming at the initiative of unions, including the Service Employees International Union.

An office worker in Boston told 9to5, "My company runs as if every employee has a wife at home to look after the kids and cook dinner. But in my house, I'm the employee and the wife."

Our choices, then, are either to provide policies for the working family, or wives to working women. The former would certainly be easier.

Barney Olmsted, Co-director

Suzanne Smith, Co-director,
New Ways to Work

TIME TO BALANCE WORK/FAMILY RESPONSIBILITIES

"Time is a scarce resource and families too often get what's left over." Management consultant Dr. Rosabeth Moss Kanter noted this almost a decade ago, long before dual-career, two-paycheck families became the norm. With more women entering the labor force, good day care for young children still hard to come by, and senior dependent care emerging as a growing family concern. the issue of how to find time for family responsibilities has become acute for many workers. The need for alternative work time policies, programs, and services which help reduce the stress on working family members is critical.

Three areas which need attention are: (1) opportunities for leave time; (2) increased availability of flexible and reduced work time options; and (3) development of policies which protect the status and employment rights of employees who take leaves or choose alternative work schedules. Employers, labor leaders, and legislators all have a role to play in improving the options available to working parents.

The United States is still the only industrialized country that does not have a national policy which provides some period of job-protected leave time for workers who become mothers. Since 47% of employed mothers currently return to work within the first year after childbirth, leave policy is an area which demands the attention of employers, legislators, and labor leaders.

Child Care: Not Just a Personal Matter

Employers are beginning to recognize that the resolution of child care and other work/family conflicts is not just a personal matter. The way a firm's personnel policy affects working parents also has "bottom line" ramifications. A survey of 1,200 families in the Philadelphia area found that working parents with children under the age of 13 lose an average of eight days from work a year because of child care problems. Another recent study revealed that two-thirds of 5,000 Midwest respondents believed that child care concerns have an adverse effect on productivity.

Some employers are beginning to take the responsibility for developing leave policy which is sufficiently long to allow for a transition period within the family and which guarantees a return either to the same job or to the same level position. A recent survey by Catalyst, a research group in New York, showed that 95% of the country's 384 largest firms offer disability leave and 52% offer unpaid maternity leave in addition to disability leave. Job security was not as positive, however. Only 38% of the women returned to the same job and 43% to one comparable to their previous position. This indicates that family leave policy is a field in which union leaders need to take a strong lead as well, negotiating family leave time with job protections for both men and women.

Until recently, the federal government has not taken a particularly active role in developing working parent/child care policies or initiatives. The House Select Committee on Children, Youth and Families, working closely with the Congressional Caucus for Women's Issues, has recently become more active in this area. A Parental and Disability Leave Bill of 1985 (H.R. 2020), introduced by Rep. Patricia Schroeder of Colorado, would require employers to furnish a minimum of four months' leave time for parents who choose to stay home with a newborn, newly adopted, or seriously ill child; require six months' leave time for pregnancy-related and other temporary disabilities; and would guarantee job reinstatement upon return to work. As of this writing, it was not known whether this bill would be passed. If it is not, Congress should pass federal legislation which establishes minimum leave time requirements with job protections and, ideally, some process for replacing income lost during unpaid time off work.

> Employers are beginning to recognize that the resolution of child care and other work/family conflicts is not just a personal matter.

New Scheduling Arrangements

Upon return to work, many working parents experience a great need for flexible and reduced work time options. A number of national polls have indicated that inflexible, 40-hour-plus workweeks are a major source of individual and family stress. Flextime, job sharing, and part-time employment schemes that grant the same rights and benefits as full-time work have been identified again and again by working parents as desirable scheduling arrangements. If they are to become viable options, a number of things must happen:

• Employers need to identify and eliminate policies that constitute barriers to less than full-time work.

• Inflexible "head counts" which discourage managers from using part-time personnel, should be replaced by full-time equivalency systems.

• Employees choosing less than full-time schedules should have the same status as full-timers, and should receive the same rates of compensation, including fringe benefits, seniority accrual, job protections, and so forth. The introduction of flexible benefits plans could greatly facilitate the creation of this kind of equity. Although some employers currently prorate the salary and cost of benefits for regular part-time employees, others hesitate either to allow at all or to expand this kind of employee option because they fear the cost will be too great, particularly in the area of fringe benefits. Most are unaware that some firms prorate these costs and have identified appreciable savings in other areas as a result of introducing options like job sharing. Becoming knowledgeable about new, equitable reduced work time policies and programs should be a first step for employers.

Labor leaders have been largely opposed to flexible and part-time work arrangements on principle, fearing that they are inherently unfair and exploitive. They must become better informed about their members' need for a wider range of work time choice and the current status of new options like flextime, job sharing, and permanent part-time employment. It is the conditions under which these scheduling arrangements are offered and the lack of employees' rights and protections which must be addressed. Too often part-timers are still refused fringe benefits, including health insurance, and are the first to be laid off — no matter how long their tenure. Some of the best reduced-work-time programs and policies have been negotiated by unions whose members expressed a need for this type of option and whose leaders developed equitable guidelines for contracts covering permanent part-time, split codes, and job sharing.

Legislation to protect the rights and status of part-timers and to facilitate employing workers on a less than full-time basis should also be developed. Existing fiscal disincentives must be removed. Contributions for FICA and UI should be assessed in such a way that employers do not pay more for job sharers and other part-timers. Legislation which encourages the expanded use of flexible or "cafeteria style" fringe benefit policies should be passed.

The area of work time as a family-related issue has been largely overlooked until recently. Introduction of new scheduling options can be an efficient, cost-effective means of addressing working parent stress.

**Jerome M. Rosow, President,
Work in America Institute**

WORK AND FAMILY: THE PRODUCTIVITY CONNECTION

The signs of change are clear and compelling: The interaction between work and family issues today is more extensive and intensive than ever before. No longer do the rigid boundaries of the past divide the home and the workplace, and no longer can employers ignore the effects of family pressures on productivity and performance. The issue is not a social one, but an economic response to a feminized work force. To survive in a highly competitive marketplace, enlightened management and labor leaders must be attentive to the new work force, examine avenues to diminish conflicts without invading privacy, and establish equitable policies to enable employees to function well on the job.

Dramatic demographic, economic, and social developments over the past two decades have radically altered the profile of the American worker. Fewer than 10% of our population lives in the "classic" family headed by a single male breadwinner. The labor force has feminized and diversified. It is better educated, more likely to live in a family of multiple breadwinners, and more likely to have children in outside care. The labor force is marrying later or not at all, divorcing more often, and choosing to have fewer children at an older age. And the labor force is in an economic squeeze.

Pressured to keep pace with the wage slowdown and the decline in real income, families have sent every potential worker into the labor force.

The competitive employer, sensitive to labor market forces, recognizes that efforts to ease work/family conflicts and sustain the mental well-being of employees will redound tenfold to the corporation.

And with more of its members in the work force full time, the American family faces squarely the dilemma of dependent care, both for young children and aging parents. Divorced, widowed, and single-parent households are increasingly caught by economic pressures, as are the "single cell families," the single-career men or women who juggle work, family, and social life alone. One-third of our work force is single; one-quarter lives alone.

Changes Not Acknowledged by Managers

Although the statistical evidence of these changes in the labor force has been available for some time, its application to the workplace has lagged by years, with adverse effects on productivity. Many of today's managers and supervisors are insensitive to the extent of the changes or unwilling to acknowledge their influence. These managers matured in a more traditional work environment, where the separation between work and home life was inviolate. Home concerns were not to be raised at the workplace, and when conflicts arose, the loyal worker, supported by family members, would never question the supremacy of work over family, especially in a male-dominant work environment.

But today's manager is facing a different work force, a work force in conflict, a work force under economic, social, and psychological strain. The adverse effect of that strain on individual productivity and quality of work is clear; in situations of marital separation or divorce, performance at work suffers. In situations of overwhelming family stress, the worker may even resign, draining valuable experience and training from the employer. The professional employee is no longer considered the property of management. Likewise, a total devotion to work at the exclusion of family today is suspect and is acknowledged to engender other risks to the health of the employee and balanced performance at work.

The competitive employer, sensitive to labor market forces, recognizes that efforts to ease work/family conflicts and sustain the mental well-being of employees will redound tenfold to the corporation. At the same time, however, the progressive employer rejects paternalism, and moves, instead, toward policy flexibility and freedom of choice. The employer' goals are:

• To keep work and family conflicts at a minimum;

• To assist the worker in coping with the complexities of the work and family connection; and

• To encourage the creation of a social infrastructure to meet workers' needs.

Personnel policies are the conduit for change. And greater flexibility in the application of those policies can greatly ease the conflicting demands on workers.

• *Support Groups:* Employers can take the initiative to establish support groups, either on-site or through a community agency, to allow workers to discuss common family concerns. Single parents, divorced employees, pregnant employees, workers with aging parents — each common-interest group — could meet regularly after work hours to exchange ideas and discuss common issues. The role of the employer would be to provide a meeting room and perhaps a group facilitator. As an alternative to on-site meetings, support groups could meet through a community social agency, with the employer contributing on a per-capita basis for services used by employees. Small employers within a community could pool resources to offer similar services.

• *Work Hours:* At a minimum, employers must allow for greater flexibility in work hours and vacation scheduling to let workers cover the pressure points of early morning and evening arrangements for family members. This, in turn, reduces absenteeism, tardiness, friction at work, and turnover.

• *Leave Policies:* In situations of overwhelming family demand, workers at all levels should be allowed to arrange for leave without pay to find a solution to these problems before they reach a crisis.

• *Vacations:* Where loyalty and service justify, loans or advances on unearned vacation time should be made available to employees in financial need who are faced with special family financial problems.

• *Maternity/Paternity Leave:* Not only must written policies on maternity leave, with job and pay protection, become the norm, but more open discussion needs to take place by employers on their generic policy toward maternity leave. Paternity leave options should also be examined and considered. As women elect to delay the decision on childbirth until their careers are established, and as a greater number of women join the professional ranks, the issue of maternity leave increases in importance to the employer. Too often, young women are discriminated against in job advancement because of an unspoken concern or assumption on the part of the employer that they will leave their work at some future point in favor of motherhood. Likewise, young women are unwilling to discuss their plans openly with their employers for fear of reprisals. By establishing a formal policy setting the standards on maternity leave and the broader questions of a career break, and by guaranteeing support for the workers' decisions, employers can depressurize the issue and open it for early discussion and advance planning.

• *Child Care:* A large and critical need that will continue to grow — quality child care, particularly for preschool-age children — is a key link in the work and family connection. It is not a crisis issue, but an ongoing part of workers' needs. Employer-sponsored programs are not the answer. Instead, employers should pool their political power to achieve the institutionalization of all-day child care as part of the social infrastructure provided by public education. This is the most cost-effective, long-term solution for the labor force, the employer, and the family.

Union Leaders as Intermediaries

Labor unions face many of the same issues confronting employers, particularly in education and policy advocacy. Historically, unions often pooled the resources of employers to provide for workers' unmet social needs. Today, in part because of pressure at the bargaining table, many employers provide for those basic services. The role of union leaders has become one of an intermediary that surveys its members and assesses those problems creating friction between work and family life. Unions should set up a mechanism to get feedback from members on their most critical, family-related needs, and then move to address them as an integral part of the bargaining agenda, alongside issues of wages, hours, and working conditions.

No less than the integrity of the family and its ability to function in society and in the workplace will be affected by the willingness of management and union leaders to become involved in work-and-family issues. Employers should not be expected to take responsibility for solving larger social concerns, but they have considerable power within their own economic interests to diminish the conflict and thereby improve their own performance and stabilize the broader society. Feminization of the American labor force, and the attendant strains on the family are issues that affect the entire economy and the well-being of future generations.

This chapter lists public and private organizations that can provide information about family-and-workplace issues. Each entry is accompanied by a short description of the organization and/or its goals and activities. The entries are arranged in alphabetical order:

Administration for Children, Youth and Families
Office of Human Development Services
Department of Health and Human Services
Head Start Bureau, Program Support Division
P.O. Box 1182
Washington, D.C. 20013
(202) 755-7944
Dottie Livingston, Commissioner
Patricia Divine Hawkins, Child Care Specialist

The agency conducts research programs on child care and early childhood, and is involved in a number of private sector initiatives, including the National Employer-Supported Child Care Project, a research project. Results of the project were published by Auburn House. (See Bibliography.)

AFL-CIO
Department of Community Services
815 16th St., N.W.
Washington, D.C. 20006
(202) 637-5189
Frank W. Emig, Director

The Department of Community Services has two key tasks: making certain that public and voluntary human services organizations work for union members and their families, and enlisting unions' support for human resource concerns in the community. The Department operates through a network of liaison staff with agencies at national, state, and local levels.

Agency for Child Development
Human Resources Administration
of the City of New York
240 Church St.
New York, N.Y. 10013
(212) 553-6563
George Gross, Administrator

ACD is involved in a project designed to encourage city agencies' cooperation with city employees to expand child care service availability and to facilitate the placement of children in day care in New York City.

American Association of University Women
2401 Virginia Ave., N.W.
Washington, D.C. 20037
(202) 785-7700
Jane Pettit, Director of Program Development

Through its Families and Work Project, AAUW is establishing networks for individuals and organizations concerned with family/work relationships. The project focuses on dependent care, cooperative action planning, and needs assessment.

American Nurses' Association
Kansas City, Mo.
(816) 474-5720

ANA promotes the concept of job sharing as a viable work option for health care workers.

Association of Junior Leagues, Inc.
825 Third Ave.
New York, N.Y. 10022
(212) 355-4380
Deborah Seidel, Executive Director
Sally Orr, Director of Public Policy

At the national level, the Association, which represents some 263 Junior Leagues, promotes child care and parental leave options. Individual Junior Leagues support a variety of child care activities in their communities, including developing and funding programs.

Association of Part-Time Professionals, Inc.
7655 Old Springhouse Rd.
McLean, Va. 22102
(703) 734-7975
Diane Rothberg, President

The Association was founded in 1978 to promote alternative work patterns for professionals, particularly permanent part-time employment. The association also serves as a source of information on benefits for part-time employees.

Bank Street College of Education
610 West 112th St.
New York, N.Y. 10025
(212) 663-7200
Leeda Martin, Chairman
Richard R. Ruopp, President
Ellen Galinsky, Project Director, Work and Family Life Study

The work of the College includes an international study of work and family life that evaluates the productivity of workers in relation to the quality of their home life. Seminars are offered to the business community on major sources of stress for working families.

Bureau of Labor-Management Relations and Cooperative Programs
U.S. Department of Labor
200 Constitution Ave., N.W.
Washington, D.C. 20210
(202) 523-6098
Stephen I. Schlossberg, Deputy Under Secretary
John Stepp, Assistant Deputy Under Secretary

In its programs, the Bureau encourages and assists the development and implementation of cooperative labor-management and employee participation programs to improve productivity and enhance the quality of work life. Resource materials include publications, films, and educational and training materials.

Business and Professional Women's Foundation
2012 Massachusetts Ave., N.W.
Washington, D.C. 20036
(202) 293-1200
Irma Finn Brosseau, Executive Director

BPW provides information on child care, pensions, flextime, job sharing, and parental leave. This year, BPW/USA, a separate "advocacy" group within BPW, will be meeting with business leaders to urge accommodation in the workplace to working parents' needs.

Capital Region Education Council
599 Matianuck Ave.
Windsor, Conn. 06095
(203) 688-7333
Claudia Shuster, Early Child Development Director

The Council is a non-profit child care resource and referral organization which provides worksite seminars on a variety of work-and-family issues for Connecticut employers.

Catalyst
250 Park Ave. South
New York, N.Y. 10003
(212) 777-8900
Felice N. Schwartz, President

Catalyst is a national not-for-profit organization that works with corporations and individuals to develop career and family options. The Catalyst Network is a group of independent resource centers that provide career and educational counseling and programs. All have a particular commitment to meeting the career needs of women.

Center for Human Services
1240 Huron Rd.
Playhouse Square
Cleveland, Ohio 44115
(216) 241-6400
Duane Beck, Executive Director

Center programs include employee assistance programs, corporate child care, and workplace seminars.

Center for Public Advocacy Research, Inc.
12 West 37th St.
New York, N.Y. 10018
(212) 564-9220
Caroline Zinsser, Project Director, Day Care Policy

   The Center encourages employer initiatives for working parents, in both the public and private sectors.

Center for the Study of Aging
University of Bridgeport
170 Lafayette St.
Bridgeport, Conn. 06601
(203) 576-4358
Dr. Michael Creedon, Professor of Gerontology

   One aspect of the Center is to provide consultation to corporations on the application of Dependent Care Benefit Plans. The Center also offers consultation services to older executives.

Center for Work and Family Issues
Dawson Hall
University of Georgia
Athens, Ga. 30602
(404) 542-1803
Dennis Orthner, Director

   The Center conducts research and evaluations for both the public and private sector on the costs and benefits of existing family support programs and potential programs.

Child Care Action Campaign
99 Hudson St., Room 1233
New York, N.Y. 10013
(212) 334-9595
Elinor Geggenheimer, President

   The Campaign comprises a coalition of leaders from organizations that seek to inform the public about child care problems, and about solutions and services that may be attainable through the efforts of government, corporations, and individuals.

Child Care, Inc.
125 West 109th St.
New York, N.Y. 10025
(212) 864-3310
Nancy Kolben, Director of Employer Services

   Child Care, Inc., a non-profit organization, conducts a program showing employers how to offer employees full access to child care information. The organization also serves as a resource and as an advocacy service for parents and child care programs in New York City.

Child Care Law Center
A project of the San Francisco Lawyers Committee
625 Market St., Suite 815
San Francisco, Calif. 94105
(415) 495-5498
Ms. Abby Cohen, Managing Attorney

The Center serves as a resource on legal issues concerning the child care community.

Child Care Management Resource
5620 Greentree Rd.
Bethesda, Md. 20817
(301) 897-8272
Carol Rudolph, President

CCMR was founded in 1978 to provide a variety of consulting services to both the business sector and the child care community. The Center also runs noon-time seminars for working parents.

Child Care Systems, Inc.
329 West Main St.
Lansdale, Pa. 19446
(215) 362-5070/1-800-VIP-KIDS
Tyler Phillips, President

Child Care Systems provides employers and employees with child care information and referral services, on-site parenting seminars, and studies the workplace impact of child care.

Children at Work, Inc.
A Division of Adolf & Rose Associates
65 Bleecker St.
New York, N.Y. 10012
(212) 777-4900
Barbara Adolph and Karol Rose, Co-directors

Children at Work is a national consulting firm helping employers understand and respond to the needs of working parents and employees with aging parents.

Children's Defense Fund
1520 New Hampshire Ave., N.W.
Washington, D.C. 20036
(202) 628-8787
Marian Wright Edelman, President
Helen Blank, Director of Child Care and Family Services

A national children's advocacy organization, the Children's Defense Fund provides information on federal legislation affecting child care, the status of tax credits, state standards, and statistics. The Child Care Division also provides referral and information on employer-sponsored child care.

The Children's Foundation
815 15th St., N.W., Suite 928
Washington, D.C. 20005
(202) 347-3300
Barbara Bode, President

The Foundation is a national clearinghouse of child support information. It monitors the implementation of the Child Support Enforcement Amendments of 1984 on a state-by-state basis. Those amendments to the Social Security Act require states to prescribe by 1989 procedures they will take to improve the effectiveness of child support enforcement guidelines. Staff provide information, training materials, and organizing assistance to national, state, and local groups.

Coalition of Labor Union Women (CLUW)
15 Union Square
New York, N.Y. 10003
(212) 242-0700
Joyce Miller, President

CLUW, which was founded in 1974, is a national membership organization of some 18,000 working women and men. Two of the organization's goals are to secure quality child and dependent care, and pregnancy disability benefits.

Coalition of Labor Union Women
CLUW Center for Education & Research, Inc.
2000 P St., N.W., Room 615
Washington, D.C. 20036
(202) 296-3408
Laura Walker, Executive Director

Established in 1978, the Center keeps tabs on the status of working women, and develops educational tools to provide information for labor leaders and others in making constructive changes in the workplace and the labor movement.

Conference Board
Work and Family Information Center
845 Third Ave.
New York, N.Y. 10022
(212) 759-0900
Helen Axel, Director
Dana E. Friedman, Senior Research Fellow

The Work and Family Information Center, formed in 1983, is a national clearinghouse of information for the business community, government agencies, and other organizations concerned with changes in work and family relationships. The Center's services are available to Conference Board associate firms and other businesses, government agencies, social service organizations, educational and research institutions, and other groups involved with work and family issues.

Congressional Caucus on Women's Issues
U.S. House of Representatives
Washington, D.C. 20515
(202) 225-6740
Rep. Pat Schroeder (D-Colo), Co-chair
Rep. Olympia Snowe (R-Me), Co-chair

The bipartisan caucus of 123 members monitors legislation and serves as an information resource for members of Congress and the public on issues that affect women, families, and employment.

COPE
37 Clarendon St.
Boston, Mass. 02116
(617) 357-5863
Diane A. Burrus, Director of Education, Training, and Research

COPE is a family counseling, education, and resource center that has developed, implemented, and evaluated work-and-family programs in many large corporations. COPE also has developed programs in the public sector for "women in transition," i.e., displaced homemakers.

Corporate Child Care Consultants, Ltd.
741 Piedmont Ave., N.E.
Suite 500
Atlanta, Ga. 30308
(404) 892-0689
Mary Brown, President

Incorporated in 1977, the firm provides child care information and referral services for about 10 employers in the Atlanta area. CCCC also assists in setting up on-site child care centers, performs needs assessment and feasibility studies, and conducts seminars at the worksite on work and family issues.

The Displaced Homemakers Network
1010 Vermont Ave., N.W., Suite 817
Washington, D.C. 20005
(202) 628-6767
Jill Miller, Executive Director

The Network is an umbrella organization that links people around the country who are concerned about the problems of displaced homemakers. The network initiates state and regional conferences; works with government agencies; creates demonstration projects, model programs, and training manuals; and provides technical assistance, funding information, and program resources to individuals and groups seeking to develop or expand services for displaced homemakers.

Dorothy Rich Associates, Inc.
The Home and School Institute
Special Projects Office
1201 16th St., N.W.
Washington, D.C. 20036
(202) 833-1400
Dorothy Rich, President

Dorothy Rich Associates, Inc., specializes in helping working parents manage the competing demands of job and family and develops specific approaches to enable businesses to be more responsive to the needs of working parents. Materials developed for working parents include *Careers and Caring* activity packets.

Employee Benefit Research Institute
2121 K St., N.W., Suite 860
Washington, D.C. 20037
(202) 659-0670
Dallas Salisbury, President

EBRI provides employers, employees, unions, and others with educational and research materials on employee benefits.

Employee Counseling Programs
120 West 57th St.
New York, N.Y. 10019
(212) 245-8178
Patricia Abelson, Director
Barbara Brooks, Clinical Coordinator

The organization provides both individual counseling and information and referral services to employees experiencing work/family-related problems. It also offers on-site family life education seminars.

Employee Relocation Council
1720 N St., N.W.
Washington, D.C. 20036
(202) 857-0857
H. Cris Collie, Executive Vice President

A membership association, the Council operates a clearinghouse of information for the relocation industry, primarily focusing on real estate concerns, and produces a directory of relocation services, including spousal counseling.

Family and Children Services of Kansas City, Inc.
3217 Broadway, Suite 500
Kansas City, Mo. 64111
(816) 753-5280
Kathleen Hermes, Director of the Employer Services Unit
Shirley Stubbs, Manager of Child Care Services

This organization, which grew out of The Metropolitan Child Care Project, provides information and referral services on child, elderly, and disabled adult care to Kansas City employers. The organization also conducts parenting seminars.

The Family Matters Project
College of Human Ecology
Cornell University
Ithaca, N.Y. 14853
(607) 256-3210
Christiann Dean, Director of Dissemination

The Family Matters Projects has developed a workshop series based on the "empowerment approach" to building upon families' strengths. A series of letters on *Balancing Work and Family* is scheduled for publication beginning in the fall of 1986. The letters will be accompanied by a guide for facilitators who would like to conduct worksite or community workshops based on *Balancing Work and Family*.

Family Resource Coalition
230 N. Michigan Ave., No. 1625
Chicago, Illinois 60601
(312) 726-4750
Bernice Weissbourd, President
Linda Lipton, Executive Director

The Family Resource Coalition is a national membership organization promoting the development of community-based programs to strengthen families. Coalition members include the American Association for Marriage and Family Therapy, American Home Economics Association, Family Service America, and National Council on Family Relations. The Coalition publishes a quarterly publication, *COFO Memo*.

Gil Gordon Associates
10 Donner Court
Monmouth Junction, N.J. 08852
(201) 329-2266
Gil E. Gordon, President

Gil Gordon Associates provides consulting services in the field of telecommuting to employers who want to provide their employees with the option of working at home. The firm also publishes a monthly magazine, *Telecommuting Review*.

The Greater Minneapolis Day Care Association
Parents in the Workplace Division
1006 West Lake St.
Minneapolis, Minn. 55408
(612) 823-7243
Connie Bell, Director

The Association serves as an employer's consultant on business and child care benefits, conducts feasibility studies, performs needs assessments, and conducts parenting seminars. Child care and information referral services are also provided on a subscription basis to 13 employers in the metropolitan area. The association also publishes employer-directed newsletters on child care benefits.

Institute for Family and Work Relationships
1020 Prospect St.
Suite 400
La Jolla, Calif. 92037
(619) 459-0155
Marjorie Hansen Shaevitz, Co-director
Morton H. Shaevitz, Co-director

The Institute was founded in 1978 to identify and report on the societal changes resulting from the large number of women moving into the work force, and the changes in sex roles at home and in the workplace. The Institute provides organizations with speakers, seminars, and consultation on related issues, and clinical services to individuals and couples.

National Adoption Exchange
Adoption and the Workplace
1218 Chestnut St.
Philadelphia, Pa. 19107
(215) 925-0200
Marlene Piasecki, Director

The Adoption and the Workplace project encourages more companies to consider benefit plans for employees wanting to adopt children with special needs.

National Association for Child Care Management
1255 23rd St., N.W.
Washington, D.C. 20037
(202) 452-8100
Carole Rogin, Executive Director

The Association published in 1984 an employer-related child care services directory, *Benefits to Employees for Benefits to Business*. The 28-page pamphlet contains alphabetical and state-by-state listings of professional child care management companies with notations on types of services provided. The directory also highlights legal requirements for providing employee child care benefits and options.

National Center for Clinical Infant Programs
733 15th St., N.W., Suite 912
Washington, D.C. 20005
(202) 347-0308
Eleanor S. Szanton, Executive Director

The National Center's staff is available to assist policymakers in locating research and clinical data on approaches to the question, "Who will mind the babies?"

National Commission on Working Women
2000 P St., N.W., Suite 508
Washington, D.C. 20036
(202) 737-5769
Alexis Herman, Chairman

NCWW was created to focus on the needs and concerns of those women in the work force — some 80 percent of all working women — who are concentrated in low-paying, low-status jobs in service industries, clerical occupations, retail stores, factories, and plants. The Commission publishes *Women at Work: News About the 80%* and other publications on child care.

National Committee For Adoption
1346 Connecticut Ave., N.W., Suite 326
Washington, D.C. 20036
(202) 463-7559
William L. Pierce, President

NCFA encourages, and works with, corporations to establish and broaden benefit programs for adoptive parents and the children who are adopted.

National Women's Law Center
1616 P St., N.W.
Washington, D.C. 20036
(202) 328-5160
Nancy Duff Campbell, Information on Work and Family Issues

The National Women's Law Center serves as a national resource for individuals and organizations that are committed to advancing the status of women through the law. In the area of the family, the Center has developed a public education program to inform lower-income families of the various ways they can obtain financial assistance to meet their dependent care needs.

New Ways to Work
149 Ninth St.
San Francisco, Calif. 94103
(415) 552-1000
Barney Olmsted and Suzanne Smith, Co-directors

New Ways to Work is a clearinghouse for information on reduced work time options, such as job sharing and work sharing, and has issued a number of publications on the subject.

The Parent Connection, Inc.
5606 Knollwood Rd.
Bethesda, Md. 20816
(301) 652-4600
Deborah Benke, Director

The Parent Connection is a non-profit organization which consists of a team of multi-disciplinary, child-related professionals providing parent education, from the pre-natal period through adolescence. The firm is now setting up a computer-based match-up service for parent-to-parent child care sharing and selection.

Phoenix Institute
Business and Child Care Project
352 Denver St.
Salt Lake City, Utah 84111
(801) 532-6190
Suzanne Clow, Director

The Business and Child Care Project provides Utah businesses with information on child care services.

Prospect Hill Parents' and Children's Center
100 Fifth Rd.
Waltham, Mass. 02154
(617) 890-5438
Eleanor Nelson, President

The Center, a model program, provides a range of family support services at the workplace for a consortium of small and medium-sized companies. Among the Center's support schemes for families and children are an on-site child care center, computerized resource and referral, training programs for family day care providers, seminars for parents, forums for management, and a parent resource library.

Regional Research Institute for Human Services
Portland State University
P.O. Box 751
Portland, Ore. 97207
(503) 229-4040
Arthur C. Emlen, Director

As one of its projects, the Institute serves as an employer's consultant on child care information and surveys the work force to assess child care needs.

RESOURCE: Careers
1258 Euclid Ave.
Suite 204
Cleveland, Ohio 44115
(216) 579-1414
Marge Shorrock, Executive Director

RESOURCE: Careers, a non-profit career development and referral service for professionals, offers career services to spouses of professional employees being recruited or relocated to northeastern Ohio. The Dual Career Project has developed programs to help both corporations and dual-career families deal with issues important to couples trying to cope with the responsibilities of work and family.

Resources for Child Care Management
P.O. Box 669
Summit, N.J. 07901
(201) 277-2689
Robert Lurie, President

Among its other activities, the firm publishes *BusinessLink*, a report on management initiatives to help working parents.

Resources for Child Caring
906 North Dale St.
St. Paul, Minn. 55103
(612) 488-7284
Tom Copeland, Director of Employer Services

This private, non-profit agency provides support services for people who care for young children, and offers employers written material on choosing and using child care and on parental leave issues. Resources for Child Caring also conducts seminars for working parents, and consults on needs assessment and feasibility studies for various child care services.

Resources for Parents at Work
722 Westview St.
Philadelphia, Pa. 19119
(215) 843-2442
Stephen Segal, President

Resources for Parents at Work is a private professional firm, specializing in training and educational programs for working parents.

Select Committee on Children, Youth and Families
U.S. House of Representatives
Washington, D.C. 20515
(202) 226-7660
Rep. George Miller (D-Calif), Chairman
Alan J. Stone, Staff Director

The Select Committee has the authority "to conduct a continuing comprehensive study and review of the problems of children, youth and families, including but not limited to income maintenance . . . and . . . employment."

Vocational Education Work and Family Institute
3554 White Bear Ave.
White Bear Lake, Minn. 55110
(612) 770-3943
Joan Comeau, Director

Founded in 1980 and associated with the statewide Minnesota vocational education system, the organization helps the business community obtain quality education services on work and family issues. The project has been replicated in other states, including Alaska, Arizona, Mississippi, Nebraska, Ohio, and Oregon.

Wellesley College
Center for Research on Women
Wellesley, Mass. 02181
(617) 431-1453
Laura Lein, Director

Center programs include research on family, employment, stress and adult development, and changing male roles. The School-Age Child Care Project provides information and assistance in understanding the "latchkey" problem and in developing options for services and policies.

Wheelock College
Center for Parenting Studies
200 The Riverway
Boston, Mass. 02215
(617) 734-5200
Frances Litman, Director

In 1977, the College began offering lunch-time seminars on topics of interest to working parents.

Wider Opportunities for Women, Inc.
Mothers at Work Project
1325 G St., N.W., Lower Level
Washington, D.C. 20005
(202) 638-3143
Barbara L. Makris, Director
Carol Rudolph, Project Manager

WOW helps workers locate day care information, provides counseling in parenting skills, and provides skills training to economically disadvantaged single parents. The organization also counsels local employers interested in implementing child care services.

Wider Opportunities for Women, Inc.
Parents at Work Project
1325 G St., N.W., Lower Level
Washington, D.C. 20005
(202) 638-3143
Carol Rudolph, Project Manager

The group sponsors training seminars on a variety of subjects, with a special focus on child care for working parents. The Center also provides information on direct services and conducts an employer outreach program.

Women Employed
Women Employed Institute
5 S. Wabash, Room 415
Chicago, Ill. 60603
(312) 782-3902
Anne Ladkey, Director

The Institute publishes and disseminates corporate policies that are designed to make employers more receptive to the needs of women and families.

Women's Bureau
U.S. Department of Labor
200 Constitution Ave., N.W.
Washington, D.C. 20210
(202) 523-6611
Lenora Cole Alexander, Director
Jill Houghton Emery, Deputy Director

Congress established the Women's Bureau in 1920 and gave it the mandate to improve women's opportunities for profitable employment. One of the bureau's major activities and concerns is to encourage employer-supported child care for working parents.

Work/Family Directions
200 The Riverway
Boston, Mass. 02215
(617) 734-0001
Gwen Morgan and Fran Rodgers, Co-directors

Work/Family Directions, a joint venture of Rodgers & Associates, Inc., and Wheelock College, operates a child care project for sick children, provides resource and referral services to major corporations, and provides consultation to employers on options for employer-supported child care.

Work in America Institute
700 White Plains Rd.
Scarsdale, N.Y. 10583
(914) 472-9600
Jerome Rosow, President

A research and publishing organization, the Institute was established to advance productivity and improve the quality of working life by encouraging the more efficient use of human resources. Work and family issues are frequently addressed in the Institute's publications.

Yale Bush Center in Child Development and Social Policy
Infant Care Leave Project
Box 11A, Yale Station
New Haven, Conn. 06520
(203) 436-1592/3
Edward Zigler, Center Director
Meryl Frank, Project Director

The Yale Bush Center Infant Care Leave Project was initiated in response to a growing concern about the quality and appropriateness of out-of-home day care for the infants of employed parents. The Project is designed to contribute to a better understanding of the effects of several care options on the infant, the family, and the workplace, and to provide scholars and policymakers with the information needed to make sound public policy decisions. The Project will publish a series of articles and reports on various aspects of infant care leave that will be incorporated into a book sometime in 1986.

APPENDIX A

99TH CONGRESS
1ST SESSION

H.R. 2020

To require that employees be allowed parental leave in cases involving the birth, adoption, or serious illness of a child and temporary disability leave in cases involving inability to work due to nonoccupational medical reasons, with adequate protection of the employees' employment and benefit rights; and to authorize a study to determine ways of providing salary replacement for employees who take parental and disability leaves.

IN THE HOUSE OF REPRESENTATIVES

April 4, 1985

Mrs. SCHROEDER introduced the following bill; which was referred jointly to the Committees on Education and Labor and Post Office and Civil Service

A BILL

To require that employees be allowed parental leave in cases involving the birth, adoption, or serious illness of a child and temporary disability leave in cases involving inability to work due to nonoccupational medical reasons, with adequate protection of the employees' employment and benefit rights; and to authorize a study to determine ways of providing salary replacement for employees who take parental and disability leaves.

Be it enacted by the Senate and House of Representatives of the United States of America in Congress assembled,

SECTION 1. SHORT TITLE AND TABLE OF CONTENTS.

(a) SHORT TITLE.—This Act may be cited as the "Parental and Disability Leave Act of 1985".

(b) TABLE OF CONTENTS.

TITLE II—COMMISSION TO RECOMMEND MEANS TO PROVIDE SALARY REPLACEMENT FOR EMPLOYEES TAKING PARENTAL AND DISABILITY LEAVES

TITLE I—GENERAL REQUIREMENTS FOR PARENTAL AND DISABILITY LEAVE

SEC. 101. DEFINITIONS.

For purposes of this title:

(1)EMPLOY.—The term "employ" includes to suffer or permit to work, and includes ongoing contractual relationships in which the employer retains substantial direct or indirect control over the employee's employment opportunities or terms and conditions of employment.

(2)EMPLOYEE.—The term "employee" means any individual who is employed by an employer on a full-time or regular part-time basis.

(3)EMPLOYER.—The term "employer" means any person engaged in commerce or in any industry or activity affecting commerce who acts directly or indirectly in the interest of an employer to one or more employees, and any agent or successor in interest of such a person.

(4)PERSON.—The term "person" includes one or more individuals, governments, public agencies, political subdivisions, labor unions, joint labor-management committees, partnerships, joint ventures, corporations, legal representatives, mutual companies, joint-stock companies, trusts, trustees in bankruptcy, or receivers, estates, unincorporated organizations, associations, or employee organizations.

(5)PUBLIC AGENCY.—The term "public agency" means (A) the Government of the United States; the government of a State or political subdivision thereof; any agency of the United States that employs employees regardless of whether or how they are classified under the civil service provisions of title 5 of the United States Code, including any executive or legislative agency, the Public Health Service, any unit of the legislative or judicial branches, any military department, a corporation wholly or partially owned by the Government of the United States, a nonappropriated fund instrumentality whether under the jurisdiction of the Armed Forces or otherwise, the United States Postal Services, and the Postal Rate Commission; (B) any agency of a State or of a political subdivision of a State that employs employees regardless of whether or how they are classified under the applicable civil service law, including any executive or legislative agency and any unit of the legislative or judicial branches; or (C) any interstate governmental agency. Persons elected to public office in the government of the United States or of any State or political subdivision thereof and persons chosen by them as their immediate advisors with respect to the exercise of the constitutional or policymaking powers of their offices shall not be considered employees of a public agency within the meaning of this paragraph.

(6)STATE.—The term "State" includes any State of the United States, the District of Columbia, the Canal Zone, the Commonwealth of Puerto Rico, the Virgin Islands, American Samoa, Guam, Wake Island, and the Outer Continental Shelf lands defined in the Outer Continental Shelf Lands Act.

(7)COMMERCE.—The term "commerce" means trade, traffic, commerce, transportation, transmission, or communication (A) among the States, (B) between a State and any place outside thereof, (C) within the District of Columbia or a possession of the United States, or (D) between points in the same State but through a point outside thereof.

(8) INDUSTRY OR ACTIVITY AFFECTING COMMERCE.—The term "industry or activity affecting commerce" means any activity, business, or industry in commerce or in which a labor dispute would hinder or obstruct commerce or the free flow of commerce, and includes any activity or industry "affecting commerce" within the meaning of the Labor Management Relations Act of 1947, or the Railway Labor Act and any governmental industry, business, or activity.

(9) PARENTAL LEAVE.—The term "parental leave" means leave by reason of-

(A) the birth of a child of an employee;

(B) the placement of a child with an employee in connection with adoption of such child by the employee; or

(C) the serious illness of a child of an employee.

(10) TEMPORARY DISABILITY LEAVE.—The term "temporary disability leave" means leave by reason of an employee's inability to perform his or her job due to nonoccupational medical reasons.

(11) EMPLOYMENT BENEFITS.—The term "employment benefits" means all benefits and policies provided or made available to employees by an employer, and includes group insurance plan eligibility, health insurance, disability insurance, sick leave, annual leave, educational benefits, and pensions.

(12) SECRETARY.—The term "Secretary" means the Secretary of Labor.

(13) REDUCED LEAVE SCHEDULE.—The term "reduced leave schedule" means leave scheduled for fewer than 5 workdays per week or fewer than the employer's usual number of hours per workday.

(14) SERIOUS ILLNESS.—The term "serious illness" means an illness, injury, or condition likely to require-

(A) continuing medical treatment, or

(B) confinement for at least one month.

SEC. 102. TEMPORARY DISABILITY LEAVE REQUIREMENT.

(a) GENERAL RULE.—(1) Each employee shall be entitled to disability leave of not fewer than 26 workweeks in any one calendar year.

(2) Such leave need not be taken consecutively.

(b) UNPAID LEAVE PERMITTED.—Except as provided in subsection (c), leave granted as required by subsection (a) may consist of unpaid leave.

(c) INCREASES REQUIRED TO MEET MINIMUMS.—Any employer which provides temporary nonoccupational disability leave or benefits, or both, must provide such leave or benefits in such a manner that each employee is entitled to a minimum of 26 workweeks of disability leave in any one calendar year. If the benefits provided are paid benefits for a period of less than 26 weeks, the additional weeks of leave which are added to meet the 26-week minimum may be unpaid.

(d) VERIFICATION REGULATIONS.—The Secretary shall promulgate regulations governing employer verification of employees' eligibility for leave under this section; except that the same standards, procedures, or other requirements so imposed must apply to all temporary disabilities.

SEC. 103. PARENTAL LEAVE REQUIREMENT.

(a) GENERAL RULE.—(1) Each employee shall be entitled to parental leave of not fewer than 18 workweeks in any two years upon advance notice to his or her employer.

(2) Such leave need not be taken consecutively.

(b) UNPAID LEAVE PERMITTED.—Except as provided in subsection (c), leave granted as required under subsection (a) may consist of unpaid leave.

(c) INCREASES REQUIRED TO MEET MINIMUMS.—Any employer which provides parental leave or benefits, or both, must provide such leave or benefits in such a manner that each employee is entitled to a minimum of 18 workweeks of parental leave in any two calendar years. If the benefits provided are paid benefits for a period of less than 18 weeks, the additional weeks of leave which are added to meet the 18 week minimum may be unpaid.

(d) VERIFICATION AND NOTICE REGULATIONS.—The Secretary shall promulgate regulations governing (1) employer verification of employees' eligibility for leave under this section; and (2) the form, content, and timing requirements of the notice specified in subsection (a)(1).

SEC. 104. EMPLOYMENT AND BENEFITS PROTECTION.

(a) RESTORATION TO POSITION.—Each employee who exercises his or her right to a leave under section 102 or 103 shall, upon expiration of such leave, be entitled to be restored by the employer to the position held by the employee when the leave commenced or to an equivalent position of like seniority, status, employment benefits, pay, and other terms and conditions of employment.

(b) MAINTENANCE OF EXISTING HEALTH BENEFITS.—During any leave taken under section 102 or 103, the employer shall maintain any existing health benefits of the employee for the duration of such leave as if he or she continued in employment continuously from the dime he or she commenced such leave until the time of his or her restoration to such employment pursuant to subsection (a) of this section, regardless of whether continuation of such benefits during employee leaves is otherwise provided.

SEC. 105. REDUCED LEAVE SCHEDULES.

Each employee shall be entitled, at his or her option and subject to section 104, to take leave under section 102 or 103 on a reduced leave schedule; except that the total time period over which such reduced leave schedule is spread may not exceed 39 consecutive weeks.

SEC. 106. PROHIBITION AGAINST RETALIATION.

(a) INTERFERENCE WITH RIGHTS.—It shall be unlawful for any person to discharge, fine, suspend, expel, discipline, or in any other manner discriminate against an individual for (1) exercising any right to which such individual is entitled under the provisions of this title, (2) the purpose of interfering with the attainment of any right to which such participant may become entitled under this title, or (3) opposing any practice made unlawful by this title.

(b) INTERFERENCE WITH PROCEEDINGS OR INQUIRIES.—It shall be unlawful for any person to discharge, fine, suspend, expel, discipline, or in any other manner discriminate against any individual because such individual has filed any complaint or has instituted or caused to be instituted, or is about to institute or cause to be instituted, any proceeding under or related to this title, or has testified or is about to testify in any inquiry or proceeding or has given or is about to give any information connected to any inquiry or proceeding relating to this title.

(c) PROOF OF RETALIATION.—Any negative material change in the seniority, status, employment benefits, pay, or other terms or conditions of the position of an employee who has been restored to a position pursuant to section 104 that occurs within one year of such restoration, or of the position of an employee who has engaged in proceedings or inquiries pursuant to subsection (b) of this section that occurs within one year of the termination of such proceedings or inquiries, shall be presumed to be prohibited retaliation under this section.

SEC. 107. ENFORCEMENT.

(a) RIGHT TO BRING CIVIL ACTION.—A civil action may be brought in any district court of the United States, or any other United States court of a place subject to the jurisdiction of the United States, without respect to the amount in controversy or to the citizenship of the parties, or in any State court of competent jurisdiction, by an employee or by the Secretary against any employer, to enforce the provisions of this title; except that the Secretary may not bring an action against any public agency.

(b) JURISDICTION.—The district courts of the United States shall have original jurisdiction of civil actions brought under subsection (a), without regard to amount in controversy.

(c) VENUE.—Where an action under subsection (a) is brought in a district court of the United States or in a court of a place subject to the jurisdiction of the United States, it may be brought in any judicial district in the State in which the violation is alleged to have taken place, in the judicial district in which the employment records relevant to such violation are maintained and administered, or in the place in which the aggrieved person worked or would have worked but for the alleged violation. If the employer is not found within any such district or plan, such an action may be brought within the judicial district in which the employer resides or may be found. For purposes of sections 1404 and 1406 of title 28 of the United States Code, the judicial district in which the employer resides or may be found shall in all cases be considered a district in which the action might have been brought.

(d) RELIEF.—

(1) EQUITABLE RELIEF.—In any action brought under subsection (a), the court may enjoin any act or practice which violates or may violate any provision of this title, or order such other appropriate equitable relief as is necessary and appropriate to redress such violation or to enforce any provision of this title.

(2) DAMAGES.—Any employer which violates any of the provisions of this title shall be liable to the employee or class of employees affected in an amount equal to any wages, salary, employment benefits, or other compensation determined by the court to have been denied or lost to such employee or employees by reason of the violation, plus interest on the total monetary damages calculated at the prevailing rate, and in an additional equal amount as liquidated damages.

(3) PUNITIVE DAMAGES.—If, in the judgment of the court, the violation of this title was deliberate, the court shall award, in addition to monetary and liquidated damages, punitive damages equal to three times the total amount of monetary and liquidated damages.

(4) REASONABLE ATTORNEYS FEES AND COSTS.—The court in any action under subsection (a)(1) shall, in addition to any judgment awarded to

the plaintiff or class or plaintiffs, allow a reasonable attorney's fee to be paid by the defendant, and costs of the action. The United States shall be liable for attorney's fees and costs the same as a private person.

(e) NOTIFICATION OF THE SECRETARY; RIGHTS TO INTERVENE.—A copy of the complaint in any action under subsection (a) shall be served upon the Secretary by certified mail. The Secretary shall have the right in his or her discretion to intervene in any action brought by an employee under subsection (a). Any person aggrieved shall have the right to intervene in a civil action brought by the Secretary under subsection (a).

(f)LIMITATIONS.—

(1) STATUTE OF LIMITATIONS.—Actions brought under subsection (a) must be commenced within three years of the date of the violation.

(2) PERIOD OF RECOVERY.—An action under subsection (a) for damages may be brought only with respect to wages, salary, employment benefits, or other compensation denied or lost to any employee for periods commencing within three years before the date on which the action is brought.

(g) ATTORNEYS FOR THE SECRETARY.—In any civil action under subsection (a), attorneys appointed by the Secretary may appear for and represent the Secretary, except that the Attorney General shall conduct all litigation to which the Secretary is a party in the Supreme Court pursuant to this title.

SEC. 108. INVESTIGATIVE AUTHORITY.

(a) IN GENERAL.—To determine whether any person has violated or is about to violate any provision of this title or any regulation or order thereunder the Secretary may—

(1) make an investigation, and in connection therewith require the submission of reports, books, and records, and the filing of data in support of any information required to be filed with the Secretary under this title, and

(2) enter such places, inspect such books and records, and question such persons as the Secretary may deem necessary to enable the Secretary to determine the facts relative to such investigation, if the Secretary has reasonable cause to believe there may exist a violation of this title or any rule or regulation issued thereunder or if the entry is pursuant to an agreement with the employer.

The Secretary may make available to any person actually affected by any matter which is the subject of an investigation under this section, and to any department or agency of the United States, information concerning any matter which may be the subject of such investigation.

(b) REQUIRED SUBMISSIONS GENERALLY LIMITED TO AN ANNUAL BASIS.—The Secretary may not under the authority of this section require any employer or any plan, fund, or program to submit to the Secretary any books or records more than once in any 12-month period, unless the Secretary has reasonable cause to believe there may exist a violation of this title or any regulation or order thereunder.

(c) SUBPOENA POWERS, ETC.—For the purposes of any investigation provided for in this section, the provisions of sections 9 and 10 (relating to the attendance of witnesses and the production of books, records, and documents) of the Federal Trade Commission Act are hereby made applicable (without regard to any limitation in such sections respecting persons, partnerships, banks or common carriers) to the jurisdiction, powers, and duties of the Secretary or any officers designated by him or her.

SEC. 109. REGULATIONS.

The Secretary may prescribe such regulations as he or she finds necessary or

A CHANGING DYNAMIC   255

appropriate to carry out this title.
SEC. 110. AUTHORIZATION OF APPROPRIATIONS.
There are authorized to be appropriated such sums as may be necessary to enable
the Secretary to carry out the Secretary's functions and duties under this title.
SEC. 111. EFFECT ON OTHER LAWS.
    (a) FEDERAL LAWS.—
    (1) The requirements of this title may not be provided in any manner that dis-
criminates on the basis of race, religion, color, national origin, or sex, within the
meaning of title VII of the 1964 Civil Rights Act; on the basis of age within the
meaning of the Age Discrimination in Employment Act; or on the basis of
disability within the meaning of section 501, 503, or 504 of the Rehabilitation Act.
    (b) STATE AND LOCAL LAWS.—Nothing in this title shall be construed to
excuse noncompliance with, or to diminish any rights or protections established
under, any provision of the law of any State or any political subdivision of a State
which provides rights and protections which are greater than rights and protections established pursuant to this title.
SEC. 112. EFFECT ON EXISTING EMPLOYMENT BENEFITS.
Except as required by sections 102, 103, 104, and 105, no provision of this title
shall excuse noncompliance with any collective bargaining agreement or other
employment benefit program or plan in effect on the date of enactment of this
Act, nor justify any employer in reducing employment benefits provided by it
which are in excess of those required by this title.
SEC. 113. EFFECTIVE DATE.
This title shall take effect six months after the date of the enactment of this Act.

TITLE II COMMISSION TO RECOMMEND MEANS TO PROVIDE SALARY REPLACEMENT FOR EMPLOYEES TAKING PARENTAL AND DISABILITY LEAVES

SEC. 201. ESTABLISHMENT AND COMPOSITION OF COMMISSION.
    (a) ESTABLISHMENT.—There is established a commission to be known as
the Paid Parental and Disability Leave Commission (hereinafter referred to as the
"Commission").
    (b) COMPOSITION.—The Commission shall consist of twenty-one members
as follows:
    (1) five members of the Commission shall be appointed by the majority
leader of the Senate;
    (2) five members of the Commission shall be appointed by the Speaker of the
House of Representatives;
    (3) five members of the Commission shall be appointed by the President of
the United States, which members shall include the Secretary of Health and
Human Services, the Secretary of Labor, and the Chairperson of the Equal
Employment Opportunity Commission; and
    (4) six members of the Commission shall be appointed jointly by the majority
leader of the Senate and the Speaker of the House of Representatives to ensure a
broad representation among the members of the Commission of child advocacy,
women's rights, labor, management, and academic interests.
    (c) QUALIFICATIONS.—The members of the Commission shall be individ-
uals who possess the demonstrated capacities to discharge the duties imposed on
the Commission.
    (d) REMOVAL.—The Speaker of the House of Representatives and the
Majority Leader of the Senate jointly may remove a member of the Commission
only for neglect of duty or malfeasance in office.

(e) VACANCIES.—Any vacancy in the Commission shall not affect its powers, but shall be filled in the same manner in which the original appointment was made.

(f) CHAIRPERSON AND VICE CHAIRPERSON.—The Commission shall elect a Chairperson and a Vice Chairperson from among its members.

(g) QUORUM.—Fifteen members of the Commission shall constitute a quorum for the transaction of business, but the Commission may establish a lesser number as a quorum for the purpose of holding hearings, taking testimony, and receiving evidence.

SEC. 202. POWERS AND DUTIES OF COMMISSION.

(a) FUNCTIONS OF THE COMMISSION.—The Commission shall—

(1) engage in a comprehensive study of existing and proposed systems to provide workers with full or partial salary replacement or other income protection during periods of nonoccupational temporary disability leave, parental leave, and dependent care leave, both within the United States and in other countries or territories;

(2) produce a comprehensive written study analyzing the plans it has considered, with emphasis on their suitability for implementation on a nationwide level in the United States, which study shall include the Commission's recommendations for implementation of a system for salary replacement for all workers in the United States during periods of nonoccupational temporary disability leave and parental leave;

(3) pursuant to the analyses and recommendations of the study under paragraph (2), and within two years of the effective date of this Act, propose legislation to Congress to implement such a system of salary replacement for temporary nonoccupational disability leave;

(4) pursuant to the analyses and recommendations of the study under paragraph (2), propose legislation to Congress to implement such a system of salary replacement for parental leave.

(b) AUTHORITY TO CONDUCT HEARINGS.—The Commission or, on the authorization of the Commission, any subcommittee thereof or any member authorized by the Commission may, for the purpose of carrying out this Act, hold such hearings and sit and act at such times and places, take such testimony, have such printing and binding done, enter into such contracts and other arrangements (with or without consideration or bond, to such extent or in such amounts as are provided in appropriation Acts, and without regard to section 3709 of the Revised Statutes (41 U.S.C. 5)), make such expenditures, and take such other actions as the Commission or such member may deem advisable. Any member of the Commission may administer oaths or affirmations to witnesses appearing before the Commission or before such member.

(c) ACCESS TO INFORMATION.—The Commission is authorized to secure directly from any officer, department, agency, establishment, or instrumentality of the Government such information, suggestions, estimates, and statistics as the Commission may require to carry out its duties, and each such officer, department, agency, establishment, or instrumentality shall furnish, to the extent permitted by law, such information, suggestions, estimates, and statistics directly to the Commission upon request made by the Chairperson or Vice Chairperson.

(d) USE OF FACILITIES.—Upon request of the Commission, the head of any Federal agency is authorized to make any of the facilities and services of such agency available to the Commission or to detail any of the personnel of such agency to the Commission, on a reimbursable basis, to assist the Commission in carrying out its duties unless the head of such agency determines that urgent, overriding reasons will not permit the agency to make such facilities, services, or personnel available to the Commission and so notifies the Chairperson in writing.

(e) USE OF MAILS.—The Commission may use the United States mails in the same manner and under the same conditions as other departments and agencies of the United States.

(f)NO CLEARANCE TO BE REQUIRED.—No officer or agency of the United States shall require the Commission to submit any report, recommendation, or other matter to any such officer or agency for approval, comment, or review before submitting such report, recommendation, or other matter to Congress.

SEC. 203. ADMINISTRATIVE PROVISIONS.

(a) GENERAL ADMINISTRATIVE AUTHORITY.—Subject to such rules and regulations as may be adopted by the Commission, the Chairperson shall have the power to—

(1) appoint, terminate, and fix the compensation without regard to the provisions of title 5, United States Code, governing appointments in the competitive service, and without regard to the provisions of chapter 51 and subchapter III of chapter 53 of such title, or of any other provision of law, relating to the number, classification, and General Schedule rates of such personnel as it deems advisable to assist in the performance of its duties, at rates not to exceed a rate equal to the maximum rate for grade GS-18 of the General Schedule; and

(2) procure, as authorized by section 3109 of title 5, United States Code, temporary and intermittent services to the same extent as is authorized by law for agencies in the executive branch but at rates not to exceed the daily equivalent of the maximum annual rate of basic pay in effect for grade GS-18 of the General Schedule.

(b) EFFECT OF SERVICE.—Service of an individual as a member of the Commission, or employment of an individual by the Commission as an attorney or expert in any business or professional field, on a part-time or full-time basis, with or without compensation, shall not be considered as service or employment bringing such individual within the provisions of any Federal law relating to conflicts of interest or otherwise imposing restrictions, requirements, or penalties in relation to the employment of persons, the performance of services, or the payment or receipt of compensation in connection with claims, proceedings, or matters involving the United States. Service as a member of the Commission, or as an employee of the Commission, shall not be considered service in an appointive or elective position in the Government for purposes of section 8344 of title 5, United States Code, or comparable provisions of Federal law.

(c) INTERNAL RULES OF OPERATION.—The Commission may adopt such rules and regulations as may be necessary to establish its procedures and to govern the manner of its operations, organization, and personnel.

SEC. 204. COMPENSATION OF MEMBERS.

(a) PAY.—Each member of the Commission who is in the service of the Government of the United States shall serve on the Commission without additional compensation. Each member of the Commission who is not in the service of the Government of the United States shall be paid at a rate not to exceed a rate equal to the maximum daily rate for grade GS-18 of the General Schedule, for each day such member is engaged in the actual performance of duties as a member of the Commission.

(b) EXPENSES.—All members of the Commission shall be reimbursed for travel and per diem in lieu of subsistence expenses during the performance of duties of the Commission in accordance with subchapter I of chapter 57 of title 5, United States Code.

SEC. 205. REPORTS AND TERMINATION OF THE COMMISSION.

(a) INTERIM AND FINAL REPORTS.—The Commission shall prepare and submit to the Congress such interim reports as the Commission deems to be appropriate, except that its report and proposed legislation to provide salary replacement for employees on nonoccupational temporary disability leave must be submitted to Congress within two years of the date of enactment of this Act.

(b) TERMINATION OF COMMISSION.—Thirty days after the submission to the Congress of its final report the Commission shall cease to exist.

*   *   *

APPENDIX B

Dr. T. Berry Brazelton, M.D.

BNA INTERVIEW WITH DR. T. BERRY BRAZELTON, M.D.

[Dr. Brazelton is Associate Professor of Pediatrics at Harvard Medical School and Chief of the Child Development Unit at Children's Hospital in Boston. His most recent book, *Working and Caring*, was published in 1985 by Addison-Wesley Publishing Co., Inc. Following is a transcript of an interview with Dr. Brazelton.]

I think the role of women has been changing very rapidly in the past 15-20 years toward women feeling more empowered to do their thing, to get things done, and with that empowerment has come the realization that if they get their thing done, so to speak, they're going to have to make compromises at home. They're going to have to have decent substitute care for their children if they're going to be in the workplace, and they're going to have to learn how to split themselves in two — which is the job I think they're up to now. We're in a very big transition in our society in which women are realizing something that so far men haven't really realized: that if you're going to nurture a family and do a good job in the workplace, you have to be able to compartmentalize yourselves, split yourself in two, and I don't think women can do that alone. I think they've got to have help from the workplace and so far the workplace is beginning to be responsive, but I don't believe it will ever be able to be responsive enough to manage what I think would be ideal for both families and children, and that is subsidized leave around a new baby, the ability to be home when the baby needs you, when he or she is sick, or when he has to come home from school, and these are going to demand a kind of flexibility of the workplace that I don't know how individual situations can possibly respond to them without help.

I think our national government has got to be responsive and back up the workplace and the individual person who has a new baby and who needs help with substitute care and so forth. I think that without the government it's going to be too whimsical. Some big businesses may well be responsive, but small businesses can't afford it and so women are going to be at the mercy of whether they can get into a firm that is responsive or not. Now you could say, "Well, that ought to push firms into getting into providing on-site day care, providing flextime, providing leave around a new baby," but I suspect that there wouldn't be a uniform response from the workplace, so the government's got to do it.

I have no question but that four months [leave] is the minimum, six months would be much better, around a new baby. Ideally, even a year for a mother or a father to be with that baby, but in our country at present, we're not really family oriented or child oriented in the U.S. I'm fighting for four months paid maternity leave or paternity leave because I think that's probably what we can get.

In terms of national legislation, I don't believe in this Administration we're going to get more than four months. I'd like to pump eventually for six months. We now have a bill called HR 2020 that Representative Pat Schroeder from Colorado has introduced to the Congress and is having hearing on, which I got a chance to testify for. [The bill] will protect four months of maternity or paternity leave around a new baby or an adopted baby. That's a first step, but people can't afford that if they have to do it without pay.

I've always wished parents could be home the first year, the mother anyway, and maybe sharing it with her husband, but at least somebody could be home with the baby the first year.

I think four months is a minimum for a baby to know that that parent is his or hers and know which is his parent and who is the day care person, which is the sitter, and before four months I think it would be iffy whether a baby ever feels a sense of basic trust that Erik Erikson talks about. I don't know. I don't think we have any data to back us up.

However, I think a baby probably adjusts to two or three caregivers better than young parents can. I believe the parents are going to be the ones that will pay the biggest price if they have to leave a baby before four months of age because I don't think a parent ever really has a feeling of getting through those terrible first three months of colic and getting on with the job of seeing that baby smile up in their face and look at 'em like, "Oh, there you are?" Every time they say "Oooh," you say "Yeah," and they say, "Oooh" a second time and you say, "That's right," and you get locked into this lovely interaction and if you've had time to really develop that with the baby, you know it's for you. And to me that is a goal for every parent. Every parent is going to learn that they're responsible for that baby's vocalizing, smiling, development. Before four months I don't feel like they can believe they've done it. They might feel like their mother did it or the sitter did it or the next door neighbor did it, but they wouldn't be sure they'd done it.

Every industrialized nation in the world is ahead of us in terms of taking care not only of their small children, but taking care of families, and I think we're paying the price.

I don't think we are a child-oriented society. Every industrialized nation in the world is ahead of us in terms of taking care not only of their small children, but taking care of families, and I think we're paying the price. You know, 58% of children will have been raised in a single-parent family in this country by the time they're 18 — over half because of marital breakdown. That's a very serious indictment of how sick our society is. It's time we thought about that and backed up families for nurturing each other and I think this is a chance to do that.

We've been studying the conditions in the U.S. for children and families in the workplace at the Yale-Bush Center and the Bush Foundation has backed up a three-year study to try to evaluate what needs to be done to back up children and families. We had a meeting about three days ago in which we came to some agreements. The ones that I feel the best about and feel like I participated the most in were subsidizing day care and being sure that we had decent, well-paid day care for all children in the U.S.A. The other way is six months protected and partially funded parental leave. And it can be divided between either parent, but each parent can be protected both in the workplace and with $750 of their salary for three months — umm, for six months . . . . I would like to have seen it full protection, full salary. I'd like to have seen it protecting either parent as it does, but with the assurance that they can get back their jobs and have benefits while they're away. All the things that we're fighting for. I would rather see full benefits for four months than partial benefits for six months because I think more people will feel like taking them.

I guess I wonder what will happen to the American family and to children if we don't do these things to protect them around a new baby and around the cementing of a family that goes on around a new baby. The main thing that worries me is that the marital breakdown is going to continue and maybe get worse and it's already affecting over half of our children, so . . . .

I blame the strain in families for a marital breakup. I don't think young people today expect to have to work at a marriage for some reason. We all had to work at it and I think that the stresses must be so great around them that when a stress in the family comes up they just can't take it anymore, so they break up. This is tragic, and it's very hard on children.

[U]nless there are cushions within the workplace, such as counseling, such as parent groups, such as ways to find decent care for your children, that it's bound to contribute to stresses in the family that families just don't feel like facing.

I think that the stresses on families when both of them are working must be enormous and unless there are cushions within the workplace, such as counseling, such as parent groups, such as ways to find decent care for your children, that it's bound to contribute to stresses in the family that families just don't feel like facing. The trouble is that then the woman gets left with her children or the man may get left with his children, and he becomes a one-salary family and he sinks to the bottom of the pay scale and he really can't afford to raise his children or her children in a decent way, so the workplace has got to be more responsive, I think, to protect families, but also to protect themselves because I don't think [employers] get very much from people who are under stress — I can't believe they do.

Sweden, as in most social reform [countries], has been one of the leading countries to come to some of this and they have a year, I think, that can be divided up among parents and I think six months of it is full pay. They have all sorts of cushions around a sick child and around sharing jobs with other people, things like that that make a big difference to the parents of small children. I think Japan is coming to a new reform in which they're protecting families around a new baby and then providing on-site day care in most work situations for the children, so everybody feels like they're in on the family. So these are two countries — all of the socialist countries, Russia, China, Israel — are all way ahead of us on their policies.

I don't think we're family oriented at all. I think we still have a pioneering ethic that a family ought to take care of itself and that the extended family is going to cushion each family. This came from our pioneering ancestors. Trouble is, the extended family isn't there to cushion them anymore and grandma is usually working as much as her daughter, so she's not available, and we really don't have any cushions for the family these days and the stresses are increasing very rapidly — the financial stresses and all the rest.

I think if we don't do some providing of cushions for our families, we're really endangering our future children. For children to grow up in single-parent families is obviously not ideal and the kind of neuroses, psychosomatic problems, that they get are out of proportion to anything they need to have if the family were a cushion for them.

I guess the thing that bothers me the most is parking children. Fifty percent of the mothers do not have a choice about where they leave their children, so they leave them next door, leaving them alone, leaving them in situations that are designed to really deny these kids a decent future and I think we can expect more terrorism, more psychosomatic disease, more outcomes in which people are going to cost us a great deal to take care of, that we really don't need to have in this country. We're affluent enough to provide decent solutions for people that we haven't done yet.

*   *   *

APPENDIX C

RESOLUTION ON CHILD CARE AND SOCIAL SERVICES
ADOPTED AT THE AFL-CIO BIENNIAL CONVENTION IN OCTOBER 1985

The country is experiencing a growing incidence of child abuse, family breakup, and rapidly increasing untreated mental and emotional illness.

Growing numbers of working parents are searching for frequently nonexistent child care arrangements and the risk of job loss is an ever-increasing concern of pregnant women as they face the delivery and care of newborn children. In addition, the need for child care services for young children whose parents must work away from home is increasing so dramatically that by 1990 an estimated 30 million infants and children will require such care. As life expectancy increases and older Americans comprise a growing percentage of the population, more and more working families find themselves responsible for the care of elderly parents.

In 1981, at the urging of the Administration, the Congress abdicated a vital federal role in providing services to the nation's most vulnerable citizens by cutting 23 percent from the already-inadequate amounts of federal funding for child care and other social services and turning the remainder over to the states with no restrictions as to how the money was to be spent. Any federal commitment to child care has been virtually eliminated with the Administration urging instead that parents look to the free market place — proprietary centers and employer-sponsored programs — as a substitute. Even the source of federal support for child care services now provided by the existing tax credit is being threatened by the Administration's efforts to change the tax credit to a tax deduction — making it far less advantageous to lower-income families.

The AFL-CIO urges the Congress to reverse the retrenchment of federal commitment to essential social services and begin to repair the program authorized by Title XX of the Social Security Act, designed to provide these vital services. The funding for this program should be increased so as to meet the needs of abused children, the mentally ill, and the elderly. In addition, a substantial portion should be designated for child care services for low-income working mothers.

The tax credit now allowed for child care expenses should be retained, and legislation should be passed insuring that parents can take a reasonable parental leave to care for newborn children without risking loss of their jobs.

Financial incentives should be provided to states to encourage programs for early childhood education and child care services as well as services for the elderly and the disabled. Assistance should be made available to improve the licensing, regulatory, and monitoring standards for center and home-based care, as well as for training and providing technical assistance for child care workers. Every effort should be made to assure the safety of child care services and to enhance and expand them.

While continuing our efforts to achieve a broad-based comprehensive national program available to every child who needs care including those whose parents work nights and weekends, the AFL-CIO continues to urge our affiliates, wherever possible, to establish child and dependent care services through the collective bargaining process. This will involve assessing the needs of members and pursuing all options including employer-sponsored centers, information and referral services, allowances for care in existing centers, time off when the child or dependent is sick, and establishing flexible working hours to accommodate caring for children or other dependents.

*   *   *

APPENDIX D

1986 AFL-CIO RESOLUTION AND FACT SHEETS
ON WORK AND FAMILY

[Following is the Resolution on Work and Family adopted by the AFL-CIO Executive Council at its annual winter meeting in Florida in February 1986.]

The family is the key to social stability, community progress and national strength. To strengthen the family is at the heart of the labor movement's long struggle to raise wages and living standards, to democratize education, leisure and health care, to broaden individual opportunity and secure dignity in old age.

In the conviction that work, and the rewards of work, are the foundations of the stable, hopeful family life that engenders self-reliance, self-respect and respect for others, unions have sought to advance the welfare of working people and their families through collective bargaining and through legislative and political activity.

As a result, generations of Americans have benefited through higher wages, negotiated pensions and health and welfare programs, increased job security and increased leisure for enjoying family life. The entire society has gained through union-won wage, hours and overtime laws, child-labor laws, Social Security, Medicare and Medicaid, equal employment opportunity, pay equity, day care and a wide range of other programs that support, protect and advance the quality of family life.

Changes are underway that make work and family issues more vital than ever to the health of America's society. Women are vastly increasing their participation in the workforce. The number of single-parent families is growing rapidly, and so are families that require two incomes.

Many who label themselves "pro-family" are in fact the architects and supporters of government policies that have drastically weakened public policies that benefit children, the elderly and the unemployed.

Two out of three jobless workers receive no unemployment benefits at all. Those who do, receive no more than 35 percent of previous wages. More and more low-wage, year-round workers fail to earn enough to lift their families out of poverty. In 1985, a full-time worker at the minimum wage earned only $7,000, less than half of the $17,000 needed, according to the Bureau of Labor Statistics for a "minimum but adequate" living for a family of four and far below the official $11,000 poverty line for such a family.

At the same time, more and more working families need day care for small children and other dependents, including elderly and handicapped family members.

Many families with one and even two earners find that the cost of day care consumes 25 to 50 percent of their income, at the rate of $3,000 per year per child.

Clearly, both the availability and the affordability of child care have reached crisis proportions.

There are no simple, easy, or cheap ways to meet the needs of America's families who have diverse and sometimes conflicting interests. But unions have special responsibilities and opportunities to promote and defend family-oriented programs, both public and private.

For example, among benefits to be won through collective bargaining are equal employment opportunity, pay equity, maternity and paternity leave, child care for union members, flexible work schedules to help working parents, the right to refuse overtime, and anti-sex-discrimination.

The AFL-CIO continues to urge affiliates, whenever possible, to pursue such family strengthening programs through the collective bargaining process, including joint employer-union sponsored day care centers, information and referral services, allowances for care in existing centers, time off when the child or dependent is sick, and establishing flexible working hours to accommodate caring for children or other dependents.

Unions should work cooperatively with parents, child care activists, churches and other civil groups to ensure that care provided meets quality standards.

The AFL-CIO also urges support for a broad range of federal action to strengthen the American family, including opportunities to work and earn enough for decent family life, including:

* National economic policies aimed at full employment in line with the Humphrey-Hawkins Full Employment and Balanced Economic Growth Act of 1978.

* Improved unemployment insurance, health care protection and mortgage and rental relief for unemployed workers.

* Quality health care for all families.

* More vigorous enforcement of anti-discrimination and equal opportunity laws and promotion of pay equity.

* An increase in the minimum wage to assure more adequate income for the working poor.

* A shorter workweek, reduced work hours per year and higher overtime penalties to increase opportunities for family life.

Specifically, the AFL-CIO urges the Congress to:

* Enact a broad-based national program to make day care available to all who need it and to provide financial incentives to states for encouragement of programs in early childhood education and child care services, as well as services for the elderly and the disabled, and to improve licensing and monitoring of day care.

* Pass legislation to insure that parents can take a reasonable parental leave to care for newborn, newly adopted or seriously ill children without risking loss of their jobs.

* Restore funding to family support programs including Aid to Families with Dependent Children, food stamps, and Medicaid.

* Restore and increase funding for social services under Title XX of the Social Security Act to meet the needs of abused children, the mentally ill, and the elderly, as well as to provide child care services for low-income working mothers.

* Retain the tax credit now allowed for child care expenses. Congress should resist the Reagan Administration's efforts to change the tax credit to a tax deduction — making it far less advantageous to lower-income families.

Work and family problems are complex. They will not yield easily or soon to the private and public efforts we are proposing. The AFL-CIO pledges its continued support of efforts to solve these problems.

FACT SHEET ON

WORK INCOME AND FAMILIES

In March 1985, there were 62.7 million families in the United States. Their median income in 1984 (50% above, 50% below) was $26,433.

Family incomes, after allowing for inflation, were less in 1984 than in 1974. This drop in real income came after a strong rise in the previous 10 years.

FAMILIES AND INCOMES

	Number of Families (Millions)	Prior Year Median Income (1984 Dollars)	Pct. Change in Income
1965	48.0	$21,970	--
1975	55.7	27,175	+23.7%
1985	62.7	26,433	-2.7%

The real income drop would have been even larger,had it not been for the rising percentage of families with working wives.

The percentage of families with a working wife rose from 29 percent of all families in 1965 to 43 percent in 1985. This happened even though married couple families as a group fell from 87 percent of all families in 1965 to 80 percent in 1985.

COMPOSITION OF FAMILIES, 1965-1985

	1965	1975	1985
Number of Families	48.0 Mill.	55.7 Mill.	62.7 Mill.
Percent	100%	100%	100%
Married Couple	87	85	80
Wife in labor force	29	37	43
Wife not in labor force	58	48	37
Male head, wife not present	3	3	4
Female head, husb. not present	10	13	16

Considering married couple families separately, the majority now have a wife in the labor force:

MARRIED COUPLE FAMILIES WITH WIFE IN LABOR FORCE

	1965	1975	1985
Number of families	41.6 Mill.	47.0 Mill.	50.3 Mill.
Percent	100%	100%	100%
Wife in labor force	33	43	54
Wife not in labor force	67	57	47

Between 1974 and 1984, real family incomes rose only for the families with a wife in the labor force. This increase was very small, however, -- only 1.5 percent.

FAMILY INCOME: TYPE OF FAMILY

| | Median Income in 1984 Dollars | | |
	1974	1984	Percent Change
All families	$27,175	$26,433	-2.7%
Married couple	$29,312	$29,612	1.0
Wife in labor force	34,149	34,668	1.5
Wife not in labor force	25,749	23,582	-8.4
Male head, no wife present	24,543	23,325	-5.0
Female head, no husb. present	13,659	12,803	-6.3

The one-earner family is increasingly a rarity. Families with one earner dropped from 44 percent of the total in 1965 to 29 percent in 1985. While the percentage with no earners increased (from 8 percent to 15 percent of the total), those with two or more earners rose from 49 percent in 1965 to 56 percent in 1985.

NUMBER OF EARNERS IN FAMILIES*

	1965	1975	1985
All Families	100%	100%	100%
No earners	8	11	15
One earner	44	35	29
Two or more earners	49	54	56

*Refers to number with earnings in previous year.

An important ingredient in the erosion of real family incomes between 1974 and 1984 was the drop in the real work earnings of men, (measured in 1984 dollars). Over the decade, the median real earnings of all male workers fell by 11 percent, with most of the decline taking place in the last 5 years. Even for those working year-round full-time, the drop was 7.2 percent over the 10-year period.

WORK EARNINGS FOR MEN
(In 1984 Dollars)

	All Male Workers		Year Round Full-Time		Percent Who Worked YRFT
	Number (Millions)	Median Earnings	Number (Millions)	Median Earnings	
1974	59.9	$ 19,202	37.9	$ 25,009	63%
1979	64.6	18,524	42.4	24,340	66%
1984	66.5	17,026	43.8	23,218	66%
Pct. Change:					
1974-79	8.0%	-3.5%	11.9%	-2.8%	
1979-84	2.8	-8.1	3.2	-4.6	
Total 1974-84	11.0	-11.3	15.5	-7.2	

Work earnings for women fared better, as many more women moved into the work force, and a steadily enlarging percentage became year-round full-time workers -- moving from 40 percent of the total in 1974 to 48 percent in 1984. The work earnings for all women workers rose 16 percent over the 10-year period, but with nearly all of the increase coming in the first 5 years. Earnings for year-round full-time workers hardly changed at all during the decade.

WORK EARNINGS FOR WOMEN
(In 1984 Dollars)

	All Female Workers		Year-Round Full-Time		Percent Who Worked YRFT
	Number (Millions)	Median Earnings	Number (Millions)	Median Earnings	
1974	42.9	$ 7,501	16.9	$ 14,674	40%
1979	50.9	8,551	22.1	14,522	43%
1984	55.2	8,675	26.5	14,780	48%
Pct. Change:					
1974-79	18.8%	14.0%	30.3%	-1.0	
1979-84	8.5	1.5	19.9	1.8	
Total 1974-84	28.9	15.7	56.2	.7	

Average weekly earnings of production and non-supervisory workers (private, nonfarm) include the wages of both men and women, and include both full-time workers and part-time workers.

Over the 1974-84 period, these earnings (in terms of 1984 dollars) dropped by 8.8 percent. The larger part of the drop came in the last 5 years, with earnings in 1984 declining 5.3 percent from their 1979 levels.

In 1985, real earnings showed a further decline of 1.0 percent.

AVERAGE WEEEKLY EARNINGS OF NON-FARM PRODUCTION AND NONSUPERVISORY WORKERS (ANNUAL AVERAGES)

	In 1984 Dollars
1974	$322.42
1979	310.61
1984	294.05
1985	290.98
Pct. Change:	
1974-79	-3.7
1979-84	-5.3
Total 1974-84	-8.8
1984-85	-1.0

In the decade 1964 to 1974, the percentage of families below the poverty line dropped sharply -- from 15.0 percent to 8.8 percent. In the decade since 1974, family poverty has risen -- reaching 11.6 percent as of 1984.

FAMILIES IN POVERTY

(Income Year)	Number of Families	Number in Poverty	Percent in Poverty
1964	47,835	7,160	15.0%
1974	55,698	4,922	8.8%
1979	59,550	5,461	9.2%
1984	62,706	7,277	11.6%

(Note: These figures relate to family units, not to number of persons.)

Over the same period the share of aggregate family income going to the families in the bottom 20 percent of income receivers showed much the same pattern. The bottom 20 percent of families received 5.1 percent of total family income in 1964. This rose to 5.5 percent in 1974, but dropped off to 4.7 percent in 1984.

At the same time, the share of the top 5 percent of families, which was 15.9 percent in 1974, fell to 15.5 percent in 1974. But it rose to 16.0 percent in 1984.

SHARES OF TOTAL FAMILY INCOME

	1964	1974	1984
	100.0%	100.0%	100.0%
Lowest 20 percent	5.1	5.5	4.7
2nd	12.0	12.0	11.0
3rd	17.7	17.5	17.0
4th	24.0	24.0	24.4
Highest	41.2	41.0	42.9
Top 5 percent	15.9	15.5	16.0

How much does it cost a family to live?

To live at a level officially defined as "poverty," the cost for a 4-person family was $10,609 in 1984. As of 1985, the poverty line will come out close to $10,988 when the official estimates are made . On a weekly basis, this translates to $204 in 1984 and $211 in 1985.

POVERTY LINE FOR A FAMILY OF FOUR

Income Year	Annual	Weekly
1984	$10,609	$ 204
1985 (est.)	$10,988	$ 211

While most families do not live in poverty, most of them fail to reach anything like a "comfortable" living standard.

The Bureau of Labor Statistics has abandoned the living cost budgets it used to prepare for a 4-person urban family (employed husband, non-working wife, two children) for "lower," "intermediate," and "higher" living levels. The last set was for Autumn 1981.

The intermediate level originally represented a "modest but adequate" living standard. The "lower" budget was originally intended to represent a "minimum adequacy" standard, (although by the time it was actually published, this description had been dropped.) The higher budget was a "more comfortable" level.

Updating the 1981 figures to take account of price changes and changes in Federal income and social security taxes, produces estimates for Autumn 1984 and Autumn 1985 as follows:

ESTIMATED LIVING COST BUDGETS FOR A FOUR-PERSON FAMILY

	Lower		Intermediate		Higher	
	Annual	Weekly	Annual	Weekly	Annual	Weekly
Autumn 1984	$16,859	$ 324	$29,432	$ 528	$40,913	$ 787
Autumn 1985	17,404	335	28,302	544	42,212	812

Families of different sizes would of course have different living cost requirements.

If adjustments are made to take account of differing family sizes (using the ones developed for the poverty line calculations), it is possible to make a fairly good guess at how many families meet the different budget standards. Using the latest detailed income statistics (which are for 1983), the figures come out as follows:

PERCENTAGE OF FAMILIES
BELOW POVERTY LEVEL AND URBAN BUDGETS
1983

Below Poverty Level (Official)	Below Lower Budget (Estimate)	Below Intermediate Budget (Estimate)	Below Higher Budget (Estimate)
12.3%	23%	44%	67%

Thus while 12 percent of families were in poverty in 1983, a considerably larger fraction -- 23 percent -- failed to meet a "minimum adequate" standard. Forty-four percent were below the "modest but adequate "standard and fully two-thirds were below a "comfortable "standard.

*　　*　　*

FACT SHEET ON CHILD CARE

Over two-thirds of the entrants into the labor force in the past decade have been women and two-thirds of these women have children — most of whom are under six years of age. By 1990 it is predicted that at least half of the labor force will be female and an estimated 30 million infants and children will be in need of child care services.

Overall, some 65 percent of the mothers of children under 18 and 52 percent of children under six are now in the workforce. One in five of all children live in a single parent home and by 1990 nearly one in four will be living with a single parent — double the 1970 rate. Over half of all black children now live with their mothers only.

Most mothers are working full-time, making child care a problem that cannot be resolved by arranging work hours to coincide with school hours. Flextime work schedules are available to only about six percent of all full-time workers. In 1980, 10 percent of the dual earner couples were able to work different shifts so that one parent would always be at home with the children.

There are currently 24 million children under the age of thirteen in need of care while their parents are out of the home. The most current reports from the Department of Health and Human Services and the Census Bureau indicate that there is space available in existing licensed centers and family homes for around 6 million children. (These official figures do not indicate the percentage of day care arrangements which are in for-profit centers. One estimate is that there are 22,000 for-profit centers nationwide.)

There are significant variations in the cost of child care based on geography, age of child and type of care ranging anywhere from $1,500 to $10,000 per year. The majority of parents pay about $3,000 per child per year for child care.

The median income of two parent households with two children was $25,338 in 1984; with two children in need of full day care the cost in most cases would be $6,000 or nearly 25 percent of their income. The median income of single parent families in 1984 was $12,803; the cost of care for one child would likely be 25 percent of this income and 50 percent if two children needed care. For the person earning the minimum wage, $6,968 a year, the cost of caring for two children would be nearly 100 percent of his or her income. For all families, both the availability and the affordability of child care are of crisis proportions.

Background of Federal Role in Child Care

The federal government became significantly involved in supplying child care services during World War II. In the Lanham Act of 1942, Congress provided grants to states to provide care for children of mothers working in wartime industries. The program ended when the war ended.

Since then, the only comprehensive child care legislation to be passed by the Congress was enacted in 1971. The bill was vetoed by President Nixon on the grounds that enacting a comprehensive child care bill would destroy the American family and lead to sovietization of child rearing in this country. That message from the President has served to reinforce right wing advocates in their efforts to successfully prevent the passage of any comprehensive legislation since then. Since 1971, bills which have been introduced to create a comprehensive federal child care program have never reached the floor of either House.

Some assistance for child care did make it through Congress in the 70's. In 1976, Congress enacted a child care tax credit for families of children under 15.

The 1976 flat rate credit for dependent care was expanded in 1981 and made slightly more generous to low-income households, allowing a 30 percent credit for expenditures up to $2,400 for taxpayers with incomes of $10,000 or less. The credit is reduced gradually between incomes of $10,000 and $28,000 and those with incomes of $28,000 and up receive a 30 percent deduction. A family earning $10,000 a year would have to pay $2,400 per year, nearly one-fourth of its income to receive the maximum credit of $720. Over two-thirds of the annual $1.7 billion tax savings from this program goes to families with above median incomes.

The Social Service Block Grant under Title XX of the Social Security Act was passed in 1974. The program provides grants to states to provide a wide variety of human services — of which child care is one — to families on welfare. (Technically, low-income working families not on welfare were eligible, but rarely was any funding available for these families.) In order to encourage the states to begin to address child care needs, the law required that a portion of the original $2 billion appropriation be set aside specifically for child care.

Some additional support programs were enacted during the 70's such as the Child Care Food Program which helps offset the cost of food in child care programs. The CETA program was a source of funds for child care employees, and federal minimum standards for federal funded day care programs existed throughout the decade. Those standards, the Federal Interagency Day Care Requirements, were never adequately enforced, but they did represent a federal policy that certain minimum protection should be provided to children in programs funded by the federal government.

As inadequate as the federal response to the critical need for child care was in the 70's, consisting primarily of some help for upper income families through the tax code, and some assistance for welfare families through Title XX, things got far worse in the 80's during the Reagan Administration. First the Congress suspended the Federal Interagency Day Care Requirements, abdicating any federal responsibility or role in requiring quality standards in the care provided to young children. In 1981, 21 percent was cut from the entire Title XX appropriation reducing it from $3.1 billion to $2.4 billion and the earmarking for child care services was eliminated. The CETA program has been abolished and the Child Care Food Program was cut by 30 percent.

A much pared down Title XX remains the only source of direct federal support for child care services (outside of Head Start which is in most cases a half-day program and not meant to provide care to children of working mothers). In fiscal 1986, the program is funded at $2.7 billion and about 20 percent of that money is being spent on child care services. This funding is slated for a 4.3 percent reduction on March 1, 1986 and an additional conservatively estimated 18 percent cut in October 1986, as a result of the Gramm-Rudman Act.

As a result of the continued efforts of children's advocates, and evidence gathered at hearings conducted in 1984 by the Select Committee on Children and Youth documenting the seriousness of the situation, three omnibus bills were introduced in the Congress in 1985 which addressed the need for child care. Congress has not passed any of these child care initiatives, nor has it funded the extremely modest program ($20 million per year) it authorized in 1984 for start-up costs for school-age care and resource and referral programs.

Maternal and Parental Leave

Although not directly relating to child care services, a bill being introduced in the Congress would improve parental leave policies in the workplace. The proposed Parental and Disability Leave Act would require employers to allow all female workers six months of unpaid maternity leave. It would also require employers to allow either parent four months of unpaid leave to care for a newborn, newly adopted or ill child which ensuring job security and continuing the worker's health insurance coverage during absence from work. Additional hearings are scheduled for late February or early March.

Criminal Record Checks

Other federal involvement in the provision of child care resulted from the exposure in 1984 of instances of sexual assault and child abuse cases occurring in centers in Florida and New York. While child care advocates recommended higher salaries (earnings of day care professionals are about half of those of public school teachers with equivalent degrees) and better training to attract competent workers to child care, Congress instead mandated that states institute state and national criminal record checking systems to be used on prospective employees. As no federal money was appropriated, the cost of setting up national criminal record checking systems is expected to cut deeply into the meager amount of federal funds for training of child care workers.

Insurance Crisis

The child abuse crisis has led to another dilemma in child care: lack of affordable liability insurance. With no concrete statistics on numbers of claims, insurance companies nationwide placed the child care industry in the same high-risk category as nuclear power plants. Liability policies for Head Start programs, child care centers and family day care homes were cancelled mid-term or premiums were hiked as much as 1,000 percent. Since most states require centers to have liability insurance, many facilities were forced to close. Congressional leaders and state officials recognize the problem, have held some hearings, but have provided no relief. One national organization has been receiving 200 calls a week from frantic center-based providers. A coalition of child care advocates has been meeting with insurance carriers in efforts to find a solution.

State and Local Government Response

Although, by and large, the availability of funding for child care is still well below 1981 levels, at the urging of child care advocates, state and local governments have shown some movement in responding to the situation. Between 1984 and 1985 thirty states increased state funding by four percent or more. With inflation factored in, however, 35 states were spending less for child care services in 1985 than in 1981. Some states increased their child care budgets and/or adopted other measures to improve their child care systems.

Massachusetts, New Jersey and Pennsylvania, for instance, have all increased state funding to help families afford child care and improved the wages for child care workers. Others, such as North Carolina and Ohio, while increasing state funding for child care services, have also created positions to strengthen their family day care licensing capacity and ability to respond to reports of licensing violations. Some states, like Iowa and New Jersey, have appropriated money to set up resource and referral offices in order to guide parents to care where it exists. Wisconsin, Michigan, California , Florida and others are providing money for child care specifically to make it possible for some of the more than 550,000 adolescent females who give birth each year to finish high school.

A number of states, notably California and Massachusetts, have funded sizable child care programs as a part of the increasingly widespread and controversial workfare programs. California will spend $134 million a year to provide child care for children of welfare recipients while their parents participate in job training and placement programs. The program will provide up to $2,100 per child per year for care of school-age children.

Five states have loan or grant programs to help with the extremely prohibitive cost of the construction of new or renovation of existing day care facilities. Iowa provides some grant money to make physical improvements in existing centers. California offers an interest free revolving fund for child care facilities. The city of San Francisco has responded to the high cost of constructing or renovating space for child care in downtown urban areas by requiring that any new building constructed in the center city be required to have free space set aside for child care or that the builders contribute a certain amount of money to pay for child care.

Public School Based Care

As state governments have begun to pay more attention to the plight of school-age children whose parents work outside the home (of whom up to 10 million under the age of thirteen are estimated to be left home alone in early morning and late afternoon), the schools are being encouraged to provide before- and after-school child care programs. Seven states have recently approved some amount of money to be spent on care for school-age children. Many programs involve schools contracting with community groups to provide care in a school setting.

There is also increased activity around the country in school based pre-school programs. Those initiatives are in response both to the need for child care for working mothers and the desire to duplicate the success of the Head Start program's positive impact on the development of young children. In the past two years an estimated seven states have been added to the twelve which have been providing some state funding for pre-school programs. Each new state takes a somewhat different approach.

Massachusetts, for example, has authorized $20 million to help local schools deal with both child care and child development programs — $2 million will be used in 1985-86. Initiatives include setting up pre-school programs for three- and four-year-olds, expanding and improving kindergarten programs, and sponsoring new programs that meet the needs of the community. Schools may contract with Head Start and other child care programs to provide services. The state board of education must establish a state office of early childhood education, develop new criteria and standards, involve parents and child development specialists and in general take all the steps necessary to re-focus its efforts in a manner that would be suitable for the care and development of infants. California, Washington and Maine appear to be taking a similar approach, whereas some other state plans are less comprehensive.

Employer and Union Involvement in Child Care

The number of union and non-union employers offering some kind of child care assistance to employees has tripled in the past three years. However, this increase brings the total to only about 1,800 of the estimated six million U.S. employers, and the benefits range from providing actual child care services to offering noon-time seminars on parenting. An estimated 855 offer some kind of financial assistance including vouchers; about 550 provide on or near site care (400 of these employers are hospitals); 300 provide information and referral services; and others offer a sick child program which permits a parent leave to care for a sick child.

The success of unions which have pursued child care at the bargaining table has been limited, but in many ways accounts for the increase in the number of employers looking into child care. The negotiating process on this issue is extremely arduous and in many cases, where the union is able to overcome employer resistance, the result has been merely an agreement to set up a joint labor-management committee to study the problem. This is followed in many cases by years of struggle which may or may not culminate in the employer participating in the actual provision of child care services. Far more often the result has been employer involvement in information and referral services or holding seminars on child care.

Some unions, such as the International Ladies' Garment Workers in New York City have started centers themselves and have then been able to get employer contributions. The Amalgamated Clothing and Textile Workers Union was one of the first to open and operate child care centers for its members which were financed from the union's health and welfare funds. The Service Employees International Union has successfully negotiated a number of contracts with hospitals beginning with Kaiser in California. A United Food and Commercial Workers Local Executive Board recently authorized its officers to purchase a child care center in Colorado for its members. A local of the Communications Workers of America in Florida put together a detailed directory of child care centers in the area and distributed it to potential members as an organizing technique.

The New York City Chapter of the Coalition of Labor Union Women (CLUW) recently acted to fill the void created by the lack of information and hard data on what has been done so far and what could be done through the collective bargaining process. CLUW published a report which lays out the variety of issues involved, such as assessing the needs of workers, flexible work schedules, creating information and referral services, and providing center care. The document includes contract language that various unions have successfully negotiated and recommended additional model language.

There is a clear need for ongoing and reliable data and further assistance provided to unions in negotiating for child care benefits. However, as the CLUW report aptly observes, "Bargaining for child care does not eliminate or diminish the need for political action to assure sufficient public funding and appropriate regulation of child care facilities. Unless child care facilities exist in a community, employer-provided subsidies will assist only a small number of workers. If state building and health code regulations are lax, permitting substandard centers to exist, working parents will endure the added stress of constant concern for their children's welfare."

While there is visible progress on the state level with 25 percent of the states enacting some child care programs, movement is slow and funding is less than adequate. Thirty-five states provided care for fewer children in 1985 than in 1981 and with the serious budget cuts expected, spending on child care is not likely to accelerate at a rate that comes close to filling the need. With the urgent focus on deficit reduction, action on the federal level is likely to continue to be negligible. The need is clear for labor unions along with other advocates for families and children to press ahead to seek increased State and Congressional support for child care.

*   *   *

APPENDIX E

AFL-CIO DRAFT RESOLUTION ON PART-TIME WORK

[Following is the text of an AFL-CIO Resolution on Part-Time Work that was introduced at the biennial convention of the AFL-CIO in October 1985.]

RESOLUTION NO. 222 — By the Office and Professional Employees International Union.

WHEREAS, The AFL-CIO and its affiliated unions reject the increasing use made of part-time work and the false argument put forward to justify its implementation, namely that it is a means of reducing unemployment. Most forms of part-time work currently being introduced are discriminatory in nature, are not covered by collective bargaining agreements, and do not provide social security benefits;

WHEREAS, Women are the group hardest hit, especially by capacity-oriented variable working time and job-sharing. Another argument put forward to justify these working time systems is that women actually desire such "flexible" working hours because they have to reconcile family and professional responsibilities. In reality, such practices merely reinforce the traditional distribution of roles in the family;

WHEREAS, The AFL-CIO notes that the extension of part-time work and the introduction of individual flexitime do not represent a suitable way of counteracting unemployment, but that, on the contrary, they bring great disadvantage to all workers. In addition, attempts by the trade unions to incorporate a working time policy into collective bargaining agreements are undermined, and their policies threatened in the long term;

WHEREAS, The extension of part-time work — especially where it replaces full-time job or takes the form of capacity-oriented variable working time or job-sharing — leads to increased rationalization with no social provisions made, with the outcome that jobs are eliminated and the workload intensified. From the company's point of view, part-time positions are often seen as a means of reducing salary costs. Such forms of part-time work increase the work stress of all employees. Moreover, part-time workers are virtually excluded from promotion and access to higher qualifications within the company, salaries are reduced, and there is a corresponding drop in social security benefits; therefore, be it

RESOLVED: That in order to tackle the problem of the uncontrolled extension of part-time work, the AFL-CIO demands that part-time workers 1) be protected from the social point of view through an overall inclusion into social security schemes; 2) be guaranteed all benefits accruing from company and collective bargaining agreements; 3) be covered by the provisions laid down in the collective bargaining agreements also when they work on a capacity-oriented working time basis; 4) be eligible for promotion, further training and retraining in the same way as full-time workers; and 5) be protected against the introduction of job-sharing; and, be it further

RESOLVED: That all employees 1) be granted a reduction in working time with no loss of salary or wages, taking into account that women give priority to the daily shortening of working hours; 2) be provided with more social facilities such as day nurseries and day schools; and 3) be granted parental leave to look after young children (both fathers and mothers).

Referred to the Committee on Resolutions.

*   *   *

APPENDIX F

DEPENDENT CARE ASSISTANCE PLANS

[The following detailed discussion on dependent care assistance plans is taken from the 1985 Tax Management, Inc., portfolio No. 397 on "Cafeteria Plans."]

Dependent Care Assistance

1. General Description

Dependent care assistance programs are described in §129, enacted as part of the Economic Recovery Tax Act of 1981.[199] Under most dependent care assistance programs employers pay or reimburse dependent care expenses incurred by employees for qualifying dependents — i.e., dependents who are either under age 15 or physically or mentally incapable of caring for themselves.[200] Alternatively, an employer may offer dependent care services directly — for example, by offering a day care center on or near the employer's premises.

2. Tax Treatment in General

If an employer's dependent care assistance program satisfies all the requirements of §129, discussed below, any amounts paid or incurred by the employer for dependent care assistance provided to an employee will be excluded from the employee's gross income.[201]

The amount excluded from the employee's income in any taxable year may not exceed the employee's earned income for the taxable year or, if the employee is married at the end of the year, the lesser of the employee's or the spouse's earned income.[202] The term "earned income" generally includes wages, salaries, tips and other employee compensation, plus any net earnings from self-employment within the meaning of §1402(a).[203] Earned income does not include any amounts paid or incurred by the employer for dependent care assistance.[204] Thus, employees receiving dependent care assistance under a salary reduction cafeteria plan are effectively prevented from excluding from income dependent care assistance expenses in excess of 50 percent of salary before the reduction for dependent care assistance (and after any reductions for other benefits).

Example: Under a cafeteria plan, an employee with a $12,000 annual salary elects to reduce that salary by $6,000 for a given year, and the employer agrees to make up to $6,000 of payments and reimbursements for that year under a §129 dependent care assistance program. Since the employee has $6,000 of earned income after making his election, he may exclude from gross income up to $6,000 of dependent care payments or reimbursements for the year, provided he is unmarried or his spouse has earned income of at least $6,000. However, if the employee had elected to reduce his salary to $5,000, and had received dependent care payments and reimbursements totalling $7,000, he would not have been able to exclude the full $7,000 from his gross income under §129.

---

[199] P.L. 97-34, §124(e)(1).
[200] §129(e)(1); §21(b)(1).
[201] §129(a).
[202] §129(b)(1).
[203] §129(e)(2); §32(c)(2).
[204] §129(e)(2).

Observation: The earned income limitation of §129(b) appears to apply to amounts *paid* with respect to a cash-basis employee in any taxable year, and not to expenses *incurred* during the year. Thus, it is not sufficient for a plan to limit the maximum amount available as reimbursements for expenses incurred each year; the actual dollars paid in any year must also be monitored.

For purposes of the above limitation, an employee's spouse is treated as having at least $200 of earned income ($400 if the employee has two or more qualifying dependents) for each month that the spouse is a full-time student at an educational institution, or is physically or mentally incapable of caring for himself or herself.[205]

Example: If, in the preceding example, the employee's spouse were a full time student at an educational institution, and if the employee and his spouse had two or more children under age 15, the spouse would be deemed to have at least $400 of earned income for each month as a full time student. If the spouse were a full time student for all 12 months of a year and had no other earned income, the employee could exclude from gross income up to (but not exceeding) $4,800 of his employer's dependent care assistance payments or reimbursements under the dependent care assistance program.

The §129(a) exclusion does not apply to any amount paid by the employer for dependent care assistance to any individual who is a child under age 19 of the employee, or to any other dependent of the employee or his spouse.[206]

In addition to the exclusion from gross income for federal income tax purposes, any dependent care payments or reimbursements by the employer will not be subject to federal income tax withholding,[207] or included in wages for FICA tax purposes,[208] if the employer reasonably believes that the amounts are excludable from income under §129.

3. Advantage of Inclusion Within a Cafeteria Plan

a. General Desirability

Unlike medical, disability, accident, and life insurance benefits, dependent care assistance is a benefit that is generally of interest only to a minority of an employer's employees. While some employers are willing to establish an on-premises day care center for the benefit of employees, few are willing to pay or reimburse employees' outside dependent care expenses on top of the employee's existing compensation and fringe benefits. In addition to the substantial expense that may be involved, there is concern that employees not eligible for the payments or reimbursements will perceive them as unfair.

Thus, dependent care assistance is an ideal benefit for inclusion in a cafeteria plan. To the extent the employer is willing to supplement compensation to provide dollars for dependent care assistance, employees without dependent care needs can apply those dollars towards other benefits suiting their own needs. If an employer is unwilling to supplement existing compensation, employees with dependent care needs can at least reduce their existing cash compensation or forgo other benefits and elect to have the same amount applied toward their dependent care needs. If, under the cafeteria plan, the employer pays or reimburses an employee's qualify-

---

[205] §129(b)(2); §21(d)(2).

[206] §129(c).

[207] §3401(a)(18).

[208] §3121(a)(18); *see* IX, A *infra* concerning FICA tax treatment where the dependent care assistance is offered under a cafeteria plan.

ing dependent care expenses, those payments and reimbursements will be excluded from the employee's gross income (subject to the earned income limitation described above). If the employee were to pay those expenses with after-tax dollars, those dollars would have been subject to federal income tax withholding and included in wages for FICA tax purposes, although a limited income tax credit is available with respect to the dependent care expenses.[209]

b. Effect of Dependent Care Tax Credit

Section 21 (formerly §44A) provides an income tax credit with respect to dependent care expenses incurred to enable the taxpayer to be gainfully employed. The expenses that qualify for the credit are the same as those that qualify for the §129(a) exclusion if paid by the employer under a qualifying dependent care assistance program. However, any expenses paid or reimbursed by the employer and excluded from income under §129(a) may not be taken into account in computing the §21 credit.[210]

The amount of the §21 credit varies, depending on several factors. It is computed by multiplying the "applicable percentage" times the employee's qualifying dependent care expenses for the year, referred to as "employment-related expenses." [211] The applicable percentage is between 20 percent and 30 percent, inclusive, depending on the taxpayer's adjusted gross income for the year.[212] If adjusted gross income is $10,000, the applicable percentage is 30 percent. The percentage then decreases by one percentage point for each $2,000 of additional adjusted gross income, except that the applicable percentage is 20 percent where adjusted gross income is $30,000 or more.

The "employment-related expenses" are subject to the same earned income limitation as applies under §129(b),[213] and are also limited to $2,400 per year ($4,800 if there are two or more qualifying dependents).[214]

As noted above, the §21 credit is unavailable for any qualifying dependent care expenses for which payments or reimbursements have been made by an employer and excluded under §129.[215] Some employees, especially lower-paid employees, may be better off paying their own dependent care expenses with after-tax dollars and claiming the §21 credit, or at least that portion of their dependent care expenses as to which the credit is available. Others may be better off having the employer pay or reimburse all dependent care expenses under a §129 plan, and claiming the exclusion from gross income under §129. If the employee participates in a cafeteria plan, under which the employee must forgo cash compensation or other benefits equal in value to the employer's dependent care payments or reimbursements, the employee's decision whether to elect dependent care assistance under the the cafeteria plan as to those expenses for which the credit is available will be motivated principally by the choice between the §129 exclusion (if dependent care assistance is elected under the cafeteria plan) and the §21 credit (if dependent care assistance is not elected under the cafeteria plan).

---

[209] §21.

[210] §129(e)(7).

[211] §21(a)(1).

[212] §21(a)(2).

[213] §21(d).

[214] §21(c).

[215] §129(e)(7).

Example: An employer establishes a cafeteria plan under which each employee may elect to have his salary reduced, with the amount of the reduction applied toward dependent care payments or reimbursements excludable from income under a qualifying §129 plan. The employer makes no amount available toward dependent care assistance aside from the amount of the employee's salary reduction.

Employee A is a married employee who in 1985 has two qualifying dependents, dependent care expenses of $4,800, joint adjusted gross income of $20,000, and joint taxable income of $16,000.

Employee B is also married and has two qualifying dependents in 1985, but his joint adjusted gross income is $30,000 and his joint taxable income is $24,000.

Employee A will be better off declining to elect dependent care assistance under the cafeteria plan, and claiming the §21 credit. Employee B, however, will be somewhat better off electing dependent care assistance under the cafeteria plan.

	Employee A	Employee B
I. Section 21 Credit		
Employee A: (.25)x($4800)	$1,200	
Employee B: (.20)x($4800)		$960
II. Reimbursement Under the Plan		
1. Salary Reduction not Elected		
(a) Pre-salary reduction adjusted gross income	$20,000	$30,000
(b) Less itemized deductions	(4,000)	(6,000)
(c) Pre-salary reduction taxable income	16,000	24,000
(d) Tax owed on 1(c) [216]	1,741	3,333
2. Salary Reduction Elected		
(a) Pre-salary reduction adjusted	20,000	30,000
(b) less salary reduction	(4,800)	(4,800)
(c) Post-reduction adjusted gross income	15,200	25,200
(d) less itemized deductions	(4,000)	(6,000)
(e) Post-reduction taxable income	11,200	19,200
(f) Tax owed on 2(e) [217]	(987)	(2,317)
3. Tax Savings from the Plan		
Tax from line 1(d)	1,741	3,333
less tax from line 2(f)	(987)	(2,317)
Tax savings	$754	$1,016
III. Comparison of Tax Savings		
Tax Savings From Section 21 Credit	$1,200	$960
Tax Savings from the Plan	$754	$1,016

Note: The effect of the §21 credit is to provide a disincentive for many lower-paid individuals to elect dependent care expense reimbursements under a qualifying dependent care assistance program that is included under a cafeteria plan. This may make it difficult to satisfy the nondiscrimination requirements of §125

[216] 1985 tax rates used.
[217] §129(e)(7).

or §129, or both. To the extent a discretionary facts and circumstances test is applied under either or both of these sections, it is unclear whether the existence of the §21 credit will "excuse" plans from covering those employees reaping greater tax benefits from the credit.

Nothing in §21 or §129 precludes an employee with substantial dependent care expenses from taking advantage of both the §21 credit and the §129 exclusion, as to different portions of his or her expenses. For example, since the credit is only available for up to $2,400 of dependent care expenses if the employee has only one qualifying dependent, and if the employee actually incurs $4,800 of dependent care expenses per year, the employee could elect to receive the maximum §21 credit and obtain excludable reimbursements of the remaining $2,400 of dependent care expenses under a §129 plan that is included under a cafeteria plan.

4. Requirements of Section 129

The exclusion of §129(a) applies to amounts paid or incurred by an employer for "dependent care assistance" that is furnished pursuant to a "dependent care assistance program" meeting the requirements of §129(d).

a. Dependent Care Assistance

Section 129(e)(1) defines dependent care assistance to mean "the payment of, or provision of, those services which if paid for by the employee would be considered employment-related expenses under §21(b)(2)" relating to the dependent care tax credit. These expenses must satisfy the following conditions:

(i) The expenses must be incurred for either (A) a dependent under age 15 for whom the employee may claim the §151(e) exemption on the employee's federal income tax return, or (B) a spouse or other dependent of the employee who is physically or mentally incapable of caring for himself or herself.[218]

(ii) The expenses must be incurred for the care of a dependent described above, or for related household services.[219]

(iii) The expenses must be incurred to enable the employee to be gainfully employed.[220]

(iv) If the expenses are incurred for services outside the employee's household, they must be incurred for the care of a dependent under age 15 or for the care of a dependent who regularly spends at least eight hours per day in the employee's household.[221]

(v) If the expenses are incurred for services provided by a dependent care center (defined as a facility that provides care, for a fee, for more than six individuals not residing at the facility), the center must comply with all applicable state and local laws and regulations.[222]

In addition, as discussed above, the §129(a) exclusion will not apply to payments or reimbursements of dependent care expenses in excess of the earned income limitation described above,[223] or payments or reimbursements to a child under age

---

[218] §21(b)(1).
[219] §21(b)(2)(A).
[220] Id.
[221] §21(b)(2)(B).
[222] §21(b)(2)(C) and (D).
[223] §129(b).

19 of the employee or to any other dependent of the employee for whom a §151(e) exemption is available.[224]

b. Dependent Care Assistance Program

Section 129(d) includes the following requirements for a dependent care assistance program:

(i) The program must be a "separate written plan of an employer for the exclusive benefit of his employees to provide such employees with dependent care assistance . . . ." [225]

Note: A self-employed individual is included within the term "employee" under §129.[226] However, this is not the case under §125. Thus, while self-employed individuals (for example, partners of a partnership) may participate in a dependent care assistance program, they may not participate in a §125 cafeteria plan, and may not elect their dependent care assistance coverage under a cafeteria plan. Nonetheless, it appears that the same dependent care assistance program may cover common law employees who elect participation under a cafeteria plan and self-employed individuals who become participants outside of the cafeteria plan. Moreover, as a practical matter, the taxable compensation of sole proprietors or partners who participate in the dependent care assistance program will often be adjusted to take into account the value of the dependent care assistance plan coverage.[227]

(ii) The contributions or benefits provided under the plan must not discriminate in favor of employees who are officers, owners, or highly compensated, or their dependents.[228] However, under §129(e)(6), the plan will not fail to satisfy this nondiscrimination rule "merely because of utilization rates for the different types of assistance made available under the program."

Note: The meaning of §129(e)(6) is unclear, but it appears to recognize that different employees will have different dependent care needs, and the mere fact that officers, owners, or highly compensated employees make greater use of one or more types of dependent care assistance under the plan would not cause it to be treated as discriminatory, assuming the *available* contributions and benefits under the plan are not more favorable for officers, owners, or highly compensated employees or their dependents. This interpretation is supported by the title of §129(e)(6), "Utilization Test Not Applicable." However, where a dependent care assistance plan is included under a cafeteria plan, the proposed §125 regulations provide that the nondiscrimination rules of §125 *will* apply based on actual utilization of nontaxable benefits, including dependent care assistance.[229]

(iii) The dependent care assistance program must benefit either all employees of the employer, or a classification of employees that is found by the IRS not to discriminate in favor of officers, owners, or highly compensated employees, or their dependents.[230] Again, under §129(e)(6), the nondiscriminatory classification

[224] §129(c).
[225] §129(d)(1).
[226] §129(e)(3).
[227] *See* text following footnote 76.
[228] §129(d)(2).
[229] Prop. Regs. §1.125-1 (Q&A-19).
[230] §129(d)(3).

test should presumably be applied to all employees who are eligible to participate in the dependent care assistance program, and not merely those who actually elect to participate. However, in the absence of regulations under §129, this issue is not settled. In testing the eligible classification for discrimination, employees excluded from the dependent care assistance program need not be taken into account if they are covered by a collective bargaining agreement, and if there is evidence that dependent care benefits were the subject of good faith bargaining with the union.[231]

(iv) Not more than 25 percent of the amounts paid or incurred by the employer for dependent care assistance in any year may be provided for the group of individuals, if any, who own 5 percent or more of the stock (or of the capital or profits interests) in the employer.[232]

(v) Reasonable notification of the availability and terms of the dependent care assistance program must be provided to eligible employees. In addition, each participant must be furnished, on or before January 31, with a written statement showing the amounts paid or expenses incurred by the employer in providing dependent care assistance to the participant during the preceding calendar year.[233]

5. Special Rules of the Proposed Section 125 Regulations

The proposed §125 regulations contain special rules, in Q&A-18,[234] concerning how §129 is to be applied when coverage under a dependent care assistance program is offered as a benefit under a cafeteria plan. These rules are similar to the special rules of Q&A-17 that apply to medical benefit options under a cafeteria plan.[235]

a. Forfeiture of Unused Benefits

The proposed regulations under Q&A-18 provide that a dependent care assistance program does not include an arrangement under which a participant may receive dependent care expense reimbursements up to a specified amount and, if the full amount is not used for dependent care reimbursements, may receive the balance in the form of cash or any other benefit. The regulations state:

"Dependent care assistance provided under a cafeteria plan will be treated as provided under a dependent care assistance program only if, after the participant has elected coverage under the program and the period of coverage has commenced, the participant does not have the right to receive amounts under the program other than as reimbursements for dependent care expenses."

This rule applies whether the maximum dependent care expense reimbursements are available as a result of a corresponding salary reduction agreement, or whether they are made available by the employer in addition to normal salary. In addition, any adjustment of the participant's compensation or other benefits as a result of unused reimbursements under the dependent care assistance option will be taken into consideration.

Example: Under a cafeteria plan, a participant may elect, for any plan year, to reduce his salary by $2,000 and to receive employer reimbursements of up to

---

[231] *Id.*

[232] §129(d)(4).

[233] §§129(d)(6) and (7).

[234] Prop. Regs. §1.125-1 (Q&A-18).

[235] *See* IV, C, 5 *supra.*

$2,000 for dependent care expenses incurred during the year. If a participant elects the dependent care expense reimbursements, those reimbursements will not be treated as made under a dependent care assistance program, and therefore will not be excludable from gross income under §129, if (1) a participant may revoke his election during the plan year and resume receiving his full salary, or (2) any portion of the $2,000 unused for dependent care expense reimbursements is available in cash or as a contribution toward any other benefit. Even if the unused amount is forfeitable under the terms of the plan, the dependent care expense reimbursements actually received by the employee will not be excludable under §129 if the employee receives, independent of the cafeteria plan, increased salary or other compensation or benefits in an amount equal to the unused reimbursements.

Comment: This rule has no clear basis in the provisions of §129, just as the corresponding rule for medical care expense reimbursements has no clear basis in §105 or the regulations thereunder.[236]

b. Expenses Must be Incurred During Period of Coverage

The proposed regulations provide that dependent care assistance is not excludable under §129 "unless the care is provided during the period for which the participant is covered by the program." *See* Prop. Regs. §1.125, Q&A-18.

Example: a participant in a cafeteria plan may elect under the plan to receive dependent care assistance for any calendar year. The participant makes the election by agreeing, prior to the beginning of the year, to reduce his regular salary by any multiple of $500 (not to exceed $6,000). Under the dependent care assistance program, the employer will make dependent care expense reimbursements for the year up to the amount of the participant's salary reduction for the year. If the participant elects in 1985 to reduce his 1986 salary by $4,000 and to receive up to $4,000 of dependent care expense reimbursements, those reimbursements must be available only for dependent care expenses incurred during 1986. Dependent care expenses incurred in 1985 may not be reimbursed from the 1986 dependent care reimbursement account, even if the participant had identical dependent care reimbursement coverage in effect for 1985.

Note: In limiting reimbursements to expenses incurred during a specified period of coverage, the proposed regulations will result in some administrative complications. Employers maintaining dependent care expense reimbursement plans will, in effect, have to maintain separate accounts for each period of coverage reflecting the maximum available reimbursements for that period and amounts already paid for expenses incurred during that period.

For purposes of this rule, dependent care expenses are treated as having been incurred when the dependent care is provided and not when the participant is billed, charged for, or pays for dependent care.[237]

As specifically provided by Q&A-18, expenses incurred before a dependent care assistance program is in existence, or before the date the participant is enrolled in the program, will not be treated as having been incurred during a period of coverage of the participant. Thus, reimbursements of such expenses will not be excludable under §129. Even if dependent care assistance is furnished in kind — that is, through an employer-maintained child care facility — the value of the assistance will be excluded from gross income under §129 only if it is provided during a period of coverage of the participant.

---

[236] *See* text accompanying footnotes 153-55.

[237] Prop. Regs. §1.125-1 (Q&A-18).

c. Duration of Periods of Coverage

According to Q&A-18, dependent care assistance under a cafeteria plan will not be eligible for the §129 exclusion if the plan operates in a manner that enables participants to purchase dependent care assistance coverage "only for periods during which the participants expect to receive dependent care assistance." Thus, month-by-month or expense-by-expense coverage presumably will not qualify for the §129 exclusion, although the proposed regulations omit the specific statement to this effect that was included in Q&A-17 relating to medical coverage. However, Q&A-18 does include the same 12-month safe harbor as Q&A-17. That is, dependent care assistance coverage provided for a 12-month period of coverage (or for a shorter initial plan year) will qualify for the §129 exclusion, so long as the participant may not select specific amounts of coverage, reimbursement, or salary reduction for less than 12 months during the period of coverage. By reference to Q&A-8, the proposed regulations appear to permit dependent care assistance coverage to be revoked during a period of coverage on account of a change in family status.

The proposed regulations do not dictate which 12 month period may be used as a period of coverage under a dependent care assistance program. Hopefully, cafeteria plans have some flexibility in this regard. A plan may wish to use a calendar or plan year for this purpose, or a different fiscal year of the employer if pay increases normally coincide with the beginning of that year. Alternatively, plans may choose the year beginning September 1 and ending August 31, since employees may have the best idea of their dependent care needs for the upcoming 12 months when a new school year is about to start.

Comment: As discussed in IV, C, 5, d above, the use of periods of coverage other than the cafeteria plan year ought to be permissible, and seems to be recognized by Q&A-3 of the proposed regulations. Hopefully, the final regulations will confirm this more explicitly.

The partial year exception to the 12-month safe harbor of Q&A-18 refers to the "initial plan year" of a cafeteria plan. Presumably, this was not intended to indicate that the plan year is the only permissible 12-month period of coverage. Whatever period of coverage is used, if the initial period when the plan is established is less than 12 months, the initial period should suffice under the proposed regulations for the same reasons that an initial plan year would suffice. Furthermore, if a new employee becomes employed during a 12-month period of coverage, the new employee should be able to elect dependent care assistance coverage for the balance of the period of coverage in progress, without having to wait for the next full period of coverage. However, the proposed regulations do not address these issues.

d. Relationship of Sections 125 and 129

Finally, the proposed §125 regulations confirm that where a dependent care assistance program is offered as one benefit under a cafeteria plan satisfying the requirements of §125, §129 will still govern whether the dependent care assistance is a taxable or nontaxable benefit. The dependent care assistance program must meet all of the requirements of §129 summarized above,[238] and the dependent care expense reimbursements or other assistance provided under the plan will be excludable from gross income under §129 only to the extent they do not exceed the earned income limitation discussed above.[239]

---

[238] *See* IV, F, 4 *supra.*

[239] *See* IV, F, 2 *supra.*

*   *   *

APPENDIX G

DEPENDENT CARE TAX CREDIT NOTICE

[This notice on the dependent care federal tax credit, which may be posted for employees, was provided by the National Women's Law Center.]

January 1986

SAVE ON YOUR TAXES!
You may be eligible for the DEPENDENT CARE TAX CREDIT
on your FEDERAL INCOME INCOME TAX!

Are you paying for the care of a child or an adult who lives in your home and is physically or mentally incapable of caring for himself or herself?

If you are working or looking for work, you may qualify for the dependent care tax credit.

If you are married, both spouses must be working or looking for work, *or* one spouse must be a student, *or* one spouse must be unable to care for himself or herself.

THE DEPENDENT CARE TAX CREDIT

• reduces the amount of federal income taxes you owe by as much as $720, if you have one dependent, or as much as $1,440, if you have two or more dependents. The size of the credit depends on your income and the amount you pay for care.

• equals from 20% to 30% of the amount you pay for care, depending on your income. For lower incomes, the percentage that applies is higher. You may claim up to $2,400 in expenses for the care of one person and up to $4,800 in expenses for the care of two or more persons.

• will reduce your federal income taxes by $500 if you pay $2,000 for the care of your dependent while you work and your income is $20,000 ($2000 x 25% = $500).

You may claim the DEPENDENT CARE TAX CREDIT on the federal short form, FORM 1040A, or on the long from, FORM 1040.

For more information or for tax forms, contact your local IRS office or tax preparer, or call the IRS toll-free information number 1-800-424-1040.

You may also be eligible for state and local tax benefits for dependent care. Contact state and local taxing authorities for more information.

*   *   *

APPENDIX H

SELECTED CORPORATE POLICY STATEMENTS

Following are selected corporate policy statements on work and family issues, including maternity leave, child care and parenting leaves of absence, and flexible work time arrangements. Included in the section are the company policies of Lotus Corporation, of Cambridge, Mass.; General Foods Corp., of White Plains, N.Y.; Fel-Pro Inc., of Chicago, Ill.; and Merck & Co., Inc., of Rahway, N.J.

Lotus Corporation
Cambridge, Mass.

[Following is the corporate policy of the Lotus Corporation of Cambridge, Mass., on parenting leaves of absence.]

PARENTING LEAVE OF ABSENCE

Policy Summary

Lotus recognizes that today's workforce includes generally younger individuals and a greater percentage of women. Many Lotus employees are at a stage in their lives when they may be concerned about the impact on their careers of having children. The company is pleased to offer a plan that will address the issues of new parenthood, and that will protect the employment status and benefits of Lotus employees who take a leave of absence because of pregnancy or adoption.

Lotus is also aware that later it may be necessary for an employee to take a leave of absence because of an emotional or physical hardship with a son or daughter. A parenting leave may be available for this purpose if discussed with and approved by the employee's manager and Human Resources.

Various leave options are available for all employees requesting parenting leave, and can be explained by the Human Resources staff in detail. The options are more extensive if the employee has been with Lotus longer than one year at the anticipated effective date of the parenting leave. All leave arrangements must be made in advance by discussing the options with the employee's manager and the Human Resources staff and a Parenting Leave of Absence Agreement must be signed by the employee. Final approval of any leave arrangement rests with the manager, in concurrence with the Human Resources Department.

References

- For details of this policy, refer to Parenting Leave of Absence.
- Benefits coordinator in the Human Resources Department.

Lotus recognizes that today's workforce is changing to include generally younger individuals and a larger percentage of women. Many Lotus employees are at a stage in their lives when they may be concerned about the impact of having children on their careers. The company is pleased to offer a plan that will address the issues of new parenthood, and that will protect the employment status and benefits of Lotus employees who take a leave of absence because of pregnancy or adoption.

Lotus is also aware that later it may be necessary for an employee to take a leave of absence because of an emotional or physical hardship with a son or daughter. A parenting leave may be available for this purpose, and would be mutually agreed upon with the manager and Human Resources.

The following leave options are available to Lotus employees experiencing new parenthood:

— Pregnant women employed at Lotus **less than one year** may receive.

• Short term disability usually for up to six weeks for normal delivery which can be extended for caesarean section delivery or other pregnancy-related medical reason.

• Long term disability leave if medically unable to return to work after short term disability expires.

• Use of any accrued vacation time.

— Primary caretakers, men or women, employed at Lotus **one year** or longer may be able to receive:

• For women short term disability leave usually for up to six weeks which can be extended for caesarean section delivery or other pregnancy-related medical reason.

• For women long term disability leave if medically unable to return to work after short term disability expires.

• Up to four weeks paid parenting leave which accrue at a rate of 2.5 days per month from the one year anniversary date until the date the leave commences to a maximum of 20 days. (Not available to women during periods of actual disability.)

• Use of any accrued vacation time.

• Unpaid personal leave of absence of no longer than four weeks OR a flexible work schedule for a maximum of three months.

— An adoptive parent employed at Lotus **less than one year:**

• Use of any accrued vacation time.

— A primary caretaker adopting a child who has been employed at Lotus **one year** or longer may be able to receive:

• Up to four weeks paid parenting leave after placement of the child in the home. Days accrue at the rate of 2.5 per month from the one year anniversary date until the date the leave commences to a maximum of 20 days.

• Use of any accrued vacation time.

• Unpaid personal leave of absence not to exceed four weeks OR a flexible work schedule for a maximum of three months if the child is less than three years old.

Exceptions to the above options will be discussed on an individual basis. Employees are paid for the parenting leave when they return to Lotus and have worked four weeks.

When there are discretionary aspects of an individual's leave the arrangements will be mutually agreed upon by the employee and the manager through the Human Resources Department taking into account the needs of each party and the following criteria:

• Length of employment at Lotus
• Strength and consistency of past performance
• Current workforce needs in the employee's department
• Ease of transfer of the employee's existing workload to other employees
• General economic needs of the company

Final approval of any leave arrangement rests with the manager in concurrence with the Human Resources Department.

We have made an investment in the individuals in the company by offering equitable compensation and a progressive benefits package. In return, we expect employees to communicate with us and show a commitment to the company. In terms of parenting leaves this means discussing and mutually agreeing on work and leave arrangements in advance and informing the manager and Human Resources Department of any potential changes. In addition, we require a commitment that the employee eventually will return to work full time or, if impossible, that the employee will return on a temporary basis until a replacement can be hired. Employees sign a parenting leave agreement when arranging for leave, so that we can document that they have been fully informed of the terms of the leave. The agreement becomes a part of the employee's personnel file.

Scope

Exempt and non-exempt Lotus employees working 28 hours or more are eligible. Excluded from the policy are regular employees working less than 28 hours a week, and agency temps, Lotus temps, contract employees, students, and interns working on a temporary basis at Lotus.

Definitions

• Adoption — The placement of a child in a home by a licensed adoption agency.

• Benefits — Included in the benefits addressed in this policy are vacation leave illness and personal days, health and life insurance the vesting of stock options and the CAP3/Program.

• Flexible work schedule — A mutually agreed upon arrangement where the employee works a schedule that is different than the usual permanent schedule. A flexible work schedule is not a possibility in every case and may be used only when the manager determines that the schedule is compatible with the department's goals and the employee's job demands. Variations may include fewer hours or days per week, work at home, or longer hours and fewer days per week. This type of schedule may be used for a maximum period of twelve weeks and is not available in addition to an unpaid personal leave of absence. Benefit accrual ceases if the scheduled arrangement amounts to less than 28 hours per week.

• Long Term Disability — A leave of absence for medical reasons that is documented by a physician's statement. The employee receives 67% of her base pay while on long term disability. A doctor's statement that the employee is able to return to work is required before the employee can begin working again. Life insurance coverage continues to accrue during this time, and the employee is covered by Lotus health insurance until accepted for Social Security benefits. Lotus will use its best efforts to find the employee a comparable position upon return.

• Parenting Leave — Up to four weeks of paid leave are available to the primary caretaker of the child. To be eligible for parenting leave the employee must have been with the company for at least one year. The employee accrues 2.5 days for every month between the one year anniversary date and the anticipated commencement of leave, to a maximum of 20 days. Benefits will continue to accrue during this time and the employee is guaranteed her/his job upon return.

• Personal Leave of Absence — An unpaid leave that is arranged in advance and may not exceed four weeks. A personal leave is possible only when the manager determines that the leave is compatible with department goals and the employee's job demands. Personal leave is not available in addition to a flexible work schedule. Benefits do not accrue during a personal leave. Lotus will use its best efforts to find the employee a comparable job at the end of leave.

• Primary Caretaker — A single parent, or the person in the immediate family who has elected to remain at home and care for the child.

• Short Term Disability — A leave of absence of up to twelve weeks for medical reasons, documented by a physician's statement. Six weeks is the usual amount of leave for childbirth. Two extra weeks is considered usual for caesarean section delivery or other pregnancy related medical reason.

The employee is paid her full base salary or wage during the first month for short term disability; she is paid 67% of her salary or wage for the duration of the leave.

The medical reasons that the employee is unable to work are documented by a doctor's statement at the onset of leave. The doctor also must verify in writing that the employee is able to return to work. During short term disability, the employee is entitled to the same or a similar job upon return and benefits continue to accrue in the usual manner. If the employee is still unable to return to work after short term disability expires, she begins using long term disability.

Procedure

Any leave arrangement (other than short and long term disability where it is not always possible) must be mutually agreed upon in advance with the employee's manager and the Human Resources Department. The decision will take into account the employee's needs as a parent, the work demands of the employee's job, and whether the department can spare the employee for the amount of time being discussed.

The employee is expected to give two weeks' notice of the anticipated commencement of leave, if possible, so that the Human Resources Department and the employee's manager can process the paperwork and make arrangements for a temporary replacement if necessary.

To document the leave arrangements the following paperwork must be completed:

— Leave Agreement

Employees taking parenting leave sign an agreement with the Human Resources Department detailing the leave arrangements and outlining the responsibilities of both Lotus and the employee. A copy is forwarded to Payroll with a Disability Payroll Authorization Form attached.

— Disability Forms

Pregnant employees are given a disability form that the doctor will complete when the doctor feels the employee is no longer medically able to work. Short term disability goes into effect on the date stated on the form. When the employee is medically able to return to work. the doctor must submit another statement to this effect.

If the employee is still medically unable to return to work after short term disability expires the doctor must complete another disability form which will initiate the employee's long term disability. As with short term disability, when the employee is medically able to return to work, the doctor must submit a statement to that effect.

— Proof of Adoption

An employee adopting a child will submit proof that the child has been placed in the home with the approval of a licensed adoption agency.

Once the employee returns to work any merit increases are pro-rated to take into account the amount of time during the merit review period that the employee was not working.

References

- Benefits coordinator in the Human Resources Department
- For more details on short and long term disability leaves, personal leave of absence, illness days, and vacation leave, refer to the full policies on each subject.

General Foods Corporation
White Plains, N.Y.

[Following is a description of the General Foods Corporation's maternity and child care leave policy, which was presented by Kathleen C. MacDonough, director of corporate issues for the firm, at Oct. 17, 1985, joint House committee hearings on disability and parental leave. General Foods, the country's largest food processor, employs some 35,000 workers in the United States.]

General Foods Maternity and Child-Care Leave Policy encompasses multiple options for parents to balance the demands of their careers with those of their personal lives. The program provides for the following:

Maternity Leave — This leave carries the benefits authorized by General Foods' Non-Occupational Accident and Sickness Disability Plan.

Normally, maternity leave can begin up to two weeks before the expected birth of a child and up to four weeks in advance for those holding a sales job. Where job requirements and the employee's physical condition may indicate different scheduling of maternity leave, the determination is made by the General Foods doctor.

Maternity leave may continue for up to six weeks after a normal delivery and up to eight weeks after a Caesarean.

Following maternity leave, an employee is guaranteed return to her job or a similar one.

Should complications arise which extend an employee's disability, maternity leave is extended up to 26 weeks, as provided by the Disability Plan. Two weeks of eligibility under the Disability Plan begin on the date of employment; two additional weeks are added, to a maximum of 26 weeks total, on each anniversary of employment. Basic benefits during a disability leave equal an employee's base salary. Should an employee's disability continue beyond the period of eligibility, supplemental benefits, at the rate of 60 percent of base salary, are paid throughout the period of disability.

Child Care Leave is unpaid leave with the same return guarantee as maternity leave. Employees, both men and women, may take up to six weeks of child-care leave following the birth of a baby or the adoption of a child. Child-care leave may be taken in addition to maternity leave. All medical, dental and life insurance coverage continues during this period so long as the employee submits his or her regular contributions to the plans.

Personal Leave may be requested in addition to maternity and child-care leave for a period of up to 12 months including child-care leave. Such personal leave may be granted depending on the needs of the business. Personal leave carries neither pay nor return to work rights, although employees' desires to return to active employment at General Foods will be accommodated where possible.

Flexible Time, Part-Time or Job-Sharing arrangements can be arranged, where possible according to the needs of the business up to a year after the birth or adoption of a child. It is General Foods policy to be as accommodating as possible in facilitating these arrangements, but they must be arranged according to the needs of the business unit.

General Foods believes this policy to meet the twin tests of responsiveness to contemporary employees' needs and competitiveness with parental leave plans of other employers. We believe that these policies reflect society as it is and allow us to continue to attract and retain superior employees in the fulfillment of our business objectives.

Fel-Pro, Inc.

Skokie, Ill.

[Following are excerpts from the employee handbook of Fel-Pro, Inc.]

This Is Fel-Pro

Fel-Pro was founded in 1918 . . . .

The family concept is important at Fel-Pro. A family-owned company, the fourth generation is active in day-to-day operations. The family concept extends through the rest of the organization. Preferential treatment is given to relatives of current employees for vacancies and new positions. Almost all temporary summer help is made up of employees' children. Fel-Pro is filled with parents, children, cousins, aunts, and uncles of other Fel-Pro employees, creating a very stable work force and an "esprit de corps" unusual in manufacturing operations of our size.

The greater "Fel-Pro family" embodies the best of the American dream. Members of almost every racial, ethnic, and religious group found in America are working under one roof at Fel-Pro. Many languages are spoken and many cultures are represented.

Other Information You Should Know

Employing Relatives

We have many employees working with us who are related to each other, and we are delighted to have them. However, when relatives are hired, we ask that they work in different departments.

Plus

Fel-Pro provides these other benefits:

— TIME OFF: Leaves of Absence: Time allowed off for personal, maternity, or military leaves.

— SCHOLARSHIP PLAN: Pays your children up to $2,200 toward annual school costs ($1,100 each semester).

— TRIPLE R: Triple R is a recreational facility established by Fel-Pro which provides a lake, swimming pool, picnicking facilities and other sports facilities. A summer day camp (with transportation provided by Fel-Pro) is available for employees' children. Also, employees may be assigned mini-farms for planting their own gardens. (Tools, water, and "plowing" are provided by Fel-Pro.)

A word about maternity expenses

Eligible expenses resulting from pregnancy will be covered just like any other medical expense.

(Fel-Pro will also help you pay for some legal expenses connected with adopting a child. See the "SPECIAL BENEFITS" section for more information.)

If you incur maternity benefits:

No benefits will be paid for a newborn infant unless you elect to continue dependent coverage while on maternity leave. In this case, you must pay your portion of the insurance premium.

Leaves of Absence

After you have worked for Fel-Pro at least three months, you may be granted leave of absence under special circumstances:

• **Personal leave** — If you would like a leave of absence, for personal reasons, get in touch with your department head. For a leave of absence of more than one week, you will also have to get approval from the Personnel Office. Any accrued vacation time at the time of your leave must be taken before your leave of absence begins. It is important to remember that requests for a leave of absence during popular vacation periods or when your department has heavy production demands are practically impossible to grant.

• **Maternity leave** — All pregnant female employees are eligible for a leave of absence. At different intervals during your leave, your doctor will be requested by the company to complete medical information forms.

If you have worked for the company as a full-time employee for more than three years, your children (or other children who are dependent upon you for complete support) may be eligible to apply for a scholarship. Dependents of eligible retirees may also apply.

Dependents who are receiving financial assistance through academic or athletic scholarships will be paid only for amounts which are not covered by their scholarships.

Fel-Pro will pay up to $2,200 toward annual school costs, or $1,100 for each semester. If the school's schedule is based on the quarter system, a proportionate amount of money will be paid each quarter.

Application must be made to the company at least one month before school starts. No special examinations are necessary. The school must be accredited, must require at least a high school diploma, and must be approved by the company.

Financial assistance will be granted for up to four academic years — or up to a total amount of $8,800. Proof of satisfactory completion of each year of school must be furnished to the company. The company reserves the right to accept or reject any student who applies, and may withdraw assistance at any time.

One more thing, any amount you receive is taxable income. This income must be reported on your tax return each year. You may want to check with a tax expert to see what effect, if any, this will have on your tax situation.

COUNSELING SERVICES

We all should be able to discuss our personal or legal problems with someone whose interest and competence we value. That's why Fel-Pro provides the services of professional counselors and lawyers who will assist you, free of charge.

Employee Counseling and Referral Service

Through Fel-Pro you can contact counselors, who will assist you either in the solution of your problems or direct you to the proper agency where assistance is available.

The counselors are available to all employees on all shifts to assist in such areas as:
• Marital and family difficulties,
• Child guidance and school problems,
• Alcohol and drug abuse, and
• Inter-personal conflicts.

Appointments outside of working hours may be made by using the telephone number listed on the bulletin boards. All discussions will be strictly confidential.

Legal Information Service

You have the opportunity to receive free legal information during working hours. On certain days an attorney will be on hand in our Personnel Office to assist you.

The attorney will not personally handle your legal work, but will give you legal information concerning your rights and advice and methods on employing economical legal aid. Replies to your questions will either be given immediately or be sent to you by mail as soon as possible.

Appointments to see the attorney may be made through the Personnel Office. Translation service, if necessary, will be supplied. Of course, any discussion between you and the attorney will be strictly confidential.

Tutoring Benefit

If you have a child with a learning problem, your child may receive comprehensive diagnostic testing and individual tutoring based on the needs of the child. The intensity of the program and the individualized help can allow children to make important educational gains.

While Fel-Pro pays the majority of the cost for this benefit, you are asked to pay a small amount. When there is an unusual need for tutoring services, you may be asked to be placed on a waiting list.

All tutoring and testing is conducted by the professional services of the One-to-One Learning Center.

MATCHING GIFTS PROGRAM

All full-time eligible employees making contributions to non-profit organizations are eligible to receive dollar-for-dollar matching gifts from Fel-Pro to the same organization for up to a total of $500 per employee per year.

In order to qualify for a matching gift, the organization must be designated by the Internal Revenue Service as meeting the requirements of Section 501(c)(3) of the IRS Code. Here are some examples of eligible organizations:
- Alcoholism and Drug Abuse Services
- Colleges and Universities
- Community and Neighborhood Organizations
- Day Care Programs

TRIPLE R

To give employees and their families a place to get away from "city life," Fel-Pro has established a recreation area called Triple R.

Located in Cary, Illinois, Triple R is over 200 acres of beautiful hills, woods, lakes for fishing, and an olympic-size swimming pool, with private lockers, changing rooms, and showers.

There is an enclosed pavilion with picnic tables and a fireplace as well as individual tables and barbecue units located conveniently throughout the area.

Facilities are available for basketball, volleyball, softball, soccer, frisbee, golf and horseshoes; equipment for these sports is available on a signout basis.

Each employee is given an identification card and may bring up to nine guests. We have a restriction on the number of guests so that the land and facilities won't get overcrowded. If you would like to bring more guests, you may obtain an authorization from the Personnel Office.

A special brochure about Triple R, including some rules and regulations, a map showing how to get there, and nature trail maps, are available in the Personnel Office.

SUMMER DAY CAMP

A nine-week summer day camp is offered each summer for dependent children from the ages of 7 through 15. Transportation is provided by Fel-Pro. Children leave from Fel-Pro at the beginning of the first shift and return in time to go home with their parents. Trained counselors offer classes in nature appreciation, arts and crafts, swimming, and many other child development areas.

To help pay transportation costs there is a $10 a week charge per family, regardless of the number of children attending the camp.

FEL-PRO DAY CARE CENTER

The Fel-Pro Day Care Center recognizes that each child is unique and special. Fel-Pro's program is designed to stimulate and foster your child's individual strengths and abilities to their fullest potential. By providing warm supportive environment and well-balanced curriculum, your child will grow and develop physically, emotionally, socially and intellectually. The center offers an accredited, state-licensed kindergarten program, taught by an experienced kindergarten teacher.

To qualify, you must be a full-time employee, and your child must be between the ages of 2 years and 5 years, must be completely toilet trained and able to feed himself or herself. A birth certificate may be required.

The center operates from 7:00 a.m. to 5:00 p.m. Parents are required to pay a reasonable amount towards the weekly tuition while Fel-Pro pays the balance.

SPECIAL GIFTS

After you've been with Fel-Pro at least three months, you are eligible for these special gifts:

• **New baby**—Fel-Pro will purchase a $1,000 treasury security for your newborn baby (including adopted children) that will be redeemable 20 years later. You will also receive a pair of baby shoes engraved with the baby's name and date of birth.

• **Adopting a child**—Fel-Pro will pay up to $1,000 toward the legal expenses of adopting a child. See the Personnel Office for more information.

• **Wedding**—If you get married, Fel-Pro will give you a check for $100 to help you begin your married life.

• **High school graduation**—When you or your children graduate from high school, Fel-Pro will present each of you a check for $100.

• **Death in the family**—A check for $200 will be sent to you if a close member of your family dies. This applies to the death of a spouse, parent, child, mother-in-law, father-in-law, or sister or brother. This check is intended as a substitute for flowers; it is hoped that it may help pay for the many expenses connected with the funeral.

Merck & Co., Inc.
Rahway, N.J.

[Following is the text of the maternity/child care leave policy of Merck & Co., Inc., of Rahway, N.J.]

LEAVES/DISABILITY/REINSTATEMENT

Requesting a leave of absence is a very important decision — one that affects not only your income but your reinstatement to work. This section briefly outlines the different types of leaves of absence available and how disability benefits are applied in the Maternity/Child Care Program.

In the case of pregnant employees, there are two key points to keep in mind when making your plans:

1. Your Maternity and Child Care Leaves (if you are granted both) will be counted as *one leave of absence.* This is very important because the length of your total leave will have a direct bearing on your reinstatement privileges.

2. The time that you are absent due to disability is *not counted* as part of your leave of absence.

For example, let's say a pregnant employee was granted a three-week maternity leave before her child was born, stayed out for six weeks due to disability following the childbirth, then was granted an additional six weeks Child Care Leave. Although she was out of work for 15 weeks, her total Leave of Absence would be counted as nine weeks (three for maternity, six for Child Care).

The following information briefly describes the leaves of absence and disability benefits included in the Merck Maternity/Child Care Program and how they affect job reinstatement.* For more detailed information and the schedule for determining disability benefits, please read Personnel Policies B-2 (Leaves of Absence) and B-10 (Disability Benefits) included in this package.

MATERNITY LEAVE

This is a leave of absence, granted without pay, that applies only to pregnant employees. Maternity leave may be requested at any time during the pregnancy and ends automatically when the child is born or when the pregnancy ends. It is not intended, however, for disabled pregnant employees — they are covered by disability benefits. All medical and dental benefits will continue during maternity leave. You may continue your group life insurance by paying the necessary premium.

CHILD CARE LEAVE

This leave of absence, also granted without pay, is meant to help employees prepare and care for a new child. It may be requested by any employee, male or female, for the birth or adoption of a new child. The age of the child is not a factor — child care leave may be granted to prepare or care for either an infant or an older new child. The key words, however, are "new child." This leave is not intended for employees who wish to care for ill children — those situations are covered by personal leaves of absence. As with all leaves of absence, medical and dental benefits will continue and you may continue your group life insurance by paying the necessary premium.

DISABILITY (SICK) BENEFITS

As it applies to the Company's Maternity/Child Care Program, this policy would be used only by a pregnant or recently pregnant employee. If *at any time during her pregnancy and while she is working* the employee becomes physically disabled (that is, unable to work) and both her personal physician and the Company's Health Services Department agree on the disability, she then may receive disability pay according to the schedule published in Personnel Policy B-10. As we explained earlier, maternity leave automatically ends when the pregnancy ends. At that time, the employee becomes eligible, in accordance to the policy, for disability benefits.

REINSTATEMENT*

For the purposes of determining reinstatement options, maternity and child care leaves (granted for a single pregnancy, childbirth, or adoption) are counted as *one leave of absence.* Please remember, we are describing the leave of absence only — this does not include the time you are absent due to disability. The length of your absence is important for you to consider, because the job to which you return may depend in part on the length of your leave. Here are your options if your Leave of Absence lasted:*

• Up to six months — you will be returned to your former position (if feasible) or one of like status and pay, barring any unforeseen circumstances.

• More than six months, less than 18 months — you *may not* be granted your former position or one of like status. Instead, every effort will be made to assign you to a vacant position that is consistent with your qualifications, provided one is available. If no such job is available, you will continue to be on a leave of absence during which time the Company will continue to seek a position for you. This total leave time shall not exceed 18 months.

• More than 18 months — your employment with Merck & Co., Inc. ends. A leave of absence cannot be extended beyond 18 months; to do so constitutes automatic termination. After 18 months, your supervisor will initiate a closure (resignation) action on your Personnel Profile form.

*IMPORTANT: In areas or divisions where local practices have differed from corporate policy, those traditional differences will continue to be applied.

*   *   *

APPENDIX I

Following are selected contract provisions on adoption, alternative work schedules, child care, dependent care assistance plans, family responsibility leave, and use of sick leave to care for an ill family member.

[The following contract clauses were drawn from contracts in BNA's *Collective Bargaining Negotiations and Contracts*.]

[From the contract between the State of Illinois, Department of Central Management Services, and American Federation of State, County and Municipal Employees, AFL-CIO. The contract expires June 30, 1986.]

Section 7. Adoption Leave

Employees shall be granted leaves of absence without pay for a period not to exceed one (1) year for the adoption of a child. Such leave may be extended pursuant to Section 1 of this Article.

Section 8. Child Care Leave

Employees shall be granted leaves of absence without pay for a period not to exceed six (6) months for the purposes of child care in situations where the employee's care of the child is required to avoid unusual disturbances in the child's life. Such leave may be renewed pursuant to Section 1 above.

Section 9. Family Responsibility Leave

A) An employee who wishes to be absent from work in order to meet or fulfill responsibilities, as defined in subsection (F) below, arising from the employee's role in his or her family or as head of the household may, upon request and in the absence of another more appropriate form of leave, be granted a Family Responsibility Leave for a period not to exceed one year. Such request shall not be unreasonably denied.

B) Any request for such leave shall be in writing by the employee reasonably in advance of the leave unless precluded by emergency conditions, stating the purpose of the leave, the expected duration of absence, and any additional information required by agency operations.

C) Such leave shall be granted to any permanent full-time employee, except that an intermittent employee shall be non-scheduled for the duration of the required leave.

D) 'Family Responsibility' for purposes of this Section is defined as the duty or obligation perceived by the employee to provide care, full-time supervision, custody or non-professional treatment for a member of the employee's immediate family or household under circumstances temporarily inconsistent with uninterrupted employment in State service.

E) 'Family' has the customary and usual definition for this term for purposes of this Section, that is:

1) group of two or more individuals living under one roof, having one head of the household and usually, but not always, having a common ancestry, and including the employee's spouse;

2) such natural relation of the employee, even though not living in the same household, as parent, sibling or child; or

3) adoptive, custodial and 'in-law' individuals when residing in the employee's household but excluding persons not otherwise related of the same or opposite sex sharing the same living quarters but not meeting any other criteria for 'family'.

F) Standards for granting a Family Responsibility Leave are:

1) to provide nursing and/or custodial care for the employee's newborn child, whether natural born or adopted;

2) to care for a temporarily disabled, incapacitated or bedridden resident of the employee's household or member of the employee's family;

3) to furnish special guidance, care or supervision of a resident of the employee's household or a member of the employee's family in extraordinary need thereof;

4) to respond to the temporary dislocation of the family due to a natural disaster, crime, insurrection, war or other disruptive event;

5) to settle the estate of a deceased member of the employee's family or to act as conservator if so appointed and providing the exercise of such functions precludes the employee from working; or,

6) to perform family responsibilities consistent with the intention of this Section but not otherwise specified.

G) If an agency requires substantiation or verification of the need by the employee for such leave, the substantiation or verification shall be consistent with and appropriate to the reason cited in requesting the leave, such as:

1) a written statement by a physician or medical practitioner licensed under the "Medical Practices Act" (Ill. Rev. Stat. 1981, Ch. 111, pars. 4401 et seq.) or under similar laws of Illinois or of another state or country or by an individual authorized by a recognized religious denomination to treat by prayer or spiritual means, such verification to show the diagnosis, prognosis and expected duration of the disability requiring the employee's presence;

2) written report by a social worker, psychologist, or other appropriate practitioner concerning the need for close supervision or care of a child or other family member;

3) written direction by an appropriate officer of the courts, a probation officer or similar official directing close supervision of a member of the employee's household or family; or

4) any reasonable independent verification substantiating that the need for such leave exists.

H) Such leave may not be renewed; however, a new leave may be granted at any time for any appropriate reason other than that for which the original leave was granted.

I) If an agency has reason to believe that the condition giving rise to the given need for such leave no longer exists during the course of the leave, it should require further substantiation or verification and, if appropriate, direct the employee to return to work on a date certain.

J) Failure of an employee upon reasonable request by the employing agency to provide such verification or substantiation timely may be cause on due notice for termination of the leave.

K) Such leave shall not be used for purpose of securing alternative employment. An employee during such leave may not be gainfully employed full time, otherwise the leave shall terminate.

L) Upon expiration of a Family Responsibility Leave, or prior to such expiration by mutual agreement between the employee and the employing agency, the agency shall return the employee to the same or similar position classification that the employee held immediately prior to the commencement of the leave. If there is no such position available, the employee will be subject to layoff in accordance with the Section on Voluntary Reduction and Layoff.

M) Nothing in this Section shall preclude the reallocation or abolition of the position classification of the employee during such leave nor shall the employee be exempt from the Section on Voluntary Reduction and Layoff by virtue of such leave.

[From the 1984-86 Collective Bargaining Agreement between The Legal Aid Society and The Association of Legal Aid Attorneys of the City of New York, District 65, UAW]

*   *   *

5. Dependent Care Assistance Plan

The Society will establish a Dependent Care Assistance Plan, which it will use its best efforts to qualify under the Internal Revenue Code, which will permit staff attorneys with children under the age of 15 or with disabled dependent children of any age to designate a portion of their gross salary as a child care allowance "set aside" and which will be exempt from taxation. The inability to establish a qualified program which permits a tax exempt set aside for child care shall not result in any liability to the Society.

*   *   *

ARTICLE IV
LEAVES

*   *   *

2. (a) A Staff Attorney may request a leave of absence without pay and after every three (3) years of service, shall have the right to such leave for a maximum period of one (1) year subject to paragraph 1(d) above. Requests for unpaid leave shall be submitted at least three (3) months in advance of the requested starting date of such leave. Within twenty (20) days of the receipt of the request, the Society shall have the right, for staffing purposes, to postpone by written notice the starting date of such leave for a maximum of ninety (90) days. Staff Attorneys may not engage in private practice during such leaves. If such leave is granted or taken, the Staff Attorney upon her return, shall be paid at the then current rate for the salary level at which she was last employed prior to her leave, unless the Society, in its discretion, determines that the nature of the Staff Attorney's work experience while on leave justifies a higher level.

(b) Upon return from authorized leave of absence, an attorney shall have the right to return to the Division in which the attorney worked prior to the leave of absence, absent a showing of reasonable necessity by management.

(c) A leave of absence without pay for up to ten (10) months shall be granted to a Staff Attorney for the sole purpose of remaining at home to care for a newborn natural or adopted child of said Staff Attorney. Requests for such leave shall be submitted at least three (3) months in advance off the approximate starting date of such leave.

(d) A pregnant Staff Attorney may elect to use a portion of said ten month leave prior and continuous to her pregnancy disability leave.

*   *   *

(f) The Society shall continue insurance coverage for Staff Attorneys on unpaid leave, at the Staff Attorney's expense, upon advance written request accompanied by payment of the premium involved.

(g) The Society will give the serious consideration to requests by attorneys who have completed one (1) year of service for unpaid leave for the purposes of extending paid leave beyond that which has accrued and up to the full yearly allowance. At the end of that anniversary year, the attorney, upon her request, shall be paid for accrued and unused paid leave which was in effect borrowed by the attorney.

3. Any leave requested by a Staff Attorney, other than as set forth, may be granted in the discretion of the Society.

ARTICLE V
CHILD CARE

1. The primary objective of the Society is to provide the highest quality representation for its clients. The Society recognizes, however, that child-rearing places demands on parent-attorneys which, on occasion, render it difficult for those attorneys to adhere to rigid worktime schedules. To accommodate such child-raising demands, when they arise, the Society shall continue to provide a flexible work environment when not inconsistent with preservation of the Society's primary obligation to its clients.

2. Part-time Employment

In the Criminal Appeals Bureau only, part-time employment shall be available during an authorized parental leave.

3. Half-Time Employment

An experimental program shall be established for the Civil Appeals and Law Reform Unit, Juvenile Appeals and Criminal Appeals Bureau proper, only. This program, which shall permit half-time employment under the circumstances described, may be terminated by the Society, in its discretion, at the expiration of this Agreement. If the Society elects to terminate the program it shall provide the Association with an explanation of the reasons for such decision.

Each of the three offices involved in the program shall have an evaluation team consisting of one member designated by the Association and one member designated by the Society. Each evaluation team will establish its own evaluation methodology and will be responsible for submitting an interim report to the Attorney-in-Chief at the midpoint of this Agreement and a final report ninety (90) days prior to the expiration of this Agreement.

There shall be the following number of half-time positions available:

    Criminal Appeals - eight
    Civil Appeals - two
    Juvenile Appeals - two

In both Civil and Juvenile Appeals, the two positions must be "matched," e.g. must begin and terminate together.

Nothing herein shall require any addition to the number of full time equivalent positions in any office or require that any "available" position be filled by the Society with half-time attorneys.

It is understood and agreed that only incumbent employees in the three respective offices shall have the right to convert to half-time employment. All other applicants for employment or transfer shall be subject to the respective office's normal hiring and/or transfer standards and the Society's exercise of discretion with respect thereto.

If an employee applicant is equally qualified and acceptable for the position, she shall be granted preference over outside applicants. A rejected employee applicant shall, upon request, be given the reason for her rejection. Disputes arising under this paragraph shall be grievable to the receiving Attorney-in-Charge only and shall not be arbitrable.

With respect to incumbents within an office, should there be more applicants for conversion than there are half-time positions, seniority shall be the standard for selection.

It is understood and agreed that this program and these half-time positions shall be available solely to the attorneys or applicants who will be using the remaining half-time to be an "at-home" parent with responsibility for the care of the child during those hours. Other gainful employment or professional activities, etc. except for bar association activities, are prohibited during the half-time hours not at work.

It is understood and agreed that the Society shall not incur any additional payroll or fringe benefit costs as a result of this program. The salary rate shall be reduced so that the total costs to the Society for salary, fringe benefits, insurance and payroll taxes for the two half-time employees shall not exceed the cost for one full time employee at salary rate of the last full time incumbent in the position. Half-time employees shall advance one step on the salary schedule every two years.

It is understood and agreed that during that part of the work week when the half-time attorney is not at work, he or she shall be available for emergencies, court appearances or conferences or for necessary telephone consultation with other Society attorneys and/or support staff.

In Criminal Appeals, a full time attorney who has converted to half time and wishes to return to full time employment may do so on thirty (30) days written notice. In Civil and Juvenile Appeals such attorney shall have the right to return to full time employment upon the occurrence of the first available vacancy. The other member of the "matched" pair shall either be matched with another acceptable half-time attorney or applicant, if available, or be converted into full time employment at the same time as the other member of the pair.

Although the Society will make reasonable efforts to find another acceptable half-time applicant to "match" with the remaining member of the original pair, if no such acceptable match can be made, the half-time attorney shall be obligated to accept full time status immediately or be terminated.

Should the Society exercise its option to terminate the experiment at the expiration of this Agreement, the then incumbent half-timers will be permitted to phase back into full time positions as vacancies arise, as described above.

4. Childcare Committee

There shall be a Joint Childcare Committee consisting of three representatives appointed by each party. This Joint Committee shall study and explore the scope of the childcare problem in the Society, consider various childcare options available and their potential costs, possible funding sources and the types of programs tried by other non-profit organizations. The Committee shall not consider flex time, part time or job sharing.

The Committee shall report its findings to the Attorney-in-Chief and the Association within 5-6 months after contract ratification.

[Side letter of clarification on a child care agreement reached during negotiations for the collective bargaining agreement between The Village Voice and District 65, UAW, effective July 1, 1984.]

1. *Child Care* — The Publisher shall pay up to $500 per year towards child care expenses per family for children of pre-school age (up to 1st grade). The payment will be prorated for part-timers. The Voice will advance the funds to the Union based upon employee's registration at the Voice. The Union will thereafter administer the payments based on vouchers proving child care expenses. Any amount of funds not spent will be applied towards the Security Fund Voice accounting.

[The following contract clauses are taken from *Bargaining For Child Care: Contract Language for Union Parents*, and are included with permission of the publisher, the Coalition of Labor Union Women.]

Association of Flight Attendants and United Airlines, 1983-86 Flight Attendant Agreement

Section 23 (C) 1. A flight attendant shall immediately notify the Company upon knowledge of pregnancy. Such flight attendant may in accordance with Company policy, either continue to fly or to be placed on leave status.

2. A flight attendant on leave status due to pregnancy must be available to return to active service as a flight attendant within ninety (90) days following the date of the delivery. If, due to the health of the flight attendant's newborn child, additional time off is deemed necessary by the Company's medical examiner, return to active status may be delayed for up to but in no case exceeding an additional ninety (90) days. Return to active service is contingent on passing a Company physical examination.

3. A flight attendant on leave status due to pregnancy shall retain and accrue seniority during the leave. She shall not, however, accrue vacation or sick leave during the period of the leave.

Association of Flight Attendants and United Airlines, 1983-86 Flight Attendants Agreement

Section 23 1. A flight attendant who adopts a child may request or shall be granted a parental leave of absence for a period not to exceed three (3) months from the date of the adoption.

2. When a male flight attendant desires to remain at home with his newborn child, he may request and shall be granted a paternal leave of absence for a period not to exceed thirty (30) days from the date of delivery.

3. A flight attendant while on a parental leave of absence shall continue to retain and accrue seniority.

Local 680, United Service Employees International Union and Leland Stanford Junior University, Stanford Employees (Reprinted in Bargaining for Equality — U.S., published by the Women's Labor Project of the National Lawyers Guild, pp. 51-52)

When serious illness in the worker's close family requires the worker's absence to care for the ill family member, the worker may take sick leave of up to 10 working days in any year. The worker's "close family" is limited to the worker's spouse, children, parents, parents-in-law, brothers or sisters, grandparents or grandchildren, or other dependent family member living the worker's household.

Office and Professional Employees International Union
Local 30, and Margolis, McTernan, Scope & Sacks
(Reprinted in Bargaining for Equality — U.S., p. 52)

Employees whose children are at day care centers or being cared for by baby sitters shall receive, in addition to the overtime outlined in the Article, seventy-five cents (75 cents) per hour baby sitting allotment for each overtime hour.

Service, Office and Retail Workers Union of Canada
and Simon Fraser Student Society Service
(Reprinted in Bargaining for Equality — U.S., pp. 60-62)

The employees in each department shall decide what form of day they will work and ensure that the departments are adequately staffed between 8:30 a.m. and 4:30 p.m.

District 65, International Union, UAW
and Barnard College
(Reprinted in Bargaining for Equality — U.S., pp. 60-62)

Flexible hours shall be arranged for any employee who has need, provided the operation of the department continues to function. Reasons for such flexibility may be but are not limited to school needs for children, medical needs, or daytime classes which are not available outside of regular working hours.

American Federation of State, County, and Municipal Employees
Model Contract Language

Flexitime: Flexitime shall be defined as a work schedule structure requiring that all employees be in work status during a specified number of core hours with scheduling flexibility allowed for beginning and ending times surrounding those core hours.

*   *   *

APPENDIX J
FAMILY EMPLOYMENT AND EARNINGS STATISTICS

[Following are selected data on family employment and earnings characteristics through the fourth quarter 1985. The figures were released by the Bureau of Labor Statistics Feb. 10, 1986.]

[Table 1. Families by employment status of members and type of family, quarterly averages, not seasonally adjusted]

(Numbers in thousands)

Characteristic	Number of families		Percent distribution	
	IV 1984	IV 1985	IV 1984	IV 1985
Married-couple families	50,082	50,424	100.0	100.0
With no members in the labor force	7,396	7,487	14.8	14.8
With at least one member in the labor force	42,666	42,937	85.2	85.2
No member employed	931	881	1.9	1.7
Some member employed	41,756	42,056	83.4	83.4
Husband only	12,377	11,898	24.7	23.6
Wife only	2,336	2,332	4.7	4.6
Husband and wife	22,730	23,542	45.4	46.7
Husband and wife only	18,037	18,705	36.0	37.1
Other combinations	4,313	4,284	8.6	8.5
Families maintained by women	9,788	10,055	100.0	100.0
With no members in the labor force	2,474	2,527	25.3	25.1
With at least one member in the labor force	7,314	7,528	74.7	74.9
No member employed	753	742	7.7	7.4
Some member employed	6,561	6,786	67.0	67.5
Householder employed	5,326	5,492	54.4	54.6
Householder only	3,357	3,503	34.3	34.8
Householder and other(s)	1,969	1,989	20.1	19.8
Other combinations	1,235	1,294	12.6	12.9
Families maintained by men	2,324	2,436	100.0	100.0
With no members in the labor force	275	303	11.8	12.4
With at least one member in the labor force	2,049	2,134	88.2	87.6
No member employed	130	148	5.6	6.1
Some member employed	1,919	1,985	82.6	81.5
Householder employed	1,618	1,697	69.6	69.7
Householder only	852	912	36.7	37.4
Householder and other(s)	766	785	33.0	32.2
Other combinations	301	288	13.0	11.8

[Table 2. Families with children under 18 years old by the employment status of parent(s) and type of family, quarterly averages, not seasonally adjusted]

(in thousands)

Characteristic	IV 1984			IV 1985		
	Total	With children 6 to 17 years old, none younger	With children under 6 years old	Total	With children 6 to 17 years old, none younger	With children under 6 years old
Total families	30,955	16,937	14,018	31,416	17,148	14,268
Married-couple families	24,248	12,700	11,548	24,386	12,802	11,584
With employed parent(s)	23,108	12,082	11,027	23,309	12,238	11,071
Neither unemployed	21,853	11,439	10,415	22,070	11,603	10,467
Father employed	8,385	3,639	4,746	7,984	3,480	4,504
Mother employed	433	303	131	413	287	126
Both employed	13,035	7,497	5,538	13,673	7,836	5,837
One unemployed	1,254	643	612	1,239	635	604
Father unemployed	505	285	220	483	267	216
Mother unemployed	749	358	392	756	368	388
With no employed parent	1,140	618	521	1,077	564	513
Father unemployed	398	146	252	381	140	240
Mother unemployed	46	29	17	39	28	11
Both unemployed	125	58	67	115	43	72
Neither in labor force	571	385	185	542	353	190
Families maintained by women	5,875	3,682	2,193	6,134	3,754	2,380
Mother employed	3,467	2,467	1,000	3,637	2,594	1,043
Mother not employed	2,409	1,215	1,193	2,496	1,160	1,336
Unemployed	511	296	214	524	258	266
Not in labor force	1,898	919	979	1,972	902	1,070
Families maintained by men	832	556	277	897	592	304
Father employed	704	471	233	729	486	243
Father not employed	128	85	43	168	106	61
Unemployed	63	35	28	81	43	38
Not in labor force	65	50	15	87	63	23
Total families with unemployed parents	2,397	1,207	1,190	2,379	1,147	1,231

314   WORK AND FAMILY

[Table 3. Families by employment status of members and type of family, annual averages]

(Numbers in thousands)

Characteristic	Number of families		Percent distribution	
	1984	1985	1984	1985
Married-couple families	49,737	49,991	100.0	100.0
With no members in the labor force	7,367	7,466	14.8	14.9
With at least one member in the labor force	42,370	42,526	85.2	85.1
No member employed	996	920	2.0	1.8
Some member employed	41,374	41,606	83.2	83.2
Husband only	12,668	12,274	25.5	24.6
Wife only	2,358	2,368	4.7	4.7
Husband and wife	21,922	22,550	44.1	45.1
Husband and wife only	17,251	17,761	34.7	35.5
Other combinations	4,426	4,414	8.9	8.8
Families maintained by women	9,897	10,122	100.0	100.0
With no members in the labor force	2,465	2,484	24.9	24.5
With at least one member in the labor force	7,432	7,638	75.1	75.5
No member employed	781	801	7.9	7.9
Some member employed	6,652	6,837	67.2	67.5
Householder employed	5,397	5,540	54.5	54.7
Householder only	3,410	3,463	34.5	34.2
Householder and other(s)	1,987	2,077	20.1	20.5
Other combinations	1,255	1,297	12.7	12.8
Families maintained by men	2,247	2,395	100.0	100.0
With no members in the labor force	273	281	12.1	11.7
With at least one member in the labor force	1,974	2,114	87.9	88.3
No member employed	132	144	5.9	6.0
Some member employed	1,842	1,970	82.0	82.3
Householder employed	1,558	1,680	69.3	70.1
Householder only	825	913	36.7	38.1
Householder and other(s)	733	767	32.6	32.0
Other combinations	284	290	12.6	12.1

[Table 4. Families with children under 18 years old by the employment status of parent(s) and type of family, annual average]

(in thousands)

Characteristic	1984 Total	1984 With children 6 to 17 years old, none younger	1984 With children under 6 years old	1985 Total	1985 With children 6 to 17 years old, none younger	1985 With children under 6 years old
Total families	30,953	16,940	14,014	31,158	17,003	14,155
Married-couple families	24,130	12,621	11,508	24,080	12,587	11,494
With employed parent(s)	22,937	11,997	10,940	22,954	12,004	10,951
Neither unemployed	21,612	11,353	10,258	21,684	11,370	10,315
Father employed	8,710	3,817	4,893	8,349	3,630	4,719
Mother employed	451	317	134	429	302	127
Both employed	12,451	7,219	5,231	12,906	7,438	5,469
One unemployed	1,325	643	682	1,270	634	636
Father unemployed	559	293	266	504	265	239
Mother unemployed	766	350	416	766	369	397
With no employed parent	1,193	625	568	1,125	582	543
Father unemployed	430	149	281	393	138	254
Mother unemployed	44	25	19	40	27	14
Both unemployed	127	62	65	118	52	66
Neither in labor force	592	389	203	574	365	209
Families maintained by women	5,987	3,756	2,231	6,147	3,800	2,346
Mother employed	3,548	2,541	1,007	3,647	2,620	1,027
Mother not employed	2,439	1,216	1,223	2,499	1,180	1,319
Unemployed	518	304	214	542	292	250
Not in labor force	1,921	912	1,009	1,957	888	1,069
Families maintained by men	837	562	275	931	616	316
Father employed	694	474	220	766	507	258
Father not employed	142	97	55	166	108	58
Unemployed	65	36	29	79	45	34
Not in labor force	77	51	26	87	63	24
Total families with unemployed parents	2,509	1,219	1,290	2,442	1,188	1,254

X. BIBLIOGRAPHY

ALTERNATIVE WORK SCHEDULES/WORKPLACES

Aikin, Olga. "Part-Time Option for Parents?" *Personnel Management*, vol. 16 (October 1984): 59.

Automation of America's Offices. Washington, D.C.: U.S. Congress, Office of Technology Assessment. 1985.

Bohen, Halcyone H., and Anamaria Viveros-Long. *Balancing Jobs and Family Life: Do Flexible Work Schedules Help?* Philadelphia: Temple University Press, 1981.

Chin, Kathy. "Home Is Where the Job Is." *Infoworld*, vol. 6, no. 17 (1984).

Christensen, Kathleen. *Impacts of Home-Based Work on Women and Their Families.* Washington, D.C.: Office of Technology Assessment (January 1985).

Christensen, Kathleen. *Women and Home-Based Work.* Center for Human Environments, City University of New York, 1984.

Costello, Cynthia. "On the Front: Class, Gender, and Conflict in the Insurance Workplace." Ph.D. dissertation. University of Wisconsin (1984).

Cross, Thomas B. "Telecommuting — the Next Frontier in Work." *ICP Business Software Review*, vol. 3 (June/July 1984): 24, 26.

Devine, Richard Q., and Ruth V. Joscelyn. "An Employee Benefit with a $0 Price Tag: Flexible Work Schedules." *National Law Journal*, vol. 4 (June 7, 1982): 17.

Finn, Peter. "The Effect of Shift Work on the Lives of Employees." *Monthly Labor Review* 104 (October 1981).

"Flexible Working Hours: A Selected Bibliography." *Ontario Ministry of Labour Library, Labour Topics*, vol. 7 (May 1984).

Gluckin, Neil D. "The Office Is Where the Workers Are." *Telecommunication Products & Technology*, vol. 3 (June 1985): 56-60.

Honan, Patrick. "Telecommuting: Will It Work for You?" *Computer Decisions*, vol. 16 (June 15, 1984): 88-98.

"If Home Is Where the Worker Is." *Business Week* (May 3, 1982).

Job Sharing: Analyzing the Cost. San Francisco: New Ways to Work, 1981.

Job Sharing: A Union Approach. San Francisco: New Ways to Work, 1982.

Job Sharing: General Information. San Francisco: New Ways to Work, 1980.

Johnson, Louise, and Lois A. Meerdink. "Job Sharing: An Employment Alternative for the Career Service Professional." *Journal of College Placement* (Winter 1985): 29-30.

Kraut, Robert. *Telework: Cautious Pessimism.* Bell Communications Research, 1984.

Lee, Patricia. "Job Sharing." *The Secretary* (January 1984).

Long, James E., and Ethel B. Jones. "Married Women in Part-Time Employ-ment." *Industrial & Labor Relations Review* (April 1981).

Morgan, Philip I., and Kent H. Baker. "Taking a Look at Flexitime." *Supervisory Management*, vol. 29 (February 1984): 37-43.

Mortenson, Patricia. "Telecommuting: The Company Perspective." *Best's Review, Property-Casualty Edition* (November 1983).

Niles, Jack. "Teleworking: Working Closer to Home." *Technology Review* (April 1982).

Nollen, Stanley D. *New Work Schedules in Practice: Managing Time in a Changing Society.* New York: Van Nostrand Reinhold/Work in America Series, 1982.

Olmstead, Barney, and Suzanne Smith. *The Job Sharing Handbook.* New York: Penguin Books, 1983.

Olson, Magrethe H. "Remote Office Work: Implications for Individuals and Organizations." *Women & Environments*, vol. 5, no. 3 (1982).

Olsten, William. "Effectively Managing Alternative Work Options." *Supervisory Management*, vol. 29 (April 1984): 10-15.

Pratt, Joanne H. "Home Telecommuting: A Study of Its Pioneers." *Technological Forecasting and Social Change*, vol. 25, no. 1 (1984).

Regenye, Steve. "Telecommuting." *Journal of Information Management*, vol. 6 (Winter 1985): 15-23.

Rothberg, Diane S., and Barbara Ensor Cook. *Part-Time Professional.* Washington, D.C.: Acropolis Books Ltd., 1985.

Saloman, Ilan, and Meera Saloman. "Telecommuting: The Employee's Perspective." *Technological Forecasting and Social Change*, vol. 25, no. 1 (1984).

A Selected Bibliography on Work Time Options. San Francisco: New Ways to Work, 1983.

Staines, Graham L., and Joseph H. Pleck. *The Impact of Work Schedules on The Family.* Ann Arbor: The University of Michigan Survey Research Center, Institute for Social Research, 1983.

V-Time: A New Way to Work. San Francisco: New Ways to Work, 1985.

Winnett, R.A., and M.S. Neale. "Results of Experimental Study on Flexi-Time and Family Life." *Monthly Labor Review* 103 (November 1980).

Wise, Deborah C., and Aaron Bernstein. "Part-Time Workers: Rising Numbers, Rising Discord." *Business Week* (April 1, 1985): 62-63.

Work Times. Part Time/Shared Job Project, New York State Department of Civil Service, vol. 1, no. 5 (May 1985).

THE CHANGING AMERICAN FAMILY

"America's New Labor Force: Working Couples." Cleveland, Ohio: RE-SOURCE: Careers (1985).

Belsky, Jay, Maureen Perry Jenkins, and Ann C. Crouter. "The Work-Family Interface & Marital Change across the Transition to Parenthood." *Journal of Family Issues*, vol. 6 (1985): 205-220.

Families and Work: Traditions and Transitions. Washington, D.C.: American Association of University Women, 1982.

Finch, J. "Work, the Family & the Home — A More Egalitarian Future." *International Journal of Social Economics*, vol. 12, no. 2 (1985): 26-35.

Kamerman, Sheila B. *Parenting in an Unresponsive Society: Managing Work and Family.* New York: The Free Press, 1980.

Levitan, Sar A., and Richard S. Belous. "Working Wives and Mothers: What Happens to Family Life?" *Monthly Labor Review* 104 (September 1981).

Levitan, Sar A., and Richard S. Belous. *What's Happening to the American Family?* Baltimore: Johns Hopkins University Press, 1981.

Programs that Strengthen Families. Chicago: Family Resource Coalition, 1983.

Segal, Stephen. "The Working Parent Dilemna." *Personnel Journal* (March 1984).

Sekaran, U. "The Paths to Mental Health — An Exploratory Study of Husbands & Wives in Dual-Career Families." *Journal of Occupational Psychology*, vol. 58, no. 2 (1985): 129-138.

CHILD CARE

Adolf, Barbara, and Karol Rose. *Child Care and the Working Parent: First Steps Toward Employer Involvement in Child Care.* New York: Children at Work, Inc., 1982.

Adolf, Barbarba and Karol Rose. *The Employer's Guide to Child Care: Developing Programs for Working Parents.* New York: Praeger Publishers, 1985.

Alden, Philip M., Jr. "A No-Cost Way to Provide Dependent Care Benefits." *Pension World*, vol. 19 (May 1983): 31-32.

Bargaining for Child Care: Contract Language for Union Parents. New York City Coalition of Labor Union Women Child Care Committee, 1985.

Bergstrom, Joan. *School's Out — Now What? Creative Choices for Your Children — Afternoons, Weekends, Vacations.* Berkeley, Calif.: Ten Speed Press, 1984.

Blank, Helen, and Amy Wilkins. *Child Care: Whose Priority? A State Child Care Fact Book.* Washington, D.C.: Children's Defense Fund, 1985

Burud, Sandra L., Pamela Aschbacher, and Jacquelyn McCroskey. *Employer-Supported Child Care: Investing in Human Resources.* Dover, Mass.: Auburn House Publishing Co., Inc., 1984.

Child Care Fact Sheet. Washington, D.C.: National Commission on Working Women, 1985.

"Child Care Information Service: An Option for Employer Support of Child Care." New York: Catalyst, Research Report No. 7 (1983).

"Child Care Programs and Developments." Employee Benefit Research Institute, Issue Brief No. 42 (May 1985).

Comfort, Randy L., and Constance D. Williams. *The Child Care Catalog: A Handbook of Resources & Information on Child Care.* Littleton, Colo.: Libraries Unlimited, Inc., 1985.

"Corporate Child Care Options." New York: Catalyst, Research Report No. 1 (1985).

"Day Care at Work Makes a Comeback." *Nation's Business* (July 1980).

"Details of Sweden's Child Care System Discussed at Seminar on Working Family." *White Collar Report*, The Bureau of National Affairs, Inc. (May 23, 1984): 605.

Emlen, Arthur C., and Koren, Paul E. *Hard to Find and Difficult to Manage: The Effects of Child Care on the Workplace.* Portland, Ore.: Regional Research Institute for Human Services, Portland State University, 1984.

"Employers and Child Care: Establishing Services Through the Workplace." U.S. Department of Labor, Women's Bureau, Pamphlet 23 (August 1982).

Families and Child Care: Improving the Options. A Report by the Select Committee on Children, Youth, and Families, U.S. House of Representatives, Ninety-eighth Congress, Second Session, with Additional Views. Washington, D.C.: U.S. Government Printing Office (1985).

Fernandez, John P. *Child Care & Corporate Productivity: Resolving Family-Work Conflicts.* Lexington, Mass.: Lexington Books, 1986.

Frank, Mary, ed. "Child Care: Emerging Legal Issues." *Journal of Children in Contemporary Society*, vol. 17, no. 2 (Winter 1984).

Frank, Mary, ed. "Marketing Child Care Programs: Why & How." *Journal of Children in Contemporary Society*, vol. 17, no. 2 (Winter 1984).

Fried, Mindy, and Elaine O'Reilly. *How Does Your Community Grow? Planting Seeds for Quality Day Care.* Commonwealth of Massachusetts, Office for Children (August 1985).

Friedman, Dana E. "Corporate Financial Assistance for Child Care." The Conference Board, Research Bulletin No. 177 (1985).

Friedman, Dana E. "Raising Child Care Issues at the Workplace." *Child Care ActioNews*, vol. 1, no. 3 (May/June 1984).

Friedman, Dana E., ed. *Shaping the Employer Role in Child Care.* Washington, D.C.: National Association for Education of Young Children, 1982.

Galinsky, Ellen, and William H. Hooks. *The New Extended Family: Day Care That Works.* New York: Houghton Mifflin, 1977.

Grams, Marilyn, and Itoko Takeuchi, illus. *Breastfeeding Success for Working Mothers.* Jacksonville, N.C.: Achievement Press, 1985.

Improving Child Care: What Can Be Done?: Report of Hearings before the Select Committee on Children, Youth, and Families, U.S. House of Representatives, Ninety-eighth Congress, Second Session. Washington, D.C.: U.S. Government Printing Office (1985).

Kamerman, Sheila B. "Child Care and Family Benefits: Policies of Six Industrialized Countries." *Monthly Labor Review* 103 (November 1980).

Kamerman, Sheila B., and Alfred J. Kahn. *Child Care, Family Benefits & Working Parents.* New York: Columbia University Press, 1981.

Keniston, Kenneth, and the Carnegie Council on Children. *All Our Children.* New York: Harcourt, Brace & Jovanovich, 1977.

La Marre, Sandra E., and Kate Thompson. "Industry-Sponsored Day Care." *Personnel Administrator* (February 1984): 53-65.

Long, Thomas, and Lynette Long. *Handbook for Latchkey Children and Their Parents.* New York: Arbor House, 1983.

Magid, Renee Y. *Child Care Initiatives for Working Parents.* New York: American Management Associations, 1983.

McMurray, Georgia L., and Dolores Kazanjian. *Day Care & the Working Poor: The Struggle for Self-Sufficiency.* New York: Community Service Society of New York, 1982.

"A Needs Assessment Approach to Corporate Child Care Policy Planning." A Position Paper by Catalyst, Research Report No. 8 (1983).

"On-Site Child Care — Pros and Cons." *Catalyst Perspective* (February 1985).

Schiller, Judith D. *Child Care Alternatives & Emotional Well-Being.* New York: Praeger, 1980.

"Sick Child Care: A Problem for Working Parents and Employers." Minneapolis, Minn.: Parents in the Workplace, 1983.

Smith, Kim L., Susan N. Satterfield, and Mary McLean, eds.; Earl Bateman, illus. *The Metropolitan Mothers at Work Book: A Complete Guide to Child Care in Metropolitan Washington, Maryland & Virginia.* Washington, D.C.: Metro Mothers Work, 1985.

Smith, Larry. "Corporate-Funded Day Care." *Employment Relations Today*, vol. 12 (Autumn 1985): 267-271.

Travers, Jeffrey, and Barbara D. Goodson. *Research Results of the National Day Care Study.* Cambridge, Mass.: Abt Bks., 1981.

Weintraub, M., and B.M. Wolf. "Effects of Stress and Social Supports on Mother-Child Interaction in Single and Two Parent Families." *Child Development*, vol. 54 (1983).

White, Burton L. *The Child Care Crisis.* New York: Viking, Inc., 1985.

"Who Cares for Kids? A Report on Child Care Providers." Washington, D.C.: National Commission on Working Women, 1985.

Women's Bureau Regional Employer Sponsored Child Care Initiatives: A Program Review Study. Washington, D.C.: Creative Associates, Inc., 1985.

"Working Parents Lose Work Time Because of Child Care Problems." *Employee Benefit Plan Review*, vol. 39 (June 1985): 52, 54.

Youngblood, Stewart, and Kimberly Chambers-Cook. "Child Care Assistance Can Improve Employee Attitudes and Behavior." *Personnel Administrator* (February 1984): 45-46, 93-95.

Zigler, Edward F., and Edmund W. Gordon, eds. *Day Care: Scientific & Social Policy Issues.* Dover, Mass.: Auburn House, 1981.

Zippo, M. "Employer-Sponsored Child Care Comes of Age." *Personnel*, vol. 57, no. 6 (November/December 1980).

THE CORPORATION'S ROLE IN WORK AND FAMILY MATTERS

Adoption Benefits Plans: Corporate Response to a Changing Society. Philadelphia: National Adoption Exchange, 1985.

Bains, Leslie E. "Banks Must Cope with Dual-Career Marriages." American Bankers Association's *Banking Journal,* vol. 77 (October 1985): 117-120.

"Beyond the Transition: The Two-Gender Work Force and Corporate Policy." New York: Catalyst, 1984.

A Corporate Reader: Work and Family Life in the 1980's. Washington, D.C.: Children's Defense Fund, 1983.

"Corporations and Families: Changing Practices and Perspectives." New York: The Conference Board, Report No. 868, 1985.

"Corporations and Two-Career Families: Directions for the Future." New York: Catalyst, 1985.

Dilks, Carol. "Employers Who Help with the Kids." *Nation's Business* (February 1984).

McGroskey, Jacquelyn. "Work and Family: What is the Employer's Responsibility?" *Personnel Journal* (January 1982).

"Nepotism Policies and Company Couples." *Catalyst Perspective* (April 1985).

Nollen, Stanley. "The Work-Family Nexus: Issues for Business." New York: The Conference Board, 1986.

Sekas, Maria Helene. "Dual-Career Couples — A Corporate Challenge." *Personnel Administrator* (April 1984): 37-45.

Whitebook, Marcy. "What Can Employer-Supported Programs Do for Child Care Staff?" *Day Care and Early Education* (Summer 1984): 16-19.

"Work-and-Family Seminars: Corporations Respond to Employees' Needs." *Catalyst Perspective* (February 1984).

DEMOGRAPHICS & RESEARCH

Brinkerhoff, Merlin B., ed. *Family & Work: Comparative Convergences.* Series: Contributions in Family Studies, no. 8. Westport, Conn.: Greenwood Pr., 1984.

Demographic and Social Trends: Implications for Federal Support of Dependent-Care Services for Children and the Elderly: Report of the Select Committee on Children, Youth and Families, U.S. House of Representatives, Ninety-eighth Congress, First Session, with Additional Views. Washington, D.C.: U.S. Government Printing Office, 1984.

Employed Parents and Their Children: A Data Book. Washington, D.C.: Children's Defense Fund, 1982

Geerken, Michael, and Walter Gove. *At Home & at Work: The Family's Allocation of Labor.* Series: New Perspectives on Family. Beverly Hills, Calif.: Sage, 1983.

Hareven, Tamara K. *Family Time & Industrial Time: The Relationship Between the Family & Work in a New England Industrial Community.* Series: Interdisciplinary Perspectives on Modern History. New York: Cambridge University Press, 1982.

Hayghe, Howard. "Husbands and Wives as Earners: An Analysis of Family Data." *Monthly Labor Review* 104 (February 1981).

Hayghe, Howard. "Marital and Family Patterns of Workers: An Update." Washington, D.C.: U.S. Department of Labor, Bureau of Labor Statistics, 1983.

Hayghe, Howard. "Married Couples: Work and Income Patterns." *Monthly Labor Review* 107 (December 1984).

Hayghe, Howard. "Working Mothers Reach Record Number in 1984." *Monthly Labor Review* 107 (December 1984).

Hewlett, Sylvia A., ed. *Parents & Work: Family Policy in Comparative Perspective.* Cambridge, Mass.: Ballinger Publishing Co., 1986.

Horvath, Francis W. "Working Wives Reduce Inequality in Distribution of Family Earnings." *Monthly Labor Review* 103 (July 1980).

Johnson, Beverly L. "Marital and Family Characteristics of Workers, 1970 to 1978." Washington, D.C.: U.S. Department of Labor, Bureau of Labor Statistics, 1979.

Johnson, Beverly L., and Elizabeth Waldman. "Most Women Who Maintain Families Receive Poor Labor Market Returns." *Monthly Labor Review* 106 (December 1983).

Major, Brenda, and Blythe Forcey. "Social Comparisons & Pay Evaluations: Preferences for Same-Sex & Same-Job Wage Comparisons." *Journal of Experimental Social Psychology*, vol. 21, no. 4 (1985): 393.

Mandelbaum, Dorothy R. *Making Life Choices: Current Research Findings on Work, Family & Children.* New York: Praeger, 1984.

"Maternity Benefits for the Federal Employee." Washington, D.C.: U.S. Office of Personnel Management, 1981.

Oppenheimer, Valerie. *Work & the Family: A Study in Social Demography.* Series: Studies in Population. Orlando, Fla.: Academic Press, Inc., 1982.

Rogers, Carolyn C., and Martin O'Connell. "Child Care Arrangements of Working Mothers, June 1982." Washington, D.C.: U.S. Department of Commerce, Bureau of the Census, U.S. Government Printing Office, 1983.

Rueschemeyer, Marilyn. *Professional Work & Marriage: An East-West Comparison.* New York: St. Martin's Press, 1986.

Spain, Daphne, and Stephen Nock. "Two-Career Couples, a Portrait." *American Demographics*, vol. 6 (August 1984): 24-27.

The Changing Situation of Americans and Their Families: Information from the March Current Population Survey. Washington, D.C.: U.S. Department of Commerce, Bureau of the Census, 1984.

Voydanoff, Patricia. *Implications of Work-Family Relationships for Productivity.* Series: Work in America Institute Studies in Productivity, vol. 13. Elmsford, N.Y.: Pergamon, 1982.

Waldman, Elizabeth. "Labor Force Statistics from a Family Perspective." *Monthly Labor Review* 106 (December 1983).

Watts, Harold W., and Felicity Skidmore. "The Implications of Changing Family Patterns and Behavior for Labor Force and Hardship Measurement." Washington, D.C.: National Commission on Employment and Unemployment Statistics, 1978.

"Women at Work: A Chartbook Corporate Source: United States." Washington, D.C.: U.S. Department of Labor, Bureau of Labor Statistics, 1983.

Women, Work & Demographic Issues. Washington, D.C.: International Labour Office, 1984.

EMPLOYEE BENEFIT PROGRAMS

America in Transition: Implications for Employee Benefits. Policy Forum Proceedings. Washington, D.C.: Employee Benefit Research Institute, 1982.

"Benefits to Employees for Benefits to Business." Washington, D.C.: National Association for Child Care Management, 1984.

"Corporate Relocation Practices: A Report on a Nationwide Survey." New York: Catalyst, Research Report No. 6 (1982).

"Employee Benefits for Part-Timers." McLean, Va.: Association of Part-Time Professionals, 1985.

"Flexible Benefits: An Analysis of the Issue." New York: Catalyst, 1983.

"Flexible Benefits Update." *Catalyst Perspective* (November 1985).

Friedman, Dana E. *Encouraging Employer Supports to Working Parents: Community Strategies for Change.* New York: Distributed by the Center for Public Advocacy Research, 1983.

Fundamentals of Employee Benefit Programs. Consumer Education Series. Washington, D.C.: Employee Benefit Research Institute, 1985.

Meyer, Mitchell. *Flexible Employee Benefit Plans: Companies' Experience.* The Conference Board, Report No. 831 (1983).

MATERNITY, PATERNITY LEAVE ISSUES

Berger, Lesly. "Maternity Leave: The Corporate Scene." *Working Woman* (February 1984).

Brozan, Nadine. "Infant-Care Leaves: Panel Urges Policy." *The New York Times* (Nov. 28, 1985).

"Career and Family: Maternity and Parental Leave." *Catalyst Perspective* (March 1983).

Chavkin, Wendy. "Parental Leave — What There Is and What There Should Be." *Ms.* (September 1984): 115-118.

"Corporate Guide to Parental Leaves." New York: Catalyst, 1986.

"Denial of Unemployment Benefits to Otherwise Eligible Women on the Basis of Pregnancy: Section 3304(a)(12) of the Federal Unemployment Tax Act." *Michigan Law Review*, vol. 82 (August 1984): 1925-1957.

"Disability Leave for Pregnancy: Short and Not So Sweet." *Compflash*, American Management Associations (March 1984).

Employers and Child Care: Development of a New Employee Benefit. Washington, D.C.: The Bureau of National Affairs, Inc., 1984.

Freedman, Elizabeth I. "Parental Leaves of Absence for Men." *Buffalo Law Review* (Winter 1982): 273-299.

Galante, Mary Ann. "No Sex Bias Found in Maternity Leave." *National Law Journal*, vol. 7 (April 29, 1985): 3.

Johnson, Theresa. "The Legal Background and Implications of Pregnancy Benefits." *Labor Law Journal* (June 1984): 352-359.

Kamerman, Sheila B., and Alfred J. Kahn, "Company Maternity-Leave: The Big Picture." *Working Woman* (February 1984).

Kamerman, Sheila B., Alfred J. Kahn, and Paul W. Kingston. *Maternity Policies and Working Women.* New York: Columbia University Press, 1983.

Leeds, Mark H. "Legal Trends: Child Care Leaves." *Personnel Administrator*, vol. 29 (May 1984): 5-8.

"Maternity Leave Survey." *Glamour* (February 1985): 3.

"Maternity Provisions: Part 1." *Industrial Relations Review and Report*, no. 317 (April 3, 1984): 2-7.

"Memo to Managers: Parental Leave." *Catalyst Perspective* (August 1985).

Milofsky, David, and Charlene Canape. "The Baby vs. the Corporation/The Forgotten Parents: When Working Women Adopt." *Working Woman* (June 1985).

"Montana High Court Upholds State's Maternity Leave Act." *Women and the Law* (January 1985).

Morrone, Wenda Wardell. "Your Boss, Your Baby and You: How to Take a Maternity Leave That Suits All Three." *Glamour* (May 1984).

Norman, Nancy, and James T. Tedeschi. "Paternity Leave: The Unpopular Benefit Option." *Personnel Administrator* (February 1984): 39-43.

Paulson, Jane H. *Working Pregnant: A Guide to Having It All During Pregnancy.* New York: Fawcett Books, 1984.

Pearce, Diana M. "Toil and Trouble: Women Workers & Unemployment Compensation." *Signs: Journal of Women in Culture & Society*, vol. 10, no. 3 (1985): 439-459.

"Preliminary Report on a Nationwide Survey of Maternity/Parental Leaves." New York: Catalyst, Research Report No. 17 (June 1984).

"Report on a National Study of Parental Leaves." New York: Catalyst, 1986.

Shreve, Anita. "The Maternity Backlash: Women vs. Women." *Working Woman* (March 1985).

"Survey of U.S. Companies' Maternity, Paternity and Childcare Policies." New York: Bernard Hodes Advertising, 1985.

Sylvester, Kathleen. "How Firms Cope with Motherhood: Examining the Options." *National Law Journal*, vol. 6 (Nov. 7, 1983): 1.

"Time Off for Family Responsibilities: Maternity/Paternity Leave." *European Industrial Relations Review*, no. 141 (October 1985): 17.

Walker, Greta. "When Maternity Leave Ends." *Parents* (November 1984).

RELOCATION AND COMMUTER MARRIAGE

"Catalyst Explores Two-Career Families." Dallas: Consultants in Relocation, Inc., 1984.

"Catalyst Relocation Seminars: The Human Factors for Employees and Employers." *Catalyst Perspective* (May 1984).

Crandall, H.B. "Career Women Move Families to Where Opportunity Knocks." *Direct Marketing*, vol. 48 (October 1985): 36-40.

Dickinson, Jan. *Complete Guide to Family Relocation.* Northbrook, Ill.: Runzheiner and Co., 1983.

Employee Relocation Council, ed. *A Guide to Employee Relocation & Relocation Policy Development, Third Edition.* Washington, D.C.: Employee Relocation Council, 1985.

"Human Factors in Relocation: Corporate and Employee Points of View." Catalyst, Research Report No. 9 (October 1983).

Mathews, Patricia A. "Changing Work Force: Dual-Career Couples and Relocation." *Personnel Administrator* (April 1984): 55-62.

"Options for International Relocation." *Catalyst Perspective* (July 1985).

Pave, Irene. "Move Me, Move My Spouse: Relocating the Corporate Couple." *Business Week* (Dec. 16, 1985): 57, 60.

Protzko, Barbara Stokel. "Relocation Procedure for Dual-Career Couples: Policy and Practice." Boston: Massachusetts Institute of Technology, 1984.

Trippel, Alan. "Spouse Assistance Programs: Relocating Dual-Career Families." *Personnel Journal*, vol. 64 (October 1985): 76, 78.

Tucker, Michael F., and Vicki Eaton Baier. *Research Background for the Overseas Assignment Inventory*. Boulder: Moran, Stahl and Boyer, Inc., 1982.

Winfield, Fairlee G. *Commuter Marriage: Living Together, Apart*. New York: Columbia University Press, 1985.

WORKING WOMEN

Alvarez, William F. "The Meaning of Maternal Employment for Mothers & their Perceptions of their Three-year-old Children." *Child Development*, vol. 56, no. 2, (1985): 350-360.

Baker, Margaret. "Career Women & Self-Concept." *International Journal of Women's Studies*, vol. 8, no. 3 (1985).

Brown, Clair. "An Institutional Model of Wives' Work Decisions." *Industrial Relations*, vol. 24, no. 2 (1985): 182-204.

Coffey, Kitty R. "Solving Family and Work Role Problems: An Academic Department Case Study." *Journal of Home Economics* (Spring 1985). Washington, D.C.: American Home Economics Association.

Davidson, M., and C. Cooper. "Women Managers — Work, Stress & Marriage." *International Journal of Social Economics*, vol. 12, no. 2 (1985): 17-25.

"Displaced Homemakers: Programs and Policy, An Interim Report." Washington, D.C.: U.S. Congress, Office of Technology Assessment (October 1985).

"Equality in the Workplace: Is That Enough for Pregnant Workers." *Journal of Family Law*, vol. 23, no. 3 (1985): 401-418.

"Family and Work: A National Survey." New York: Newsweek, Inc., 1984.

Harkess, Shirley. "Women's Occupational Experience in the 1970's: Sociology and Economics." *Signs: Journal of Women in Culture & Society*, vol. 10, no. 3 (1985): 495-516.

Hoffecker, Pamela Hobbs. "Will the Real Working Mom Please Stand Up?" *Parents* (April 1985).

Koblinsky, Sally A., and Kathleen Mikitka. "Job Sharing: A Part-Time Career for a Fuller Life." *Journal of Home Economics* (Winter 1984). Washington, D.C.: American Home Economics Association.

Iglehart, A.P. "Wives, Work, and Social Change: What About the Housewives?" *Social Science Review*, vol. 54, no. 3 (September 1980): 23-28.

Keown, Ada Lewis, and Charles Keown. "Factors of Success for Women in Business." *International Journal of Women's Studies*, vol. 8, no. 3 (1985).

Klemesrud, Judy. "Working Women: Easing the Burden." *New York Times* (Feb. 6, 1982).

Lawhon, Tommie M. "Work and Stress in the Home: 'How Do You Help in the Family?'" *Journal of Home Economics* (Winter 1984). Washington, D.C.: American Home Economics Association.

Locksley, A. "On the Effects of Wives' Employment on Marital Adjustment and Companionship." *Journal of Marriage and Family*, vol. 42, no. 2 (May 1980).

Rothman, S.M. "Going Public — Historical Perspectives on Working Women." *American Journal of Psychoanalysis*, vol. 45, no. 2 (1985): 167-175.

Sacks, Karen, and Dorothy Remy. *My Troubles Are Going to Have Trouble with Me: Everyday Trials & Triumphs of Women Workers*. New Brunswick, N.J.: Rutgers University Press, 1984.

St. Pierre, Tena Lloyd. "Addressing Work and Family Issues Among Extension Personnel." *Journal of Home Economics* (Winter 1984). Washington, D.C.: American Home Economics Association.

Strober, M.H., and C.B. Weinberg. "Strategies Used by Working and Networking Wives to Reduce Time Pressures." *Journal of Consumer Research* (March 1980.)

Wallace, Joanne. *The Working Woman*. Old Tappan, N.J.: Revell, 1985.

Washington, Valerie, and Ura Jean Oyermade. "Employer-Sponsored Child Care: A Movement or a Mirage?" *Journal of Home Economics* (Winter 1984). Washington, D.C.: American Home Economics Association.

Woods, Nancy F. "Employment, Family Roles, & Mental Ill Health in Young Married Women." *Nursing Research*, vol. 34, no. 1 (1985): 4-10.

"Women Who Maintain Families." Fact Sheet No. 85-2 (July 1985). Washington, D.C.: U.S. Department of Labor, Women's Bureau.

"Working Mothers and Their Children." Fact Sheet No. 85-4 (July 1985). Washington, D.C.: U.S. Department of Labor, Women's Bureau.

ADDITIONAL MATERIAL

Aldous, Joan. *Family Careers: Developmental Change in Families*. New York: Wiley, John, & Sons, Inc., 1978.

Aldous, Joan. *Two Paychecks: Life in Dual Earner Families*. Series: Sage Focus Editions, vol. 56. Beverly Hills, Calif.: Sage Publications, Inc., 1982.

Barrett, Karen. "Two Career Couples: How They Do It." *Ms.* (June 1984).

"Bibliography on Work and Family Issues." New York: The Conference Board, 1984.

Burtman, Andrea I. "New Latchkey Kids: What Children Do After School." *Working Mother* (February 1984).

Clark, D., K. McCann, K. Morrice, and R. Taylor. "Work & Marriage in the Offshore Oil Industry." *International Journal of Social Economics*, vol. 12, no. 2 (1985): 36-47.

Conrad, Pam. *Balancing Home & Career*. Los Altos, Calif.: Crisp Publcations, Inc., 1986.

Daniell, D. "Love & Work — Complementary Aspects of Personal Identity." *International Journal of Social Economics*, vol. 12, no. 2 (1985): 48-55.

Eisenberg, R. "How Employers Can Help." *Money* (November 1980).

"Equal Opportunities and Equal Treatment for Men and Women Workers: Workers with Family Responsibilities." Geneva: International Labour Office, Report V (2), 1981.

Fulmer, Robert M. "The Fragile Family: Implications for Planners." *Managerial Planning*, vol. 33 (January/February 1985): 60-61.

Genovese, Rosalie G., ed. *Families & Change: Social Needs & Public Policy.* South Hadley, Mass.: Bergin & Garvey, 1983.

Grollman, Earl A., and Gerri L. Sweder. *The Working Parent Dilemma: How to Balance the Responsibilities of Children and Careers.* Boston, Mass.: Beacon Press, 1986.

Le Play, Frederic, and Catherine Silver, eds. *Frederic Le Play on Family, Work, & Social Change.* Series: Heritage of Sociology. Chicago: University of Chicago Press, 1982.

Moynihan, Daniel P. *Family and Nation.* New York: Harcourt, Brace, & Jovanovich, 1986.

Of Cradles & Careers: A Guide to Reshaping Your Job to Include a Baby in Your Life. New York: New American Library (Plume), 1985.

Papkin, Robert D. "The New Nepotism: No-Spouse Rules and the Working Couple." *America's New Labor Force: Working Couples, Seminar Manual.* Cleveland: RESOURCE: Careers.

Pleck, Joseph H., Graham L. Staines, and Linda Lang. "Conflicts between Work and Family Life." *Monthly Labor Review* 103 (March 1980).

Pleck, Joseph H., and Graham L. Staines. "Work Schedules & Family Life in Two-Earner Couples." *Journal of Family Issues*, vol. 6, no. 1 (1985): 61-82.

Report on the Activities in the Ninety-eighth Congress of the Select Committee on Children, Youth, and Families. Washington, D.C.: U.S. Government Printing Office, 1985.

Rowatt, G. Wade, Jr., and Mary Jo Rowatt. *The Two-Career Marriage.* Series: Christian Care Books, vol. 5. Philadelphia: Westminster, 1980.

Schwartz, Felice N. "New Policies for a Two-Gender Work Force." *Catalyst Perspective* (March 1984).

Segal, Stephen. "The Working Parent Dilemma." *Personnel Journal* (March 1984).

Trunzo, C.E. "Mixing Children and Jobs." *Money* (November 1980).

Voydanoff, Patricia, ed. *Work & Family: Changing Roles of Men & Women.* Gloversville, N.Y.: Mayfield Publishing, 1983.

Work and Family in the United States: A Policy Initiative. A Report of the Family Policy Panel of the Economic Policy Council of UNA-USA. New York, N.Y.: United Nations Association of the USA (December 1985).

Zigler, Edward F., Sharon Lynn Kagen, and Edgar Klugman, eds. *Children, Families and Government: Perspectives on American Social Policy.* New York: Cambridge University Press, 1983.

S

805-810, see HR 2867

LEISURE TIME

Sweden 167

LIFE INSURANCE COMPANIES

Transamerica Occidental Life Insurance Co. program 75

LONGSHOREMEN (ILA)

Alcoholism treatment program 96

M

MAINE

Child care legislation 145

MARYLAND

Adoption leave for state employees 147
Child care, Private Sector Day Care Initiatives Task Force 147
Leave without pay, seasonal leave available to state employees 147
State employee personnel policies 146

MASSACHUSETTS

Boston Bar Assn. child care program 148
Child care proposals 147
Parental leave study 149

MATERNITY BENEFITS

ILO Global Survey, 180

MATERNITY LEAVE

In general 102, 231
Arizona legislation 138
Bibliography 324
Foley, Hoag & Eliott, law firm program 114
Iowa state employee programs 143
Wisconsin state employee programs 157
Union policies 104

MICHIGAN

Alternative work schedules for state employees 150
Child care proposals 149
Parental leave legislation 149
Work sharing policy for state employees 150

MINNESOTA

Adoption leave legislation 150
Alternative work schedules for state employees 151
Child care for state employees 151
Family Task Force 151
Parental leave for state employees 151

MORALE OF EMPLOYEES

Employee assistance programs 99

MORTGAGE ASSISTANCE PROGRAMS

Diamond Shamrock Corp., relocation program 126

N

NATIONAL ASSOCIATION OF WORKING WOMEN

Views of the experts 224

NEW JERSEY

Child care programs 152

NEW YORK

Child care 195
Employee assistance program 94
Part-time employment for state employees 155
Work sharing program for state employees 154
Worksite day care programs for state employees 154

O

OIL WORKERS (OCAW)

Child care policies 198

ON-SITE DAY CARE

In general 34
Boston City Hospital and SEIU program 37
Fel-Pro Inc. program 38
New York state employee programs 154
San Francisco, Calif., ordinance requiring office developers to provide space for on-site day care or to contribute to city fund 61

ORGANIZATIONS

Resource directory 233

ORGANIZING

Union Activity Spurred by Changes 208

P

PARENTAL BENEFITS

See also ADOPTION ASSISTANCE; MATERNITY BENEFITS; PATERNITY BENEFITS
Trends 106

WISCONSIN—Contd.

Child care, state employees programs 157
Maternity leave for state employees 157
Sick leave, use by state employee to care for
  immediate family members 158

WOMEN EMPLOYEES

See also CHILD CARE
Stress and absenteeism 29

WORK SCHEDULES

See ALTERNATIVE WORK SCHEDULES

WORK SHARING

Michigan, state employee policy 150
New York, state employee program 154
Rolscreen Co. program 78

WORKPLACES

Bibliography 317

WORKWEEKS

See VOLUNTARY REDUCED WORKWEEKS